Police Misconduct:
Legal Remedies

third edition

JOHN HARRISON has worked as an information officer, editor, lecturer and law centre worker. He is a solicitor, deputy head of legal services for a London borough and a Harkness Fellow at Harvard Law School. He has written on policing and other issues for *Legal Action*, the *New Law Journal*, *Law Society's Gazette* and *Solicitors' Journal*.

STEPHEN CRAGG is the Project Solicitor for the Public Law Project. Before this, he worked at Hackney Law Centre where he specialised in police misconduct litigation. He has written and taught widely on the police and on public law, has had articles published in all the major practitioners' journals, and is a major contributor to the Public Law Project's *Applicant's guide to judicial review* to be published in late 1995. He is an ex-Vice Chair of the Law Centres' Federation and has a master's degree in socio-legal studies.

Police Misconduct:
Legal Remedies

third edition

John Harrison, SOLICITOR

and

Stephen Cragg, SOLICITOR

Legal Action Group
1995

Third edition published in Great Britain 1995
by LAG Education and Service Trust Limited
242 Pentonville Road, London N1 9UN

First edition 1987
Second edition 1991

© John Harrison and Stephen Cragg 1995

The right of John Harrison and Stephen Cragg to be identified as the authors of this work has been asserted by them in accordance with the Copyright, Designs and Patents Act 1988.

British Library Cataloguing in Publication Data
A CIP catalogue record for this book is available from the British Library.

ISBN 0 905099 58 3

Phototypeset by J&L Composition Ltd, Filey, North Yorkshire
Printed in Great Britain by Bell & Bain Ltd, Glasgow

Preface

Taking action against police misconduct is difficult. The individual whose civil liberties have been violated must brace him or herself for a struggle with one of the largest and most powerful institutions of the state. The procedures are imperfect and complicated. Aggrieved people will invariably find themselves fighting a 'battle for the truth': police officers involved in the case will often provide an account that absolves them, and their force, from guilt. Taking a stand against police wrong-doing is often lonely and bewildering.

Lawyers and advisers in this area can provide important expert support in community struggles for social, economic and political change, and for those groups and individuals who are singled out for police harassment. Even the knowledge that such expertise exists can have an effect on curbing police misconduct, if it can be demonstrated that the legal limits to police power cannot be breached with impunity. As legal action in response to police misconduct increases, however, lawyers who advise the police have built up an expertise in this area which only the few lawyers who specialise in police misconduct law on behalf of complainants and plaintiffs can hope to match.

In this book, we aim to explain in detail the procedures and tactics of the two major routes to remedying police misconduct: police complaints and civil actions. Police complaints and discipline procedures are tightly controlled by a statutory framework of primary legislation, regulations and guidance. Civil actions against the police have highly unusual rules and procedures due to the nature of the torts involved, the availability of exemplary and aggravated damages and, of course, the availability of trial by jury. As well as describing the advantages, we have attempted to indicate the pitfalls of the two procedures and how best to avoid them.

There is no single action which effectively ensures both that indivi-dual officers are punished for misconduct *and* that victims are ade-quately compensated for the wrongs committed against them. We have described at some length the complicated inter-relationship between the complaints system and civil actions, in particular in the light of the landmark ruling by the House of Lords in *R v Chief Constable of West Midlands Police ex parte Wiley*, where it was held, finally, that public interest immunity does not apply in general to the use of police complaints documents in civil actions against the police.

In addition, we have outlined other remedies which might be appropriate in cases of police misconduct and in this edition we have provided a detailed analysis of the use of the private prosecution by individuals against police officers who it is alleged have committed criminal offences. More detailed treatment has also been given to remedies whose use is (or is likely to be) on the increase: the European Convention on Human Rights, judicial review, and the new criminal appeals procedures where wrongful conviction is alleged. Our aim is to point to the most important of the legal structures and procedures (and some extra-legal strategies) that might be effective in these cases and to equip the reader with the essentials for advising on the full range of remedies available.

Acknowledgements

Many people contributed to this book. Some, particularly those who have brought civil actions against the police, cannot be identified; our debt to them is none the less for that. Others encouraged us with ideas, suggestions and practical help, without which this book would be immensely poorer. In particular, we acknowledge our thanks to:

Michael Aspinall, Keith Bevell, Helen Bramford, the staff of the British Library of Political and Economic Science, HM Inspectorate of Police, Mark Guthrie, the staff of the Law Society library, Nathaniel Matthews, Fiona Murphy, Peter Moorhouse (PCA), Patrick O'Connor QC, Inspector Randolph Otter, the staff of the Legal Action Group, Brian Sedgemore MP, Graham Smith, John Wadham, Sally Weston.

The Police Complaints Deadline Targets (appendix 1) and extracts from the Police Discipline Code (appendix 2), the Guidelines for the Police on the Use of Firearms (appendix 5), the Home Office Circular 62/1992 (appendix 12) and the Home Office Guidance on *R v Edwards* (appendix 13) are Crown copyright and reproduced with the sanction of the Controller of HMSO.

The views expressed in this work are those of the authors and not of their employers.

The law is stated as at 1 June 1995 but in some places it has been possible to include later developments.

Contents

List of tables

Table of cases

Table of statutes

Table of Statutory Instruments

Abbreviations

ACPO	Association of Chief Police Officers
AEAC	Atomic Energy Authority Constabulary
Code(s)	Codes of Practice issued by Home Office under PACE s66 (3rd edition 1995)
Complaints General Regs	Police (Complaints) (General) Regulations 1985 SI No 520
CPS	Crown Prosecution Service
DIS	Defendants' Information Service
Discipline Regs	Police (Discipline) Regulations 1985 SI No 518
Dispensation Regs	Police (Dispensation from Requirement to Investigate Complaints) Regulations 1985 SI No 672 (formerly Police (Anonymous, Repetitious etc Complaints) Regulations, renamed by 1990 SI No 1301)
DPP	Director of Public Prosecutions
ECHR	European Court of Human Rights
GCO	Guidance to Chief Officers on Police Complaints and Discipline Procedures, HMSO 1985
HAC	Home Affairs Committee (House of Commons)
HC	House of Commons
HO	Home Office
HO Memo	Home Office Memorandum of 23 June 1982 on miscarriages of justice
Informal Resolution Regs	Police (Complaints) (Informal Resolution) Regulations 1985 SI No 671
Mandatory Referrals Regs	Police (Complaints) (Mandatory Referrals) Regulations 1985 SI No 673

PACE	Police and Criminal Evidence Act 1984
PCA	Police Complaints Authority
PII	public interest immunity
PMCA	Police and Magistrates' Courts Act 1994
Police Regs	Police Regulations 1995 SI No 215
PTSD	post-traumatic stress disorder
Senior Officer Discipline Regs	Police (Discipline) (Senior Officers) Regulations 1985 SI No 519
SOCO	scene of crime officer
TSG	Territorial Support Group
UKAEA	United Kingdom Atomic Energy Authority

CHAPTER 1

What can be done?

Introduction

A young man comes to you in some distress. He says that he was arrested and beaten by the police last night and he wants to know what he can do about it. His face is swollen and his eye is turning colour.

At about 11.30pm he was walking down the High Street when he was stopped by two uniformed police officers. They took his name and address. He continued walking and at the corner of the street met two more uniformed officers. They stopped him. He again gave his name and address and he showed them the contents of his pockets. He walked on and was stopped for a third time as he went into the public lavatories in the town square. This time he became angry. He told the police to get lost and ran off. The officers chased him on foot and called for assistance. He was eventually arrested by officers from a police van.

When he saw that the van was full of police, he stopped and let himself be taken. The officers put him in an arm lock and one of them said, 'You cheeky spade. You're nicked. You'll be sorry you were on the street today.' His arm was pulled back hard and he was bundled into the back of the van where he was hit in the face a couple of times by one of the officers.

At the station the young man was left in a cell. Eventually a police surgeon arrived, looked him over briefly and said, 'You'll be OK.' He was then taken up to the police sergeant who said, 'Pity you fell over and hurt yourself on the steps. As long as it stays that way we'll leave it shall we. Goodbye.' He was thus released at about 4am the following morning.

What can be done?

This book aims to guide the adviser through the law, practice and procedure available to meet this kind of situation, and other abuses of police powers. The remedies that may be open to the victim of police misconduct are frequently inadequate, illogical and contradictory, and the adviser will need to select the correct remedy, or mixture of remedies, to meet the objectives of the client and the particular circumstances of each case.

A civil claim for damages will usually be the preferred option, but an official complaint could be brought, either as an alternative to suing or in tandem with the civil action (see p200). This could lead to disciplinary action or even a criminal prosecution against the officers responsible (see p87). If the action complained of is part of a systematic course of police conduct or part of a pattern of police abuses, other remedies besides civil litigation, including extra-legal remedies, may be appropriate (see p12).

Secondly, the adviser must help the client decide if s/he wants to take the matter further. At this preliminary stage s/he does not have to decide if s/he will take proceedings but merely whether to keep the option open. People are often apprehensive about possible police retaliation if they make a complaint, and the client may need to be reassured both that this is rare and that the law can provide further protection should harassment occur (see p179).

There may, however, on reflection, be reasons why the client would not wish to encourage too close an examination of his/her circumstances by the police. Previous criminal convictions are no bar to making a complaint or suing and should not in themselves dissuade people from exercising their rights, but they should be weighed in the balance with everything else. It is said that some defendants facing criminal charges submit a complaint in the belief that this will assist their defence. However, such a tactic may focus police attention and make the criminal case especially hard fought.

Thirdly, if the client is to sue or pursue a complaint, s/he must act immediately to gather evidence to support the allegations. The police will start to construct their case immediately, 'agreeing' their version of events amongst themselves, interviewing witnesses, possibly shaping statements from themselves and witnesses to fit their story, and compiling their report as fully or incompletely as required. In the meantime the client may have been held in custody unable to identify or contact witnesses. It is crucial to impress upon the client the importance of identifying witnesses at the earliest possible stage. There may be none. Incidents of police misbehaviour may take place in the back of police vans or in police stations where only other officers are present. But passers by may, for example, have seen the motion of the van as the client took a kicking or prisoners may have heard sounds from an adjoining cell. If the incident took place in the street, the client should

go back immediately and ask around, talk to shopkeepers and neighbours and tell them how to get in touch if a witness should turn up.
There is more advice on witnesses at p5.

Fourthly, the adviser should take steps to record and preserve evidence.
At the initial interview (see below) the adviser should arrange for the client
to be seen by a doctor, arrange for photographs to be taken of any injuries
or of the scene of the incident and contact the police to ask them to
preserve any physical evidence that may otherwise be lost or destroyed. An
independent record of any injuries should be made immediately.[1]

Finally, the adviser should do what s/he can to check on the police
version of events. A telephone call to the officer involved, if s/he can be
identified, or to the custody officer on duty at the time may reveal
invaluable information. It is a simple matter to say that the client was
arrested last night, that s/he seems rather the worse for wear this
morning and could they tell you what happened? There is more advice
on obtaining the police version of events at pp19–33.

Advisers should beware of making a judgment: it is not their role to
believe or disbelieve the client's story. People should not be discouraged
from exercising their civil rights by scepticism on the part of their
advisers. On the other hand, clients need to appreciate any apparent
weaknesses or inconsistencies in their account. Furthermore, the story
may turn out to be more complicated than originally told. In the
example of the young man above, for instance, it might emerge that a
package containing heroin was found near the lavatories. The police are
checking it for fingerprints, which they suspect to be the client's. This
has no relevance to the allegations of assualt. Nevertheless, the young
man may want to consider his position in the round and, on reflection,
may feel that it is not in his interest to pursue the matter.

Initial interview

The first step is to interview the client and prepare a detailed statement.
Provided the statement is made soon after the incident, and preferably
at the earliest opportunity, and the complainant read it and signed it
while the facts were still fresh in his/her mind, s/he will be able to use it
in court to refresh his/her memory while giving evidence.[2]

---

1 Aside from the client's own statement, a statement describing the injuries
  should be made by someone other than the client's own lawyer, as s/he may
  be prevented from acting in the case if s/he is required to give evidence.
2 *R v Mills, R v Rose* [1962] 3 All ER 298, 301; *Attorney-General's Reference
  (No 3 of 1979)* (1979) 69 Cr App R 411. See also Civil Evidence Act 1968
  s3(2).

The initial interview is the crucial interaction between adviser and client. It offers the best opportunity to get the story straight from the outset while the events are still at their freshest in the client's mind. However, it also carries the greatest risks that the adviser will misunderstand, or that the client will omit a crucial detail. If it is the first time the adviser and client have met, there is a danger both may seek to test out the other, the client perhaps being wary of authority figures, and worried that s/he may be disbelieved, and the adviser wary of an embroidered account.

There may be a tendency on the part of the client to leave out the damaging parts of a story, such as provocation by the client, and to exaggerate injuries or the conduct of the police. The adviser should constantly ask him/herself during the interview whether the story is credible, and particularly try to get to the bottom of any action, whether by the police or the client, which seems inexplicable, motiveless or irrational.

The adviser should aim to produce a full narrative of the entire incident, including all that preceded the conduct complained of, and all that followed. The account should seek to present a rounded picture of the client and of his/her character and way of life. If this appears favourable, it may compound the conduct of the police; if it appears unfavourable, it may provide a motive for conduct the police will seek to deny took place.

In all this the adviser must seek to win and maintain the confidence of the client. A structured interview can help achieve this and should include the following.

Interview checklist

1 Date, time and place of the incident. A sketch map may assist at this stage, and scale plans may need to be drawn at a later stage to illustrate what happened, where witnesses were standing etc. A visit to the scene and photographs[3] of the area may be necessary.
2 What preceded the incident? How did the client become involved? What had s/he been doing that evening, that day, that week?
3 How did the client arrive at the scene? By foot, vehicle, public transport?

---

3 For precautions to be taken in relation to photographs and other items likely to be produced in evidence, see chapter 2 p19.

4 How did the police arrive? What vehicles were involved? Are any registration numbers or police vehicle identification numbers known? The type, make or colour of any vehicles. Which officers arrived in which vehicles?

5 The number of officers involved, their names, numbers, ranks, force, division or station. An inability to name or identify an officer is not fatal to either a complaint or a civil action (see pp16 and 204), but in practice if an officer cannot be traced the police may deny the incident ever took place.

6 If an officer cannot be identified by the client, a detailed description, together with the time and place of the incident, will assist the police to establish who was in the area. The description should cover sex, age, size, weight, height, clothing/uniform, hair colour, hairstyle, headgear, accent, complexion, and whether a man was clean shaven or had facial hair.

7 If more than one officer was involved, precisely which officer was responsible for which acts.

8 Who said what, and to whom? Who else was present when the words were spoken?

9 Details of any witnesses: names, addresses, ages, relationship to client. If there were witnesses but they cannot currently be identified, how might they be contacted? Were any witnesses involved in the incident, or arrested or interviewed by the police? Did they give any statements, information or physical evidence to the police?

10 The exact sequence of events. How long each act or element of the incident took. How long was the client held? If the client is unsure of the time of an incident, it should be estimated (noting in the statement any uncertainty) by reference to known earlier events such as pub closing time or the time a TV programme ended. A detailed chronology will need to be drawn up.

11 Had the client, any witnesses or the police taken any drink or drugs? (Alcohol is a factor in 23% of complaints against the police.) Was the client or any witness in possession of drink or drugs?

12 Did the client know or recognise any of the officers? What previous dealings has the client had with the officers?

13 What previous convictions does the client have? List all previous incidents, confrontations, arrests, attendances at police stations, trials, sentences, contacts with probation, parole and other criminal justice services. It will be necessary to compile a full schedule of the client's (and possibly any witnesses') antecedents

in due course, particularly noting any convictions relevant to the incident, eg, assault, or that go to credibility, eg, offences of dishonesty (see pp182–185).[4]

14 Injuries. What injuries did the client sustain? How were they caused? Precisely which officers were responsible? Were any officers injured?

15 Has the client been seen by a doctor with a view to preparing a medical report? If not, ensure this is done immediately, and that the doctor knows and records how the injuries are alleged to have occurred (as they may later have to give evidence as to whether the injuries they treated or observed were consistent with the client's account of how they happened).[5]

16 Have colour photographs of the injuries been taken?[6] If not, ensure this is done *immediately.* It may be necessary to take further photographs later of bruising, as bruises change colour and may be at their height at one, two or three days after the incident.[7] However bruising on a black skin may not show distinctly, in which case photographs should be supplemented by detailed, measured drawings, preferably made by a doctor.

17 What lasting effects or impairment (including psychological damage) have the injuries caused? See pp134 and 177.

18 If the client has been injured, take a medical history including prior injuries, conditions and illnesses. Prepare a form of release for all medical and psychiatric records, including any held by prison authorities (see p17).

---

4 It is not usually prudent to accept the client's recollection at face value: the police will disclose previous convictions if there is to be a criminal trial arising out of the incident; if there is not, previous convictions may only be disclosed at the discovery stage of a civil action (see p232), but a request to the police should nevertheless be made at the outset.

5 Clinical notes from a hospital or the client's GP which were merely prepared in the course of treatment, rather than with a view to legal proceedings, while potentially valuable if there is no other contemporaneous medical evidence, are not ideal, as their quality varies enormously.

6 Ideally this should be done by a professional photographer, although this may involve some expense. If this is not possible, amateur snapshots may suffice. Some complainants have called the press and used photographs taken by a press photographer.

7 Langlois and Gresham, 'The Ageing of Bruises: A Review and Study of the Colour Changes With Time', *Forensic Science International*, 50 (1991) 227–238.

19 Weapons. did the client have or use a weapon during the incident? Did the police use, or threaten the use of, handcuffs (bracelet or rigid Quik Kufs, see p62), conventional truncheons or US-style batons?[8] Were police dogs (see p63), CS or CN or other gas or sprays,[9] or firearms involved (see p59)?

20 Was the client subjected to any neck holds, arm locks or martial arts techniques (see p62)?

21 How was the client treated while in custody? Was the client allowed to make a phone call, allowed food and drink, use of lavatory, medical treatment including medicines, or seen by a police surgeon? Consider whether any breach of PACE Codes of Practice has occurred. (Breach of a code may justify disciplinary action but does not of itself render an officer liable to civil or criminal proceedings; see p14).

22 Was the client charged with any offence arising out of the incident? Current status? Name and address of lawyer acting? Secure notes or transcripts of any criminal trial/other civil actions/coroner's inquest (see pp 24 and 292–293).

23 If a search was conducted, was there a warrant and was it shown to anyone at the premises? (See pp168–169).

24 Description of anything seized, damaged or destroyed by the police. How did the damage or destruction occur? Photographs of any damage to premises or property are compelling evidence and must be arranged immediately.

25 Description and whereabouts of any physical evidence. The production of physical evidence in court can have a dramatic impact. A blood-stained shirt or the remains of a smashed-in front door will provide graphic evidence of an assault or a violent entry which could not be matched by a dry cleaning receipt or a carpenter's invoice.

26 Did the client make any oral or written statement to the police?

8 A variety of US-style batons, both fixed and telescopic frinction-locking, have been tested and issued in recent years, including the straight 21" Arnold and 26" Celayaton batons, the two-piece 24" Monadnock, the three-piece telescopic ASP (armament systems and procedures), CASCO (counter assault systems), PPCT (pressure point control tactics) batons which extend to 21", and the extendable side-handled baton, which is like a 24" Monadnock but with side handle: see Laux, 'Baton-Age on trial', *Police Review*, 30 September 1994, pp16–17.

9 CS gas sprays (but not the allegedly carcinogenic OC 'pepper sprays') have been tested in 18 forces since July 1994: *Police Review*, 17 March 1995 p9, 19 May 1995, p6.

Was it under caution? Did the client give a statement to anyone else about the incident? Has there been any press publicity (see p191)?

27 Has the client suffered any other loss aside from physical or psychological damage, eg, loss of employment or employment prospects, past and future loss of earnings, medical or psychiatric counselling expenses, loss of reputation (see pp193–194)?

28 Any previous complaints or civil actions against the police.

29 Whether the client was rude to the police, questioned their authority or did anything to provoke the police, resisted arrest or other lawful or unlawful instruction from the police; whether the client struck or attempted to strike the police.

30 The client's family, education, employment and medical history, noting particularly anything that may attract sympathy or hostility, or may affect credibility, eg, psychiatric problems, work record, military service record, voluntary work or church activities.

31 The client's perception or explanation for the police misconduct, including any allegations of prejudice or discrimination on the basis of race, sexual orientation, age, sex, lifestyle, political or other affiliation.

32 What remedy or outcomes the client seeks to achieve by taking action against the police, eg, damages, clear name, restore reputation, expose police abuses, punish offender, apology, seek publicity, shun publicity, political/social change.[10]

Initial options

There are two principal routes available to those who seek to air a grievance about police misconduct: suing for damages in the civil courts or making an official complaint. These two courses of action are sometimes unfairly contrasted as if they offered alternative remedies which were capable of comparison on an equal footing. In the authors' view this is to mistake the purpose and function of the two regimes. Suing for damages is a private law remedy which, if successful, results in the wrongdoer compensating the victim for the wrong done: essentially it is a transaction between the two or more individuals. The complaints procedure serves a quite different objective. It is a public law procedure,

10 The authors have drawn on the US work of Avery and Rudovsky, *Police Misconduct: Law and Litigation*, Clark Boardman, NY, looseleaf, in compiling this checklist.

intended to serve a public purpose for the benefit of the whole community: the upholding of standards of behaviour by public officials to whom the community has granted awesome and extensive powers. It may result in internal action through the public administration (formal or informal disciplinary action) or external action (a criminal trial). The point here is not how effectively the complaints system works (and the authors join with numerous commentators in believing it deeply flawed), but rather that because it is intended to serve such a different purpose to the civil courts, it is pointless to ask simplistic questions such as 'Which is a better option for my client?' or to draw comparisons between 'success rates' under the two procedures.

Nevertheless, there is an important relationship between the two regimes and both are fully described, as one may help or hinder the other. The task of the lawyer is to use the battery of remedies available singly or in combination to achieve the client's objective. Most commonly the client will seek damages and the lawyer will pursue a civil claim, possibly using the complaints procedure as a supporting strategy. However, in many cases clients are motivated by wider concerns: to seek symbolic justice for the wrong done, to clear their name and restore their reputation, to establish a point of principle, to see an officer personally held to account or punished or to seek an apology and admission that the client's rights were abused. In these circumstances a civil action may (or may not) still be the best route, possibly used in combination with the complaints procedure or, more rarely, a private prosecution (see p117). But the lawyer needs to keep the client's objective clearly in mind: it is all too easy for the lawyer to focus on winning damages to the exclusion of all other considerations. Even a substantial award against a chief constable will miss the mark if it is made in an out of court settlement subject to a 'no publicity' condition, when the client was really seeking public vindication and to hold the individual officer to account.

Similarly the client may have a wider social or political agenda and be seeking to use the legal process to challenge a widespread police practice, to challenge a conventional interpretation of the law or to focus public attention on a community or political campaign. Here the usual notions of 'success' in the sense of winning the case in court may be irrelevant or secondary if the case serves its purpose of attracting publicity and stimulating debate or change in the political arena. The remedies described in chapter 9, particularly judicial review, an application under the European Convention on Human Rights or an official or unofficial inquiry, may be appropriate. Similarly a private prosecution may, in very particular circumstances, be appropriate (see p117).

However, the majority of cases that involve legal action concern an incident which may give rise to civil proceedings for, say, assault, false imprisonment, possibly the loss or damage of goods or trespass, and more rarely malicious prosecution (see chapter 5). The facts are commonly disputed, and the first tactical decision for the lawyer will be whether to use the complaints procedure and how this can be deployed to assist the civil action rather than undermine it.

Hitherto the availability of the two routes to pursuing a grievance, suing for damages and making a complaint, posed a difficult dilemma for victims of police misconduct and their advisers. Assuming that the client has a good civil claim, should s/he also make and pursue an official complaint? If s/he failed to do so, s/he might face censure when the matter came to court and the police officer might personally escape the consequences of the wrongful act. However if a complaint was pursued simultaneously with a civil action, the police investigating officers would interview all the witnesses including the complainant. The client's case would thereby be given away at a very early stage and the police would have secured a powerful advantage. This led to the controversial tactic of making a complaint but declining to co-operate with its investigation, either until the civil case had been disposed of or until an undertaking was received from the police that nothing revealed by the complaints investigation would be used in the civil case.[11] As such an undertaking would be routinely refused, the complaints investigation would in practice be stalled.

This unsatisfactory state of affairs has now changed as a result of *R v Chief Constable of West Midlands Police ex p Wiley*,[12] which held that statements created in the course of a complaints investigation can be revealed to complainants who bring civil actions. The client can therefore now take advantage of evidence compiled by the police, including any statements taken from the officers involved in the incident and any independent witnesses. This has somewhat evened up the equation and made the tactical decision of whether to sue *and* complain more subtle and finely balanced. This question is discussed at greater length at p200.[13]

Most incidents of police misconduct, however, do not result in a civil

11 See Harrison, 'Police Complaints: Pitfalls for the Unwary Litigant', *NLJ* 13 December 1985 p 1239; and Harrison and Cragg, 'Suing the Police: should plaintiffs also make a complaint?' June 1991 *Legal Action* 22.
12 [1995] 1 AC 274, [1994] 3 WLR 433, [1994] 3 All ER 420, HL.
13 See also Harrison and Cragg, 'Police Complaints and Public Interest Immunity' *NLJ* 29 July 1994 pp 1064–1065; and McNamara, 'PII and the Police', *SJ* 24 March 1995, pp 262–263.

action. In 1994 23,956 complaints cases involving 36,521 individual complaints were received by the police. A significantly smaller number of civil actions is brought.[14]

Generally, suing is only suitable in the more serious cases, both because the causes of action only concern serious abuses and because the cost of a case will not usually be justified if damages are expected to be low. A complaint, however, may be appropriate in both minor cases, such as rudeness, and also in really serious cases, since what starts as a complaint may develop into a disciplinary matter and even a criminal prosecution.

The decision to sue

There are powerful reasons to bring a civil action. Compensation can be awarded and the amount awarded may be considerable – sums of several thousands of pounds are now common in serious cases. Furthermore, a civil action keeps the case in the control of the complainant. S/he can say who should be interviewed as witnesses, what evidence should be produced, which officers must answer the allegations and how the case should be conducted. Third, if a civil action goes to court, the police must answer for their conduct in public and, if a matter of principle (such as a common police practice) is at stake, this will be brought to public attention. Fourth, a civil case has to be proved only on the balance of probabilities; a complaint must be proved on the criminal standard of proof, ie beyond reasonable doubt, which is more difficult to establish, see pp102–104.

Most advisers, therefore, start by considering whether there are grounds for bringing a civil action. This involves looking both at the question of whether there has been a technical breach of the civil law and at more practical issues, like the real chances of success. The most important civil wrongs are:

– *assault and battery* if someone is injured, hurt or searched;
– *false imprisonment* if someone is stopped, detained or arrested;
– *malicious prosecution* if someone is prosecuted when the police believe that s/he is innocent;
– *causing death* if someone dies through police brutality or negligence;
– *trespass* if the police enter premises without a warrant or other legal authority;

14 No national figures are available: HC Written Answers 9 March 1995.

- *seizure of goods* if the police take property without excuse or fail to return it;
- *damage to goods* if property is damaged, for example, when entering or searching a house.

These grounds are explained in more detail in chapter 5. The young man in our example could sue for the assault and battery in the police van that led to his injuries and the false imprisonment that arose out of his arrest and detention.

If a civil action looks like the best course of action, the legal adviser must consider carefully whether a complaint should also be made and, if so, on what conditions and whether the complainant should co-operate with the police investigation. These technical issues are explained in more detail at p200.

Other remedies

The following remedies are considered in detail in chapter 9:

- appeals and petitions in wrongful conviction cases;
- appealing under the European Convention on Human Rights;
- intervening at a coroner's inquest if someone has died;
- campaigning for an official or unofficial inquiry;
- applying for judicial review if a public body or official has acted illegally, improperly or unreasonably;
- claiming for criminal injuries compensation in assault cases if legal aid is not available;
- claiming in the magistrates' court for the return of property seized by the police.

The decision to complain

Perhaps the greatest attraction of making a complaint is that the procedure is very simple, it is completely free and it entails little effort. Once the complaint has been made, the business of proving what happened is in the hands of others – albeit other police officers.

The other advantage is the range of behaviour that can form the subject of a complaint. Any breach of the Police Discipline Code[15] or the PACE Codes of Practice[16] will be a good ground for complaint. The

15 Police (Discipline) Regs 1985 SI No 518 Sch 1.
16 Made under Police and Criminal Evidence Act 1984 s66.

TABLE 1
Completed complaints against the police, by outcome

	1985	1986	1987	1988	1989	1990	1991	1992	1993	1994
Substantiated	1,155	1,129	924	853	765	847	813	760	750	793
Unsubstantiated	11,650	12,676	10,432	9,848	8,464	11,864	11,329	10,038	9,734	8,797
Informally resolved	2,162	4,038	5,085	5,913	7,125	7,958	8,980	9,140	10,126	12,273
Withdrawn or not proceeded with	13,286	11,335	11,491	12,144	12,958	14,225	14,224	14,984	14,284	14,658
TOTAL	28,253	29,178	27,932	28,758	29,312	34,894	35,346	34,922	34,894	36,521

Source: *Home Office Statistical Bulletin* 13/95, 28 June 1995

TABLE 2
Complaints of racial discrimination against the police (all forces in England
and Wales)

	1989	1990	1991	1992	1993
Substantiated	4	5	7	3	5
Unsubstantiated[1]	107	210	240	259	281
Informally resolved	67	69	79	98	96
Withdrawn	113	125	100	101	68
TOTAL	291	409	426	461	450

[1] including complaints dealt with by dispensation.

Source: HC Written Answers, 9 March 1995

range of misconduct is thus very wide and includes rudeness, racism,
corruption, planting evidence, violence, mistreating prisoners, conducting coercive interviews and may other abuses of the rights of individuals. The potential grounds for a complaint are therefore much wider
than the narrow and technical civil wrongs for which a case for damages
may be brought.

Against this, however, there are a number of limitations to the
complaints procedure. Firstly, no compensation is payable. Secondly,
cases are currently only upheld if they could be proved on the criminal
standard of proof, that is, beyond reasonable doubt (see p102). This
imposes a very high standard which in practice often cannot be met.

Thirdly, complaints are investigated by other police officers, who
may or may not pursue their investigations with all the vigour and
thoroughness that might be hoped for.

Fourthly, the chances of a complaint being upheld are slim. In 1994
36,521 complaints were completed of which 793 (2.2%) were substantiated. Only 92 officers were charged with disciplinary offences as a
result of complaints from the public. However 14,658 (40.1%) complaints were withdrawn or not proceeded with in 1994 and a further
12,273 (33.6%) were informally resolved.

The chances of a complaint being upheld vary from one type of
complaint to another, and from one complainant to another. The
largest number of substantiated complaints is consistently for
conduct amounting to neglect of duty, usually over 25% of all
complaints that are upheld.[17] The attitude of investigating officers

17 Home Office Statistical Bulletins 1992, 1993 and 1994.

to particular types of misconduct undoubtedly affects the outcome of some investigations:

> In allegations of corruption or fraud or offences which are seen by the investigating officer to endanger the reputation of the police service, the investigating officer can be relied upon to pursue every means to bring a guilty policeman to account, but where the allegation is one of assault in the course of making an arrest an investigating officer is, perhaps, more likely to be influenced by early experiences of his own and to be more ready to accept the policeman's account of what took place than that of the complainant.[18]

The very small number of complaints of police racism that are upheld has attracted widespread criticism and suspicion. A former Metropolitan Police commissioner remarked, 'I am concerned that out of 300 cases of racial harassment only 1% of officers are disciplined.' He expressed doubts that 99% of complainants are lying and concluded 'We are failing because officers are committing offences, and we are not doing anything about it. We are not getting them.'[19]

Home Office research has also shown that complaints by black people are much less likely to be upheld by the police than those by white people.[20]

18 Police Complaints Board, Triennial Review, 1980, HMSO, para 61.9.
19 Sir Peter Imbert, *Police Review* 1 December 1989.
20 Stevens and Willis, *Ethnic Minorities and Complaints against the Police*, Research and Planning Unit Paper No 5, Home Office, 1982.

CHAPTER 2

Identification and evidence

In most cases, whether a complaint or a civil action is being considered, the issues of identification and evidence are crucial. Identification of the officer involved may prove very difficult, particularly because incidents often flare up and die down in a matter of minutes. Nevertheless, it is often possible to piece together information to identify an officer, even after the event. Other evidence may come from items such as the complainant's own statement, witness statements, photographs and certain police records that are available on request. These are described on pp19–22. Other types of evidence, such as transcripts of the criminal case or internal police records, are appropriate only in civil actions. They are also described in this chapter and advisers should be aware at an early stage of the documents which may be useful. Further procedural and evidential matters in relation to civil actions are discussed in chapters 6, 7 and 8.

Identification

If a complaint is to have any real chance of success, it must be brought against an identifiable officer rather than against a police force. A civil action may be brought against an individual officer or against the chief officer of police or both. Strictly, therefore, it is not necessary to identify the officer concerned, provided that it can be shown that the incident was carried out by an officer – any officer – under the control of the chief officer (see p203). However, in practice, if the individual officer cannot be identified, the police will be in a strong position to argue that the incident did not take place and to defend a civil action.[1]

Identification is important, but it is not essential to know the name

---

1 But see comments of Police Complaints Authority on difficulty of identifying individual police officers, despite strong evidence of assault by a group of officers – PCA Annual Report 1987 para 2.14.

or number of the officer. It is sufficient to describe his/her physical appearance and the time and place of the incident. This should enable the police to use their own records of who was in the area at the time to identify the officer concerned. Identification by physical appearance is dealt with in the interview checklist in chapter 1. In addition, following recommendations of the Police Complaints Authority (PCA), Metropolitan Police personnel carriers now prominently display an identity number.

An alternative way of identifying an officer may be to ask for one of the official records listed on pp19–33, such as the national search record or the custody record. These are available from the police on request within 12 months of the incident and should contain the names of all the officers involved.[2] In reality, if the officers deny that an incident took place, there will be no record of it. It would be difficult for officers to avoid completing a custody record (where several officers would have to be involved in the deception), but an individual officer on the beat could neglect to complete a national search record of a stop and search.

Finally, if an incident occurs at a demonstration, sympathetic magazines or trade union newspapers may agree to carry an appeal for witnesses who may have noted an officer's number. It is important to identify the time, place and incident, and if possible to give a description of the officer.

Evidence

Medical evidence

The value of medical evidence varies enormously. The complainant may have medical reports from his/her own GP or from a hospital casualty department. These may be brief and incomplete. A note that s/he had 'bruising and cuts to the face' is inadequate if it could have read 'bruising and swelling of upper lip, 2cm laceration to lower lip; 5 × 3cm abrasion and swelling of left cheek; bruising to left eye'. If the solicitor is the main witness to the injuries, then it may be that s/he should not act for that client as s/he may be called to give evidence at trial.

If a person alleges that s/he has been assaulted by the police, it is important that s/he sees a doctor as soon as possible. This could be the person's own GP or, if not available, a doctor at a hospital's casualty department. It is vital that the doctor is informed (and records) how the

2 PCA Triennial Review 1985–1988 para 3.26.

injuries occurred, as s/he may later have to give evidence as to whether the injuries s/he treated were consistent with the person's account of how they happened.

The client may have to see several doctors, not only to ensure there is a full record immediately after s/he suffered the injuries, but also to have the benefit of a consultant's opinion on whether there are likely to be any lasting effects. If the first medical report is unhelpful, a second opinion should be obtained. If the second opinion is more favourable, the existence of the first report need not be revealed to the police.

The client will need to be assessed as to whether s/he should be examined by a psychiatrist to obtain a report on the existence of a recognised mental illness, such as post-traumatic stress disorder (PTSD). This might be appropriate, for instance, if the client reports nightmares, sleeplessness or panic attacks at the sight of police officers. There are various specialist units which deal with such probems and who will provide a medical report that can be used in civil proceedings (see useful addresses appendix 14).

It should be explained to the client at the outset that the police will often want him/her to be seen by their own doctors. A civil case can be halted if the complainant unreasonably refuses this.[3] Some people are very apprehensive about seeing police doctors, and if someone is especially worried, then a legal adviser can attend with them (but see below). When being examined by a police doctor the complainant should be as consistent as possible with whatever s/he told his/her own doctors. It is also important to guard against discussing the incident with the police doctors, as the complainant may inadvertently make an admission that will get back to the police. S/he may talk about the injuries, but not about how s/he received them.

Avoiding discussion about the incident with police doctors can be especially difficult in cases where PTSD or other mental disorders are alleged. As PTSD concerns the person's response to events, the doctor will inevitably need to talk to the person about those events. This factor needs to be considered by the plaintiff's solicitors before making a claim based on mental disorder. In addition the police may be entitled to disclosure of all the plaintiff's medical records in order to ascertain if there is a history of mental probems which are relevant to the case. It is therefore advisable to obtain the plaintiff's medical records from his/her doctor in advance. Although in many cases it will be possible for the plaintiff to have someone accompany him/her to see the police doctor, it

3 *Edmeades v Thames Board Mills* [1969] 2 All ER 127, CA.

has been held that it is not unreasonable for the doctor conducting a psychiatric examination to refuse to allow that person to be present during the examination.[4]

Usually, any medical report produced in court must have been disclosed to the police before the start of the case and the police must disclose to the complainant their report before the case comes to trial[5] .

Photographs

The importance of photographs to record injuries to the plaintiff and damage to his/her property is described in chapter 1.[6] A record should be kept of the name and address of anyone who has had physical possession of the film, negatives and prints, including those who handled the film while it was being developed and printed, as it may be necessary later to prove in court that it has not been tampered with or touched up in any way.

The prints must be sent to the police solicitors at least ten days before the date of the trial.[7] If they 'agree' the photographs, they will be admitted as evidence without further contest. However, if the photographs are not so 'agreed', they must be 'proved' genuine. Everyone who has had possession of them will have to swear to this. The police solicitors are unlikely to object to photographs unless they genuinely believe that there has been some improper interference, but it is sensible to be prepared in advance with the names of everyone who has handled the photographs. This is an additional reason for employing professional photographers, who can develop and print the pictures themselves or at least have this done by someone they can easily identify. The negatives and prints should be kept sealed and under lock and key until needed at the trial, preferably by the complainant's solicitor.

Collecting evidence from the police and other official sources

Some information held by the police is available as of right. Other information will only be available to the plaintiff at the discovery stage of a civil action. Other bodies such as the Crown Prosecution Service (CPS) and the criminal courts may have information which is important to the client's case, whether s/he is pursuing a complaint, a civil action

4 *Whitehead v Avon County Council* (1995) *Times* 3 May, CA.
5 See Hodgkinson, *Expert Evidence: law and practice*, Sweet & Maxwell, 1990, for general discussion.
6 See p4.
7 RSC Order 38 r5.

or both. In all cases it is important to request the information, or request that it is preserved where there is no immediate right to disclosure, as soon as possible.

Police records available on request

Copies of two types of police record are available on request: the national search record,[8] which records stops and searches, and the custody record,[9] which records details of any time spent in a police station. These can be requested from the police at any time within 12 months of the time that the person left police detention or was taken before a court, and the police must provide copies.

There is a right to see returned search warrants.[10] After a search of premises, the search warrant must be endorsed with details of the search and returned to the court that issued it, where it is available for inspection for 12 months. If property is seized during the search, the police must keep a record of it, see pp25–26, and provide a copy of the record to the occupier of premises searched, within a reasonable time of any request.[11]

These records may be helpful in making a complaint or in bringing a civil action, for example, by establishing the identity or role of a particular officer or by providing a chronology of events. In a few cases, there may even be discrepancies between documents or between a document and the version given by the officer answering the allegation. The records should be requested before a complaint or civil action is started and so may be useful guides as to whether either course is worthwhile. The last page of the custody record lists some of the documents created in the course of detention which can be requested immediately, and which will have to be disclosed at the discovery stage of the action (see p232).

National search record[12]

Police officers who carry out stops and searches must make written records as soon as practicable, usually on the spot. The record must be made on a form known as the national search record. It should show:

8   PACE s3(7) and (8).
9   Codes of Practice for the Detention, Treatment and Questioning of Persons by Police Officers (Code C) para 2.4, revised edn, HMSO, 1995.
10 PACE s16(12).
11 Ibid s21(1) and (2).
12 Code of Practice for the Exercise by Police Officers of Statutory Powers of Stop and Search (Code A) paras 4.1–4.7A.

- the name of the person searched (or, if s/he withheld it, a description);
- a note of the person's ethnic origin;
- where a vehicle is searched, a description of it, including the registration number;
- the object of the search;
- the grounds for making the search, which must, briefly but informatively, explain the reason for suspecting the person concerned, by reference to their behaviour or other circumstances;
- the date and time of the search;
- the place where the search was carried out;
- the result of the search;
- a note of any injury or damage to property resulting from the search;
- the identity of the officers who carried out the search.

The Criminal Justice and Public Order Act 1994 s60 authorises searches based on the reasonable belief that incidents involving serious violence may take place within a locality. Authorisation for a specified period of time and for a specified geographical area for the exercise of these powers must normally be given by an officer of the rank of superintendent or above. A record of a search carried out under these powers should state the authority under which the search is made, rather than providing reasons to support the grounds for the search.[13] A written statement that a person or a vehicle has been searched under these provisions can be provided in the search record or separately.[14]

Custody record[15]
A separate custody record must be opened as soon as practicable for each person brought to a police station. If any action, such as taking fingerprints without consent, requires the authority of an officer of a specified rank, that officer's name and rank must be entered in the record. The custody officer is responsible for the accuracy and completeness of the record and for ensuring that the record, or a copy of it, accompanies any prisoner who is transferred to another police station. All entries made in the custody record and the written interview records must be timed and signed by the person making the entry.
    The person detained, or his/her solicitor, is entitled to a copy of the

13 Code A para 4.7. Likewise, the authorisation for any search under the Prevention of Terrorism (Temporary Provisions) Act 1989 must be cited.
14 Code A para 4.7A and Note for Guidance 4C.
15 Code C para 2.1–2.7

custody record as soon as practicable after the detainee has been released or taken to court, if one is requested. This entitlement lasts for 12 months.

The main information contained in the custody record includes:

- the time of detention;
- the grounds for detention;
- the detainee's signed acknowledgement that s/he has been given written notice of the right to have someone informed of the detention, and of the right to legal advice;
- a record of any property taken, signed by the detainee;
- the reasons why the police kept any article found on the detainee;
- records of all the detainee's requests to have someone informed, letters and messages sent, calls made or visits received, including the reasons for any that were refused;
- a record of meals and replacement clothes offered;
- any complaints about treatment;
- records of medical examinations, medical directions to the police and any medicines found on, or needed by, the detainee;
- a record of all the times when the detainee was not in the custody of the custody officer and the reasons, for example because s/he was being interviewed;
- the reason for any refusal to deliver the detainee out of custody;
- a record of any interpreter called to the station;
- a record of any postponement in review of detention, the outcome of the review and the grounds for any further detention;
- a record of all charges brought and anything which the detainee said when charged;
- a record of strip searches and intimate body searches, including reasons and results and, for intimate searches, which parts of the body were searched, who carried out the search and who was present;
- a record of fingerprints taken without consent, with reasons for taking them;
- a record of non-intimate samples, with reasons.

The PCA has also recommended that the custody record should have sequentially numbered pages, that cell numbers should be recorded to enable a later reconstruction of which prisoners were in which cells, and that the condition of prisoners be recorded when one custody officer hands over to the next shift.[16]

16 Annual Report 1991 p16 para 2.14.

Evidence in civil actions

Court transcripts

Evidence about what was said in any criminal trial may obviously be very important in a civil case. The police evidence may have contained damaging admissions or inconsistencies that will prove crucial to the success of a civil claim. The details of the complainant's own evidence or witnesses' evidence may also be an issue. Comments made by the judge concerning the standard of evidence provided by the police might also be important, especially in a malicious prosecution case. It is now possible for police officers to be cross-examined in criminal trials on evidence in previous trials which has been disbelieved by the jury.[17] All this information may be admissible in the civil case.[18] However, if evidence about anything that was said at the criminal trial is to be given, notice must be served on the police[19] to allow them the opportunity to apply to the court for directions as to the admissibility of the transcript.[20] Admissibility can often be dealt with between the parties by agreeing an appropriate direction (see generally pp225–231).

Crown court transcripts are usually the best evidence available, although expensive. It is, therefore, usual to ask only for transcripts of those parts of the evidence that may be useful to the case. If the client is legally aided, application should be made to the Legal Aid Board for prior authority to spend money on this. There is no rule about how long the shorthand writers should keep their notes and they should be contacted as soon as possible to ensure that they are preserved.

In magistrates' courts, shorthand writers are not used. If there is a dispute as to what was said, the complainant might have to rely on the notes of his/her solicitor, the police solicitor, the clerk of the court or the magistrate. Notes from these sources *may* be perfectly satisfactory but, on the other hand, may be incomplete, if they exist at all. Magistrates' clerks are not legally required to take notes,[21] although many do so and are very experienced at recording evidence. Lawyers *should* take comprehensive notes, but standards vary and no lawyer can write while speaking. These notes are much more likely to be destroyed than those

17 *R v Edwards* [1991] 2 All ER 266, CA (see p108). For civil cases see *Steel v Commissioner of Metropolitan Police* (1993) 18 February, CA, Lexis.
18 Civil Evidence Act 1968 ss2 and 4, and see *Brinks Ltd v Abu Saleh* (1995) *Times* 12 May: a transcript of the judge's summing up in criminal proceedings is admissible.
19 RSC Order 38 r21.
20 RSC Order 38 r28.
21 *Practice Direction* [1981] 2 All ER 831, para 4; see also *R v Clerk to Highbury Courner Justices ex p Hussein* (1986) *Times* 16 July.

of a shorthand writer, so the need to ensure that they are preserved is all the more urgent. The clerk's note of evidence and memorandum of register entry (which details the result of the case) should be provided free of charge to anyone on income support or legal aid.[22]

Special rules apply to evidence given in coroners' inquests. The written records of witnesses' statements, known as depositions, are not admissible as evidence in civil cases, although they can be used for the purposes of cross-examination.

Previous convictions

It is important to be aware of the use that the police can make of a client's criminal record in a civil action. In criminal cases, the police cannot usually produce evidence of previous convictions. In civil cases, such evidence is often admissible, and the plaintiff, defendant and witnesses can all be cross-examined on previous convictions which go to their credit. However, there are two important rules.

Spent convictions Previous convictions are usually admissible provided they are not 'spent' under the Rehabilitation of Offenders Act 1974. The police cannot bring evidence that the complainant was charged with or prosecuted or sentenced for any offence which was the subject of a spent conviction.[23] Nor can s/he be asked questions about his/her past which could be answered only by admitting to spent convictions.[24] However, if the judge in all the circumstances decides that 'justice cannot be done' unless the spent convictions are admitted as evidence then s/he has the power to so admit them.[25]

Relevant convictions The fact that the complainant has been convicted of an offence is admissible for the purpose of proving, where to do so is relevant, that s/he committed that offence.[26] The question of whether s/he committed an offence of dishonesty might, for example, be relevant to his/her credibility as a witness. On the other hand, a driving offence, say, might be irrelevant.[27]

22 For guidance on other situations in which they should be released, see para 1–34 of *Stone's Justices Manual 1995*.
23 Rehabilitation of Offenders Act 1974 s4(1)(a). A conviction is spent if the necessary period of time (calculated by reference to the severity of the sentence) has elapsed since conviction.
24 Ibid s4(1)(b).
25 Ibid s7.
26 Civil Evidence Act 1968 s11(1).
27 See also Code of Conduct for the Bar of England and Wales 1990 para 610 (h) on the limits to the challenging credibility by attacking character in cross-examination.

If the police seek to rely on this rule, they must give prior warning in their pleadings of their intention to raise the matter of the complainant's convictions.[28] If s/he denies the conviction,[29] or claims that it was wrongful or denies that it is relevant, s/he must give the police notice of such denial in his/her pleadings.[30]

Of course, the rules about evidence of criminal convictions can work to the complainant's advantage. In the unlikely event of a police officer being convicted of an offence arising out of the incident being complained of, evidence can be produced of that conviction[31] and other relevant convictions arising from separate incidents may also be admissible.[32]

Statements following complaints

When a complaint about a police officer is made, there must be an investigation by the police. This may involve taking statements from the person who makes the complaint, from the officers against whom the complaint is made and from witnesses to the incident. The difficulties that may arise where a statement has been given by a complainant who is also bringing a civil action against the police are discussed in greater detail at pp10, 75, 200–203 and 238–241.

Search register[33]

A search register must be kept at every sub-divisional police station. After any search of premises the officer in charge of the search must make a record which includes:

– the address of the premises searched;
– the date, time and duration of the search;
– the legal authority under which the search was made. A copy of the

28 RSC Order 19 r7A(1). In the county court, it seems that prior warning is not required, although it may be desirable as a matter of practice, see note to County Court Rules (CCR) Order 20 r1.
29 If the conviction is denied, it can be proved under Criminal Procedure Act 1865 s6 as amended by PACE Sch 7 Pt IV.
30 RSC Order 18 r7A(3); in the county court, see n28. The burden of proving that s/he did not commit the offence lies on the complainant: Civil Evidence Act 1968 s11(2)(a).
31 The conviction must be pleaded.
32 *R v Edwards* [1991] 2 All ER 266.
33 Code of Practice for the Searching of Premises by Police Officers and the Seizure of Property fund by Police Officers on Persons or Premises (Code B) paras 7 and 8.

warrant or consent (if any) must be attached to the record or kept in
an identified place;
- the names of the officers who carried out the search;
- the names, if known, of anyone on the premises searched;
- a list of all articles seized, or a note of where such a list is kept, and
  the reasons for seizure if they were not covered by a warrant;
- whether any force was used and the reason for it being used;
- details of any damage caused and the circumstances.

If premises are searched under a warrant, the warrant must be
endorsed to show:

- whether the articles listed in the warrant were found;
- whether any articles not listed were seized;
- the date and time of the search;
- the name of the officers who carried out the search;
- whether a copy was handed to the occupier or left on the premises
  and, if so, where.

Magistrates have been urged by the PCA to include the time as well as
the date on search warrants.[34] Search warrants, whether executed or
not, must be returned by the police to the magistrates' clerk or court
officer. The occupier of any premises to which the warrant relates can
inspect the returned warrant within 12 months of its return.[35]

Written and tape-recorded records of interviews[36]
An accurate record must be made of any interview[37] with anyone
suspected of an offence, whether or not the interview takes place at a
police station. The record must state:

- the place of the interview;
- the time it began and ended;
- the time the record was made, if not the same;
- any breaks in the interview;
- the names of those present.

The record must be made on the forms provided for the purposes or in
the officer's pocket book. At the end of a taped interview, the police
officer must make a note in his/her notebook of:

34 PCA Triennial Review 1985–88 para 3.25.
35 PACE s16(10), (11) and (12).
36 Code C paras 11 and 12 and Annex D and Code E.
37 For a definition of 'interview' see Code C para 11.1A.

– the fact that an interview has taken place and has been tape-recorded;
– the time, duration and date of the interview;
– the identification number of the master tape.[38]

Where proceedings follow the tape-recording of an interview, any written record of the interview must be prepared in accordance with national guidelines issued by the Home Secretary and the seal on the master tape may be broken in restricted circumstances only.[39] Where there are no criminal proceedings, the tape must be kept securely and the chief officer of police must establish arrangements for the breaking of the seal if necessary.[40]

Identification parade records[41]
Records of identification parades should be completed by the identification officer responsible for the parade. If a parade cannot be held for any reason, that reason must be recorded, including any refusal to participate. The names of everyone present at a parade or group identification which are known to the police must be recorded. If a parade is held without a friend or a solicitor present, a colour photograph or video of the parade should be taken and handed to the person suspected, or his/her solicitor, on request within a reasonable time. Unless the person is convicted or cautioned, the photograph or video will be destroyed at the conclusion of the proceedings.[42]

Complaints register
Every chief office of police must keep a register of complaints against members of his/her force. The register must contain a record of the steps taken in dealing with a complaint and the outcome.[43]

Discipline records
Every chief officer must keep a discipline book which records every charge made against a member of the police force. It must contain the decision on the charge and a record of the decision in any further disciplinary proceedings connected with it.[44] Relevant disciplinary

38 Code of Practice on Tape Recording (Code E) para 5.1.
39 Ibid Notes for Guidance 5A and para 6.2.
40 Ibid paras 5.2, 6.1 and 6.3.
41 Code of Practice for the Identification of Persons by Police Officers (Code D) paras 2.19–2.21 and Annex A paras 19–22.
42 Ibid Annex A para 20.
43 Police (Complaints) (General) Regs 1985 Complaints General Regs SI No 520 reg 12
44 Discipline Regs reg 29.

charges proved against the officers involved should be disclosed by the police and cross-examination concerning these matters will be allowed.[45] As the rules on admissibility of such evidence in criminal and civil trials are similar, police disciplinary records may have been revealed to the defence by the CPS already if there has been a previous criminal trial.

Information from the Crown Prosecution Service

Where there has been a previous criminal trial the CPS may have documentation which the plaintiff wishes to use in the civil proceedings. The CPS has set out the basis on which it decides whether to disclose information.[46]

> The CPS is faced with ever-increasing demands to provide copies of statements and other documents to others for a whole variety of purposes. The most common requests are from solicitors involved in civil proceedings [which include] those acting for acquitted defendants who are suing the police. . . .
>
> When dealing with any request for information from a third party, the CPS adopts a position of impartiality, and will consider each request on its merits and in accordance with a number of general principles. It has to be recognised, however, that there will be a number of exceptions to the general principles, either because of the particular status of the third party, or because of the special circumstances which may apply to certain types of proceedings.
>
> Information will only be supplied to a person with a genuine interest in the proceedings or contemplated proceedings in question. Whenever possible, the consent of the maker will be sought before a statement is disclosed. Persons who make statements to the police do so in the knowledge that the statements are likely to be used in criminal proceedings and are entitled to be consulted if their statements are to be revealed for the purpose of other proceedings. It is not usual to disclose material before the criminal proceedings are completed. . . .

Other information about police misconduct

There is often difficulty in identifying whether there is information concerning an officer's background which may be relevant in a particular case, or which may be used as background material. An organisation called the Defendants' Information Service (DIS) has set out to fill this gap. DIS runs a computer database which contains information, at the time of writing, on almost 1,000 police officers, mostly in London.

45 *R v Edwards* [1991] 2 All ER 266, CA.
46 Crown Prosecution Service Annual Report 1992–1993. London: HMSO, 1993, para 5.2.

The information includes details of convictions, complaints, relevant statements read in open court (see p247), and comments made by judges about the reliability of evidence of an officer as well as background material.[47]

Metropolitan Police records

There is no comprehensive list of all the records kept by the police. The following list is compiled from various sources by the authors,[48] who have also drawn on their own experience and that of other practitioners, and is believed to include the main documents available from the Metropolitan Police in addition to those listed above. Most forces have similar or equivalent records.

Notebooks

CID officers have only one notebook; uniformed officers have four.

Arrest report/incident report book   This includes details of arrests and other incidents such as those involving mentally disordered persons, civil disputes, dog bites, fires, meetings, processions and strikes, prostitute cautions, injury on duty, racial discrimination. Sometimes the contents will have been typed up, and transcripts can be asked for also.

Notebook   This records details of other matters such as property lost and found, absences from duty and requests for police attention.

Accident report book   This records accidents, other than those involving damage only, where there is no allegation of an offence.

Process report book   This includes details of traffic and other offences where a person will be summonsed rather than charged.

Police station records

Duty state books   Record every officer working from a particular station. They show officers who are on duty, where they are on duty and the time at which they came on and off duty, refreshments taken and overtime.

47 See *Guardian* 28 March 1995. For details contact DIS on PO Box 7459, London N16 6QQ. Tel/fax: 0181 806 4952.
48 'A guide to the Metropolitan Police (11): procedures in the police station (parts 1 and 2)', *Policing London* No 15 Nov/Dec 1984 and No 16 Jan/Mar 1985; Heaton-Armstrong 'Use of notebooks in court by Metropolitan Police Officers' May 1983 *LAG Bulletin* 64; Clayton and Tomlinson, *Civil Actions Against the Police* (Sweet & Maxwell 1992) pp122–127.

Parade books   Parades at the beginning of each shift are no longer the formal occasions they used to be and not all officers attend. The parade books contain topical information, such as current demonstrations, and football matches and may include the collator's report summarising recent crime, criminal 'intelligence' and gossip.

There should also be records of which police officers are posted to a particular car or other carrier, and records of which officers have attended a particular incident.

Message pads   Kept in the communications room of the station. Mainly, they record messages by telephone from the public. The message is recorded on a pad in a standard form, together with details of the person assigned to deal with it and the result. It may also be recorded on computer. If there is no result by the end of the shift, it must be passed on to the next relief. All messages must be signed by the station officer in the course of the shift and by the duty officer. For 999 calls see p33.

Radio messages are often recorded as computer aided despatch records and the print outs should be requested, together with any other records of radio messages.

The occurrence book   Records events in the police station. Its function has been largely replaced by the custody record (see p21), although occurrence books include details of fires, sudden deaths and illness in the street and injuries to officers on duty. Some of these entries may be kept together in the occurrence report binder. Some stations also have an occurrence book grid which abstracts information by category and shows, for example, people moved from one station to another or juveniles detained.

Records linked with custody records   are not always provided with the custody record. They include property sheets, prisoners' rights inserts, charge sheets, records of cautions.

Front office records   A variety of record books which are kept at the front counter of each station. The more important include:

- missing persons;
- minor meetings and poster parades;
- doctor's book;
- firearms certificates issued;
- firearms found;
- property lost and found;
- log of radio messages recording officers' messages;

- production of documents;
- verbal warnings to motorists.

Medical reports

Book 83 contains details of attendance at the police station and medical examinations by the forensic medical examiner (the police doctor, formerly known as the police surgeon). There may also be original notes and statements. The same records will exist if police officers or other witnesses have been examined by the doctor (see also the front desk doctor's book). If the doctor instructed that a prisoner should be transferred to hospital, this should be recorded.

Book 116 records the breathalyser test procedure carried out at the station.

Laboratory submission and result records will exist for any substance analysed.

Crime reports

The police complete a crime report on a standard computer form for every crime reported. It records details of:

- the offence;
- victims;
- witnesses;
- suspects;
- comments by the officer in charge of the investigation;
- any statements taken;
- any arrests made.

The reports are filed loose-leaf in binders according to the seriousness of the crime. Offences investigated by the CID are kept in the 'major crime book'. Records of petty thefts, car thefts, criminal damage and assaults of the kind dealt with by uniformed officers are kept in the 'beat crime book'. Records of burglaries are kept in a separate 'burglaries book'.

There should also be a report of the scene of crime officer (SOCO).

Other reports

There may be separate Territorial Support Group (TSG) and CID operational and incident reports if they have had involvement in an arrest or investigation. The police sometimes compile press reports or make press statements themselves about cases. Relevant standing orders of the police force concerned can be requested. The Association of

TABLE 3
Summary of recommended retention periods for police records

Record	Comments on retention
Reportable offences	'Weeded' 20 years after last conviction for reportable offence, except: (a) total of more than 6 months' imprisonment, including suspended sentences; (b) two or more convictions for reportable offices; (c) traces of mental history on record; (d) conviction for indecency, violence or drug-trafficking or possession of class 'A' drugs; (e) conviction for offence (not against property) where victim is child or young person, elderly or mentally or physically disabled; (f) where has been subject to proceedings of Prevention of Terrorism (Temporary Provisions) Act 1989 or convicted of offence in Sch 1 to Suppression of Terrorism Act 1978 (if committed in connection with act of terrorism). – Where one of (a) to (e) apply, deleted when subject reaches 70. – Where (d) and (e) apply and record contains only one offence, reviewed after 20 years and deleted if not required for police purposes. – Where (d) applies, and there is conviction for homicide or rape, or (f) applies, record retained for subject's life (or 100 years after date of birth if no notification of death received).
Non-reportable offences only	'Weeded' 10 years after last conviction.
Major incident reports	No longer than 6 years, unless proceedings pending.
Undetected crime reports	Reviewed every 5 years, after initial 10-year period.
Detected crime reports	No longer than 6 years, unless proceedings pending.
Criminal intelligence records	Reviewed annually, retained for long periods in cases of persistent serious offences.
Occurrence/incident reports or logs	No longer than 2 years, unless legal proceedings pending.
Personnel records	Until subject and spouse deceased, except in short employment cases where 20 years.
Adult cautions	Deleted after 5 years if no additions to record.
Juvenile cautions	Kept for 3 years.

Source: *General Rules for Criminal Record Weeding on Police Computer Systems* in agreement with the Data Protection Registrar.

Note: Not all police forces will be subject to the same retention periods. It will, in part, depend upon whether the particular record is held on a computerised system, and subject to data protection, or still held manually on paper. Retention periods vary across the UK for paper-based records.

Chief Police Officers produces documentation on a range of policing matters. Relevant communications with the CPS should be requested. Even those which attract legal privilege should be listed on the list of documents produced by the police in civil proceedings.

999 calls

All 999 calls in the Metropolitan Police area are taken by a central command and control complex. Details of the call are typed directly into the command and control computer. The computer holds up-to-date information on the whereabouts of all police vehicles. The officer taking the 999 call can dispatch the nearest available vehicle to deal with the call. The computer can provide print-outs of the details of the call and the action taken on it.

Preserving police records

Like any large bureaucracy, the police keep an enormous quantity of official records. These cover everything from lost dogs to deaths in police custody. The volume of all this paperwork means that much of it has to be destroyed after a period of time. It is, therefore, crucial that solicitors write to the police at an early stage, possibly in the letter before action, asking them to preserve all their records concerning the case. The national search record and custody record must be kept for 12 months. The Association of Chief Police Officers has produced a code of practice for police computer systems on the retention of records, and table 3 is a summary of this.

It should also be noted that the PCA only retains its files for 18 months after a case has been completed.[49]

---

49 Information provided by the PCA at meeting of the Police Actions Group, 1 February 1994.

CHAPTER 3
Police complaints

Introduction

The police complaints system allows complaints to be dealt with in one of three ways, depending on the seriousness of the allegation:

- informal resolution, for the least serious allegations, such as the use of bad language (see p44);
- formal investigation, for more serious allegations that might result in disciplinary or criminal charges against an officer (see p51);
- supervised formal investigation, for the most serious cases involving, eg, death, serious injuries, assault, corruption and other serious arrestable offences (see p52). These cases are supervised by the PCA.

The PCA has two main functions: first, to supervise the investigation of serious cases (see p52), and second, to supervise the bringing or consideration of disciplinary or criminal charges in all cases other than those that are informally resolved (see pp70–72). In addition, it has power to supervise the investigation of non-complaint matters voluntarily referred to it by the police such as shooting incidents, deaths in police custody and cases of serious corruption (see p78).

The complaints system is closely linked to the police discipline procedures which are to be significantly amended by forthcoming regulations to be introduced under the Police and Magistrates' Courts Act 1994. The anticipated changes are summarised in chapter 4 at p110 but are also referred to in this chapter where they have implications for the complaints system.

Making a complaint

The procedure for making a complaint about the conduct of a police officer is simple and informal. A complaint is best made in writing (see p42), but may be made orally.

Who can make a complaint?

Any member of the public can make a complaint; it need not be the 'victim'. So, for example, a person witnessing an officer assaulting someone in the street could make a complaint. The complaint would stand in the name of the witness, and thus the consent of the victim would not be necessary. However, the PCA will not treat a limited company as a member of the public, nor public and local authorities, local police authorities, trade unions, or pressure groups and their representatives, unless those representatives are making a complaint in their own right and not in their representative capacity. Nevertheless, such bodies can make a complaint on behalf of a member or individual. Strictly speaking the complainant must consent in writing if the complaint is made on his or her behalf,[1] although in practice the police are advised to exercise discretion before demanding written consent. In particular where a solicitor indicates that a complaint is forwarded on instructions from a client it should be accepted without challenge.[2]

If an oral complaint is made, an officer will interview the complainant and probably offer to draft a statement for him or her to sign. Even with the best will in the world, this is likely to be less satisfactory than a statement made in the complainant's own words or with the help of a sympathetic adviser. Furthermore, there is evidence that complainants who attempt to make oral complaints are often fobbed off with assurances or excuses and their complaints are not recorded. Independent research has suggested that at least one in three of those who make a definite attempt to complain are dissuaded (for good reason or otherwise) from doing so.[3]

Recording complaints

Complaints should be addressed to the Chief Constable or, in London, to the Commissioner of Police. Collectively these are known as the chief officers of police.[4] Chief officers of police are under a duty to record all complaints[5] (except for complaints against senior officers outside the Metropolitan Police, which must be recorded by the police authority,

1 PACE s84(4).
2 GCO para 3.1.
3 Maguire and Corbett 'Patterns and profiles of complaints against the police' in Morgan and Smith eds *Coming to Terms with Policing*, Routledge, 1989.
4 Police Act 1964 s62, as amended by Police and Magistrates' Courts Act 1994 s44 and Sch 5 para 15. In practice almost all the functions of the chief officer relating to complaints are delegated: Complaints General Regs reg 13.
5 PACE s85(1); GCO para 3.7.

(see p73)). Chief officers have no discretion to refuse to record a complaint, although the complaints procedure cannot be used for complaints about the way a chief officer directs or controls a police force.[6] However, the PCA makes a clear distinction between the tactical execution of plans or tactial control of detachments on the ground by subordinate officers and strategic and central command of an entire force by a chief officer.[7] Tactical decisions by officers of any rank can properly be the subject of a complaint. So, for example, a decision to take a very large number of officers to conduct a search of a small house, where no violent resistance is expected and which seems calculated to strike terror into the occupants, will not be treated as relating to the 'direction or control' of a police force.[8] Complaints that junior officers have acted improperly on the instructions or with the authority of more senior officers should be made against both the junior officers and the senior officers concerned. Criticisms of strategic decisions by a chief officer will not be recorded as a complaint and should be made instead to the police authority. Neither will a complaint be recorded if it concerns conduct which is or has been the subject of criminal or disciplinary proceedings against an officer.[9] This complements the rule against double jeopardy discussed on p95.

Investigation of a complaint, particularly one expressed in very general terms, may reveal other matters that were not specified in the original complaint. The PCA has reported that:

> Several chief officers have contended strenuously that because the complainant did not specify those detailed acts of misconduct they cannot be investigated or made the subject of disciplinary proceedings under the Act. We consider such a contention to be unjust to the point of absurdity. Ordinary people do not go about with the codes of conduct for the police in their pockets . . . We have said to chief officers that even if a ground of complaint uncovered by the investigation was not specified and recorded originally, there is nothing to prevent that happening later when the wrongdoing comes to light. But we have sometimes encountered an illiberal resistance to this idea and a determination to construe 'complaint' as that only which the complainant originally articulates.[10]

Chief officers are, therefore, now advised that where a complaint is couched in general terms and the subsequent investigation reveals a

6 PACE s84(5).
7 PCA Annual Report 1985 para 2.2.
8 PCA Triennial Review 1985–88 para 1.9.
9 PACE s84(6).
10 PCA Triennial Review 1985–88 para 1.7.

number of breaches of discipline, all such breaches arising directly from the incident and affecting the well-being of the complainant should be treated as separate items of complaint. Any other ancillary matters and breaches of discipline arising from the incident which did not affect the complainant need not be recorded.[11]

Where the police decline to record a complaint and seem to be clearly frustrating the law, the simplest course is probably to ask the PCA to make the complaint on the complainant's behalf. The PCA has said, 'On the comparatively rare occasions when we do find reluctance on the part of the police to take immediate action on receiving a complaint we make our views very clear.'[12] It has also said that it believes that the Authority and not the police should have the final decision on whether a complaint should be recorded by a police force and that it would strengthen public confidence in the complaints system if it had power to direct that a complaint be formally recorded.[13]

There have been cases of systematic failure to record complaints. In 1993 HM Inspectorate of Constabulary reported that officers in Area 8 of Metropolitan Police district were breaching PACE by treating serious complaints as if they simply related to policy questions: 'Most should have been dealt with at least by informal resolution, but many, in other forces, would have led to a full investigation.'[14] If the police persist in refusing to record a complaint, they could be compelled to do so by an application for judicial review (see p302).

The PCA is under a duty to send complaints it receives to chief officers of police unless the complainant does not wish it to do so or it would, in all circumstances, be unneccessary. However, the PCA has a discretion to forward a complaint, even against the wishes of the complainant, where it is satisfied that the public interest so requires.[15]

If a complaint is to be made (see chapter 1), it should be made early on, while events are still fresh in the minds of the complainant, the officer and any witnesses. If more than 12 months have elapsed between the incident, or the latest incident, giving rise to the complaint, the chief officer has a discretion not to investigate it, provided that s/he is of the opinion either that no good reason for the delay has been shown or that injustice would be likely to be caused by the delay, and provided that the

11 GCO para 3.14(e) (amended 4 December 1990) and PCA Triennial Review 1991–94 p5.
12 PCA Annual Report 1991 para 5.6.
13 PCA Triennial Review 1991–94 p71.
14 *A Report of Her Majesty's Inspectorate of Constabulary, Metropolitan Police Area No 8*, June 1993.
15 Complaints General Regs reg 3.

PCA agrees.[16] If the police are considering a waiver under this rule, they should write to the complainant by recorded delivery, inviting him or her to set out any reasons for the delay within 21 days. Any reply should be sent to the PCA.[17]

If a member of the public starts a civil action against the police, this will not automatically be recorded as a complaint. Instead s/he will be asked if s/he wishes to have the matter recorded as a complaint and whether s/he is willing to co-operate in the investigation (see p200).[18]

Special constables, cadets, probationers and civilian staff

Special constables and police cadets

Complaints about special constables and police cadets, who are not formally members of a police force,[19] are not within the scope of the statutory complaints system. The government's White Paper on Police Reform[20] proposed to increase the number of special constables from 19,000 to 30,000, thus increasing the ratio of special constables to regulars to one in four. Special constables have the same powers and privileges (including powers of arrest) within their own police area and in contiguous areas as regular officers[21] and, as in the future they are likely to be in greater contact with the public, the number of complaints against them is likely to increase.

Where a report, allegation or complaint is received from which it appears that a special constable may have been remiss or negligent in the discharge of his/her duty or otherwise unfit for duty, a chief officer may

16 Police (Dispensation from Requirement to Investigate Complaints) Regs 1985 reg 3(1)(aa). The Police (Anonymous, Repetitious etc Complaints) Regs 1985 SI No 672 were amended and renamed by the Police (Dispensation from Requirement to Investigate Complaints) Regs 1990 SI No 1301. The former regulations in their amended form are cited here as 'Police Dispensation Regs' 1985.
17 GCO para 4.36(v) (amended 4 December 1990).
18 Ibid. para 4.30 (amended 20 February 1989).
19 For the status of specials see Police Act 1964 s16, *Commissioner of Police v Hancock* [1916] 1 KB 190 and *Sheikh v Chief Constable of Greater Manchester Police* [1989] 2 All ER 684 at 689a; for the status of cadets see Police Act 1964 s 17, and *Wiltshire Police Authority v Wynn* [1980] 3 WLR 445.
20 *Police Reform: A Police Service for the Twenty-First Century,* Cm 2281, June 1993.
21 Police Act 1964 s19, as amended by Local Government Act 1972 ss196(5), 272(1) and Sch 30 and Police and Magistrates' Courts Act 1994 s44 and Sch 5; see Criminal Justice Act 1948 s66 for custody powers beyond constable-wick.

suspend him.[22] The suspension can last until either it is decided that no action need be taken or action is taken. A chief officer has power to require a special to retire as an alternative to dismissal where the special has been remiss or negligent, or is otherwise unfit to discharge his duty.[23]

In practice chief officers are advised to treat complaints against special constables in the same way as complaints against regular officers; however, this is not obligatory and in any event there can be no supervision by the PCA. The PCA has said that it is convinced that the inability to consider complaints against 30,000 special constables will be seen as a loophole and will therefore diminish confidence in the complaints system.[24]

If a complaint is made against a special constable or a cadet *and* a regular officer, any report to the PCA (see p71) should include details of the whole investigation, even though the part dealing with the conduct of the special constable or cadet is not its direct concern.[25] For the civil liability of special constables and police cadets, see pp206–207.

Probationers

Newly appointed constables serve a probationary period of at least two years. Probationers are full members of a police force and are as fully subject to the police complaints system as any other officer. Aside from the complaints and discipline procedures, however, a chief officer of police can discharge a probationer at any time if s/he considers that the probationer is unfit, physically or mentally, to perform the duties of his/her office, or that s/he is not likely to become an efficient or well conducted officer.[26] However, chief officers should not use this provision as a means of dismissing a probationer where disciplinary proceedings should properly be brought[27] (see p93).

Civilian staff

The police complaints system does not extend to civilian staff who are employed directly by police authorities or by commercial enterprises

22 Special Constables Regulations 1965 SI No 536, reg 1.
23 Ibid reg 3.
24 PCA Annual Report 1993 p37.
25 GCO para 3.20.
26 Police Regs 1995, SI No 215 reg 15; *R v Chief Constable of Thames Valley Police ex p Stevenson* (1987) *Times* 22 April, QBD.
27 *Chief Constable of the North Wales Police v Evans* [1982] 1 WLR 1155; [1982] 3 All ER 141 HL; *R v Chief Constable of the West Midlands Police ex p Carroll* [1994] 7 Admin LR 45, CA.

under contract to the police. There are about 42,000 civilian staff (compared to about 127,000 police officers) and there is a growing trend to transfer traditional police functions to such staff, whether as scene of crime officers, control room staff or staff handling and transporting prisoners. There are also more and more senior managerial staff within police forces who may exercise authority, although in theory not operational control, over police officers. In recent years there has also been increasing pressure from the security services, particularly MI5,[28] to take over responsibility for a number of areas of 'traditional' police work, including drug trafficking, money laundering, animal rights protests and computer fraud. The PCA has noted that 'the mere fact that certain tasks are no longer being carried out by police officers is unlikely to reduce the possibility of complaints.'[29]

Police authorities have long had power to employ civilian staff.[30] However, the Police and Magistrates' Courts Act 1994 requires that the police authority must secure that such staff are under the control and direction of the chief constable.[31] Civilian staff may be covered by local complaints procedures operated by individual police authorities; allegations of maladministration may be referred to the Local Ombudsman;[32] allegations that any proposal, decision or omission by a police authority constitutes illegality, maladministration or a breach of any statutory code of practice may be referred to the monitoring officer of the police authority who must prepare a report.[33]

The PCA has recommended that the police complaints system should be extended to cover all the providers of what were previously police services.[34]

28 The security service (MI5) has a separate complaints procedure see Security Service Act 1989 s5 and Sch 2; the complaints tribunal has *never* upheld a single complaint. A complaints procedure for the secret intelligence service (MI6) and GCHQ was established by the Intelligence Services Act 1994 s9 and Sch 1; see Wadham, 'The Intelligence Services Act 1994' (1994) 57 MLR 916. For the relationship between Special Branch and MI5, see 'Guidelines on Special Branch work in Great Britain, Home Office and Scottish Office, July 1994.
29 PCA Triennial Review 1991–94 p20.
30 Police Act 1964 s10; cf HO Circular 105/1988, Civilian Staff in the Police Service.
31 Ibid, as amended by Police and Magistrates' Courts Act 1994 s10, from a date to be appointed.
32 Local Government Act 1974 s25(1)(ca) as amended by Police and Magistrates' Courts Act 1994 Sch 4.
33 Local Government and Housing Act 1989 ss4,5, and 21(1)(g) as amended by Police and Magistrates' Courts Act 1994 Sch 4.
34 PCA Triennial Review 1991–94, p20.

For the civil liability of civilian staff see p208.

Copies of complaints

Generally copies of a complaint must be supplied on request to:

- the person who made the complaint
- the person on whose behalf the complaint was made
- the officer against whom the complaint was made.

The request must be made in writing.[35] The police are advised that for these purposes 'complaint' means the basic document or documents in which the complainant's allegations against an officer are brought to the attention of the appropriate authority. The Home Office considers that:

a letter which simply states that the writer wishes to complain, but which does not include sufficient details for the purpose of investigation, does not constitute a complaint in this sense; in such cases the complaint includes the statement which the complainant will then normally make setting out his account of the incident or conduct in question. Where a complaint is made orally, 'the complaint' includes the written record of what was said by the complainant in describing the grounds of his complaint. When a copy of a complaint is supplied to the complainant or the officer . . . it should not include any subsequent statements made in the course of the investigation.[36]

In 1989 the Home Office amended this guidance by adding:

the document or documents of which copies should be supplied to an officer under the Regulations are:
a. if the complaint is made in writing, a copy of the letter of complaint or of that part of it which relates to that officer;
b. if the complaint is made orally, a copy of the written record made of the complaint (which may include a copy of a contemporaneous entry, eg, in a pocketbook or incident register, and the formal record of the complaint made out later); and
c. copies of the relevant parts of any statements which either contain fresh complaints or explain or particularise complaints already made.

It is considered that a letter indicating a wish to complain but not detailing the substance of the complaint does not constitute a complaint for these purposes. In such cases, the complaint of which a copy shall be provided is

---

35 Complaints General Regs reg 9(1).
36 GCO para 7.8, possibly intending to follow *Conerney v Jacklin* [1985] Crim LR 234, 129 SJ 285, CA. See notes 217 and 218 below.

the relevant portion of the statement or other written record of the substance of the complaint.[37]

Complaints letter checklist

1 Name and address of member of the public on whose behalf complaint is made.[38] See pp35 and 67–68.
2 Name and address of complainant's representative. Enclose complainant's written consent.[39] See p35.
3 Date, time and place of incident.[40] See p37–38.
4 Name, number, physical description or other means of identifying the police officers involved, if possible. (A complaint can still proceed even if *none* of these details can be supplied.)
5 Registration number, police identification number, make, type of colour of any vehicle involved.
6 *Brief* description of conduct complained about; see p200.
7 Proposed venue for any interview; see p47.
8 Instructions to investigating officer to communicate only through complainant's representative and not to call on the complainant at home or at work.
9 Request to preserve any specific documents or evidence, see p19.
10 Request that any specific investigation be carried out immediately, eg, search a particular officer's locker, carry out any medical or forensic science examination, fingerprinting etc; see p43.
11 Request that any specific interviews be carried out, eg, custody officer, occupants of adjoining cells, complainant's neighbours etc.
12 Whether complainant declines informal resolution:[41] see p44.
13 Consider copying letter to PCA and inviting PCA to supervise the investigation[42] (see p52) or to take urgent legal action to preserve

---

37 GCO para 7.10A, added by Home Office Circular 21/1989 (20 February 1989) following *R v Commissioner of Police for the Metropolis ex p Ware* (1985) *Times* 31 July, QBD (not fully reported, see transcript CO/1496/83) concerning the now repealed Police (Copies of Complaints) Regs 1977 SI No 579.
38 Complaints General Regs reg 2(1); Dispensation Regs.
39 PACE s84(4).
40 Dispensation Regs reg 3(1)(aa).
41 PACE s85(2).
42 PACE s89.

> evidence in the hands of third parties, eg, CC/TV videotapes (see p44).
> 14 Do not confuse a complaints letter with a 'letter before action' in civil proceedings. If there is any possibility of a civil action, any letter should be written only by the complainant's solicitor; see pp38 and 211.
> 15 Consider whether anything in the letter is capable of being defamatory; see p82.

Chief officers have a discretion to refuse to supply a copy of a complaint if they think that it might prejudice any criminal investigation or proceedings pending at the time the request is made. They can also refuse if they think that it would be contrary to the public interest *and* the Home Secretary agrees. In either case, the refusal must be made in a written notice to the person asking for the copy. If a copy is refused, six months must elapse before another request can be made.[43]

Of course, complainants and advisers should have kept a copy of the complaint, as a matter of course. However, if this was not done, a copy should be requested as soon as possible. It is important that the complainant has a copy in front of him/her if s/he agrees to be interviewed by the investigating officer, see p46. A tactic for obtaining a copy of the complainant's statement, despite the Home Office advice, is described at p49.

Initial procedure

When a complaint is made, the police are under a duty to take any steps that appear desirable for the purpose of obtaining or preserving evidence relating to the conduct forming the subject of the complaint.[44] This might involve such things as preserving documentary records, conducting searches, taking photographs and ordering medical examinations of the parties to an assault, both the complainant and the police officer(s). Medical examinations can be carried out only by consent.[45] The Home Office advises the police that:

> Where the allegation is one of assault by a police officer it is advisable to make immediate arrangements to have the victim and the officer medically examined, with their consent. The examination should whenever possible,

43 Complaints General Regs reg 9(2).
44 PACE s84(1).
45 GCO para 3.4.

be carried out by a police surgeon or at a hospital if medical attention is required urgently. In addition, a note should be made of the general condition of the victim and the officer and this should include references to any visible signs of injury or discomfort. Photographs of both parties can also be useful.[46]

While such evidence will be used to investigate the complaint, it will also be available to the police lawyers if a civil action is brought and may be used to defend such proceedings. Tactically it will usually be preferable to arrange for an examination by an independent doctor and to release any resulting medical report to the investigating officers through the complainant's solicitor (see p17). If an examination by a police doctor is unavoidable, the complainant should be warned not to discuss the circumstances of the injury with the doctor.

If the complainant is aware of any evidence that ought to be obtained or preserved, this should be specified in the letter of complaint, even if it has been mentioned orally. Police procedures for the automatic weeding out and destruction of written and computer records have already been explained on p32. Failure by the police to obtain or preserve evidence may itself justify a further complaint. In exceptional cases the PCA may intervene to preserve evidence and it has, for example, taken legal action to obtain video footage before it could be accidentally mislaid, erased or damaged.[47]

Once steps have been taken to obtain or preserve evidence, the chief officer must establish whether any senior officers, ie, those above the rank of chief superintendent, were involved.[48] The special procedure for such officers is explained below at p73.

In practice most complaints from members of the public concern junior officers. In such cases the police must decide whether the matter can be resolved informally.[49]

Informal resolution

Informal resolution is only appropriate for the less serious complaints. It allows the complainant, if s/he chooses, to see whether the complaint can be resolved to his/her satisfaction without a formal investigation. It usually involves a minimal element of investigation with an attempt at conciliation.

46 Ibid para 7.10A (amended 20 February 1989).
47 PCA Annual Report 1988 para 4.4.
48 PACE s84(2) and (4).
49 Under PACE s85(2).

On receiving a complaint the chief officer must decide whether it is suitable for informal resolution (see below). If it is, the police must seek to resolve it informally, that is, they must ask if the complainant will agree to informal resolution. This is solely a matter for the complainant; the police cannot insist on it. Most forces deal with approximately 30%–40% of all complaints in this way.

Informal resolution may be appropriate where, for example, the complainant decides that, on reflection, the matter is too trivial to pursue. However the police often have a strong interest in seeking an informal investigation or persuading the complainant to withdraw the complaint completely so that it cannot be investigated at all (see p66). The PCA has hinted that it suspects that some informally resolved cases are not recorded so that they do not appear in the statistics.[50]

Police tactics

If the complainant is serious about pursuing a formal complaint, it is important that s/he is forewarned that the police may try to persuade him/her to agree to informal resolution or withdrawal. They commonly use various tactics, from assurances that the officer has learned a salutary lesson to pointing out that the chances of success are very slim. They may also say that the officer is young and that a complaint will blight his/her future career or conversely that s/he is nearing retirement and that a complaint will jeopardise his/her pension. Complainants are also frequently, and misleadingly, 'warned' that a formal investigation will mean that they and their witnesses will have to take a day off work in order to attend a disciplinary hearing, despite the tiny number of cases that result in such hearings. If the investigating officer attempts this tactic, it is worth pointing out that, if the police honestly believe that the case is sufficiently serious to merit a disciplinary hearing they should encourage the complainant to pursue the matter and not attempt to discourage him/her. Conversely, if they honestly believe the complaint is insufficiently serious to warrant formal investigations, it is underhand to suggest that a disciplinary hearing is likely.[51] Some other useful ways of dealing with this kind of pressure are described below.

The appointed officer's task is to achieve a position in which the complainant is satisfied that his or her complaint has been dealt with in an appropriate manner.[52] It is also important to remember that the

50 PCA Annual Report 1992 p9.
51 Maguire and Corbett *A Study of the Police Complaints System*, HMSO, 1991, pp77 and 100.
52 GCO para 4.4.

complainant is agreeing only to *attempt* an informal resolution. If, having made the attempt, the complainant is not satisfied with the outcome, s/he can still insist on a formal investigation.

Which cases are suitable for informal resolution?

A complaint can be resolved informally only if:

- the member of the public consents; and
- the conduct complained of, even if proved, would not justify a criminal or disciplinary charge.[53]

Not every breach of the Police Discipline Code would justify a charge: the chief officer has a discretion to decide that, say, a technical or trivial breach should be dealt with in some way short of making a charge. In practice, this is quite common.[54] Informal resolution does not need the consent of the officer concerned.

In deciding whether an offence is sufficiently trivial to allow informal resolution, the Home Office advises the police that trivial offences involving motor vehicles and trivial non-traffic cases, such as 'the use of obscene language or the disciplinary offence of incivility, or an assault in the nature of a mere push without aggravating features such as an endeavour to obtain an admission', need not be formally investigated. If a member of the public in similar circumstances would not be prosecuted or would be cautioned, the Home Office considers informal resolution to be permissable.[55]

None of this affects the complainant's right to refuse to consent to informal resolution: this remains a matter for him/her to decide, no matter how trivial the incident.

The PCA will supervise the investigation of certain cases of serious misconduct, including cases where the conduct allegedly resulted in death or serious injury (see p52). Although PACE does not say that such cases cannot be informally resolved it is clearly the policy of the Act that they should be fully and formally investigated.

The interview

The interview is the key event in the complaints process. It is often the only opportunity the complainant will have to get his/her version of events over to a sceptical or hostile investigating officer. It is also the

53 PACE s85(10).
54 Eg, See Cook 'The blue-coated deviant: semi-formal discipline' *Police Review* 21 January 1983 p124.
55 GCO para 4.4.

time when the complainant is likely to come under the greatest pressure to withdraw the complaint or accept informal resolution. Many complainants expect the interview to be a neutral investigation of the facts, only to find that they are subjected to forceful or intimidating interrogation at which they feel everything they say is ridiculed or disbelieved.[56] It is therefore crucial to make sure the complainant is well prepared for the interview.

It is wise for a friend or adviser to be present at the interview and to help the complainant prepare for it in advance. The complainant and the friend or adviser should discuss beforehand whether the former is prepared to accept informal resolution. If the complainant wants a formal investigation, the friend or adviser should be clear about this so that s/he can provide support if the police appear to be exerting contrary pressure.

If the complaint is to be informally resolved the investigating officer is under a duty to seek the views of both the complainant and the officer as soon as practicable.[57] The complainant should therefore be interviewed about both the incident that gave rise to the complaint and whether s/he will agree to informal resolution.

Many complainants feel uncomfortable if the interview is held at a police station, possibly the very scene of the incident they are complaining about. Equally they may be reluctant to allow the police into their home. Interviews can therefore be arranged to be held on neutral territory such as a citizens advice bureau or a solicitor's office where the complainant will feel confident and relaxed.

In certain cases, a complaint may be informally resolved as soon as it is made. This may be possible, for example, where a superior officer receives a complaint and the officer concerned is present and willing to give an explanation or apology immediately which satisfies the complainant.[58] There is a danger that the police may mistakenly think that the complainant is satisfied when, in fact, s/he still wishes to pursue the complaint. The police are, therefore, advised that, if they are satisfied with the handling of the complaint, they make a record in the complaints register and write to the complainant recording briefly their understanding of the way in which the compaint was resolved and indicating their *intention* of recording it as having been informally

56 Police Complaints Board, Triennial Review 1983 para 4.13; K Russell, *Complaints against the police which are withdrawn,* Leicester Polytechnic Reprographic Unit 1986.
57 Police (Complaints) (Informal Resolution) Regs 1985 (Informal Resolution Regs) SI No 671 reg 4(1).
58 Informal Resolution Regs reg 4(1); GCO para 4.8.

resolved.[59] This allows the complainant the opportunity to object and make a formal complaint. If s/he fails to do so, a later complaint may be debarred as being repetitious.[60]

In some cases, there will be irreconcilable differences in the complainant's version and the police officer's version of the incident. The investigating officers are advised that 'in such a case it may be sufficient to explain the position to the complainant and invite him to accept that nothing further can be done'.[61] The police may have taken the view that someone – either complainant or police officer – is lying, but this is not in itself a good reason for allowing the investigating officers to wriggle out of deciding which. If the complainant stands on his/her right to refuse informal resolution, the police will be forced to make a decision (see p69).

Strictly, a complainant does not have to agree to be interviewed about the complaint, but, not surprisingly, if s/he refuses, the chances of having the complaint upheld are reduced to virtually nil. It is most probable that the complaint would be dispensed with on the ground that it would not be reasonably practicable to investigate it, see p67.

Legal aid may be available to pay for a solicitor's attendance at the interview, eg, if a civil action is being funded by legal aid. Even if no civil action is contemplated, the advice and assistance of a solicitor at the interview may still be funded under the green form scheme (see p185).

Interview checklist

If the complainant agrees to an interview, the adviser who is going to be present should run through the following points in advance. In particular, the adviser should discuss beforehand what, if anything, the complainant is prepared to agree with the police.

a) The adviser should be aware of all the relevant facts. A written statement about the incident should be prepared in advance so that this can be used as an *aide-memoire* in the interview. If the complainant is represented by a solicitor the statement should be prepared in a form that satisfies Criminal Justice Act 1967 s9.[62] A properly prepared s9 statement can be handed to the police at the start of the interview and will save time as the interview can then be confined to questions that clarify the complainant's allegations. The complai-

59 GCO para 4.8
60 Dispensation Regs 1985 reg 3(2)(d).
61 GCO para 4.6.
62 See also *Practice Direction* (1986) 83 Cr App R 212 on the preparation and editing of statements.

nant will also have greater control of the interview and can be confident that no mistakes will be made about the order of events, who was present at the incident, the dates and times of incidents and any other points that might otherwise be forgotten or confused. However, if there is any possibility of a civil action being brought an interview should take place, if at all, only with a solicitor present (see p200). In this event such a statement should only be drafted by the solicitor acting in the civil action.

b) Before the interview begins, agree with the police that they will supply the complainant at the end of the interview with a copy of any statement and of any notes they make. This may be the last opportunity to obtain a copy (see p201). Even where a civil action is brought there can be difficulties, both legal and practical, in obtaining copies. If the police do not agree to supply a copy, the complainant can either insist the interview takes place sufficiently slowly to allow the adviser to make a full record or call off the interview, make a fresh complaint about the investigating officer and refer the matter to the PCA.

c) Start the interview by asking whether the investigating officer has already interviewed the offending officers. If the original complaint contained sufficient detail to identify the officers it is probable that they will already have been interviewed and that their version of events will have gained credibility in the eyes of the investigating officer. The complainant then effectively has to disprove the officers' explanation.

d) The role of the adviser is to intervene if the police try to press the complainant to make an admission or if they become overbearing or oppressive.

e) The adviser should discuss beforehand whether the complainant is prepared to accept informal resolution or to withdraw the complaint. The complainant should be made aware in advance of the kinds of tactics the police use to persuade him/her to reconsider, see pp45 and 67.

f) If the questioning gets rough or new facts emerge, the adviser should call for an adjournment to discuss the matter in private.

g) At the end of the interview, press the investigating officer to give an estimate of when s/he expects to submit his/her report to the chief officer. This is the only effective way to monitor whether the investigation is likely to be delayed see p65.

Apologies and statements made during informal resolutions

All that many complainants seek from an informal resolution is a written apology from the offending officer, or from his/her superior officer. In practice this is almost never forthcoming, at least in the form of an unqualified apology. Investigating officers have power to offer an apology on behalf of the police officer concerned. However, they can do this only if the officer has admitted the conduct complained about.[63] On the other hand, investigating officers are always free to apologise on behalf of the police force without the officer's consent or admission. The reluctance of investigating officers to offer even such limited apologies needlessly pushes many eminently reconcilable complaints out of the informal resolution process into formal investigations. In practice the most that can sometimes be expected, short of a formal investigation, is a letter apologising that the complainant felt the need to complain.

If the investigating officer thinks that it would be helpful, s/he may arrange for the officer complained about to meet the complainant in order to discuss the incident and, possibly, to offer an explanation or apology in person. However the officer cannot be compelled to attend such a meeting.[64]

Any statement, whether written or oral and whether made by the complainant or the police officer, which is made for the purpose of an informal resolution of a complaint is not admissible in any subsequent criminal, civil or disciplinary proceedings.[65]

This is intended to encourage all parties to discuss the incident as freely as possible, without the fear that what they say will be used against them in a subsequent hearing. However, a statement is not inadmissible if it consists of or includes an admission which should not, because of its seriousness, be resolved informally.[66] Thus if an officer during the informal resolution of a trivial matter makes an admission about a serious matter, the serious matter is admissible in subsequent proceedings. For the relationship between formal complaints and civil proceedings, see p200.

Records of informal resolutions

The complainant is entitled[67] to a copy of the record of the outcome of

63 Informal Resolution Regs reg 4(2).
64 GCO para 4.9.
65 PACE s104(3).
66 Ibid s104(4).
67 Informal Resolution Regs reg 5.

a complaint if s/he agrees to informal resolution, provided that s/he applies within three months of:

- the date on which the informal resolution was achieved; or
- the date on which it was decided that the complaint should no longer be dealt with by informal resolution (for example, because it turned out to be more serious than was originally thought).

No record of an attempted or successful informal resolution is entered on the personal record of the officer concerned.[68]

Formal investigations

Formal investigations can be conducted in two different ways. The investigation of really serious cases (where the allegation involves death or serious injury: p52) is supervised by the PCA and a report is made to the Authority. Ordinary formal investigations are the responsibility of the chief officer of police and a report is made to him/her.[69]

Ordinary formal investigations

There must be a formal investigation of a complaint if it appears to the chief officer:

- from the outset, that it is unsuitable for informal resolution; or
- that, despite attempts having been made, informal resolution is impossible, because, for example, the complainant refuses to consent to it; or
- that, after attempts have been made, the complaint is not suitable for informal resolution, for example because it turns out to be more serious than was originally thought.[70]

A complaint is unsuitable for informal resolution unless the member of the public consents *and* the chief officer is satisfied that the conduct complained of, even if proved, would not justify a criminal or disciplinary charge.[71]

If there has to be a formal investigation, the chief officer must

68 GCO para 4.13.
69 PACE s85(9).
70 Ibid s85(3) and (5).
71 Ibid s85(10).

appoint an officer from his/her own or another force to investigate the complaint formally. It is often a major source of grievance to complainants that misconduct by the police is investigated by other police officers. In his report on the Brixton disorders Lord Scarman said, 'By and large, people do not trust the police to investigate the police'.[72]

In ordinary formal investigations, the choice of investigating officer lies with the chief officer and a complainant cannot compel the chief officer to appoint an officer from another force. In practice, outsiders are appointed only in exceptional cases which have attracted widespread public concern. Such complaints are, in any case, likely to be supervised by the PCA which has power to insist on an officer from another force (see p56). In 1989, 63 cases were investigated by an officer from another force compared with 53 in 1988.[73]

The investigating officer appointed to conduct the formal investigation must not be the officer who attempted to resolve the complaint informally.[74] Furthermore, the investigating officer must not be the chief officer of the force concerned, nor an officer in the same subdivision or branch as the officer being investigated.[75]

The investigating officer will want to interview the complainant about the complaint and to take a statement. As has been seen, arrangements should be made for a friend or adviser to be present at any interview. (For further advice on handling interviews see pp46–51.)

A complainant may feel that the interview has been handled in such a cursory manner that s/he has not been given an opportunity to expand on all the points at stake. In such a case, a letter should be sent to the investigating officer, explaining the complainant's dissatisfaction. A copy should be sent to the PCA, which may then decide to supervise the investigation and to issue a direction to conduct another interview more fully (see pp56–57).

Supervision by PCA

Which complaints will be supervised?
Mandatory referral Complaints about certain cases of serious misconduct must be referred to the PCA. These are cases where the complaint alleges:

72 *The Scarman Report* Pelican Books, 1982, para 5.43.
73 Report of HM Chief Inspector of Constabulary 1989 para 9.3; more recent figures are not available: HC Written Answers 9 March 1995.
74 PACE s85(6).
75 Discipline Regs reg 6(5).

- that the conduct resulted in death;[76] or
- that the conduct resulted in serious injury, ie, a fracture, damage to an internal organ, impairment of bodily function, a deep cut or a deep laceration.[77] Whether a wound needs three or more stitches is sometimes used as a rule of thumb for deciding whether a cut is 'deep'. The government has said it will legislate to allow the PCA a discretion to dispense with supervision where it is satisfied, on proper evidence, that the injury is minor (notwithstanding the definition in PACE s87(4)), whether this is apparent from the start or becomes so only in the course of the investigation.[78]
- assault occasioning actual bodily harm;[79]
- corruption;[80]
- a serious arrestable offence.[81]

In such cases, the complaint must be referred to the PCA within one day of the chief officer realising that the complaint alleges such conduct.[82]

The PCA can receive notification of complaints outside normal working hours by telex. If it is necessary to consult the Authority before the next working day, appropriate arrangements have been made for police headquarters to contact an Authority member out of working hours.

The statutory time limit is usually met, although there have been cases where 'an unexplainable delay' has occurred between a complaint being registered at a force outstation and notification to police head-quarters.[83]

Discretionary referral Any other type of complaint may be referred to the PCA, but the chief officer is not under a duty to do so.[84] A chief officer might choose to make such a referral if a case had attracted widespread interest or concern and s/he felt that involving the PCA

76 PACE s87(1)(a)(i).
77 PACE s87(1)(a)(i) and (4).
78 HC Written Answers col 397, 27 June 1989. Such a provision is expected in forthcoming regulations: see PCA Triennial Review 1991–94 p6.
79 Police (Complaints) (Mandatory Referrals etc) Regs 1985 ('Mandatory Referrals Regs') SI No 673 reg 4(1)(a); GCO para 6.2; *R v Miller* [1954] 2 All ER 529.
80 Ie, any offence under Prevention of Corruption Act 1906 s1: Mandatory Referrals Regs reg 4(1)(b).
81 Ie, within the meaning of PACE s116: Mandatory Referrals Regs reg 4(1)(c).
82 Complaints General Regs reg 10(1); Mandatory Referrals Regs reg 4(2).
83 PCA Triennial Review 1985–88 paras 1.27–1.28.
84 PACE s87(1)(b).

TABLE 4
Referrals to the PCA

	1991	1992	1993	1994/95*
Mandatory referrals	4,212	4,333	3,998	3,624
Voluntary referrals	103	132	129	114
Referrals required by PCA	15	11	12	17
Total referrals	4,330	4,476	4,139	3,755

*April 1994 to March 1995
Source: HC Written Answers, 9 March 1995 and PCA Annual Report 1994/95

would be a way of reassuring the public that it was receiving full and proper attention.

The PCA has a discretion to require a chief officer to submit a complaint to it.[85] This might happen where the PCA hears of a serious complaint, for example, through press coverage or directly from a complainant. The chief officer must submit the complaint within one day of receiving notification of the requirement.[86]

Mandatory supervision   The PCA must supervise the investigation of any complaint alleging misconduct resulting in death or serious injury and any other case where the Authority considers it desirable in the public interest.[87] The PCA must generally give the chief officer notification of its decision within seven days of receiving the complaint. This time limit can be extended if the PCA asks for further information to help it to make a decision or if an investigation is delayed pending the outcome of a criminal case relating to the complaint. The PCA must then notify the chief officer of its decision within seven days of receiving the further information or of being notified of the outcome of the case.[88]

Discretionary supervision   The PCA has complained that many cases suitable for discretionary supervision are more deserving of its independent scrutiny than those that must automatically be referred to it for mandatory supervision; however, it cannot call in such cases 'if we are unaware of the incident. We would therefore encourage forces to make

85 Ibid s87(2).
86 Complaints General Regs reg 10(2).
87 PACE s89(1) and (2)(a). The PCA has recommended that legislation be enacted so that it need not necessarily supervise all cases of serious injury: PCA Triennial Review 1988–91 paras 2.1–2.11.
88 Complaints General Regs reg 4(2) and (3).

greater use of the section which allows them to refer a complaint to us voluntarily.'[89] The PCA has also said it 'has no set rules as to which cases we accept and which we reject. Rather we consider each case on its merits. By adopting this method we find that we supervise a wide spectrum of cases, including allegations of perjury, indecent assault, planting drugs, improper disclosure of information, unlawful detention and many others.'[90]

Complainants should therefore be encouraged to refer such cases, and other cases which may be novel or complex or raise important issues of general application, to the PCA, requesting it to exercise its discretion and supervise the investigation.

The PCA has said that it will usually look for some special factor in the case, for example, if the complainant is in any way disadvantaged (being, say, very elderly, or a juvenile or mentally ill), or if there is an allegation of corruption or conspiracy to pervert the course of justice.[91] However, the complainant is free to draw the PCA's attention to any complaint and it may be worthwhile doing so in any serious case.

The purpose of supervising an investigation is to ensure that the investigating officer is answerable to the PCA for the conduct, speed, strategy and tactics of the investigation. In supervised cases, responsibility for the supervision is delegated to an individual member of the PCA. The degree of involvement of that member will depend on the nature of the case, but the member will at least confer with the investigating officer at the outset, to ensure that steps have been taken to preserve evidence and to identify all possible witnesses and suspects. There will also be discussion and agreement on the plan of investigation and the general lines of enquiry. Usually supervision is conducted by telephone and letter, and perhaps will include a meeting with the investigating officer.[92] The member may attend when complainants, witnesses and even the officers about whom the complaint has been made are being interviewed and asked to make statements.[93]

In 1993 individual members of the PCA made 130 visits to various parts of the country in carrying out their supervising responsibilities, and 220 meetings with investigating officers were held at the PCA's headquarters.[94]

89 PCA Annual Report 1992, p17, para 2.2.
90 PCA Annual Report 1991, p17, para 2.16.
91 PCA Annual Report 1985 para 3.19.
92 Ibid paras 3.3–3.4.
93 *R v PCA ex p Thompson* (1989) *Times* 24 October; [1990] COD 205, DC; PCA Annual Report 1989 para 5.4.
94 PCA Annual Report 1993, p19.

TABLE 5
Supervision by the PCA

	1991	1992	1993	1994/95*
Mandatory supervision	421	420	625	574
Discretionary supervision	308	337	326	425
Total	729	757	951	999

*April 1994 to March 1995
Source: HC Written Answers, 9 March 1995, and PCA Annual Report 1994/95

In 1994/95, 3,755 cases were referred to the PCA for it to decide whether or not the investigation should be supervised. In 574 of these cases supervision was mandatory (as they involved death or serious injury) and in a further 425 the PCA judged that the investigation should be supervised in the public interest. Thus in 1994/95 the PCA supervised a total of 999 cases.[95]

The PCA's powers
If the PCA supervises the investigation, it can require the chief officer to obtain its approval of his or her choice of investigating officer. If the investigating officer has already been appointed and the PCA is dissatisfied with the appointment, it can require the chief officer to select another officer who meets its approval.[96] In many cases, the PCA's interest in the appointment will not go beyond the broad question of whether the officer should come from a different division of the force, or from outside the force.[97]

In serious cases, complainants often prefer to have their cases investigated by an officer from another force. If this is the case, it is a good idea to ensure that the complaint receives wide publicity and to make it clear to the PCA that an investigation by an insider will not enjoy public confidence. A chief officer must provide an investigating officer if the chief officer of another force asks him or her to do so.[98]

A police officer must comply with any directions from the PCA imposing additional reasonable requirements as to the conduct of any

95 HC Written Answers 9 March 1995 and PCA Annual Report 1994/95. See also table 4 above.
96 PACE s89(4).
97 *Police Complaints and Discipline Procedures* Cmnd 9072, HMSO, 1983, para 20.
98 PACE s85(7).

particular investigation.[99] This might cover directions, for example, to interview particular witnesses or to carry out searches or forensic tests. However, if at any stage the possibility of criminal proceedings arises, the PCA cannot give directions to obtain or to preserve evidence of a crime without the consent of the Director of Public Prosecutions.[100] Before giving any directions about the resources which a chief officer should make available for the investigation (for example, a direction to release extra officers to assist the investigating officer), the PCA must consult the chief officer and have regard to what s/he says.[101] Some cases have involved substantial teams of investigating officers supported by civilian staff, computers and incident rooms. Exceptionally, the team investigating 754 arrests made by the West Midlands police serious crime squad consisted of 28 officers and two civilians.

One of the major reasons for the lack of public confidence in the police complaints system has been the impression that investigating officers do not always pursue their enquiries into police misconduct as rigorously and as conscientiously as they would if they were investigating an offence by a member of the public. There has been criticism in the past that, in a significant minority of cases, investigations have not been as thorough as might have been expected and that more thorough cross-examination and tracing of witnesses might have resulted in better evidence to substantiate the complaint.[102]

While it remains the case that police wrongdoing is still investigated by other police officers, each supervised investigation is individually scrutinised by a named member of the PCA:

'In every case one of our first and most important functions is to ensure that the complainant is given the opportunity to make a full statement of his complaint(s). He will also be encouraged to nominate witnesses and to draw attention to evidence which he believes will support him . . . The investigating officer is responsible directly to the supervising member for the conduct of the investigation. Statements from witnesses, evidence such as medical or forensic science reports, photographs, relevant police records, interview tapes and video film are collected and submitted to the member for scrutiny. We require the investigating officer to submit monthly reports on the progress of an investigation, but in a few cases much closer liaison has to be maintained. After examining the papers the member may conclude

99 Ibid s89(5); Mandatory Referrals Regs reg 5(2).
100 Ibid reg 5(3).
101 Ibid reg 5(4).
102 News report, *Times* 8 April 1981. Published in amended form as Stevens and Willis *Ethnic minorities and complaints against the police* Research and Planning Unit Paper No 5, Home Office, 1982.

that the complainant or witnesses should be interviewed or re-interviewed
to clarify or enlarge on their evidence or that further lines of enquiry should
be developed.'[103]

The individual member of the PCA who is responsible for supervising the case is available by telephone to discuss the investigation with
complainants or their representatives.[104] Complainants and their representatives should take advantage of this opportunity and in serious cases
should consider arranging a meeting between themselves, the PCA
member and the investigating officer in order to discuss the progress
and direction of the investigation. At least they should ask the PCA
member to keep them regularly informed of developments in the case.

Of course, the overwhelming majority of cases are not scrutinised by
the PCA. So, where it seems that the police are, for example, failing to
interview a particular witness, the complainant should inform the PCA,
inviting it to supervise the investigation and to issue directions ordering
the police to conduct the interview.

At the end of the investigation, the investigating officer sends a
report to the PCA with a copy to the chief officer.[105] The PCA then
considers the report and sends a statement to the chief officer. The
statement must show whether it is satisfied with the investigation and, if
not, the Authority must give details.[106] The PCA has said that in 'the
rare cases where we come across bias and less than thorough investigations we point them out and will persist until we are satisfied that we
can issue the "appropriate statement" declaring our satisfaction with
the investigation.'[107] The statement may also include details of any
respects in which the PCA thinks its satisfaction with the conduct of
the investigation ought to be recorded, or it can deal with other matters
relating to the investigation or supervision that the Authority feels
should be dealt with in the public interest or brought to the attention
of the chief officer, the complainant or the officer under investigation.[108]
If it is practicable, a copy of the statement must be sent to the
complainant (or person on whose behalf the complaint was made)
and to the officer whose conduct has been investigated.[109] The PCA

103 PCA Annual Report 1987 paras 1.8–1.9.
104 PCA Annual Report 1992, p8; see appendix 14.
105 PACE s89(6). Public interest immunity attaches to the report: *Taylor v
Anderton* [1995] 1 WLR 447, CA.
106 PACE s89(7) and (10).
107 PCA Annual Report 1991, p17, para 2.17.
108 Complaints General Regs reg 7.
109 PACE s89(8) and (9). It will not be practicable if, for example, the
complainant or the officer cannot be identified.

can issue separate statements on the disciplinary and criminal aspects of the investigation.[110] This might happen where it is appropriate to press ahead with criminal charges without delay.

The general policy is that the PCA should have an opportunity to comment on the effectiveness of an investigation before further action is taken. Thus, no disciplinary charge can be brought before the Authority has submitted its statement to the chief officer.[111] This prevents chief officers bringing minor disciplinary charges in order to pre-empt criticism of investigations from the PCA. Similarly, neither the DPP nor the chief officer can bring criminal proceedings before the PCA has submitted its statement, unless there are exceptional circumstances which make it undesirable to wait.[112]

PCA policy on particular types of conduct

Use of 'reasonable force'
There has been criticism that the PCA is reluctant to find that officers have used unreasonable force. In reply it has been said that it 'fully accepts that today's police officer is more likely to encounter violence than his predecessors. Nevertheless, there have been a number of instances in which the Authority have felt it necessary to express concern that the use of 'reasonable force' had almost been pre-determined with little or no attempt been made to defuse a situation'.[113]

Shooting incidents
If the police use firearms and kill or wound a member of the public, any complaint will be supervised by the PCA, and even if a complaint is not made it is likely that the police will voluntarily invite the PCA to supervise the investigation.[114] In fatal shooting cases it is usual to appoint an investigating officer from another force. The individual supervising member of the PCA will usually travel to the area of the incident as soon as practicable – sometimes within hours of the incident. S/he will aim to make him/herself known to all interested parties, including families of those killed or wounded and any appropriate groups such as police consultative groups or community organisations.

110 Ibid s89(11).
111 Ibid s89(12).
112 Ibid s89(13) and (14).
113 PCA Annual Report 1993, p32.
114 PCA Annual Report 1991, pp14–15, paras 2.7–2.10; see p78.

The PCA usually declines to make public statements about such cases other than to explain their role and procedure. They do, however, comply with formal requests from coroners for copies of the statements gathered in the course of the investigation.[115] The PCA has agreed procedures whereby the recommendations and lessons learned from shooting incidents are made available to the Association of Chief Police Officers' Joint Standing Committee on Police Use of Firearms, the body responsible for firearms policy and training.[116] The PCA aims to complete investigations into shooting incidents within three months.

Deaths in custody
Deaths in custody or while the deceased is otherwise with the police are, as a matter of police practice, usually referred to the PCA on a voluntary basis even if no complaint is made (see p78). The PCA must supervise the investigation of such cases if a complaint has been made, and until 1991 it would always do so as a matter of policy even if no complaint had been made.[117] However, since 1991 less than half of all investigations into deaths in custody have been supervised.[118] Most deaths occur in police cells and the actions of the custody officer come under close scrutiny. Deaths are treated as being 'otherwise with the police' even if, for example, the death occurs at a hospital or in other circumstances where the deceased could be regarded as being under the care or protection of the police.

Hanging is the most common cause of all deaths that occur at police stations. Of the 68 cases that occurred during 1991–94, 32 were due to hanging, of which 25 had certainly or possibly involved the use of the cell hatch. Often there are no protrusions within a cell but if the hatch is left open an item of clothing etc can be attached to the bolt holes in the framework or to the handles on the outside of the door. Most force orders require hatches to be kept closed, but if this is obeyed ventilation within the cell becomes totally inadequate. In other forces the custody officer has a discretion as to whether to leave the hatch open.

The PCA has drawn attention to 'the problems facing custody

115 PCA Annual Report 1991, pp14–15, para 2.9.
116 PCA Annual Report 1992, p19, para 2.7; see *Manual on the Police Use of Firearms*, ACPO; cf the leading US text, Geller and Scott, *Deadly Force: What We Know – A Practitioner's Desk Reference Guide on Police Involved Shootings*, Police Executive Research Forum, $30 pb, fax 001 202 466 7820.
117 PCA Annual Report 1991, p15, para 2.11.
118 Police Complaints Authority – The First Ten Years, HMSO 1995, p14.

TABLE 6
Firearms incidents in England and Wales 1985–94

Year	1983	1984	1985	1986	1987	1988	1989	1990	1991	1992	1993	1994
Number of notifiable offences in which firearms reported as used	7,962	8,376	9,742	9,363	9,002	8,524	9,502	10,373	12,129	13,305	13,951	N/A
Number of police firearms operations	3,180	2,667	2,488	2,453	2,185	2,227	2,583	2,874	3,722	4,479	5,625	N/A
Number of occasions when shots fired by the police*	3	6	7	1	7	2	4	3	5	12	6	6
Number of authorised firearms officers	13,044	11,873	10,244	8,395	7,349	7,194	7,311	7,411	7,717	6,850	6,769	N/A
Civilian casualties due to police use of firearms Deaths	0	0	1	0	5	0	2	3	3	3	3	2
Injuries	3	5	3	0	6	3	0	0	2	8	2	3

*These figures do not include accidental discharges by police officers
Source: Police Complaints Authority – the First Ten Years, HMSO 1995 p12.

officers in deciding whether someone was simply "falling down drunk" or was suffering from something more serious.' There have been cases of people being detained as drunks who then died from alcohol poisoning, drugs overdoses or fractured skulls. The PCA has endorsed the recent view of the BMA Medical Ethics Committee that it is 'unreasonable and dangerous' to rely on non-medically trained police officers to maintain close, clinical observation of apparently drunken detainees.[119]

Neck holds and armlocks
The PCA has compiled a substantial body of expert opinion on the effect of neck holds and certain armlocks after a number of high profile cases. It accepts expert opinion that a neck hold which exerts any pressure on the carotid artery or which compresses the airway involves, except in extreme circumstances, an unacceptably high element of risk. The PCA believes that this advice must be emphasised in police training to avoid the risk of deaths resulting from this kind of restraint.[120] Despite this advice, the use of such techniques appears to be increasing, and indeed the use of strangulation, in which the supply of blood to the head through the carotid artery is restricted, has been seriously advocated as a 'not unpleasant experience' which, if properly taught, 'has a place in the repetoire of techniques required for realistic police arrest'.[121]

Quik Kufs and 'tweaking'
Traditional handcuffs, linked by a chain, are generally used to hold a prisoner who is not or is no longer offering resistance. Quik Kufs, which are rigid, are capable of being used by the police as a means of positive restraint in their own right: an officer attaches one cuff to the suspect's wrist and pulls or 'tweaks' the other cuff to hurt the restrained wrist. The PCA has said, 'Despite their obvious merits in allowing speedy restraint of an arrested person, not least by a smaller officer, the Authority question the use of rigid handcuffs for the purpose of ensuring "compliance through pain". We appreciate that a number of armlocks are methods of restraint which involve the inflicting of pain. Nevertheless, under normal circumstances, the practice alleged in some cases, of giving a prisoner "a tweak" by manipulating the rigid

119 *Police Complaints Authority – The First Ten Years*, HMSO 1995, p14.
120 PCA Annual Report 1993, p34. See also Home Office Self-Defence and Restraint Manual, unpublished; *Facing Violence*, HM Inspectorate of Constabulary, 1995.
121 M Finn, 'Going for the Jugular', *Police Review*, 5 August 1994 p26; cf S Fraser, 'Legal Moves', *Police Review*, 10 June 1994 p23.

handcuff and thereby causing pain to the wrist, is neither acceptable nor reasonable force. It would be a matter for concern if an item of equipment which is a considerable improvement on its predecessor came under suspicion as a result of misuse.'[122]

The Home Office circular guidance to the police on the use of handcuffs is reproduced at Appendix 12.

Police dogs

Complaints arising from the use of police dogs typically result from bites inflicted during arrests. The PCA has noted that these 'are sometimes serious enough to require plastic surgery. If injuries on a similar scale had been directly inflicted by a police officer they would have justified consideration of criminal charges. The "force" exerted by a police dog may exceed "reasonable force" by a considerable margin. Clearly, disciplinary action cannot be taken against the dog nor can negligence or abuse of authority be proved against the handler.'[123] (A civil action under the Animals Act 1971 may be possible.)

The PCA has recommended that the use of police dogs in an 'off-lead' arrest role should be strictly limited.

High-speed pursuits

In 1993 the PCA supervised investigations into eight police pursuit cases which resulted in a total of seven deaths. Such cases are only supervised if a complaint is made or it the police voluntarily refer a case to the PCA (see p52). The PCA would prefer all cases of death or serious injury arising from police pursuits to be referred to it so that it could consider the possibility of supervision; in the meantime, pursuit cases that do come to their attention 'will be given particularly close attention'.[124]

The Association of Chief Police Officers' Police Driving Report,[125] prepared in 1989, included comprehensive recommendations covering police pursuits, including their control and management aspects.

Investigations of allegations of child abuse

The PCA has considered complaints alleging either that the police have acted too hastily, thereby destroying reputations, or that they have acted too slowly, thereby allowing abuse to continue. After a major

---

122 PCA Annual Report 1993 p33; cf S Howe, 'Safety Links', *Police Review*, 17 June 1994 p220.
123 PCA Annual Report 1993, p32.
124 PCA Annual Report 1993, p45.
125 Unpublished; see also *Roadcraft: the Police Drivers' Handbook* HMSO, 1994.

investigation into the police response to complaints made against Frank Beck, the PCA published an extensive summary report. This included its findings and recommendations concerning interview procedures, the proper recording of allegations and the possible disclosure of sensitive information to employers.[126]

Forcible entry techniques
The police on occasions use sledgehammers to break open doors, particularly during drugs raids, when speed of entry to a building is necessary if evidence is to be preserved. The PCA has commented that 'such drastic action, which often attracts media attention, is not only disturbing to innocent householders and onlookers but is potentially dangerous. Anyone about to open the door, especially old or young persons who may be directly behind it, could receive serious injuries. Forces should be encouraged to use alternative methods for which equipment is available.'[127]

Demonstrations, crowds and public order
In situations where the police are dealing with large crowds or demonstrations, some complaints are of a general and unspecific nature:

> alleging, for example, excessive use of force, misuse of mounted police, or inappropriate use of dogs or truncheons. The Authority is not empowered to investigate these general matters unless the incident has been referred to them under Section 88 of the [Police and Criminal Evidence] Act, in which case we would consider all aspects of the policing at the incident including the plans prepared in advance, the command arrangements and the methods used. Here we may make a public statement explaining the findings of an investigation into general complaints and drawing attention to errors of judgment in the planning and organisation of an operation. But our powers are limited to recommending, or if necessary, directing disciplinary charges to be brought against identified officers under a specific paragraph of the Discipline code. Errors of judgment in planning and organising can seldom be so culpable as to amount to a breach of discipline.[128]

Misuse of police national computer
There have been repeated complaints about improper access to the police national computer and about the improper disclosure of information

126 PCA, *Inquiry into police investigations of complaints of child and sexual abuse in Leicestershire children's homes: a summary*, February 1993.
127 PCA Annual Report 1989 p17 para 3.9.
128 PCA Annual Report 1986, para 2.5.

obtained from it. In 1986 the PCA issued a special report[129] following an investigation into allegations of improper use of the computer which made a number of recommendations, some of which have still not been implemented. The PCA has dryly remarked that, 'It is of further concern that not all force standing orders deal with this matter with the clarity that might be expected in an area of potential abuse by officers.'[130]

Tenure in specialist units

One of the PCA's central recommendations in its 1991 report on the notorious West Midlands Serious Crime Squad was that there should be a time limit on continuous service in any specialised serious crime unit. The next year HM Inspectorate of Constabulary recommended that such service should not exceed six years. However, some forces refuse to impose any such limit and according to the PCA Annual Report for 1994/95, others have postponed the introduction of such a limit or have doubled the period to 12 years. If a complaint involves an officer from such a unit, enquiries should therefore be made as to force policy and as to how long the particular officer has served in the unit.

Delay

Delays in resolving complaints have been a perennial problem. The PCA has said it is 'constantly being told that the complaints procedure is too slow', and a former chairman said, 'Since I arrived here I have been dismayed by the time taken to process complaints.'[131] Delays are not only frustrating and discouraging for complainants but can also serve to undermine the outcome of any resulting disciplinary action or criminal prosecution (see p97 and 116).

The police organisations have opposed statutory time limits,[132] and when the PCA drew up a voluntary Statement of Intent intended to cut down on delays, the Home Office watered it down to such an extent that the PCA felt it necessary to say that 'We were disappointed that . . . the Home Office, after consulting with ACPO, submitted a number of amendments which appeared to reduce the "up-beat" tone and the effectiveness of the statement, which had seemed to us to accord with the

129 *The Police National Computer: Report to the Secretary of State . . . by the Police Complaints Authority,* 16 June 1986, HC 425.
130 PCA Annual Report 1992, p24, para 3.6.
131 PCA Annual Report 1991, p21.
132 Home Affairs Committee, *Police Complaints Procedures,* HC 179, HMSO 1992 px para 19.

thinking in the majority of progressive and forward-thinking forces.'[133]

The Statement of Intent, which came into operation on 1 January 1991, is set out in appendix 1. It provides that reports on complaints should be completed within a target period of 120 days from the time the investigation became 'live'. The Statement of Intent does not define when an investigation becomes 'live'; however, provided a complaint is capable of investigation (see p67), it is submitted that it should be treated as becoming live on its receipt by the police. If it is apparent at the outset of an investigation, or if it becomes clear during the course of it, that the investigation cannot be completed within 120 days, the assistant chief constable responsible for complaints and discipline in unsupervised cases, or the supervising member of the PCA in supervised cases, will be consulted and a new completion date agreed. There is no requirement to inform complainants of such extensions of time, although many forces do so in practice. If there is any serious delay beyond a target date, the complainant should write to the chief officer seeking an explanation. If a complaint seems to have been unnecessarily delayed, the PCA should be asked to take up the matter with the chief officer concerned.[134]

By 1994/95, 68% of supervised complaints (by their nature the most complex cases) were being completed within the 120-day target, a decline from 72% in 1993. Some forces had voluntarily set themselves a target of 90 days.[135] However, the targets for arranging and holding disciplinary hearings are not being met (see p97).

The PCA's target for completing its own consideration of the disciplinary aspects of cases (see p58) is 28 days from receipt of the chief officer's memorandum. The average time taken in 1994/95 was 31 days.[136]

Withdrawal of complaints

The complainant can withdraw a complaint or tell the police that s/he does not want them to take any further action on a complaint at any time. This must be done in writing and be signed by the complainant or his/her solicitor or other authorised agent.[137] Once s/he has done so, the

133 PCA Annual Report 1991 para 4.5.
134 Police Complaints Board Triennial Review 1983 para 3.7.
135 PCA Annual Reports 1994/95 p20 and 1993 p46.
136 PCA Annual Report 1994/95 p20.
137 Complaints General Regs reg 11(1).

police are no longer under a duty to seek an informal resolution or to conduct a formal investigation.

In 1994, 40% of complaints were withdrawn or not proceeded with.[138]

Some are withdrawn for good reason but there have been suggestions in the past that high rates of withdrawal may be partly because of intimidation by the police.[139] These fears have, to some extent, been borne out by independent research which indicates that, while some investigating officers are neutral or truth seeking, others are partial, discouraging or intimidating. The same study suggested that almost a third of all complaints that are withdrawn are substantially valid.[140]

Police pressure to withdraw can take the form of suggestions that the complaint is too trivial to pursue or that it is so serious that officers' jobs are at risk. It is also sometimes suggested that, if the complaint is pursued, the complainant will have to attend a disciplinary or court hearing to give evidence. In reality, this is extremely unlikely (see p14) and in any event would usually occur only in very serious cases, that is, the very cases where investigating officers should not be encouraging complainants to withdraw.

In most cases where the PCA has already been made aware of the complaint, the police must send the PCA a copy of any withdrawal,[141] but the PCA does not have any system for checking whether the complaint was withdrawn under pressure. However, there is nothing to prevent the police continuing with the investigation after the complaint has been withdrawn. The investigation is most likely to continue if the complaint alleged that an officer committed a crime.[142]

Complaints which cannot or need not be investigated

A complaint can, with the agreement of the PCA, be dispensed with if it is not reasonably practicable to complete the investigation. A complaint may similarly be dispensed with if it is anonymous, repetitious, vexatious, oppressive or otherwise an abuse of the procedures for dealing

---

138 Home Office Statistical Bulletin 13/95: *Police Complaints and Discipline, England and Wales,* 1995 p10.
139 *Police Complaints Procedures* Home Affairs Committee 1981/2, HC 98–II, paras 157–60.
140 Russell, *Complaints Against the Police which are Withdrawn,* Leicester Polytechnic School of Law, 1986.
141 Complaints General Regs reg 11(2).
142 GCO para 4.35.

with complaints,[143] or if it is made more than 12 months after the incident (see p37).

It is not regarded as reasonably practicable to complete an investigation if, for example, the police cannot communicate with a complainant or other injured person, or if the complainant or other injured person fails or refuses to make a statement.[144] There may be tactical reasons for declining to co-operate with a complaints investigation until a civil action has been resolved, or at least delaying such co-operation until witness statements are exchanged by the parties (see p200). A bald refusal to make a statement until after a civil action has been resolved (which may be two years or more away) may be treated as an outright refusal justifying a dispensation.[145] However, it is submitted that provided a plaintiff's civil case is started promptly after the incident occurred and pursued reasonably vigorously, the exchange of witness statements should not occur so long after the incident that it would be reasonable for the PCA to grant a dispensation.[146]

A complaint is anonymous only if it reveals neither the name and address of the complainant nor the name and address of any other injured person and it is not reasonably practicable to discover them.[147]

In 1994/95 the PCA agreed to dispense with 7,721 complaints.[148] Of these, the majority were cases where it was not reasonably practicable to complete a satisfactory investigation.

A dispensation will not be granted, however, if the PCA judges that there is sufficient evidence in the original complaint on which to base a satisfactory investigation. In 1993, nine requests for dispensations were refused for this reason and an ordinary investigation followed.

In granting a dispensation the PCA is, in effect, removing the citizen's statutory right to have his/her complaint investigated. Furthermore, if the PCA does grant a dispensation where a complainant declines to be interviewed until after witness statements in a civil action have been exchanged, it will be excluding from the complaints system many of the most serious allegations of misconduct. The PCA states that it is 'insistent that forces give complainants every opportunity to co-operate

143 Dispensation Regs 1985 reg 3(1).
144 Ibid Sch para 4.
145 *R v PCA ex p Broome* (1988) 6 December, unreported but cited in PCA Annual Report 1988 para 4.5.
146 See Harrison and Cragg, 'Police Complaints and Public Interest Immunity', *NLJ* 29 July 1994, p1064.
147 Dispensation Regs 1985 Sch para 2.
148 Home Office Statistical Bulletin: *Police Complaints and Discipline, England and Wales* 1994 p10 n2.

TABLE 7
Dispensations from investigations granted and refused 1989–93

	1989	1990	1991	1992	1993
Granted	2,133	2,991	4,083	6,035	7,075
Refused	28	42	37	20	9

Source: HC Written Answer, 9 March 1995

with the investigation, including sending a final letter by recorded delivery which states that unless the complainant responds positively within 21 days the force will request dispensation from carrying out an investigation.'[149]

The PCA has noted that there has been an upward trend in the number of complaints concluded by dispensation. While the reasons have not been statistically analysed, it has suggested that this may be due to:

- new regulations introduced in July 1990 adding new grounds for dispensation (including vexatious complaints, delayed complaints and abuse of the procedures);
- an increase in the tactical use of the complaints procedure to 'aid' the defence of a criminal charge, at the end of which proceedings the complainant is unwilling to co-operate further; and
- complainants being released on bail and subsequently failing to answer to bail so that it is not practicable to communicate with the complainant.[150]

When are complaints upheld?

While a complaint may result in criminal or disciplinary proceedings, the question of whether a complaint is substantiated does not depend on such proceedings being brought against an officer or on the outcome or such proceedings, but rather on the extent to which evidence tends to support the complainant's allegation. The police are advised[151] that there:

> will be circumstances in which a complaint is shown to have been justified but disciplinary proceedings are not possible (because, for example, the

149 PCA Annual Report 1992 para 3.4.
150 PCA Annual Report 1992 para 3.4.
151 GCO para 3.13.

conduct complained of cannot be attributed to a particular officer or officers, or the officer has left the force) or are inappropriate (because, for example, the conduct complained of is not sufficiently serious to warrant formal proceedings, or the officer's youth or inexperience or other extenuating circumstances makes advice a more suitable course).

In such cases the complaint is upheld and recorded for statistical purposes as substantiated.

After the investigation

When the investigation has been completed, whether or not it was supervised by the PCA, a number of 'safeguards' come into play. These are intended to ensure that the possibility of bringing disciplinary or criminal proceedings is properly considered.

Duties of chief officers

When a chief officer receives the investigating officer's report, s/he must consider whether it indicates that a criminal offence *may* have been committed by one of his/her officers. If it does so indicate, s/he must consider whether the offence is such that the officer ought to be charged with it. If s/he considers that the officer *should* be charged, s/he must send the report to the DPP.[152]

> Many chief officers took this as a general invitation to consider whether a criminal charge would be likely to suceed and, not surprisingly, they often took the view that having regard to their opinion of the complainant, his antecedents and his witnesses, it would not. We [the PCA] moved at once to correct this interpretation which we thought was quite wrong and a usurpation of the functions and prerogative of the Director of Public Prosecutions. A circular letter was sent to all chief constables the burden of which was to urge that the Section required only that the appropriate authority should consider whether the report disclosed a prima facie case for the Director of Public Prosecutions to consider and that it was for him to weight the evidence and determine the prospects of successfully bringing proceedings.
>
> As to the second consideration, we urged that the words "such that the officer ought to be charged with it" referred to the *quality* of the offence and its circumstances and not to the available proof. If, for example, an officer were to park his vehicle on a double yellow line in order to arrest a deranged man brandishing a gun, the traffic offence would not in the circumstances be "such that the officer ought to be charged with it" regardless of whether the proof of it was good, bad or indifferent.[153]

152 PACE s90(3) and (4).
153 PCA Triennial Review 1985–88 paras 1.39–1.40.

Despite this clear advice, many chief officers persisted in their interpretation of the law. Consequently, the Home Office has advised that it is not sufficient for the chief officer 'to refer only those cases where he feels that a criminal charge would be likely to succeed'; all such cases should be referred to the DPP.[154] The Police and Magistrates' Courts Act (PMCA) 1994 will remove from chief officers the duty to consider whether the criminal offence is such that the officer ought to be charged with it.[155] From a date to be appointed the chief officer will have no discretion and this will be a matter for the DPP alone.

Once the DPP has dealt with the question of bringing a criminal charge, the chief officer should send the PCA a memorandum stating whether s/he has brought any disciplinary proceedings. If no proceedings have been brought, s/he must usually explain the reasons for this (but see below).[156]

If a chief officer considers that an investigating officer's report does not indicate that any criminal offence may have been committed, s/he must send the PCA a memorandum stating whether s/he has brought any disciplinary proceedings and if s/he has not, stating his or her reasons for not doing so.[157]

The PCA has powers to recommend, and ultimately to direct, that disciplinary proceedings be brought.[158] In doing so, however, the PCA will be mindful of the fact that disciplinary proceedings must be proved beyond reasonable doubt, that is, to the criminal standard of proof.[159] It is expected that this requirement will be abolished when the new disciplinary procedure is introduced under the Police and Magistrates Courts Act 1994.[160] The PCA approach to reviewing evidence against the criminal standard of proof has been a major source of dissatisfaction to complainants. In 1990 the PCA said:

> Proof [beyond reasonable doubt] is often not easy to obtain because many of the incidents which we examine take place where there are no independent witnesses. In these circumstances we have to rely on the accounts given by the police on the one hand and by the complainant, and sometimes his

154 GCO para 5.8 (amended 4 December 1990).
155 s35.
156 PACE s90(5), to be amended by PMCA 1994 s35 from a date to be appointed.
157 PACE s116; to be amended by PMCA 1994 s35 from a date to be appointed..
158 PACE s93; to be amended by PMCA 1994 s36 from a date to be appointed..
159 Discipline Regs reg 23..
160 PMCA 1994 s37. See *Review of Police Discipline Procedures*, Home Office consultation paper, 1993.

friends, on the other. Regrettably it is frequently the case that it is impossible to reconcile the two accounts. In such cases we can only attempt to explain to complainants that we do not disbelieve their story but that it cannot be proved beyond reasonable doubt.[161]

However by 1991 the PCA had indicated that it was prepared to take a more robust approach:

> There is still a belief in some forces and amongst some police officers that if the complainant tells his side of the story and the officer he is complaining about denies the allegation and if there are no independent witnesses then it is not possible to prove a case at a disciplinary hearing. The argument is that it is one man's word against the other's and that therefore it cannot be proved to the required standard of proof, which is 'beyond reasonable doubt'. We do not take such a rigid view in those cases in which there is circumstantial or other evidence which strongly supports one side or the other. Nor do we hesitate in recommending that disciplinary charges be preferred against a police officer in a 'one against one' situation if there are compelling reasons for believing the complainant's story.[162]

The requirement that there must be 'compelling reasons' for believing a complainant's story sets an exceptionally high test which often cannot be demonstrated in advance of a hearing when the officer's and the complainant's stories can be compared and tested by cross-examination. It is submitted that a more appropriate test would be that there should be a reasonable prospect of the complainant's story being believed over that of the police officer.

The power of the PCA to direct chief officers to refer reports to the DPP for possible prosecution is to be abolished by the Police and Magistrates Courts Act 1994.[163] Henceforth chief officers will have no discretion, and will be under a duty to refer all cases to the DPP if the report indicates that a criminal offence *may* have been committed.

Action short of a disciplinary charge

Given the rigidity of the current disciplinary procedures, there are many cases that fall into a grey area between those that require a formal disciplinary charge and those that can be dismissed with no action at all being taken against the officer. There is currently no clear or official procedure for dealing with such cases The PCA has said that in such cases, 'management action may be taken in the form of an admonishment or a warning, or by "advice". The latter is a term well understood

---

161 PCA Annual Report 1989 para 2.15.
162 PCA Annual Report 1990 para 2.9.
163 PACE s92; as amended by PMCA 1994 s37 from a date to be appointed.

by the police service but widely misunderstood by complainants. "Advice" can be given by a senior officer who may be any rank from a superintendent to a deputy chief constable, depending upon the severity of the cases, and can vary from a severe rebuke to an expression of disapproval or advice as to how to handle a similar situation in future. It is most certainly not the case, as some complainants believe, that an officer who has been "advised" has not been fully taken to task.'[164] If this is the case, and in practice many complainants are not even told of such management action, it is incumbent on the police to explain clearly what action they have taken rather than rely on arcane language that appears designed to protect their officers from embarrassment.

Complaints against senior officers

Complaints against senior officers, that is, officers holding a rank above that of superintendent[165] are handled slightly differently from those against junior officers.

Apart from in the Metropolitan police, complaints against senior officers are dealt with by the police authority.[166] Inside the Metropolitan police, complaints against a deputy assistant commissioner or commander are dealt with by the commissioner. Officers of assistant commissioner rank and above are appointed and may be removed by the Queen and fall outside the statutory police complaints system.[167] If a complaint about a senior officer is made to a chief officer outside the Metropolitan police, s/he must refer it to the appropriate authority, which must record all complaints received. Because it may be necessary to carry out, say, examinations or searches within hours of receiving a complaint, all chief officers are under a duty to take any steps that appear desirable for the purpose of obtaining or preserving evidence, even though the responsibility for investigating the complaint lies with the police authority.[168] For the procedure on the suspension of senior officers see p91.

164 PCA Annual Report 1991 p44 para 15.
165 PACE s84 as amended by PMCA 1994 Sch 5 para 24; 'senior officer' included all officers above chief superintendant until 1 April 1995, when that rank and the rank of deputy chief constable were abolished: Police Regulations 1995 SI No 215 reg 6, and PMCA 1994 s6.
166 PACE s86. The police authority and the commissioner are collectively known as the 'appropriate authority'.
167 See GCO para 10.1 (amended 4 December 1990).
168 PACE s84(1).

PACE does not provide a procedure for the informal resolution of complaints against senior officers. The commissioner or police authority need not even investigate a complaint if it is satisfied that the conduct complained of, even if proved, would not justify a criminal or disciplinary charge.[169] The appropriate authority, accordingly, has a wide discretion as to how it handles such cases and a complainant cannot insist on a formal investigation (unlike where the complaint concerns a junior officer). If the conduct would justify a charge, however, the commissioner or police authority must investigate it and must appoint an officer from the same or another police force to carry out the investigation. The investigating officer must be of at least the same rank as the officer against whom the complaint is made, but must not be serving in the same sub-division or branch.[170] Because complaints against senior officers are rare and are likely to be potentially serious, they are more likely to merit the appointment of an investigating officer from outside the senior officer's own force, see p56). The investigating officer's report must be submitted to the appropriate authority unless the investigation is supervised by the PCA, in which case it goes to the PCA.[171]

The PCA has the same powers and duties here as in the supervision of investigations of complaints made against junior officers.[172] The section on supervision by the PCA (see p52 above), therefore, applies equally to senior officers. As has been seen, an appropriate authority (the police authority or, in London, the commissioner) need not investigate all complaints against senior officers; it has a wide discretion as to how it handles complaints that would not justify a criminal or disciplinary charge. If the appropriate authority does investigate, the PCA has power to supervise any investigation if it considers such supervision desirable in the public interest. However, the PCA cannot insist on an investigation; that is a matter for the appropriate authority alone.

When the appropriate authority receives a report on a senior officer either from the investigating officer or, where the investigation was supervised, from the PCA, it must send a copy to the DPP unless it is satisfied that no criminal offence has been committed.[173] Neither the authority nor the PCA has a discretion to decide whether or not the

169 Ibid s86(2).
170 Police (Discipline) (Senior Officer) Regulations 1985 SI No 519 reg 5.
171 Ibid s86(6).
172 Ibid s89.
173 Ibid s90(1).

officer ought to be charged with the offence; that is a matter for the DPP alone. Neither has the PCA any power to recommend or direct that disciplinary charges be brought; that is a matter for the appropriate authority alone.[174]

Disclosure of information

The PCA must not disclose any information it receives in connection with its work except:

- to the Home Secretary, eg, so that s/he can refer a miscarriage of justice case to the Court of Appeal (see p261);
- to other persons (eg, the complainant or his/her representative), so far as may be necessary for the proper discharge of the PCA's functions;
- in the form of a summary or other general statement which does not identify the person from whom information was received or any person to whom it relates;
- for the purpose of any criminal, civil or disciplinary proceedings.[175]

The PCA takes this to prevent it making public the outcome of disciplinary cases, and only three out of the 42 police forces are known to inform complainants of the results of disciplinary proceedings voluntarily as a matter of policy.[176] Complainants can therefore be left completely in the dark as to the final result, even when their complaint has been upheld and has resulted in disciplinary proceedings with a punishment being imposed. The Home Affairs Committee of the House of Commons has recommended that all forces should adopt a policy of giving the complainant full information on the outcome of disciplinary hearings and that HM Inspectorate of Constabulary (see p79) should monitor the implementation of this policy.[177]

Using complaints documents in civil actions   The release of documents created in the course of a complaints investigation for use in civil proceedings is not straightforward (see p200). In 1981 the Court of Appeal held that public interest immunity attached to all such documents as a class.[178] Thus statements made by the police officers against

174 Ibid s90(3).
175 PACE s98(1).
176 Home Affairs Committee, *Police Complaints Procedures* HC 179, HMSO 1992, pp xiv-xv para 34.
177 Ibid.
178 *Neilson v Laugharne* [1981] QB 736.

whom the complaint had been made would not be released for inspection by complainants. This was followed by a string of cases leading to increasingly questionable results, which included preventing the disclosure of the statements of witnesses who had consented to the disclosure.[179] It also led plaintiffs' lawyers, for tactical reasons, to advise against making, or at least pursuing, a complaint if a civil action was contemplated[180] (see p200). This unsatisfactory position was resolved in 1994 when the House of Lords in *R v Chief Constable of the West Midlands Police ex p Wiley*[181] reversed the 1981 decision and held that public interest immunity does not attach to all documents created in the course of a police complaints investigation as a class and they may therefore be disclosed for use in civil proceedings. Not all such documents will necessarily be released, and the PCA argued in the House of Lords that 'protection was still necessary for certain types of complaints material. Foremost among these were reports from investigating officers conveying assessments of the quality and credibility of witnesses and recommendations for action. Other examples were documents indicating the identity of informants or containing sensitive information about internal police policy or operational matters'.[182] The House of Lords left open the question of whether such documents, if protected at all, are protected as a class or only on the basis of the particular contents of a particular document.[183] However, the Court of Appeal has subsequently held that investigating officers' reports as a class of documents attract public interest immunity and therefore should not be routinely released for inspection.[184]

Using complaints documents to defend criminal prosecutions or to fight criminal appeals   Where a prosecution witness is of bad character, there is a general duty on the prosecution to disclose that fact and any material upon which the defence could cross-examine the witness as to his/her character.[185] The government has published proposals to restrict the general duty of the prosecution to disclose information to

---

179 *Makanjuola v Commissioner of Police of the Metropolis* [1992] 3 All ER 617, CA (decided 16 March 1989).
180 See Harrison, 'Police complaints: pitfalls for the unwary litigant', *NLJ* 13 December 1985, p1239; Harrison and Cragg, 'Suing the police: should plaintiffs also complain?' June 1991 *Legal Action* 22.
181 [1994] 3 WLR 433, [1994] 3 All ER 420.
182 PCA Triennial Review 1991–94 p13–14.
183 *Ex p Wiley* [1994] 3 All ER 420 per Lord Woolf at 446.
184 *Taylor v Chief Constable of Greater Manchester Police* [1995] 1 WLR 447.
185 *R v Collister and Warhurst* (1955) 39 Cr App R 100.

the defence and to estend the requirement on the defence to give advance notice of the nature of it case.[186]

In 1991 *R v Edwards*[187] extended this to require disclosure of certain police discipline records. In a criminal case in which a police officer's credibility is in issue it is permissible to cross-examine the officer about any criminal or disciplinary charges proved against him/her in respect of other matters which cast doubt on his/her credibility. Thus if a disciplinary charge has been proved in respect of, say, tampering with a notebook or fabricating confessions, that must be disclosed to the defence. The practice of the police and the Crown Prosecution Service (CPS) on the disclosure of discipline records is examined in greater detail at p108. The CPS internal guidance to the police on *Edwards* and the duty to disclose discipline records is reproduced in full as appendix 13.[188]

The mere fact that a complaint has been made against an officer who is to be a witness in a criminal trial will not usually be disclosed to the defence, but if an officer is suspended or charged with a disciplinary matter, or if an investigation is pending into serious allegations, those facts may be disclosed (see p109). If an investigation is being supervised by the PCA (see p52), the CPS will consult the supervising member, as well as the police, before disclosing details of the investigation to the defence.[189]

The PCA has expressed its concern that the possibility of future disclosure may dissuade chief officers from finding officers guilty in disciplinary proceedings:

It is of course a matter for the police force concerned to make judgments in relation to the relevance of such disciplinary findings. From the Force's point of view, it must be of concern that such relevant findings can have an effect on the officer's credibility as a witness in criminal, or indeed civil, proceedings. There is therefore a reluctance on the part of chief officers to impose a finding upon an officer which could affect his credibility and therefore his use to the Force in terms of the giving of evidence.[190]

186 *Disclosure: a consultation document*, Home Office, Cm 2864, HMSO May 1995.
187 [1991] 2 All ER 266. See Harrison and Cragg 'Prosecution disclosure of police discipline records' September 1995 *Legal Action* 19.
188 CPS Guidance on *R v Edwards*, DPP to Chief Officers of Police, 5 October 1992 (hereafter 'CPS on *Edwards*').
189 CPS on *Edwards* para 19.
190 Letter from Mr Peter Moorhouse, Deputy Chairman PCA, to authors, 8 December 1994.

The DPP has advised that the fact that an officer was under a Regulation 7 Disciplinary Notice (see p89) at the time of giving evidence should also be disclosed to the defence and that the PCA, amongst others should give a view as to the likelihood of the officer facing disciplinary action and the further likelihood of the officer being found guilty. The PCA has declined to take part in this 'forecasting exercise', as it seems to the PCA to be an inherently unfair pre-judgment.[191]

Informal resolutions   Statements made by any person for the purpose of informal resolution of a complaint are generally not admissible in any subsequent criminal, civil or disciplinary proceedings (see p50).[192]

Confidential documents   Correspondence from the PCA to a complainant, for example explaining that a complaint does not merit a disciplinary charge or that further action will not be taken, is confidential and may not be published without the complainant's consent. An injunction may therefore be issued to prevent its publication.[193] Similarly the PCA obtained an injunction restraining Central Independent Television from disclosing the contents of its draft report on the West Midlands Serious Crime Squad.[194]

Publicity for appeal tribunal documents   The Home Secretary cannot be compelled by judicial review proceedings to supply a complainant with copies of his/her order, statement of reasons and report in relation to a hearing before a police disciplinary tribunal.[195]

The PCA and investigations not arising from complaints

A chief officer (or the appropriate authority in cases concerning senior officers) can refer any grave or exceptional matter to the PCA where it appears that an officer may have committed a criminal or disciplinary offence, even if no complaint has been made.[196] A chief officer might wish to do this where a matter comes to light by reason of internal management or through some other public route (including civil

191 Ibid.
192 PACE s104(3)and (4).
193 *PCA v Greater Manchester Police Authority* (1991) 3 Admin LR 757, (1990) *Guardian* 28 December, QBD; PCA Annual Report 1988 para 4.3; *West Midlands Police Authority and Another v Walsall MBC*, (1992) *Independent* 26 February, QBD.
194 *PCA v Central Independent Television* (1991) unreported, see PCA Annual Report 1991 p28 para 6.
195 *R v Secretary of State for Home Department ex p Goswell* (1994) *Times* 31 December.
196 PACE s88, to be amended by PMCA 1994 s34 on a day to be appointed.

actions). Typical cases include shooting incidents, deaths in custody, possible miscarriage of justice and cases of serious corruption. If the matter has attracted widespread interest or concern, s/he may decide that the involvement of the PCA would be a useful way of reassuring the public that it is receiving full and proper attention. The PCA cannot initiate such investigations itself.[197] If such a matter is referred to the PCA, it must supervise the investigation if it considers it desirable in the public interest.[198] Requests by chief officers are seldom turned down. The PCA has the same powers to veto and approve the appointment of the investigating officer as it has in the investigation of a complaint.[199]

In 1994/95 71 cases not arising from a complaint were considered by the PCA compared to 52 in 1993.[200]

Independent police forces

The PCA can agree procedures corresponding to the usual complaints procedure with any authority, other than a police authority, which maintains a body of constables.[201] It has concluded agreements with the British Transport Police, the Ministry of Defence Police, the Port of Liverpool Police, the Port of Tilbury Police, the Royal Parks Constabulary and the UK Atomic Energy Authority Constabulary. The agreement with the Royal Parks Constabulary came into effect on 1 January 1992[202] and the agreement with the Port of Tilbury Police (formerly the Port of London Authority Police) was renewed in 1992 when the port changed its title and became a private company.

This leaves a number of smaller independent police forces, of which there are at least 21, with no such agreement. If no procedure is in force, the Home Secretary can establish such a procedure.[203]

Information and reports

H M Inspectorate of Constabulary and all police authorities are under a duty to keep themselves informed about how the complaints procedure is working.[204] Some police authorities do this by holding regular

197 HC Written Answers col 398, 27 June 1989.
198 PACE s89(2)(b).
199 Mandatory Referrals Regs reg 5(1).
200 PCA Annual Report 1993 p14 and 1994/95 p15.
201 PACE s96(1), to be amended by PMCA 1994 Sch 5 para 30 from a date to be appointed; cf PMCA 1994 s38.
202 PCA Annual Report 1991 para 6.12.
203 PACE s96; HC Written Answers, 29 November 1990 cols 452-453; for accounts of a MOD police disciplinary tribunal and a MOD police board of inquiry see *Police Review* 8 July, 26 August and 2 September 1994.
204 PACE s95.

meetings of complaints sub-committees or panels. However, democratic oversight of the complaints system, and the supervision of the quality of policing generally, by police authorities has in the past been poor, and is likely to deteriorate further with the introduction of more appointed members to police authorities in the place of elected members.[205]

Chief officers should make their complaints books available for scrutiny by members of the authority.[206]

The House of Commons Home Affairs Committee has said that 'the unique position of the Home Secretary as Police Authority for the Metropolis, and the special accountability which he thereby has to Parliament on questions of discipline, means that full information on disciplinary matters must be provided to Parliament. When a recent parliamentary question asked how many Metropolitan officers were reduced in rank as a result of disciplinary hearings, the Parliamentary Under–Secretary replied that these were "matters for the Commissioner". This unwillingness to provide information is unacceptable.'[207]

The PCA must make an annual report to the Home Secretary about how it has carried out its functions in the previous year.[208] It may make additional reports on any specific matters to which it thinks the Home Secretary's attention should be drawn.[209] For example, the PCA prepared a special report on the working practices of the West Midlands Serious Crime Squad after the longest and most complex case it had handled, involving 96 complaints cases, 11 non-complaints cases and interviews with almost 700 individuals.[210]

In 1994, for the first time, the PCA issued summaries of its annual report in Punjabi, Urdu, Gujarati and Bengali.

The requirement on the PCA to publish triennial reviews of the workings of the complaints system is to be abolished by the Police and Magistrates' Courts Act 1994 s93 and Sch 9 Pt I.

---

205 Police and Magistrates' Courts Act 1994 s3 and Sch 2 amending Police Act 1964 s3A and Schs 1B and 1C.
206 GCO para 8.3.
207 Police Complaints Procedures, Home Affairs Committee 1991–92, HC 179 pviii para 11.
208 PACE s97(3). It must contain a statement of any guidance issued to it by the Secretary of State under s105(4).
209 PACE s97(2).
210 *A Report on the Investigation into the West Midlands Police Serious Crime Squad*, PCA, 1 November 1991; PCA Annual Report 1991 para 2.6.

Police complaints 81

The PCA and wrongful convictions

A complaints investigation may reveal evidence of a miscarriage of justice. Surprisingly, there appears to be no procedure for directly informing the victim of a wrongful conviction (whether or not s/he is the complainant) or his/her lawyers of such evidence. Instead, the PCA ensures that the investigating officer informs either the DPP or the division of the Home Office that deals with wrongful convictions (see p271). The DPP will be informed as head of the Crown Prosecution Service in all cases in which the person whose conviction is in doubt has a continuing right of appeal, whether or not it is 'out of time'; C3 Division of the Home Office will be informed where there is no such right of appeal, ie, either where the convicted person pleaded guilty, or where a person pleaded not guilty and has had his/her appeal rejected. This procedure has the approval of the DPP, the Home Office and the Court of Appeal.[211]

Even the PCA regards this arrangement as unsatisfactory, although only because 'C3 Division, Home Office could be perceived to be motivated by a desire to uphold Court decisions; while the Director of Public Prosecutions is in an invidious position in dealing with a complaint where a man may have been unjustly convicted as the consequence of a prosecution which was conducted by the Crown Prosecution Service in the first instance.'[212]

The PCA has supported the establishment of an independent body to review allegations of miscarriages of justice[213] to which it could refer evidence of doubtful convictions. It has given no indication, however, that it would directly inform people who have been wrongly convicted about the existence of evidence that could exonerate them.

For the legal remedies available to those who have been wrongfully convicted and other victims of miscarriages of justice, see p258.

False complaints

There may be serious consequences for anyone who makes a false complaint, especially where the allegation against an officer is serious. There are three main courses of action which the police can take in response to complaints which they feel are unfounded:

211 PCA Annual Report 1991 pp27–28 paras 6.5–6.6.
212 PCA Annual Report 1991 p28 para 6.7.
213 The Criminal Cases Review Commission is to be established by the Criminal Appeal Bill 1995.

- a civil action for defamation;
- a criminal prosecution for libel;
- a criminal prosecution for wasting police time.

Civil actions for defamation

The civil law of defamation (libel and slander) seeks to protect a person's reputation from false attack. It is conventionally said that a defendant may be liable for defamation if s/he makes (or 'publishes') a statement or other representation about the plaintiff to a third party which tends to lower that person in the estimation of right-thinking people, or tends to make people shun or avoid him/her. Clearly, to suggest falsely that a police officer has committed a criminal offence, or has seriously breached the Police and Criminal Evidence Act Codes of Practice, is capable of being defamatory.

It is beyond the scope of this book to consider the law and practice of defamation except in two narrow respects that particularly affect police misconduct proceedings:

- the privilege that may attach to complaints of police wrongdoing; and
- the production and inspection of police complaints and statements made in the course of complaints investigations.

Privilege

Privilege may be absolute or qualified. It is a complete defence to an action for defamation to show that the statement was made in circumstances where it was absolutely privileged, no matter what the motivation of the defendant in making the statement or his/her belief in its truth. A statement made in court proceedings, whether orally in court or in written pleadings, is absolutely privileged. So too is any statement made in proceedings before certain quasi-judicial tribunals. It is submitted that as a police disciplinary tribunal bears so many of the characteristics of a court, including the power to impose fines and to hear witnesses who have been compelled to attend by court order,[214] absolute privilege should apply.[215]

Qualified privilege may attach to statements where there is a 'competing public interest in permitting men to communicate frankly and freely with one another about matters in respect of which the law

214 RSC Order 38 r19; GCO para 5.19. See also *Currie v Chief Constable of Surrey* [1982] 1 All ER 89.
215 See, however, *R v Lancashire County Council Police Authority ex p Hook* [1980] 1 QB 603 (police authority committee proceedings not priviliged).

recognises that they have a duty to perform or an interest to protect in doing so'.[216] Qualified privilege is a defence to defamation provided the statement was made in good faith, but the privilege is lost if the statement was made maliciously, as where the maker does not believe it to be true.

If a citizen has grounds to make a police complaint, s/he has a public duty to do so and qualified privilege will attach to the letter of complaint.[217]

It is submitted that statements, ie, formal written witness statements, made in the course of a police complaints investigation also attract qualified privilege on the ground that there is a public interest in bringing allegations of misconduct to the attention of the authorities and a public duty to do so.[218]

There is also a practical reason why the courts should be slow to allow actions for defamation to be based on statements. Statements, although of course signed by complainants, will often have been drafted by the investigating officer. Such a document will usually be the officer's own version of the complainant's account, and never in reality a verbatim record of what a complainant actually said. It would be wrong to hold a complainant liable for every jot and comma produced by such an imperfect process.

Any communication made to the police for the purpose of a *criminal* investigation will attract qualified privilege, which will be lost if not made in good faith.[219]

Production and inspection

In the ordinary course of events, a potential plaintiff cannot conduct a 'fishing expedition' against third parties to discover whether a potential

216 *Horrocks v Lowe* [1975] AC 135 per Lord Diplock at 149–150.
217 *Fraser v Mirza* 1993 SLT 527 at 531D, HL; note that *Conerney v Jacklin* [1985] Crim LR 234, 129 SJ 285, CA is not reliable: in substance the case appears to concern (and was originally pleaded in terms of) privilege but was, in the authors' view mistakenly, argued and decided in terms of public interest immunity.
218 Note that in *Conerney v Jacklin* (supra) the Court of Appeal, because it had taken a wrong turning in deciding the case in terms of public interest immunity (PII), needlessly strained to draw a distinction between letters of complaint and formal statements taken in the course of complaints investigations, the latter having earlier been held to attract PII: *Neilson v Laugharne* [1981] 1 QB 736, itself now overruled by *R v Chief Constable of West Midland Police ex p Wiley* [1995] 1 AC 274, [1994] 3 WLR 433, [1994] 3 All ER 420, HL, see p201.
219 *Collins v Cooper* (1902) 19 TLR 118.

defendant published a defamatory statement. However a police officer against whom a complaint has been made is in an advantageous position in this respect. S/he is statutorily entitled to be supplied with a copy of the complaint if s/he so requests in writing.[220] The chief officer may refuse to supply a copy if s/he thinks that to do so:

a) might prejudice any criminal investigation or proceedings pending when the request is made; or
b) would be contrary to the public interest and the Home Secretary agrees that no copy should be supplied.

In *R v Commissioner of Police for the Metropolis ex parte Ware*[221] it was held that an officer is entitled (in addition to any initial letter of complaint) to the statutory record of any oral complaint, the reduction into writing of any oral complaint and extracts from any statements, whether they are in the course of investigation into these complaints or not, which amount, in themselves, to complaints, ie, which either make fresh complaints in addition to those already made or explain or particularise complaints which have already been made. Documents cannot be withheld on the grounds of common law public interest immunity given the statutory procedure for refusing copies with the Home Secretary's agreement.

A constraint on free speech?
The Police Federation has wide power to use its funds for any purpose it thinks necessary or expedient in the interests of the Federation or its members.[222] In practice, it has been assiduous in financially supporting actions for defamation brought by its members. Members of the public who face such civil actions cannot obtain legal aid, no matter how small their financial resources, as the bringing and defending of defamation actions is one of the few types of case specifically excluded from legal aid.[223] In practice, therefore, only the very wealthy can even contemplate defending such an action.

220 Police Complaints General Regs reg 9.
221 (1985) *Times* 31 July, but not fully reported, see transcript CO/1496/83. The case concerned the now repealed Police (Copies of Complaints) Regulations 1977, but they were in similar terms to the Complaints General Regs reg 9.
222 Police Federation Regs 1969 SI No 1787 reg 19(2) as amended by Police Federation (Amendment) Regs 1990 SI No 1575 reg 6.
223 Legal Aid Act 1974 Sch 1 Pt II para 1.

There is concern that such actions have a chilling effect in dissuading people from commenting on police matters of general concern.[224] Even quite inadvertent comments may be libellous. In 1983, Granada Television was ordered to pay £20,000 to an officer who appeared in a two-and-a-half second shot of a police station for which the commentary was: 'Since 1969 repeated investigations have shown some CID men take bribes.'[225] After another case, the general secretary of the National Council for Civil Liberties (now Liberty) said: 'We are very concerned that the possibility of being sued for libel is going to deter people who have genuine complaints against the police coming forward.'[226]

However, the fear of libel proceedings should not deter the ordinary member of the public from making a genuine complaint, particularly as libel is usually a civil action and any officer about whom a complaint has been made will know that it is pointless to sue someone who does not have the means to pay damages.

Criminal prosecutions for libel

As well as being a civil wrong, libel can also be a crime. The offence has largely fallen into disuse, although much of the old law which was frequently used to silence critics of the establishment still remains in force.[227]

There are two offences, both contained in the Libel Act 1843. The less serious offence of publishing a libel is punishable by up to one year's imprisonment and an unlimited fine, and the more serious offence of publishing a libel knowing it to be false is punishable by up to two years' imprisonment and an unlimited fine.[228]

Prosecutions of members of the public who complain about the police seem to be very rare. However, in 1965, one man received a total of three years' imprisonment (two consecutive terms of 18 months) on two counts of libelling a Flying Squad officer by suggesting that he had

224 Police Complaints Procedures, HC Home Affairs Committee, HC 179, 1992, pp27–28 paras 148–151; see Chalet, 'Police libel actions', *NLJ* 11 February 1994 p194, and reply, Taylor, *NLJ* 4 March 1994 p312.
225 *Guardian* 15 June 1983.
226 *Guardian* 6 October 1979.
227 JR Spencer 'Criminal libel – a skeleton in the cupboard' [1977] Crim LR 383 and 465. Reform has been proposed in *Report on Criminal Libel* Law Commission No 149, 1985, Cmnd 9618.
228 Libel Act 1843 ss4 and 5.

stolen £10,[229] and, in 1971, another man received a six-month sentence for hiring five men to distribute 5,000 handbills accusing an officer of drunkenness.[230]

Convictions that tend to compromise free speech may breach the European Convention on Human Rights see p275). In *Thorgeirson v Iceland*[231] the conviction and fining of an Icelandic journalist for 'defaming a public servant' by publishing two newspaper articles which made allegations of police brutality against unnamed officers and described them as 'wild beasts in uniform', was held to breach the European Convention. Because of the importance of the subject-matter and because the purpose of the articles was to promote a debate about the need to reform the police complaints system, it was held that the language used was not excessive.

Wasting police time

A person who makes a false complaint against a police officer is much more likely to be charged with the offence of wasting police time. The offence is committed if any wasteful employment of the police is caused by making to any person a false report tending to show that an offence has been committed, or to give rise to fears for the safety of any person or property, or to show that the maker has information that is material to any police enquiry.[232] The offence is committed if a false report is made to *any* person; thus it would be no defence to show that the report was made to, say, the PCA. A false allegation that did not amount to wasting police time might nevertheless amount to an attempt the pervert the course of justice.[233] Any prosecution for wasting police time must be authorised by the DPP, and the penalty is a fine at level 4 on the standard scale or up to six months' imprisonment or both.[234]

229 *Forbes*: news report *Times* 24 September 1965; (1965) 130 JP 688; 1965 *Police Review* 830.
230 *R v Leigh*: news report *Times* 9 and 19 March 1971; see also *R v McMahon* (1933) 24 Cr App R 95.
231 (1992) Series A, No 239; 14 EHRR 843.
232 Criminal Law Act 1967 s5(2).
233 *R v Machin* [1980] 3 All ER 151, CA.
234 Criminal Law Act 1967 s5(3); s5(2) as amended.

CHAPTER 4

Discipline procedures and criminal prosecutions

If a complaint is upheld, the police may take disciplinary proceedings against the officer or, if a criminal offence has been committed, the DPP may decide that a prosecution should be brought. In either case the complainant has a very limited role to play and members of the public often complain that they are left in the dark about how the case is progressing. This chapter explains what goes on behind the scenes and describes how, in exceptional cases, to bring a private prosecution.

In 1993 the government issued a consultation paper on the reform of police discipline procedures, and the Police and Magistrates' Courts Act 1994 made provision for change at a future date.[1] However, the substance of most of the changes will be contained in regulations which have not been published at the time of writing.[2] The current discipline procedures, introduced by the Police and Criminal Evidence Act 1984, are therefore described, noting the major anticipated changes. A brief description of the new system, which will largely replace the existing legalistic and adversarial procedures with a system characterised by greater management discretion, is given at p110.

Police discipline

The police disciplinary system is, in theory, distinct from the complaints procedure. In practice, however, if a disciplinary matter arises as a result of a complaint, the one runs into the other almost imperceptibly. Most disciplinary matters do not arise from complaints (see Table 8); it is much more common for them to arise as the result of internal management by the police themselves. This may, in part, explain why the existing system often seems ill-suited to dealing with complaints from

1 By ss37, 44 and 93 and Schs 5 and 9.
2 The regulations are expected to be laid before parliament in November 1995 with the intention that they should come into effect in April 1996.

TABLE 8
Police disciplinary charges[3] 1988–93

Arising out of	1988	1989	1990	1991	1992	1993
COMPLAINTS						
Officers charged	108	84	102	121	101	121
Officers found guilty	63	61	75	100	70	106
OTHER CIRCUMSTANCES						
Officers charged	358	278	258	271	269	N/A
Officers found guilty	329	265	246	264	259	256*
Total charged	466	362	360	392	370	N/A
Total found guilty	392	326	321	364	329	362*

* The 1993 figure relates to officers receiving disciplinary punishments.
Source: HC Written Answers, 25 April 1995.

members of the public. The proposed new discipline system would distinguish between cases of poor performance and cases of misconduct and introduce separate procedures for each type of case.

Investigation

Investigations of disciplinary offences that come to light because of a complaint from a member of the public are handled by the investigating officer who dealt with the complaint. Other investigations, such as those that arise from internal police management, are handled by an investigating officer appointed for the purpose. Such an officer must be appointed where it appears that a disciplinary offence may have been committed, unless the chief officer decides that no proceedings need be taken.[4] There is, therefore, a wide discretion not to investigate matters formally, and in practice many technical breaches, such as lateness in reporting for duty, are properly treated as 'management' issues which are dealt with informally, if at all.[5] However, as we have seen, there must be formal investigations of matters that arise as a result of a complaint

3 England and Wales, excluding Metropolitan Police.
4 Discipline Regs reg 6.
5 See, eg, Cook 'The blue-coated deviant: semi-formal discipline' *Police Review* 21 January 1983 p124; 'The blue-coated deviant: discretion and supervisory tolerance' *Police Review* 28 January 1983 p170.

from a member of the public, unless the member of the pubic agrees to informal resolution and the chief officer is satisfied that the conduct complained of, even if proved, would not justify a criminal or disciplinary charge (p44).[6] But a formal investigation is not necessary if a complaint is withdrawn (p66–67).

Written notice to accused officer

As soon as is practicable, the investigating officer must notify the officer who is subject to investigation of the report, allegation or complaint. The written notice, known as a 'regulation 7 notice', must inform the officer that s/he is not obliged to say anything concerning the matter, but that s/he may, if s/he so desires, make a written or oral statement. Such a statement may be used in any subsequent disciplinary proceedings.[7]

The requirement to serve the notice is directory, not mandatory, thus a failure to serve the notice, or a failure to serve it as soon as practicable, is not necessarily a bar to disciplinary proceedings.[8] However, a delay in serving the notice may lead to any subsequent disciplinary proceedings being quashed if the delay causes injustice, or the risk of injustice, to the officer, as, for example, where an officer is not told of the nature of a complaint or given an opportunity of responding to it[9] (see p97). As to whether delay may also prejudice subsequent criminal charges, see p116.

While officers are entitled to decline to make a statement, and about 3% of police officers actually do so,[10] the PCA takes the view that:

> Every police officer should be prepared to give his own account of an incident and it will usually be to his advantage to do so. If, however, he refuses and the evidence given by the complainant seems convincing, then, if there is nothing to counter that evidence, we would not feel inhibited from using our powers to ensure that charges are preferred.[11]

It is expected that under the new disciplinary system (see p110) a refusal to give a full and accurate account of an incident should be capable of

6 PACE s85(3), (5) and (10).
7 Discipline Regs reg 7.
8 *R v Secretary of State for Home Department ex p Miller* (1983) 4 May, unreported.
9 *R v Chief Constable of Merseyside Police ex p Calveley and Others* [1986] 1 All ER 257; *R v Chief Constable of Merseyside Police ex p Merrill* [1989] 1 WLR 1077.
10 January 1994 *Legal Action* 28.
11 PCA Annual Report 1987 para 2.18.

raising an inference casting doubt on the officer's conduct and fitness for service.[12]

Medical retirement

Every year a small but significant number of officers escape disciplinary action by retiring on medical grounds before the investigation has run its course. The Home Office advises: 'If at any stage of the disciplinary process an accused officer's medical condition . . . is found to be such that he would normally be granted medical retirement, the disciplinary process should not necessarily prevent or delay retirement.'[13] The advice was modified in 1992 so that, in cases where the accused officer is entitled to legal representation and the chief officer has doubts about the medical condition, every effort should be made to determine the disciplinary proceedings before any decision is taken on medical retirement.[14]

The official advice has been ineffective. The PCA has reported:

'In a number of high-profile cases prior to the Authority being able to announce disciplinary proceedings we have been faced by a considerable volume of both early retirements and medical retirements which have removed officers from the scope of discipline . . . . The announcement in major cases of an exodus from the service, some leaving under privileged conditions, continues to damage the image of a service which should be seeking to ensure publicly either an acquittal or a penalty in discipline cases. Justice should not be seen to be denied. Yet the appearance for some is one of evasion.[15]

The PCA has said it is particularly concerned about cases where officers have been judged unfit for further service but where there are no grounds for believing that they are unfit to face a disciplinary hearing.[16] However, if a chief officer decides that an officer could or should take medical retirement, it has been held that that decision takes effect immediately and cannot thereafter be postponed pending possible disciplinary proceedings.[17]

12 *Review of Police Discipline Procedures*, Home Office, 30 March 1993, para 58.
13 GCO para 9.34.
14 GCO para 9.34 as amended by HO Circular 8/92.
15 PCA Annual Report 1992, p9; cf p27 para 4.1.
16 PCA Annual Report 1993 p34.
17 *R v Chief Constable of Northumbria Police ex p Charlton* (1994) *Times* 6 May; cf *R v Kent Police Authority ex p Godden* [1971] 2 QB 662, sub nom *Re Godden* [1971] 3 All ER 20, CA.

TABLE 9
Resignations among officers in England and Wales (excluding the Metropolitan
Police) facing criminal or disciplinary proceedings

	1988	1989	1990	1991	1992	1993
Resignations after criminal charges preferred but before completed	25	17	22	21	20	15 (4)*
Resignations after disciplinary charges preferred but before completed	20	21	32	12	15	18 (10)*
Resignations while under suspension (but before charges preferred)	33	37	31	14	24	19 (3)*

* Figures for Metropolitan Police (only available from 1993).
Source: HC Written Answers, 25 April 1995.

Suspension

A chief officer has power to suspend an officer if it appears that s/he might have committed a disciplinary or criminal offence, whether or not the matter has been investigated.[18] Officers are suspended with pay but without some allowances, and the opportunity to earn overtime is lost.[19] It is not necessarily unlawful to prevent a suspended officer from attending Police Federation meetings in appropriate circumstances.[20] The suspension may be lifted once the disciplinary matter has been dropped or dealt with, or earlier if the chief officer so decides.[21]

An officer cannot retire or give notice while suspended for disciplinary reasons without the consent of the chief officer.[22] Nor can an officer be dismissed once his or her resignation has become effective.[23] A proposal to suspend a senior officer is subject to the approval of the

18 Discipline Regs reg 27(1).
19 Discipline General Regs reg 27(2).
20 *R v Chief Constable of North Wales ex p Hughes* [1991] ICR 180, CA.
21 Discipline Regs reg 27(2).
22 Police Regs 1995 reg 18(1).
23 *Cooper v Wilson* [1937] 2 All ER 726; 2 KB 309.

PCA, and the suspension does not generally take effect until its approval is given.[24]

Action after investigation

Once the investigation has been completed, a number of 'safeguards', intended to ensure that the possibility of disciplinary or criminal proceedings is properly considered, come into play. These include requiring the chief officer to report to the PCA and to send files to the DPP, and the power of the PCA to direct the chief officer to bring disciplinary charges, see pp70–72.

Formulating disciplinary charges

The chief officer decides whether an officer should be charged with a disciplinary offence, after considering the investigating officer's report and any statement made by the officer.[25] In formulating the charge s/he must 'have regard' to guidance to chief officers and other police officers issued by the Home Secretary.[26] The principal source of guidance is the *Guidance to Chief Officers on Police Complaints and Discipline Procedures* (GCO),[27] which is not generally available to the public.[28] It contains detailed guidance on the general principles of formulating charges and advice on formulating charges in respect of a number of specific offences including discreditable conduct, disobedience to orders, falsehood or prevarication and racially discriminatory behaviour.[29] The requirement to have regard to the guidance does not mean that it must be slavishly followed in every detail[30] and the consequences of a failure to follow the guidance on formulating charges are not clear. A failure to have regard to the guidance when deciding on guilt or punishment is explicitly made admissible in any appeal,[31] but this leaves open the question of whether an officer can appeal against conviction or sentence on the ground that, if the

24 Police (Discipline) (Senior Officers) Regs 1985 ('Senior Officers Discipline Regs') SI No 519 regs 23 and 24.
25 Discipline Regs reg 8.
26 PACE s105(1) to be amended by the Police and Magistrates' Courts Act 1994 Sch 5, para 34 from a date to be appointed.
27 Looseleaf issued by Home Office.
28 The only published guidance is *Police Complaints and Disciplinary Procedures*, Cmnd 9072, 1983, which was produced before PACE was enacted.
29 GCO paras 9.1–9.15.
30 *R v Police Complaints Board ex p Madden and Rhone* [1983] 2 All ER 353.
31 PACE s105(3); GCO para 9.1.

guidance had been followed, the charge would not have been laid in the first place.

The PCA has said that it is concerned that chief officers are failing to bring disciplinary proceedings because, as a result of *R v Edwards*,[32] which held that police disciplinary record can be disclosed to juries in subsequent criminal trials where the officer is a witness, the officer's usefulness to the force is thereby diminished.[33]

Disciplinary proceedings cannot be dismissed on the grounds that a complaint has only been made as a collateral attack on a criminal conviction of the complainant. Thus, where a complainant alleges that officers made false statements to secure his/her conviction, those statements can form the subject of disciplinary proceedings even though the complainant's criminal conviction still stands.[34]

Probationers

Quite apart from the discipline procedures, a chief officer can discharge a probationer constable at any time if s/he considers that the probationer is not fitted, physically or mentally, to perform the duties of his/her office, or that s/he is not likely to become an efficient or well conducted constable.[35] However, this procedure should not be used as an alternative means of dismissing a probationer where disciplinary proceedings should properly be brought. It is an unlawful breach of the duty of fairness to discharge a probationer without the opportunity of a hearing where the allegations against him/her would support disciplinary proceedings.[36]

32 [1991] 2 All ER 266.
33 PCA Annual Report 1993, p30; see p108.
34 *R v Metropolitan Police Disciplinary Tribunal ex p Police Complaints Authority* (1993) 5 Admin LR 225, [1992] COD 405, DC; cf *Hunter v Chief Constable of West Midlands Police* [1982] AC 529; [1981] 3 WLR 906; [1981] 3 All ER 727, where an allegedly collateral attack by means of civil proceedings on the plaintiffs' criminal convictions was struck out.
35 Police Regs 1995 reg 15; *R v Chief Constable of Thames Valley Police ex p Stevenson* (1987) *Times* 22 April, QBD; see also p29.
36 *Chief Constable of North Wales Police v Evans* [1982] 1 WLR 1155, [1982] 3 All ER 141, HL; *R v Chief Constable of West Midlands Police ex p Carroll* (1994) 7 Admin LR 45 CA; GCO para 9.38 advises that where disciplinary proceedings are appropriate and justified, they should be brought; where they are not brought, a probationer should not be left with the impression that he has been suspected of an offence and given no chance to defend himself at a disciplinary hearing.

94   *Police Misconduct / Chapter 4*

Special constables

Special constables are not formally members of a police force.[37] They are appointed by, are under the direction and control of, and are subject to dismissal by, chief officers.[38] They thus fall outside the regular complaints and disciplinary procedures, and, because they are volunteers, there are concerns that they are not susceptible to any of the usual management or discipline constraints that regulate the conduct of other officers.[39]

Where a report, allegation or complaint has been received from which it appears that a special constable may have been remiss or negligent in the discharge of his/her duty or otherwise unfit for the same, the chief officer may suspend him/her from the office of constable. Alternatively, the chief officer may require a special constable to retire.[40] There is no statutory provision for a disciplinary hearing. For the civil liability of special constables, see pp203 and 207.

Police officers acting in a group

There are sometimes allegations that a complainant has suffered misconduct, such as assault, at the hands of one or more of a group of officers, but that the complainant is unable to identify the actual member or members of the group. This was previously thought to be an insurmountable obstacle to successful disciplinary proceedings. However, the PCA has now concluded that:

provided there was strong evidence of the complainant having been assaulted by someone and strong evidence of the presence of the group during the assault, there were two practicable courses of action –

a)   to charge the entire group jointly with the offence of using excessive force, on the basis that the evidence showed a concerted action in which all participated although not all may have struck blows;

b)   to charge each officer in the alternative with an individual neglect of duty in failing to prevent the commission of an offence, or failing to protect a prisoner or, at the very least, failing to report an incident.

Thus officers who claimed by way of defence not to have participated in the assault, or even to have disapproved of it, might none the less be brought to book for a shameful silence in the knowledge of disgraceful misconduct.[41]

37   *Sheikh v Chief Constable of Greater Manchester Police* [1989] 2 All ER 684 at 689.
38   Police Act 1964 s16.
39   See, eg, Leon, 'Rank Outsiders' *Policing* Vol 9 Winter 1993 pp280–301.
40   Special Constables Regulations 1965 SI No 536 regs 2 and 3.
41   PCA Annual Report 1987 para 2.15.

The 'double jeopardy' rule

An officer who has been convicted or acquitted of a criminal offence cannot be charged with an offence against discipline which is in substance the same as the criminal offence.[42] This rule against 'double jeopardy' is intended to protect officers from being tried twice over for the same offence.

The question of whether two offences are 'in substance the same' is not straightforward. The police are advised[43] that the elements of a criminal charge and a disciplinary charge:

> may not be as similar as appears at first sight: the mental element of the criminal offence may be lacking in the disciplinary offence, or the conduct involved may differ. Where this is so, there is no bar to disciplinary proceedings, because the two offences are not in substance the same. As examples, in criminal proceedings against a police officer for corruption it is necessary to establish that the officer agreed to show favour to the person from whom he agreed to accept a gift or consideration, but this element is absent from the disciplinary offence of accepting a gratuity; a criminal charge of perjury involves proof that an allegedly false statement was material to the proceedings in which it was made, but a disciplinary charge of falsehood does not; and a Theft Act charge will require proof of an intention permanently to deprive a person of his property or permanently to evade payment of a debt, whereas these elements are absent from disciplinary offences relating to the care of property or failure to discharge debts. By contrast the criminal charge of assault and the disciplinary charge of unnecessary violence is the most common example of such charges being in substance the same.

The rule against double jeopardy does not apply to the disciplinary offence of 'criminal conduct' which is committed where an officer has been found guilty of a criminal offence by a court of law, including a conviction which leads to probation, or conditional or absolute discharge.[44] Thus if an officer is convicted of the criminal offence of, say, assault, s/he may not be charged with the disciplinary offence of unnecessary violence, but may be charged with the disciplinary offence of criminal conduct.

In cases that arose from a complaint, it used to be the practice of the old Police Complaints Board to refuse to recommend or direct a chief officer to bring disciplinary charges in any case where the DPP had already decided not to bring a criminal prosecution for substantially the

42 PACE s104(1).
43 GCO para 5.14.
44 PACE s104(2); Discipline Regs Sch 1 para 16; *R v Secretary of State for Home Department ex p Thornton* [1986] 3 WLR 158.

same offence on the ground of lack of evidence. This practice was justified as an extension of the principle against double jeopardy. It was successfully challenged in the High Court in 1982, when it was decided that double jeopardy meant that no one should be *tried* twice for the same offence.[45] The consideration of a case by the DPP was not the same as trying a case. Thus, the Board should have considered whether or not to recommend or direct that an officer be charged with a disciplinary offence, even if the DPP had decided not to prosecute. As a result of the High Court decision the Board changed its policy,[46] and the guidance to chief officers has been amended.[47]

The rule against double jeopardy is to be abolished by the Police and Magistrates' Courts Act 1994 s93 and Sch 9 Part I, from a date to be appointed. Thereafter it will be possible to bring disciplinary proceedings against police officers either before or after any criminal proceedings and irrespective of the outcome of such proceedings. However, a police complaint by a member of the public will not be recorded or investigated if it wholly or partly relates to conduct which is or has been the subject of criminal or disciplinary proceedings.[48]

Legal representation
An officer cannot be dismissed, required to resign or reduced in rank as a result of disciplinary proceedings without having been given an opportunity to be represented by a lawyer.[49] Police Federation funds are available for legal representation,[50] but officers are not given the opportunity of representation automatically, and it is for the officer responsible for formulating the charge to decide whether to offer the opportunity to be legally represented. Legal representation is usually only offered if there is a genuine prospect of the chief officer considering dismissal.[51]

If the officer responsible for formulating the charge underestimates the seriousness of the case, whether blamelessly or otherwise, and does

---

45 *Ex p Madden and Rhone* n30.
46 Police Complaints Board Triennial Review 1983 paras 3.23–3.27.
47 GCO para 5.13.
48 PACE s84(6); see p36.
49 PACE s102(1); minor amendments are to be made by PMCA 1994 Sch 5 para 33 from a date to be appointed. The government's original proposal to repeal s102 was reversed by a government amendment: House of Commons Standing Committee D, 14 June 1994, col 366.
50 Police Federation Regs 1969 SI No 1787 reg 19(2), as amended by Police Federation (Amendment) Regs 1990 SI No 1575 reg 6.
51 Discipline Regs reg 12; GCO para Annex H para 6.

not allow the accused the opportunity of legal representation, the chief officer will be prevented from imposing any punishment more serious than a reduction in pay. The House of Commons Home Affairs Committee has commented that 'These powers afford senior officers the opportunity to allow officers, even if found guilty, to escape with a far lighter punishment than might reasonably be regarded as appropriate. While this opportunity exists, the efforts of police and the [Police Complaints] Authority to improve public confidence in the complaints system are seriously hampered.'[52]

However, more recently the PCA Annual Report for 1994/95 (p35) has criticised senior officers for 'playing safe' and allowing legal representation too freely to cover every eventuality, however remote, with the result that hearings are delayed, take longer to hear than is necessary and involve greater expense.

If an officer is not given an opportunity to be legally represented, s/he may be represented only by another police officer.[53] The Police Federation may represent a member of a police force, including a cadet, at any disciplinary proceedings or appeal.[54]

Delay

There has been considerable concern at the delay between deciding to bring disciplinary charges and holding a hearing. The PCA itself has complained of delays of 11 months, a year and even 16 months.

> One of the main reasons for delay is the availability of chief constables to hear disciplinary cases which can last for days and even weeks – especially when legal representation is involved . . . Another cause of delay has recently become apparent: that of the non-availability of a particular counsel to represent the accused officer. While we recognise that ideally an officer should be represented by counsel of his choice, this may not always be possible and we are not willing to accept this as an excuse for delay in all circumstances, any more than it is in the criminal courts . . . Delays have been such that in some instances it has appeared to us that Forces are trying every conceivable tactic to dissuade the [Police Complaints] Authority from pressing charges . . .[55]

52 Police Complaints Procedures, HC Home Affairs Committee, Fourth Report, Session 1991–92, HC 179, pxvi para 38.
53 PACE s102(3), to be amended by PMCA 1994 Sch 5 para 33 from a date to be appointed; see *Maynard v Osmond* [1977] QB 240; [1977] 1 All ER 64, CA.
54 Police Act 1964 s44(1)(1A)(1B) and (6) as amended, to be further amended by the PMCA 1994 s44 and Sch 5 Part I para 11 from a date to be appointed.
55 PCA Annual Report 1987 paras 2.19–2.20.

A Joint Statement of Intent on delays was agreed by the PCA, the CPS and ACPO, see appendix 1. The target within which disciplinary hearings should be arranged is four months from the decision to bring proceedings, and in all cases within six months, unless the circumstances are wholly exceptional. The Statement provides that while 'every effort will be made to meet the accused officer's wishes, a hearing will not be unreasonably delayed because of the inability of a particular friend or counsel to attend'. The PCA has reported that the objectives set out in the Joint Statement of Intent 'are not being met and in the Authority's view it is the presented case rather than the defended case which suffers. Civilian witnesses, inexperienced as they are in the giving of evidence, are likely to be more vulnerable to cross-examination after a significant lapse of time.'[56] In cases of serious delay, and where no reasonable explanation is forthcoming, there is inevitably a suspicion that senior officers are colluding with accused officers to defeat the purpose of the disciplinary process.

A delay in holding a hearing can result in an application being made that because of the passage of time it would be an abuse of process and contrary to natural justice for the officer to face disciplinary proceedings. A chief officer's refusal to discontinue proceedings on the grounds of prejudicial delay can be quashed by judicial review.[57] It has even been held, exceptionally, that judicial review may be available to quash a decision to find disciplinary charges proved against officers after a two-year delay in serving a Regulation 7 notice (see p89), even though the officers had exercised their statutory right of appeal.[58] However, other than in exceptional circumstances, the courts ought not to exercise their discretion to grant judicial review until the elaborate disciplinary framework of the statutory appeals process has been exhausted. Since the issue is one of delay, to entertain applications for judicial review in advance of the appeals process is simply to delay further the hearing of the case. A disciplinary tribunal should make its own decisions on matters such as delay, and any review of such a decision should generally be made through the appeal process.[59]

A chief officer will not be liable in damages for an unreasonable delay (eg, in respect of loss of overtime payments or damage to reputa-

56 PCA Annual Report 1993 p46.
57 R v Chief Constable of Merseyside Police ex p Merrill [1989] 1 WLR 1077, CA.
58 R v Chief Constable of the Merseyside Police ex p Calveley [1986] QB 424, [1986] 2 WLR 144, [1986] 1 All ER 257, CA; cf R v UK Central Council for Nursing, Midwifery and Health Visiting ex p Thompson and Others [1991] COD 275 (no breach of natural justice for 48 months' delay). See p000.
59 R v PCA and Another ex p Wells [1991] COD 95.

tion), either in negligence, breach of statutory duty or misfeasance in a public office.[60]

Disciplinary hearings

Disciplinary hearings are usually heard by the chief constable or by an assistant chief constable sitting alone (or, in London, by a disciplinary board or a commander).[61] If the chief constable of the relevant force is a witness in the case or has some other interest in it, a chief constable from another can take his or her place.[62] In any case where the chief officer initially decided not to bring a disciplinary charge and has done so only because the PCA has recommended or directed that s/he do so, the charge must be heard by a tribunal, usually consisting of the chief officer and two members of the PCA.[63] This is intended to ensure that chief officers do not automatically dismiss, at the hearing state, charges that they were disinclined to bring in the first place. The PCA is clearly uneasy in this role. It has said that, while the two members of the PCA will have had nothing to do with the case prior to sitting on the tribunal, it can still be perceived as acting as judge and prosecutor. It has also complained that some cases are not presented with the force and clarity that it would have expected. The PCA may direct that a charge be heard by a tribunal in other cases where it considers it desirable because of any exceptional circumstances affecting the case.[64] These might be the intrinsic seriousness of the charge, the complexity or difficulty of the case, or any grave public disquiet or other special considerations.[65]

The Police and Magistrates' Courts Act 1994 ss37(c) and 93 and Sch 9 Pt I will abolish disciplinary tribunals and it seems that henceforth there will be no independent oversight of cases that chief officers were reluctant to bring and that have only proceeded because the PCA has directed that they must be heard. Thus an important safeguard has been lost and the value of the PCA being able to direct that a hearing take place has all but been thrown away.

If a disciplinary hearing is delegated to an assistant chief constable,

60 *Calveley v Chief Constable of Merseyside* [1989] AC 1228, HL.
61 Discipline Regs regs 13 and 16 and Sch 3; as amended by PMCA 1994 s6 from 1 April 1995 and Police Discipline (Amendment) Regulations 1995, and Police Discipline (Amendment No 2) Regulations 1995.
62 Ibid reg 14.
63 PACE s94(1).
64 Ibid. s94(2).
65 GCO para 6.37.

s/he may not impose a punishment of dismissal, requirement to resign or reduction in rank.[66] This could raise the suspicion that, if a chief officer were so minded, s/he could manipulate the proceedings by delegating a serious case to his/her deputy so as to protect an officer facing a charge.

The disciplinary hearing is of a quasi-judicial character and the rules of natural justice must be observed.[67] While the procedure is prescribed by regulations (see p102), the hearing should not be conducted as if it were a criminal trial and it need not be bound by technical rules of evidence.[68] Nor will a verdict inevitably be quashed merely because a procedural flaw gives the appearance of justice not being seen to be done.[69]

> These matters are, perhaps, being obscured by the introduction of legal representation at disciplinary hearings. We [the PCA] wonder whether some of the lawyers presenting and defending cases are aware of these important differences. The presenting officer or counsel has a special responsibility to spell out these considerations at disciplinary hearings and to safeguard the rights of complainants and their right to hear the evidence as to fact.[70]

The existing scheme of discipline regulations will be abolished in due course by the Police and Magistrates' Courts Act 1994.[71]

Attendance of complainant
If a disciplinary hearing arises from a complaint, the complainant is allowed to attend the hearing while witnesses are being examined, or cross-examined, on the facts alleged in the charge.[72] Home Office advice is rather broader and says simply that s/he may 'be present throughout the proceedings and until a finding is reached'.[73] However, if the complainant is to be called as a witness, s/he cannot attend before s/he gives evidence (although s/he should be allowed to stay afterwards); and s/he can be excluded if a witness may say something in evidence

---

66 Discipline Regs reg 16.
67 *Ridge v Baldwin* [1964] AC 40, [1963] 2 All ER 66, HL.
68 Discipline Regs reg 18(8); GCO paras 9.18–9.19 and Annex H.
69 *R v Chief Constable of South Wales ex p Thornhill* (1986) *Times* 12 May.
70 PCA Annual Report 1988 para 2.14.
71 Sections 37(e) and 93 and Sch 9 Part I repeal PACE s101 from a date to be appointed; discipline regulations may be made pursuant to Police Act 1964 s 33(2)(e).
72 Discipline Regs reg 22(1) and (2).
73 GCO Annex H para 25.

which ought not to be disclosed to a member of the public.[74] It seems that a complainant is not entitled to be present when punishment is being considered, where there are no witnesses or when the accused pleads guilty.[75]

> As a result the process gives the appearance of being shrouded in mystery, which detracts from the credibility of the system. After a disciplinary hearing most forces will go no further than to say that the charges against the officer were proved at the disciplinary hearing and that suitable action was taken, or that the case was not proved . . . We [the PCA] ask ourselves why the complainant is not entitled to know the outcome of a case which has been brought at his or her instigation.[76]

If the officer conducting the hearing thinks it appropriate, because of the complainant's age or otherwise, s/he may be accompanied by a friend or relative.[77] This is not intended to allow the complainant to bring a lawyer, but, of course, if the friend were a lawyer, there would be no obligation to mention this fact. The existence of the rule against admitting lawyers has sometimes led to the ludicrous but unavoidable practice of complainants' lawyers sitting outside the hearing room and complainants periodically calling for adjournments in order to seek the advice of the lawyer outside.

If the accused gives evidence, the complainant may, after any cross-examination, put his/her own questions either through the officer conducting the hearing or, at that officer's discretion, directly.[78] In effect, this gives the complainant a valuable opportunity to cross-examine the accused about the incident and to draw out any inconsistencies in the officer's evidence. It is, therefore, helpful to make a detailed note of the evidence presented to the hearing as a reminder of the points which are open to challenge. Effective cross-examination of the accused may have a real influence on the final decision. However, there is no point in cross-examining an officer if the presenting officer has already done the job satisfactorily. The complainant should be careful not to intervene or interrupt without the permission of the officer conducting the hearing. If s/he behaves in a disorderly or abusive manner or otherwise misconducts him/herself, s/he can be excluded from the rest of the hearing.[79]

74 Discipline Regs reg 22(2)(a) and (b).
75 GCO Annex B.
76 PCA Annual Report 1989 para 2.19.
77 Discipline Regs reg 22.
78 Ibid reg 22(3).
79 Ibid reg 22(4).

If the complainant is called to attend a disciplinary hearing *as a witness*, s/he is entitled to reasonable expenses at the discretion of the chief officer and the police authority.[80] A reluctant witness, including a complainant, can be compelled by a court order to attend a hearing in order to give evidence.[81]

Procedure at the hearing

Disciplinary hearings are held in private. The accused officer may be accompanied by a 'friend', that is, another police officer acting as his/ her representative and adviser. There will be a presenting officer who explains the case against the accused. In addition, in cases where the accused officer has had the opportunity of legal representation, there may be lawyers both for the defence and for the presenting officer. There may also be administrative staff and a shorthand writer present.

The PCA has repeatedly complained that some cases are not presented (or prosecuted) with the 'vigour and accuracy' that might be expected. This is particularly a problem where the case is being heard on the recommendation or direction of the PCA and, therefore, fundamentally against the wishes of the prosecuting force.

> For example, we were dismayed when three men who had given their names and addresses as witnesses and all of whom had made statements to the investigating officer, which, on the face of it, proved the complainant's case, were not called by the presenting officer to suppor the complaintant's case at the hearing. We will never convince the public of the soundess of the system while such anomalies exist.[82]

Decisions and the standard of proof

The officer conducting the hearing must either dismiss the charge or find it proved. A charge will be found proved only if either the officer admits it or if the case is proved beyond reasonable doubt.[83] This high standard of proof is, therefore, the same as in criminal cases and not, as in civil cases, merely on the balance of probabilities.

The civil standard of proof applies to other disciplined forces such as

---

80 GCO Annex H para 40.
81 RSC Order 38 r19; GCO para 5.19; see also *Currie v Chief Constable of Surrey* [1982] 1 All ER 89.
82 PCA Triennial Review 1988–91 para 3.18.
83 Discipline Regs reg 23.

TABLE 10
Punishments awarded as a result of disciplinary proceedings, England and
Wales 1989–94

Most serious punishment	1989	1990	1991	1992	1993	1994
Dismissed	33	28	42	54	47	27
Required to resign	48	40	51	55	55	64
Reduction in rank	20	16	25	12	20	21
Reduction in pay	15	19	20	25	24	38
Fine	182	157	165	134	184	114
Reprimand	83	115	118	126	117	88
Caution	25	33	27	27	38	35
Total	406	408	448	433	485	390

Source: HO Statistical Bulletins 1994 and 1995, 13/94 and 13/95.

the fire service and, more pertinently, the prison service.[84] Civilian employers, in justifying the fairness of a dismissal before an industrial tribunal, do not even need to meet the civil standard of proof. They need only show that they had reasonable grounds for believing an employee had committed misconduct. Unlike members of the armed forces, to whom the criminal standard also applies, police officers face nothing more severe than dismissal as a result of a disciplinary hearing, while a court martial may impose a term of imprisonment.

The police seek to justify the higher standard of proof on the ground that a significant proportion of complainants have come into contact with the police through their own misdeeds and may, therefore, have an ulterior motive for making the complaint. However, the PCA has said that there are some complaints in which most of the available evidence seems to point to the police over-reacting or breaking the Discipline Code but where there is insufficient evidence to prove the case beyond reasonable doubt and it is, therefore, inhibited from pressing a disciplinary charge. It has concluded that the standard of proof is unnecessarily causing the disciplinary process to fall into disrepute.[85]

The Home Office has tentatively suggested that in the proposed new discipline system allegations of misconduct 'will be assessed on the

84 *R v Hampshire CC ex p Ellerton* [1985] 1 All ER 599, CA; *Police Complaints Procedures*, HC Home Affairs Committee, Session 1991–92, HC 179 p xviii para 47.
85 PCA Annual Report 1989 para 2.16; PCA Triennial Review 1988–91 para 3.15.

basis of the level of evidence normally acceptable in everyday life and according to where, on that basis, any reasonable person would think the truth most likely to lie.'[86]

Punishments

If a charge is found proved, the officer must receive *one* of the following punishments:[87]

- dismissal from the force;
- a requirement that s/he resign from the force;
- reduction in rank;
- reduction in rate of pay, for not more than 12 months;
- a fine;
- a reprimand;
- a caution.

As we have seen, an officer cannot be dismissed, required to resign or reduced in rank without having had the opportunity of being legally represented.[88] If a disciplinary hearing is delegated to an assistant chief constable, s/he may not impose a punishment of dismissal, a requirement to resign or a reduction in rank.[89] A reduction in pay or a fine cannot be imposed for the disciplinary offence of criminal conduct.[90] The officer conducting the hearing must, therefore, either decide effectively that the offence was relatively minor or treat it as so serious as to make the officer unfit to remain in the force or to remain in his/her current rank. If a case is heard before a chief officer from outside the force, s/he can only recommend a punishment; the final decison lies with the accused officer's own chief officer.[91]

Internal appeals

If responsibility for hearing a charge has been delegated, for example to an assistant chief constable, the accused officer has a right of appeal to

86 *Review of Police Discipline Procedures: Consultation Paper,* Home Office, March 1993, para 75. It is expected that the test to be included in the forthcoming regulations will set a standard that lies somewhere between the test suggested in the consultation paper and criminal standard.
87 Discipline Regs reg 24.
88 PACE s102.
89 Discipline Regs reg 16 as amended.
90 Discipline Regs reg 25.
91 Ibid reg 24(3) and (5).

the chief officer against the finding and punishment or against the punishment alone.[92] It seems that a complainant has no right to attend such internal appeal hearings, although it is possible that s/he could be called as a witness.

Disciplinary charges against senior officers

Senior officers are defined as officers above the rank of superintendent, ie, assistant chief constables, chief constables and some equivalent ranks in the Metropolitan police and the City of London police.[93]

The disciplinary procedure is broadly similar to that for more junior officers, although the appropriate authorities (the police authority or, in the Metropolitan Police, the commissioner)[94] are allowed greater discretion to dispense with the procedure and the accused officer is, in practice, largely protected from less serious allegations. Furthermore, although the PCA has the same functions in supervising complaints as against senior officers as in respect of junior officers, it has no role in the disciplinary procedure.

When the appropriate authority first hears of a report, allegation or complaint, it has wide power to decide that no disciplinary proceedings need be taken.[95] It must, however, in discharging its functions, have regard to any guidance issued by the Secretary of State.[96]

In formulating a charge, the commissioner or police authority is advised[97] that although:

> it has not been thought necessary to frame a special discipline code for senior officers, clearly some of the offences or some part of the offences listed will not be applicable to officers of that rank. Care should therefore be taken to ensure that charges under the discipline code are not brought against a senior officer which are obviously inappropriate.

92 Ibid reg 26.
93 PACE s84 as amended by PMCA 1994 Sch 5, para 24; 'senior officer' included all officers above chief superintendent until 1 April 1995 when that rank and the rank of deputy chief constable were abolished: Police Regulations 1995 SI No 215, reg 6 and PMCA 1994 s 6.
94 In the Metropolitan police the appropriate authority in respect of deputy assistant commissioners and commanders is the commissioner himself; officers of assistant commissioner rank and above are appointed (and may be removed) by the Queen and fall outside the statutory complaints and discipline procedures.
95 Senior Officer Discipline Regs reg 5(3).
96 PACE s105(1), to be amended by the PMCA 1994 Sch 5 para 34 from a date to be appointed.
97 GCO para 10.3.

If an officer admits a disciplinary offence, the commissioner or police authority can impose a punishment without a hearing, but has a wide discretion not to impose any punishment at all.[98]

A police authority, acting with the approval of the Home Secretary, can call on a chief constable or assistant chief constable to retire in the interests of efficiency, but before seeking such approval, it must allow the chief constable an opportunity to make representations and must consider them.[99] By analogy with the position of probationary constables (see p93), it might be an abuse of process to require a chief constable to resign under this procedure when s/he should more properly be charged with a disciplinary offence to which s/he could mount a defence.[100]

Procedure at the hearing
The disciplinary hearing is heard by a tribunal consisting of a single person chosen by the appropriate authority from a list of people nominated by the Lord Chancellor. The tribunal will be assisted by one or more 'assessors', one of whom must be a serving or former chief officer, who advises on police matters.[101] The accused officer may be represented by a lawyer and, unlike hearings against junior officers, this does not depend on the seriousness of the case and has no bearing on the punishment that can be awarded.[102]

Attendance of complainant
If the charge arose from a complaint, the complainant has the same rights to attend the hearing and to ask the accused officer questions as s/he has in hearings against junior officers, see p100. Although the accused officer may be legally represented, complainants who wish to cross-examine the officer have no such entitlement and may bring only a friend or relative. The complainant's questions must be put to the accused by the tribunal, or, at its discretion, by the complainant directly.[103]

As for junior officers, a disciplinary charge must be proved on the

---

98 Senior Officers Discipline Regs reg 8.
99 Police Act 1964 ss5 and 6 to be amended by PMCA 1994 ss5 and 6.
100 See *Chief Constable of North Wales Police v Evans* [1982] 1 WLR 1155, [1982] 3 All ER 141, HL; cf *Ridge v Baldwin* [1964] AC 40, HL.
101 Senior Officers Discipline Regs reg 12.
102 Ibid reg 13(6).
103 Ibid reg 17.

criminal standard of proof, that is, beyond reasonable doubt.[104] The tribunal must find the charge proved or not proved and make a recommendation about any punishment.[105] The commissioner or police authority may then dismiss the case, record a finding of guilt but take no further action, or record a finding of guilt and impose a punishment.[106] The only punishments available are dismissal, requirement to resign or reprimand.[107]

Appeals to the Home Secretary

Any officer can appeal to the Home Secretary against the finding on the disciplinary charge and against punishment.[108] This is so, even if the officer pleaded guilty at the original disciplinary hearing.[109] If the appeal is against dismissal, requirement to resign or reduction in rank, or if it is necessary to take evidence, the Home Secretary must appoint a tribunal of three people, chaired by a lawyer, to hold an inquiry and to report to him/her. The Home Secretary also has a discretion to appoint a tribunal in other cases.[110] If the disciplinary charge arose from a complaint, the complainant has the same right to attend any hearing and to ask questions of the accused as applied to the disciplinary hearing, see pp100 and 106.

A police officer who appeals to the Home Secretary may be represented at appeal hearings by a lawyer. However, complainants who wish to cross-examine the officer do not have the same right and may bring only a friend or relative, as they could to the disciplinary hearing.[111]

The Home Secretary is not bound to follow the findings of the appeal tribunal, and may on consideration of the papers resolve to dismiss an officer in the face of a finding that charges are not proven.[112] However, the Home Secretary cannot impose a punishment that could not have been imposed at the original disciplinary hearing, nor a punishment that is more severe than the original

---

104 Ibid reg 18(2).
105 Ibid reg 18(1)(b) and (c).
106 Ibid reg 19.
107 Ibid reg 20.
108 Police Act 1964 s37 as amended by PACE s103(1).
109 *R v Secretary of State for Home Dept ex p Chief Constable of Nottingham* (1984) *Times* 10 March.
110 Police Act 1964 Sch 5 para 3 as amended by PACE s103(2).
111 Police (Appeals) Rules 1985 (Appeals Rules) SI No 576 r14.
112 *R v Secretary of State for Home Department ex p Barr and Others* [1994] Admin LR 7, CA; cf *R v Secretary of State for Home Department ex p Harrison* (1994) *Times* 17 May.

one.[113] The Home Secretary's decision letter must adequately address the charge and give reasons for the decision.[114]

The PCA has said that the composition of appeal tribunals is misconceived in that the preponderance of ex-police officers gives the complainant the 'wrong impression'.[115] The Police and Magistrates' Courts Act 1994 will abolish the right of appeal to the Home Secretary and instead provide for appeals to be heard by a four-person Police Appeals Tribunal consisting of a legally qualified chair, a representative of the appropriate authority, a serving or former chief officer from a different police force and a retired police officer of appropriate, although not necessarily equal rank to the appellant officer.[116] Thus, there will no longer be a majority of serving or former police officers on the tribunal: in practice, however, the retired officer will be a former staff association representative.[117]

Rules to be made by the Secretary of State may govern the procedure of Police Appeals Tribunals and may enable the tribunal to require any person to attend to give evidence or to produce documents.[118]

Disclosure of police disciplinary records in criminal trials

In the past there has been uncertainty whether police disciplinary records and notice of suspensions and pending complaints investigations should properly be disclosed where this might assist the defence in a criminal trial. Where a prosecution witness is of bad character, there is a general duty on the prosecution at common law to disclose that fact and any material upon which the defence could cross-examine the witness as to his/her character.[119] In 1991 *R v Edwards*[120] extended this to require the disclosure of certain police discipline records. In a criminal case in which a police officer's credibility is in issue it is permissible to cross-examine the officer about any criminal or disciplinary charges proved against him/her in respect of other matters, as they

113 Police Act 1964 s37(4) as amended by PACE s103(1).
114 *R v Secretary of State for Home Department ex p Nelson* (1994) *Independent* 2 June.
115 PCA Annual Report 1992 p26 paras 3.13 and 15.
116 PMCA 1994 s19 and Sch 3, amending Police Act 1964 s37 and Sch 5, from a date to be appointed.
117 HC Standing Committee D, 26 May 1994, cols 316–318.
118 Police Act 1964 s37(4), to be amended by PMCA 1994 s19, from a date to be appointed.
119 *R v Collister and Warhurst* (1955) 39 Cr App R 100.
120 [1991] 2 All ER 266.

may cast doubt on his/her credibility. Where there is a right to cross-examine there is a corresponding duty upon the prosecuting authorities to volunteer disclosure to the defence. The duty to disclose discipline records to the defence applies whether the officer's evidence is to be given in person, or read out to the court or whether it merely forms 'unused material' disclosed to the defence.

As a matter of policy, disciplinary findings in respect of neglect of health, improper dress or untidiness or entering licensed premises are not reported by the police to the CPS unless the CPS specifically asks for them.[121] Subject to this, the police are required by the CPS to reveal to them details of any disciplinary findings of guilt in all cases where a full file of evidence is prepared, ie, where the defendant has been charged with an indictable-only offence, an either-way offence that the magistrates are likely to refer to the Crown Court or any type of assault and is likely to deny the offence.[122]

The DPP takes the view that the duty does not extend to records that have been expunged by the passage of time. (Records of minor disciplinary matters are removed from officers' personal records after three years, and after five for more serious matters.)[123] The DPP also takes the view that the duty does not extend to cases where there is no duty to record the finding formally; thus findings that only result in cautions are not disclosed. Nor will complaints that do not result in disciplinary findings of guilt be revealed, except in certain cases where the matter is still to be adjudicated upon (see below).[124]

The DPP requires the police to reveal to the CPS whether any officer in a case has been suspended pending completion of enquiries into his/her conduct. The police must also reveal cases where an officer has been charged but the discipline case has not yet been concluded. There is a third ill-defined category of cases where even though no charge has yet been brought 'the nature of allegations [sic] made or under investigation is such that their non-disclosure might subsequently prejudice the current case'.[125] The ACPO officer responsible for discipline (usually the assistant chief constable) is responsible for ensuring that such cases are revealed to the CPS 'where there is any likelihood that the interests

---

121 CPS Policy on *R v Edwards*, DPP to Chief Officers of Police, 5 October 1992 (hereafter 'CPS on Edwards'), para 8, reproduced as appendix 13.
122 CPS on Edwards, para 9. Likelihood of denial is judged by asking, 'Has the defendant admitted the offence, or if not, was its commission witnessed by a police officer?'
123 Police Regs 1995 SI No 215 reg 17(2).
124 CPS on Edwards para 7, see appendix 13.
125 Ibid.

of justice require this'.[126] The CPS then decides whether or not to disclose the facts to the defence, although it will do so if the defence so requests.[127]

Proposals for reform of the discipline system

In March 1993 the government published a consultation paper on proposals for reform of the discipline system,[128] and a number of these proposals have been incorporated into the Police and Magistrates' Courts Act 1994.[129] However most of the detailed proposals will require amendments to secondary legislation by regulations which have not been published at the time of writing. Some proposals for reform have been fiercely resisted by the Police Federation and others.[130]

Misconduct and poor performance
The proposals for reform aim to place discipline procedures, or whatever will replace them, within a wider context of personnel management that seeks to emphasise positive support to achieve improved performance, while recognising the need for specific procedures to deal with misconduct. Misconduct cases will therefore be distinguished from cases of poor performance, and separate procedures will apply to each type of case. Both types of case could be revealed by a complaint from a member of the public, but equally they could be revealed by internal police management.

Poor performance   Cases of poor performance may continue to be dealt with by informal management action, but any formal action will consist of a four-stage process involving:

– *first interview* with the officer's immediate superior;
– *second interview* involving the personnel department, possibly leading to a written warning;
– *unsatisfactory performance hearing* with a chief police officer and two assessors of at least superintendent rank. This may result in the

126 CPS on *Edwards* para 18.
127 Ibid paras 9 and 19. See Harrison and Cragg, 'Police Misconduct: Prosecution Disclosure of Police Discipline Records' September 1995 *Legal Action* 19.
128 *Review of Police Discipline Procedures: Consultation Paper*, Home Office, 1993.
129 The principal amendments are found in ss19, 36, 37 and 38 and Schs 5 and 9.
130 See, eg, *Response of the Police Federation of England and Wales to the Consultation Paper on Police Personnel Procedures*, 1993; *Guardian* 20 May 1993; and Baker and English, *A Guide to the Police and Magistrates' Courts Act 1994*, Butterworths, 1994.

officer being required to resign or being transferred with a reduced rank, possibly with a written warning;
- *review* of the hearing's decision by the chief officer, if the police officer is dissatisfied, usually only on the papers, and without a hearing.

Defining 'misconduct' The consultation paper acknowledges the difficulty of drawing a satisfactory line between misconduct cases and cases of poor performance. It is critical of a definition that relies upon a code such as the Police Discipline Code[131] and suggests two possible alternative definitions:

- the abuse of statutory powers in relation to a member of the public (or wilful omission to observe a statutory safeguard); or any other action, whether criminal or constituting a civil wrong, which casts doubt on his/her fitness to be a police officer; or failing to account for his or her actions while on duty when called on to do so; or
- criminal conduct; or a breach of the PACE Codes of Practice; or failing to account for his/her actions in relation to such an allegation.

Both definitions have been criticised as unduly narrow and likely to allow allegations of serious misconduct to go unpunished.[132] To take a hypothetical example, suppose an officer negligently left a known violent offender with a weak and vulnerable prisoner whom the violent offender then murders in the cells. The officer may have committed no crime or breach of the PACE Codes and under the second, narrow, test there would have been no 'misconduct'. Again suppose an officer failed adequately to investigate a racist murder for his own racist motives. It is far from clear that such behaviour would constitute 'misconduct' under either the first or second test (at least provided he did not fail to account for his actions). It could be treated as sufficiently trivial to merit only the 'poor performance' procedure. Conversely some breaches of the PACE Codes will be very minor.[133]

Standard of proof
The PCA and the Royal Commission on Criminal Justice both recommended that the criminal standard of proof for discipline cases was too

131 Discipline Regs 1985 Sch 1.
132 Harrison and Cragg, 'Police Discipline', *NLJ*, 23 April 1993, p591.
133 At the time of writing it appears neither test may be adopted and that there may be no hard and fast distinction drawn between misconduct and poor performance.

high and was bringing the discipline system into disrepute.[134] The government's consultation paper proposed that misconduct cases should be 'assessed on the basis of the level of evidence normally acceptable in everyday life and according to where, on that basis, any reasonable person would think the truth most likely to lie.' This provoked some of the angriest reactions from police officers to any of the proposals and it remains to be seen how (or indeed whether) the government will formulate the standard of proof when it brings amending regulations forward in due course.[135]

Although the consultation document was silent upon the point it can at least be expected that the standard of proof for 'poor performance' cases will be lower than the criminal standard.

Abolition of 'right to silence' and rule against double jeopardy
The consultation paper proposed to bring police officers into line with all other employees by allowing adverse inferences to be drawn by superior officers if a police officer fails to give a full account of his/her actions when called upon to do so, and by allowing disciplinary proceedings to be brought irrespective of any criminal proceedings. The rule against double jeopardy is to be repealed by the Police and Magistrates' Courts Act 1994 ss37(f) and 93 and Sch 9 Part I from a date to be appointed. Abolition of the 'right to silence' would require amendment to Discipline Regulations reg 7.

Abolition of appeals to Home Secretary
Appeals to the Home Secretary against the finding or punishment of a disciplinary hearing are to be abolished and replaced by a right of appeal to a four-person Police Appeals Tribunal; see above pp107–108.[136]

Criminal proceedings against the police

Like any other citizen, a police officer may be prosecuted at the instigation of either the Crown Prosecution Service or a private prosecutor. Provided a constable acts within his/her powers in, for example, making an arrest, conducting a stop and search, entering or searching

---

134 PCA Triennial Review 1988–91, para 3.15; Royal Commission on Criminal Justice, Report, Cm 2263, July 1993, para 103(ii).
135 At the time of writing it appears possible the government will create a test of reasonableness which would allow a sliding scale standard, requiring something more than a balance of probabilities in more serious cases, but never reaching the criminal standard of proof.
136 PMCA 1994 ss19 and 93 and Sch 9 Part I, from a date to be appointed.

premises or seizing evidence, s/he will have a complete defence to a criminal charge arising out of that act. However, if a constable acts beyond his/her powers, s/he should, in theory, be as answerable to the criminal law as a private citizen in the same position.[137] In practice, however, the decision to bring a prosecution against a police officer will often, given the current policy of the CPS, not be as straightforward as the decision to bring a prosecution against a member of the public in similar circumstances, and this can weight the decision in favour of the officer (see p114). In 1992, for example, there was widespread surprise and dismay when the DPP announced that she would not be prosecuting any of the members of the West Midlands Serious Crime Squad, following the largest police complaints investigation ever carried out which resulted in the West Yorkshire Police recommending the prosecution of at least 16 officers.[138] In addition, the close working relationship between the police and the CPS may give the impression, whatever the reality, of collusion.

In these circumstances the right of an individual to bring a private prosecution is an important constitutional guarantee of the fundamental principle that no one is above the law. It is beyond the scope of this work to consider all the offences that might come within the ambit of criminal police misconduct. However they will include various types of assault, perverting the course of justice, indecent assault (for example, arising out of intimate body searches), criminal damage (for example, caused in the course of a search), obtaining unauthorised access to computer material, perjury, corruption and false imprisonment. In one exceptional case, *R v Dytham*,[139] a police officer was convicted of the offence of 'misconduct of an officer of justice' after he stood by without intervening and watched a group of men kick another man to death.

This section considers, first, prosecutions brought by the CPS following a complaint or disciplinary investigation and, second, private prosecutions brought by members of the public.

Investigating officers' reports and the DPP

The question of criminal proceedings is usually considered at the end of the investigation of a complaint but before any disciplinary proceedings

137 In *DPP v Harris* (1994) *Times* 16 March, it was held that a general defence of necessity was not open to a police driver who failed to stop at a red light.
138 *Law Society's Gazette* 27 May 1992, p10.
139 [1979] 3 All ER 641; compare the analogous tort of misfeasance in a public office, see p176.

are brought.[140] If the chief officer considers that the report indicates that a criminal offence may have been committed, and that the officer ought to be charged, he must send a copy of the report to the DPP.[141] In all other cases, the report must be sent to the PCA, with a memorandum indicating whether the chief officer considers that a criminal offence may have been committed and if so, that s/he considers that a charge should not be brought.[142]

The requirement that the chief officer must also consider whether the officer *ought* to be charged is to be abolished by the Police and Magistrates' Courts Act 1994 s93 and Sch 9 Part I from a date to be appointed (see p71). So too will be the duty of the PCA to review such decisions and direct the chief officer to send a report to the DPP.[143]

Action by the DPP

The decision to prosecute a police officer lies with the DPP. Two tests are applied. *First,* is there sufficient evidence to justify a prosecution? *Second,* would it be in the public interest for a prosecution to be brought? The DPP will deal with the questions in turn, only asking the second question if satisfied as to the first.

In answering the first question the DPP has decided as a matter of policy that a prosecution should only be brought if there is a reasonable prospect that a jury is more likely to convict than to acquit on the evidence. This is sometimes popularly, if inelegantly, known as the '51 per cent rule'. It involves the prosecutor acting 'as a sort of socio-legal pundit, attempting to second-guess the jury.'[144] Given that juries generally tend to find police officer defendants more credible than the general run of defendants in criminal cases there is said to be a higher rate of acquittals against police officers than there would be against an ordinary defendant facing the same evidence. This phenomenon is fed back into the equation in assessing the adequacy of the evidence against police officers, with the result, it has been said, that a higher standard

---

140 GCO Annex G para 1.
141 PACE s 90(4).
142 Ibid s90(6) and (7).
143 PMCA 1994 ss37(b), 93 and Sch 9 Pt I which repeal PACE s92(1) and (2); see p71.
144 Mansfield and Peay *The DPP – Principles and practices,* Tavistock, 1987 pp10–15; see also Edwards, *The Attorney-General, Politics and the Public Interest,* Sweet & Maxwell 1984 pp 413–417; and the Guide to Crown Prosecutors issued under Prosecution of Offenders Act 1985.

TABLE 11
Police officers convicted of criminal offences

Type of principal offence	1989	1990	1991	1992	1993	1994
Criminal (non-traffic)	64	73	50	57	49	35
Traffic	403	454	371	289	240	191
Total	467	527	421	346	289	226

Source: Home Office Statistical Bulletins 13/94 and 13/95

of evidence is required against police defendants. A former DPP commented:[145]

> It is sometimes suggested that . . . we tend to favour police officers. That is certainly not our intention. We try to apply the same test . . . Our conviction rate of prosecutions against police officers is certainly lower than in other cases. But this may just be a reflection of the traditional reluctance of juries to accept the word of a citizen, with, perhaps, a criminal record, against that of a police officer – a reluctance which I find wholly understandable but which sometimes makes it rather difficult to assess the chances of success in prosecutions of police officers.

Professor Glanville Williams has argued[146] that the consequences of the rule is that, in some cases, prosecutors will not bring a charge even though they believe an officer to be guilty:

> The effect of the rule of practice is that corrupt and violent policemen are not brought to book when ordinary people would be.

A former Attorney-General has criticised the rule, saying that:

> Where there is a clear prima facie case against a police or prison officer, the greater likelihood of acquittal which he enjoys as such should be secondary to the public interest in ensuring and demonstrating that those who enjoy a position of authority do not abuse it.[147]

The DPP will inform the complainant whether or not the police officer complained about will be prosecuted. The DPP does not give reasons for the decision but, if the decision is against prosecution, the complainant will usually be told either that the evidence is insufficient

145 Sir Thomas Hetherington, reported in *Guardian* 2 June 1980.
146 Glanville Williams 'Letting off the guilty and prosecuting the innocent' [1985] Crim LR 115.
147 Sam Silkin, *Guardian* 21 April 1980, quoted in Glanville Williams, op cit.

to justify criminal proceedings (that is, that the case fails the '51 per cent rule') or that criminal proceedings are not necessary in the public interest.[148] Sometimes, the DPP will indicate to the chief officer (but not usually to the complainant) that, although criminal proceedings are not appropriate, the chief officer could still consider disciplinary action.

Delay and abuse of process

The general rule for offences tried on indictment is that time never runs against the Crown. The same rule is applied to offences triable either way which are heard in the magistrates' court.[149] For other cases tried in the magistrates' court the general rule is that the information must be laid within six months of the commission of the offence.[150] However many statutes contain individual limitation periods specific to particular offences.

In a very limited range of circumstances a prosecution may be stayed because a delay in starting the case or bringing it to trial amounts to an abuse of process.[151] In the second edition of this work the authors drew attention to the apparent expansion of this doctrine in police misconduct cases. A spate of cases arising out of the News International demonstrations at Wapping in January 1987 appeared to find that a relatively short delay which could give rise to prejudice or unfairness, rather than the stricter test of unjustifiable delay, could by itself amount to an abuse of the process of the court.[152]

This trend was decisively reversed in *Attorney-General's Reference (No 1 of 1990)*[153] which held that a stay on the grounds of delay, even unjustifiable delay, or for any other reason, should only be imposed in exceptional circumstances. Still more rarely should stays be allowed in the absence of fault by the victim or the prosecution. Even a very

---

148 GCO para 5.11.
149 Magistrates' Courts Act 1980 s 127(2) and (3).
150 Ibid s127(1).
151 See generally Andrew L-T Choo, *Abuse of Process and Judicial Stays of Criminal Proceedings*, 1993 Clarendon Press.
152 See, for example *R v Bow Street Stipendiary Magistrate ex p Cherry* (1990) 91 Cr App R 283; Annual report of the Crown Prosecution Service 1990–91, 9 July 1991, HC 487, HMSO, p28; *Police Complaints Authority – The First Ten Years*, 1995 HMSO p21.
153 [1992] QB 630, 95 Cr App R 296, [1992] 3 All ER 169 CA, approved by the Privy Council in *Tan v Cameron* [1992] 3 WLR 249.

lengthy delay will not necessarily amount to an abuse of process.[154]

It is therefore submitted that a failure to serve an accused officer with a 'regulation 7 notice' (see p89), which is, after all, only a procedural protection in disciplinary cases, will not be sufficient reason to stay a criminal prosecution, and that earlier authority to the contrary[155] can no longer be regarded as good law.

Private prosecutions

The right of a private citizen to bring a prosecution is a useful and effective safeguard against 'improper inaction' by the prosecuting authority.[156] When the potential defendants are police officers and the authority responsible for investigating offences is a police force, the potential for improper inaction becomes obvious and the right of the citizen to bring a prosecution takes on the character of a constitutional guarantee. In the notorious 'rhino whip case', for example, a Sheffield solicitor prosecuted two officers in order to expose the fact that they were systematically beating confessions out of suspects and that senior officers were turning a blind eye to wholesale abuses.[157]

Nevertheless, there are formidable obstacles to bringing a private prosecution, including the risk of the prosecution being taken over by the DPP and discontinued, the need for official consent in some cases, the expense of bringing the case (legal aid is not available) and the difficulty in obtaining evidence sufficient to meet the criminal standard of proof. For most victims of police misconduct the possibility of bringing a private prosecution will not be a viable alternative to bringing a civil action for damages. Indeed it should not be viewed as an alternative at all, as the purposes of the two procedures are so different: the former being to punish the wrongdoer, the other to compensate the

154 *R v Bow Street Metropolitan Stipendiary Magistrate ex p DPP* (1992) 95 Cr App R 9, DC (Guildford Four police case): probable 18-year delay by time case would come to trial would not amount to abuse where issue to be decided depended upon documents still in existence; *R v Central Criminal Court ex p Randle and Pottle* (1991) 92 Cr App R 323 DC (George Blake escape case): 20-year delay, on particular and exceptional facts, not an abuse.

155 *Ex p Cherry* (n152 above).

156 Report of the Royal Commission on Criminal Procedure, Cmnd 8092, 1981, p 161, para 7.50, quoted with approval in *R v Bow Street Stipendiary Magistrate and Another ex p South Coast Shipping Co Ltd and Others*, [1993] QB 645, [1993] 2 WLR 621, (1993) 96 Cr App R 405; [1993] 1 All ER 219.

157 Sheffield Police Appeal Enquiry, HMSO, 1963, Cmnd 2176.

victim. A private prosecution will usually only be an option if some wider purpose is sought, such as to demonstrate the failure of the police in investigating the incident or the failure of the DPP to bring a prosecution, to prevent the police committing contempt of court,[157A] to challenge a prosecutor's interpretation of the law[158] or to expose a pattern of malpractice or a desire to see justice done and to vindicate the rule of law.

If it is proposed to run both a prosecution and a civil action based on the same incident, a number of tactical issues will arise. Limitation periods for both the civil action and the prosecution will need to be observed. Evidence of a criminal conviction can be pleaded in a civil case, but a successful civil judgement is obviously not probative of criminal guilt. Presumably exemplary damages could be reduced to nil if a criminal court has previously imposed a punishment (see p196); on the other hand, a sentence (and any compensation order) may presumably be reduced from that that would otherwise have been imposed if exemplary damages have been awarded against the defendant (although not if only awarded against the chief officer).

If the DPP is initially reluctant to prosecute, a succesful civil action can serve to demonstrate that witnesses will come up to proof, and may thus prompt the DPP to change her mind.

The right to prosecute

As a general principle any citizen can bring a prosecution. This right is preserved by Prosecution of Offences Act 1985 s6, which, in the context of police misconduct, for all practical purposes does not restrict the right to bring a private prosecution.

The DPP has a duty to institute and have the conduct of criminal proceedings in any case where it appears to him/her that

a) the importance or difficulty of the case makes it appropriate that proceeding should be instituted by him/her or
b) it is otherwise appropriate for proceedings to be instituted by him/her.[159]

However, this does not oblige the DPP to take over the conduct of such cases, nor is there any implied limitation in the Act so as to preclude more than one prosecution arising out of the same incident, as where, for example, the DPP has already brought a minor charge and the

---

157A   Eg, where the police seek to prevent a criminal defendant identifying alibi witnesses: *Connolly v Dale* (1995) *Times* 13 July, DC.
158   *R v Lemon* [1979] AC 617.
159   Prosecution of Offences Act 1985 s3(2)(b).

private prosecutor seeks to bring a more serious charge.[160] It may, however, be an abuse of process to allow a private prosecutor to continue with a summons where the CPS has dropped a case in exchange for a defendant agreeing to be bound over to keep the peace.[161]

The choice of the charge that is to be preferred is generally in the discretion of the private prosecutor, not the magistrate.[162] In one case of a private prosecution of a police officer for malicious wounding, contrary to Offences Against the Person Act 1861 s20, the prosecutor wanted the case to be heard in the Crown Court and told the defendant that unless he agreed to elect for trial on indictment, leave would be sought to issue a summons charging an offence under s18, which could only be heard in the Crown Court. The defendant's application for judicial review of the justices' decision to grant the second summons (in respect of the s18 charge) was dismissed. The fact that the prosecutor wished to add or substitute new charges, to ensure that the case was tried either summarily or on indictment, was not a ground for refusing the issue of a summons, provided that the issue of the summons was a proper course on the facts.[163]

The issuing of a summons is, of course, a judicial act, not an automatic formality. Where the question has already been considered by the CPS, it has been held that the magistrate is entitled to have regard to the likelihood of the DPP taking over the prosecution in deciding whether to issue a summons on the information of a private prosecutor.[164] However, it is submitted that this gives insufficient weight to the principle that private prosecutions are 'a useful constitutional safeguard against inertia or partiality on the part of authority',[165] and poses the risk that magistrates may usurp the functions of the DPP.

A summons should not be refused on the grounds that a private prosecutor has a civil remedy.[166] Nor should a private prosecution be

---

160 *R v Bow Street Stipendiary Magistrate and Another ex p South Coast Shipping Co Ltd and Others* [1993] QB 645; for exceptions in drink driving cases, see *R v Moxon-Tritsch* [1988] Crim LR 46 and *R v Forest of Dean JJ ex p Farley* [1990] RTR 228.

161 *R v Grays JJ ex p Low* [1990] QB 54; see also *R v Croydon JJ ex p Dean* (1994) 98 Cr App R 76, DC.

162 *R v Nuneaton JJ ex p Parker* (1954) 118 JP 524.

163 *R v Redbridge JJ ex p Whitehouse* (1992) 94 Cr App R 332, (1992) 136 SJ (LB) 31, (1992) COD 234, [1992] LS Gaz 4 March p36.

164 *R v Tower Bridge Metropolitan Stipendiary Magistrate ex p Chaudhury* [1994] QB 340, (1994) 99 Cr App R 170, DC.

165 *Gouriet v Union of Post Office Workers* [1978] AC 435, [1977] 3 WLR 300 at 310, per Lord Wilberforce.

166 *R v Bennett and Bond ex p Bennett* (1908) 72 JP 362, 52 SJ 583, 24 TLR 681.

adjourned pending the outcome of civil proceedings concerning the same facts.[167]

Procedure
Prosecutions by the police can be commenced by laying an information before a magistrate or magistrates' clerk, either orally or in writing, or by the defendant being charged at a police station. There is some uncertainty as to whether a private prosecution can be commenced by way of a charge[168] but for all practical purposes a private prosecutor should be advised to proceed only by way of a written information. An arrest warrant may also be sought; however, careful consideration should be given as to whether this is necessary or tactically appropriate in the circumstances of the case.

Official consent
Some offences require official consent, either from the Attorney-General or from the DPP, before a prosecution can be brought.[169] For example the consent of the Attorney-General is necessary in order to bring a prosecution for bribery or corruption[170] and the consent of the DPP is a prerequisite of a prosecution for the offence of making an unauthorised disclosure of a spent conviction.[171] It is the duty of the person issuing the summons to ensure that consent has been obtained. There is a presumption that this has been done. Any objection that a necessary consent has not been obtained should be made before the prosecution case is closed, whereupon the burden passes to the prosecution to prove that the proceedings are properly authorised.[172]

Official consent is unlikely to be forthcoming if, on the same evidence, the DPP has already refused to prosecute.

---

167 R v Evans (1890) 62 LT 570, 54 JP 471, 6 LRT 248, 17 Cox CC 81, DC.
168 R v Ealing JJ ex p Dixon [1990] 2 QB 91 (disapproved in R v Stafford JJ ex p Customs and Excise Commissioners [1990] 3 WLR 656); cf R v Croydon JJ ex p Holmberg [1992] Crim LR 892; see Blackstone's Criminal Practice 1993 edn pp929–30 for a fuller discussion.
169 See Prosecution of Offences Act 1985 s25; the main offences are listed in Archbold 1995 edn, Vol 3, Table of penalties for the principal indictable offences; a fuller but less up-to-date list is given in Prosecutions by private individuals and non-police agencies, Royal Commission on Criminal Procedure Research Study No 10, HMSO, 1980, Appendix F.
170 Prevention of Corruption Act 1906 s2(1).
171 Rehabilitation of Offenders Act 1974 s9(3); see also X v Commissioner of Police of the Metropolis [1985] 1 All ER 890.
172 Price v Humphries (1958) 122 JP 423; R v Waller [1910] 1 KB 364.

Discontinuance of proceedings

The DPP has wide powers to take over the conduct of a private prosecution, even where s/he is under no duty[173] to do so, at any stage.[174] Having taken over the conduct of a prosecution, the DPP can discontinue it if the evidence is insufficient, or if the proceedings would be contrary to the public interest, or to avoid duplication or for any other good reason. His/her sole purpose in taking over the prosecution can be to bring it to an end and this is justifiable provided it is not manifestly unreasonable.[175] It is submitted that as a matter of policy the DPP should not discontinue a case on the ground of insufficient evidence unless the prosecution is motivated by malice or is otherwise baseless and a clear abuse of process. If the evidence is insufficient, that issue can be tested at the plea and directions stage; if the magistrates or the court find that there is a case to answer the DPP should not usurp the functions of the court.

If it is too late to discontinue the proceedings, the DPP may offer no evidence, or in the Crown Court, the Attorney-General may enter a nolle prosequi to bring the case to an end at any stage. The decision of the Attorney-General cannot be reviewed by the courts.[176]

Expense

The cost of bringing the prosecution will usually fall on the prosecutor. If the offences charged are tried in the Crown Court, both solicitor and counsel will in practice usually have to be engaged. While the Crown Court has a discretion to allow a private prosecutor to appear in person, this is only likely to be exercised occasionally.[177] If the offences are to be tried in the magistrates' court, a prosecutor may appear in person, although this would rarely be advisable against police defendants. If

---

173 Eg, under Prosecution of Offences Act 1985 s3(2).
174 Prosecution of Offences Act 1985 s6(2); for the DPP's policy as to when s/he will intervene, see HC Written Answers col 295 28 October 1985.
175 Ibid s23 and Magistrates' Courts (Discontinuance of Proceedings) Rules 1986 SI No 367; *Raymond v Attorney-General* [1982] QB 839; [1982] 2 All ER 487. For the Attorney-General's power to restrict vexatious prosecutions, see Supreme Court Act 1981 s42, as amended by Prosecution of Offences Act 1985 s24.
176 *R v Comptroller-General of Patents, Designs and Trade Marks* [1899] 1 QB 909; *Gouriet v Union of Post Office Workers* [1978] AC 435 at 487; *Turner v DPP* (1978) 68 Cr App R 70 at 76; *R v Solicitor-General ex p Taylor* (1995) *Times* 14 August.
177 Courts and Legal Services Act 1990 s27(2)(c); *R v Southwark Crown Court ex p Tawfick, CPS intervening,* (1994) *Times* 1 December.

the offences are triable either way, the prosecutor will not know in advance whether the defendants will opt for Crown Court trial, and this is will make for uncertainty about the likely expense of the proceedings. In addition, there will often be unforeseen costs in investigating the incident and collecting evidence.

Legal aid is not available to commence a private prosecution. However, it may be allowed in defending an appeal against conviction or sentence from a magistrates' court to the Crown Court where the prosecution has been brought by an individual 'not acting in an official capacity to resist the appeal.'[178]

If the defendant is acquitted, the prosecutor can expect to be ordered to pay the defendant's costs as well as his/her own. A successful private prosecutor can expect to be awarded costs out of central funds unless there is good reason for not doing so, for instance, where proceedings have been instituted or continued without good cause;[179] but the award may not cover the full cost of the prosecution.

Obtaining evidence

The police may have carried out extensive investigations into the incident and they or the CPS may hold copious statements, reports, photographs and other evidence. As a matter of policy the police have been advised to decline any request for such evidence,[180] and before the first court hearing the court will not order the CPS to release them.[181] It is submitted that, as a matter of policy, and so as not to impede the administration of justice, it would be preferable if the decision whether or not to release evidence lay with the CPS rather than the police.

After committal a private prosecutor could apply for a witness summons under the Criminal Procedure (Attendance of Witnesses) Act 1965 to compel the police to produce all the statements and exhibits they held in their possession.[182]

Committal proceedings were abolished with effect from 4 September

---

178 Legal Aid Act 1988 s21(1); if a private prosecutor fails to defend an appeal, the DPP may take over the conduct of the case so as not to allow a conviction to be quashed simply for want of prosecution: HC Written Answers col 295 28 October 1985.

179 *Practice Direction (Costs in Criminal Proceedings)* (1991) 93 Cr App R 89 para 3.1.

180 GCO para 7.15; such advice may be itself contrary to public policy.

181 *R v DPP ex p Hallas* (1987) 87 Cr App R 340, [1988] Crim LR 316.

182 *R v Pawsey (Gregory)* [1989] Crim LR 152.

1995,[183] and replaced by plea and directions hearings, but presumably the rule will continue to apply, so as to allow a private prosecutor to apply for a witness summons after the transfer of the trial proceedings.

The police are under a duty to supply details of a defendant's previous convictions to the defence upon request; they must also supply a proof of evidence of the defendant's antecedents (age, education, employment, date of arrest, whether on bail, summary of any previous convictions and previous findings of guilt, etc) to the prosecution counsel 'at the outset of the case'.[184] The duty applies equally to police and to private prosecutions.

Professional ethics
Lawyers who usually undertake civil actions against the police or criminal defence work but who are unused to conducting private prosecutions will need to make some mental readjustments to their new role as a prosecutor. Their duty is no longer to win their client's case, but rather to present the case fairly and allow the court to decide. Indeed their client will not be a party to the case: prosecutions are brought on behalf of the Crown. The lawyer's first duty as a prosecutor is no longer to the client, but to the wider public interest; having commenced a prosecution, the lawyer must act as an officer of the court and must be ready to distance him/herself from instructions from the client that are at variance with this public duty. Thus, for example, the duty of disclosure must be scrupulously observed.[185] It is also prudent to review the DPP's guidance (Code for Crown Prosecutors) and professional guidance from the Law Society and the Bar Council.

183 Criminal Justice and Public Order Act 1994 s44.
184 *Practice Direction* (1966) 50 Cr App R 271.
185 The government has proposed restricting the prosecution duty of disclosure and increasing the defence duty of disclosure: see Home Office *Disclosure: A consultation paper*, HMSO, 1995, Cm 2864.

CHAPTER 5

Suing the police: the law

A civil action against the police for damages can be brought only where the police have committed a civil wrong. All the causes of action described in this chapter are torts, and the grounds are much narrower than those constituting matters about which complaints can be made. The most important torts giving cause to sue the police are:

- assault;
- battery;
- false imprisonment;
- malicious prosecution;
- malicious process;
- negligence;
- causing death;
- trespass to land;
- trespass to goods;
- misfeasance in public office.

This chapter explains each cause of action in turn and describes some of the defences the police can raise to defeat a claim. Some of the less important, or more uncertain, causes of action such as intimidation, harassment, unlawful strip search, and causing nervous shock are then briefly discussed at the end of the chapter.

Assault and battery

Assault and battery are two of the torts which constitute trespass to the person. False imprisonment is the third. Clerk and Lindsell defines the principles on which the torts are based and explain the differences between them as follows:

> Interference, however slight, with a person's elementary civil right to security of the person, and self-determination in relation to his own

body, constitutes trespass to the person. . . . A battery is committed when there is an actual infliction of an unlawful physical contact with the plaintiff, and assault where the plaintiff is caused to apprehend the immediate infliction of such a contact.[1]

Battery

The fundamental principle of the tort of battery is that everybody's person is inviolate and even the slightest touching of another person may amount to a battery. The effect is 'that everyone is protected not only against physical injury but against any form of physical molestation'.[2] It is not necessary that the plaintiff suffers pain or physical injury as a result. Thus cutting hair,[3] taking fingerprints[4] and taking hold of the plaintiff's arm by a police officer in order to administer a caution[5] can all amount to battery, just as much as rough handling during an arrest or a deliberate attack.

Unless the police are exercising a power of arrest or another power (see below), they have no greater rights than members of the public and therefore any physical contact by a police officer with another person may be unlawful as a battery. They may, of course, raise the same defences to the battery that members of the public can raise. In Halford v Brookes it was held that where the battery alleged amounts to a charge of murder the standard of proof is the criminal standard of being sure beyond reasonable doubt.[6] Although it was not expressly stated in the case, Clerk and Lindsell argues that in cases that fall short of an allegation of murder, the burden of proof is on a sliding scale depending on the seriousness of the battery alleged.[7] However, there is no authority for this view and it creates an obvious difficulty as to the point at which the sliding scale would start.

Intent

The physical contact must be intentional for it to amount to a battery. Thus the plaintiff must show that the police intentionally used some physical force against him/her. There does not need to be any intention to cause the plaintiff injury or damage through the physical contact.

1 Clerk and Lindsell on Torts, 16th edition, Sweet & Maxwell 1989 p959.
2 See Collins v Wilcock [1984] 1 WLR 1172 at 1177 per Robert Goff LJ.
3 Forde v Skinner (1830) 4 C&P 239.
4 Dumbell v Roberts [1944] 1 All ER 326.
5 Collins v Wilcock [1984] 1 WLR 1172.
6 [1992] PIQR P175.
7 Clerk and Lindsell on Torts, Third cumulative supplement to 16th edition (1993) p124 para. 17–03.

Although for many years it had been argued that there must be an element of 'hostility' in the intentional contact for there to be a battery,[8] this approach has now been disapproved in *F v West Berkshire Health Authority*,[9] and this does not seem to be a necessary element of the tort. If the act was not intentional, there cannot be battery, but there may still be a claim in negligence.[10]

If a police officer intends to commit a battery against one person but mistakenly strikes a second, then a battery has been committed against the second person. In one case a soldier shot a rioter while in fact aiming for another. It was no defence to battery that he shot the 'wrong' person in those circumstances.[11]

Defences to battery

Consent There is a general principle of law that, if a person consents to something that would otherwise be an infringement of his/her rights, s/he cannot later complain about it. Thus, if the police search someone in circumstances that are otherwise illegal, but with that person's permission, then s/he cannot subsequently bring an action for battery.

In relation to the tort of battery there is an initial presumption that the plaintiff consents to such contact as is 'generally acceptable in everyday life'.[12] This was illustrated in the case of *Collins v Wilcock* thus:

> nobody can complain of the jostling which is inevitable from his presence in, for example a supermarket, an underground station or a busy street . . . Among such forms of conduct, long held to be acceptable, is touching a person for the purpose of engaging his attention, though of course using no greater degree of physical contact than is reasonably necessary in the circumstances for that purpose.[13]

In that case it was held that a plaintiff who had been grabbed by the arm

8 *Cole v Turner* (1704) Holt KB 108; *Wilson v Pringle* [1986] 2 All ER 440.
9 [1990] 2 AC 1 per Lord Goff at p74.
10 There is a tort of negligent trespass to the person which was thought to be effectively obsolete: *Letang v Cooper* [1965] 1 QB 232. However, Clayton and Tomlinson *Civil Actions against the Police*, 2nd edn 1992 pp135–136 argue that the tort is still of importance because of a lower burden of proof in negligent trespass to the person. Clerk and Lindsell on Torts disagree with this analysis (at p960) and say the burden of proof is the same for both torts.
11 *Livingstone v Ministry of Defence* [1984] 15 NIJB CA; and see Clerk and Lindsell p960.
12 *Collins v Wilcock* [1984] 1 WLR 1172 at 1177.
13 Ibid.

by a police officer could not be said to have consented to such contact, but in the case of *Donnelly v Jackman*[14] it was held that an officer who had tapped a person twice on the shoulder to question him about an offence had not exceeded the bounds of acceptable conduct and had not therefore committed a battery. The court in *Collins* felt that *Donnelly* was 'an extreme case',[15] as the touching was very slight and the plaintiff's reaction very violent. Thus, it is submitted that in the vast majority of cases where a police officer, not exercising arrest or other powers, physically contacts a member of the public, a battery will have been committed.

A number of police powers under PACE can be exercised only with the consent and/or the authority of an officer of at least the rank of superintendent. Consent to the taking of an intimate sample, eg, a swab from the anus or vagina, is required[16] and, if refused, force cannot be used to take the sample. Although consent in writing is required for the taking of a non-intimate sample,[17] such as a nail-clipping or a sample of saliva from the mouth,[18] reasonable force to take the sample may be used in certain circumstances where authorised by a superintendent (or more senior officer).[19] However, the person must be in police detention or in custody under a court order.[20] Thus the police could not raise as a defence their power to take non-intimate samples if they had taken the sample without consent in a person's home. In such circumstances that person would succeed in a claim for battery.

Similarly, consent to fingerprinting must be in writing[21] if it is given at a police station but, again, there are circumstances where fingerprints can be taken without consent.[22] 'Consent' in this context means the consent of the person if aged 17 or over, the consent of the person and the parent or guardian if between the ages of 14 to 16 and the consent of the parent or guardian alone if under the age of 14.[23] If consent is not given by the correct person, it is presumably invalid and a claim for battery should succeed, unless of course the procedures for taking samples or fingerprints without consent have been properly followed.

14 [1970] 1 WLR 562.
15 [1984] 1 WLR 1172 at 1179.
16 PACE s62(1).
17 PACE s63(2).
18 See Criminal Justice and Public Order Act 1994 s58(3).
19 PACE ss63(3) and (4).
20 PACE ss63(3) and 118(2).
21 Ibid. s61(2).
22 PACE s61(3) and (6).
23 Ibid s65.

Special problems may arise if a person signs a form to indicate his/her consent to something, but subsequently denies that the consent was freely given. There is a general principle that:

> a man cannot be said to be truly 'willing' unless he is in a position to choose freely, and freedom of choice predicates, not only full knowledge of the circumstances on which the exercise of choice is conditional, so that he may be able to choose wisely, but the absence of any feeling of constraint so that nothing shall interfere with the freedom of his will.[24]

Thus, a situation might arise where a person is arrested and told at the police station to sign a form to consent to the taking of intimate body samples and that if s/he refuses s/he will be kept there until s/he does sign. If s/he eventually signs and the samples are taken, then the 'consent' would be invalid because obtained under duress and s/he could sue for battery. Likewise, if the police obtain consent by fraudulently representing that they had powers to take samples in situations where they did not, an action for battery will also lie.[25]

Police acting within their powers The police have wide powers to make arrests, to stop and search people, to conduct searches, including intimate searches, to take fingerprints and intimate and non-intimate samples, including samples of body tissues and fluids. Where the police have any power under PACE and the power can be exercised without consent, the police may use reasonable force, if necessary, to exercise the power. Two questions will therefore arise:

– Did the police act within their powers? and
– Where the use of force is permitted in exercising those powers, was the force used reasonable and necessary?

The police have a wide range of powers and the circumstances in which they can be exercised are complicated. See, for instance, the powers of the police under PACE to search someone[26] and take samples and fingerprints.[27] If the police fail to comply with the provisions of the Act when purporting to exercise these powers, then they may lay themselves open to an action for battery and assault. Considerations of space prohibit all the powers being detailed here,[28] but the power to

24 *Bowater v Rowley Regis Corporation* [1944] KB 476 at 479.
25 See discussion, for instance, in Clerk and Lindsell, above, at p964–5.
26 PACE ss1, 32, 54 and 55, and see Criminal Justice and Public Order Act 1994 s60.
27 Ibid ss61–63.
28 Police powers are considered in detail in Levenson and Fairweather, *Police powers: A practitioner's guide* (LAG).

take body samples and make intimate searches is given below as an example. In addition to statutory powers, the police also have common law powers of arrest, most notably where a breach of the peace is, or reasonably appears to be about to be, committed.[29]

Intimate searches of body orifices[30] by the police can only be carried out by someone of the same sex[31] unless the person carrying out the search is a doctor or a nurse. Thus, if a policeman carried out an intimate search of a woman, the search would be unlawful and the woman would have an action for assault and battery. Code C also provides that nobody of the opposite sex, except a doctor or a nurse, should be present during intimate searches. The code does not have the force of law and a breach of the code does not automatically give rise to civil liability,[32] but, it is submitted, a woman will have a claim for assault and battery if a policeman were present while she was intimately searched by a policewoman.

Likewise, a strip search is permitted under the codes of practice, if the custody officer thinks it necessary in order to remove an article which the detainee would not be allowed to keep and reasons are given (if practicable) and recorded.[33] If such a search is conducted in breach of the codes, there may be an action for assault and battery if physical contact occurs, or the police may be liable for unlawfully inducing a person to remove his/her clothes if there is no contact (see p180).

As already mentioned, intimate searches may only take place in certain circumstances and must be authorised by an officer of at least the rank of superintendent.[34] The rules for taking an intimate sample are even stricter and such a sample can only be taken with the person's 'appropriate consent' in writing.[35]

Where the use of force is permitted, is it reasonable and necessary?
The police can only use force if it is necessary. Therefore, a defence of 'reasonable and necessary force' may be defeated if the plaintiff can show that s/he did consent, or that s/he would have consented to the

---

29 See, for instance, *Albert v Lavin* [1982] AC 546.
30 A search of the mouth is excluded from the definition of intimate search – Criminal Justice and Public Order Act 1994 s58(2)(c).
31 PACE s55(7).
32 PACE s67(10).
33 Code C Annex A and see *Brazil v Chief Constable of Surrey* [1983] 3 All ER 537, DC and *Mann-Cairns v Ministry of Defence* September 1988 *Legal Action* 21.
34 PACE s55(1) and (2).
35 Ibid s62.

police using their powers (for example, their power to search) if s/he had been given the opportunity to do so.[36] A claim may, therefore, still succeed even where the police used only reasonable force but that force was unnecessary in the circumstances.

If some force is justified, then whether the police used more than reasonable force must be judged on an objective test on the facts. In *Sturley v Commissioner of Police for the Metropolis*[37] a middle-aged woman arrested after a minor traffic offence was restrained by means of a hammer-lock and bar, that is holding her arm behind her back and twisting the wrist. Her wrist was twisted so forcefully that the bone was fractured and it was held that, as two officers were present, the degree of force used to restrain someone of the plaintiff's age was unreasonable and she succeeded in a claim for assault and battery. It has also been held to be unreasonable (on the facts of the case), to restrain a convicted prisoner for 24 hours in a body belt. Damages were awarded for assault.[38] However, even extreme force will be justified in some circumstances. In *Carey v Metropolitan Police Commissioner*[39] it was held that the shooting by police of two men believed to be carrying out an armed robbery, and believed to be attacking the officers, was justified. Clerk and Lindsell state that:

> The degree of force reasonable must be judged in the light of the circumstances apparent to the arrestor and he will not be found to have used unreasonable force because of a defect in the planning of the arrest or crime prevention which with hindsight can be seen to render the amount of force unnecessary.[40]

In attempting to establish whether the degree of force used was reasonable, the plaintiff's solicitor should seek access to police manuals (where they are discoverable) on practice and procedure. These are in existence, for example, in the areas of the use of firearms, roadcraft, self-defence and restraint, the training of police dogs and public order. In addition the PCA has commented on a number of methods involving the use of force, including restraint techniques,[41] neckholds and armlocks,[42] the use of 'Quik Kufs',[43] and the use of police dogs.[44]

36 See *Swales v Cox* [1981] 1 All ER 1115.
37 (1984) *Times* 27 June.
38 *Rodrigues v Home Office* February 1989 *Legal Action* 14.
39 (1989) unreported, but cited in Clayton and Tomlinson, *Civil actions against the police* 2nd edn 1992, Sweet & Maxwell, p152.
40 Clerk and Lindsell on Torts 16th edition p983.
41 PCA Annual Report 1992 p14 para 1.17.
42 PCA Annual Report 1993 p34.
43 PCA Annual Report 1993 p33.
44 Ibid p32.

The plaintiff's behaviour

It is probable that it is no defence for the police to say that the plaintiff provoked the battery, although this could reduce or eliminate any claim for aggravated or exemplary damages[45] (see p194–200). However, it is uncertain whether the plaintiff's wrongdoing (criminal or otherwise) may afford a defence to a claim for battery (and other trespass to the person torts). Thus, Lord Denning has said that:

> a man who takes part in a criminal affray may well be said to have been guilty of such a wicked act as to deprive himself of a cause of action or, alternatively, to have taken upon himself the risk.[46]

It is likely that the police will make use of opportunities to forward this defence especially where a convicted plaintiff is suing for an assault that took place during his/her arrest, but it is still far from certain how far the doctrine will extend. In *Kirkham v Chief Constable of Greater Manchester Police*[47] (where the plaintiff took his own life), the Court of Appeal rejected the argument that this 'wrongdoing' should prevent a claim. The court said that the question was whether, in all the circumstances, it would be an affront to the public conscience or shock the ordinary citizen to grant the plaintiff the relief which he seeks. It would be entirely wrong, it is submitted, for a plaintiff who has been arrested while involved in peaceful protest which breaks the law in a relatively minor way (for instance, by obstructing the highway) to be barred from bringing a successful action for battery if s/he is arrested by the police and they use unnecessary force. The situation would be more doubtful if the plaintiff had been involved in violent acts. However, in *Simpson v Chief Constable of South Yorkshire Police*[48] the Court of Appeal refused to strike out an action for assault against the police on the basis that the plaintiff had been convicted of crimes of violence, even where those crimes arose out of the same incident and a police officer was the victim. The fact of such convictions did not necessarily carry the conclusion that the plaintiff was not assaulted by the police.

Self-defence

The police have a good defence if they can show that they were acting only in self-defence against an attack or attempted attack made on

45 *Barnes v Nayer* (1986) *Times* 19 December.
46 *Murphy v Culhane* [1976] 3 All ER 533, CA.
47 [1990] 3 All ER 246 at 251, CA.
48 (1991) *Independent* 14 March, CA.

them. However, the amount of force an officer can use in self-defence must be reasonable. In the leading case this principle was described thus: 'hitting a man a little blow with a little stick on the shoulder, is not a reason for him to draw a sword and cut and hew the other'.[49]

It may be that the stress or 'unexpected anguish' of the moment will be taken into account in deciding whether the amount of force used is reasonable,[50] as may be the fact that an officer acted instinctively under pressure. The Association of Chief Police Officers' *Public Order Manual* correctly states that: 'The law . . . recognises that it is not always easy to apply careful consideration of legal niceties in stressful situations'.[51]

Anyone is entitled to use such force as is reasonable in the circumstances to prevent a crime.[52]

Prior prosecution
Battery constitutes a crime as well as a civil wrong. Usually it is no defence to a civil action for the defendant to show that s/he has already been prosecuted in the criminal courts for the same incident. However, if an officer is prosecuted for common assault, or aggravated assault on a boy under the age of 14 or a female of any age,[53] the criminal case may prevent any subsequent civil claim. The police must show that the prosecution was heard before a magistrates' court (and not a Crown Court) and that there was a hearing on the merits.[54] They must show that the officer was convicted and paid any fine or served any term of imprisonment imposed, or that the magistrates made out a certificate that the case was dismissed because the assault was not proved, was justified or was so trifling as not to merit any punishment.[55] In such cases, the officer is released from all further or other proceedings, whether civil or criminal, based on the same facts.

49 *Cockroft v Smith* (1705) 2 Salk 642.
50 *Palmer v R* (1971) 55 Cr App R 223, cited in Jason-Lloyd, 'Plastic bullets on the mainland' *NLJ* 26 October 1990 p1492.
51 Cited in Jason-Lloyd supra; see also Northam, *Shooting in the dark: riot police in Britain* 1988 Faber & Faber.
52 Criminal Law Act 1967 s3; *Farrell v Secretary of State for Defence* [1980] 1 All ER 166, HL.
53 Offences Against the Person Act 1861 ss42–43. It is submitted that the age/gender disparity is contrary to the European Convention on Human Rights.
54 *Reed v Nutt* (1890) 24 QBD 669; *Ellis v Burton* [1975] 1 All ER 395, DC.
55 Offences Against the Person Act 1861 s45.

Although the individual officer may be released from a subsequent civil action, a civil action against the chief officer of police[56] may still be possible (see p203).

Assault

To show that there has been an assault the plaintiff must prove that there has been an act by the defendant that causes the plaintiff reasonably to apprehend an immediate intention by the defendant to commit a battery.[57] Thus, there can be an assault without there in fact being a battery. However, a mere threat of violence is not enough to constitute an assault unless there is also the means to carry out the threat.[58] A person who with fists raised runs at another and would have hit that other if s/he had not been stopped will probably have committed an assault.[59] However, large numbers of people shouting abuse at others on a bus who they cannot reach do not commit an assault if they have no means of carrying out their threat.[60] The principles that govern defences to battery by the police, as described above, also apply to the tort of assault.

Damages

Assault and battery are actionable in their own right. It is not necessary to prove that there has been damage before a claim can be brought and the successful plaintiff will always be entitled to at least nominal damages, even if s/he cannot point to any real loss. All damage flowing from the unlawful act is recoverable and it is not necessary, as it is in negligence, to establish that the injuries complained of are of a reasonably foreseeable kind.

The general principles that apply to any case of personal injury apply to cases of assault. Thus, a claim can be made for:

- pain and suffering, both in the past and in the future;
- 'loss of amenity', eg, full or partial loss of a limb or organ;
- loss of enjoyment of life, eg, an amateur footballer who has to give up the game because of the injuries;

56 *Dyer v Munday* [1894–9] 2 All ER Rep 1022.
57 See Clerk and Lindsell on Torts p970.
58 *Stephens v Myers* (1830) 4 C&P 349.
59 Ibid.
60 *Thomas v National Union of Mineworkers (South Wales Area)* [1986] Ch 20.

- financial loss due to medical expenses, loss of earnings and loss of earning capacity.

Under pain and suffering can be included damages for substantial discomfort and inconvenience,[61] and for insult and injury or injury to feelings for a battery which has also caused harm.[62] In addition, damages can be recovered for nervous shock,[63] and post-traumatic stress disorder.[64]

In a very few cases, assault and battery by the police have amounted to torture and where this is the case very large awards of exemplary damages can be expected. In *Treadaway v Chief Constable of West Midlands*[65] the judge stated this in terms when summing up for the jury. The £40,000 exemplary damages in this case were four times the level of the compensatory damages. Torture is also a specific criminal offence under Criminal Justice Act 1988 s134 and a breach of the European Convention of Human Rights (see p277).

It is possible for damages to be assessed both at the conclusion of the case and again at some future date if there is a chance that the plaintiff's condition will seriously deteriorate or that s/he will develop a serious medical condition (for example, epilepsy from head injuries). S/he can, accordingly, apply to receive provisional damages when the court first gives judgment and a further award at some later date.[66]

False imprisonment

The right to freedom of movement without fear of arbitrary arrest or detention is a fundamental civil liberty. In the civil law it is protected in part by the right to sue for false imprisonment, which can arise if the police, directly and intentionally or negligently, confine a person without lawful excuse. False imprisonment most commonly occurs when the police make an arrest which is not legally justified. This may explain why it is sometimes, inaccurately, called false or wrongful arrest: there

61 *Bailey v Bullock* [1950] 2 All ER 1167.
62 *Loudon v Ryder* [1953] 2 QB 202, CA.
63 *McLoughlin v O'Brien* [1982] 2 WLR 982, HL.
64 On this see for instance, Hoare, 'Post-traumatic stress disorder', *SJ* 28 January 1994.
65 (1994) *Independent* 23 September.
66 Supreme Court Act 1981 s32A; RSC Order 37 rr7–10 and County Courts Act 1984 s51; CCR Order 22 r6A; *Practice Note* (*personal injuries action; provisional damages*) [1985] 2 All ER 895.

is no such tort in English law and the 'wrongful arrest' is usually just the act at the start of a period of false imprisonment.

There are two elements which together constitute false imprisonment:

- the confinement; and
- the lack of a lawful excuse.

The onus is on the plaintiff to prove the confinement but on the police to prove that they had a lawful excuse. The excuse that the police are most likely to provide is that they were carrying out a lawful arrest. Accordingly, confinement is explained first and the types of defence the police can raise to show that they had a lawful excuse are considered subsequently.

Confinement

Confinement may occur in many common situations: in the course of a stop and search in the street; during questioning, whether at the police station or anywhere else; or on arrest. The place of confinement is irrelevant but the restraint must be total. A person may, for example, be held in prison,[67] in a car,[68] in his/her own home[69] or in the street[70]; provided that s/he is restrained within an area set by the police, all these amount to imprisonment. A person is imprisoned even if s/he is moved from one place to another, for instance to a police station from the place of arrest. The means used for confinement need not be physical; a threat of force can be used, and an assertion of authority by a police officer, such as saying, 'You're under arrest', is enough. There is no need to show that the person was touched by the officer,[71] nor is there any need to resist arrest. In fact, use of a person's wish to avoid embarrassment to make them submit to arrest can amount to restraint.[72] A person held at gun-point for two minutes was held to have a claim for false imprisonment.[73]

---

67 *Cobbett v Grey* (1849) 4 Exch 729.
68 *Burton v Davies* [1953] QSR 26 (Queensland).
69 *Warner v Riddiford* (1858) 4 CB(NS) 180.
70 Termes de la Ley c1520; see *Merring v Grahame-White Aviation Co* (1920) 122 LT 44.
71 *Warner v Riddiford* n69 supra; *Chinn v Morris* (1826) 2 C&P 361; *Grainger v Hill* (1838) 4 Bing NC 200; *Wood v Lane* (1834) 6 C&P 774.
72 *Conn v David Spencer* (1930) 1 DLR 805.
73 *Parry v Sharples* (1991) 17 July, CA, Lexis.

Unauthorised detention by the police

An action for false imprisonment can be brought where the police
exceed their statutory powers to detain someone. The custody officer
at a police station is under a duty to determine whether there is
sufficient evidence to justify a charge against a suspect as soon as
practicable after the suspect has arrived at the station.[74] If there is
not sufficient evidence at this point, then the further detention of the
suspect should only be authorised if there are 'reasonable grounds for
believing that his detention without charge is necessary to secure or
preserve evidence relating to an offence for which he is under arrest or
to obtain evidence by questioning him'.[75]

If this 'necessity principle' is not met, then it seems that a suspect
should be released at once and, if appropriate, be given a date to return
to the station. In practice, however, custody officers almost automatically authorise detentions without taking the principle into consideration and without recording on the custody record what were the
'reasonable grounds' that made the detention 'necessary'.[76] This failure
by custody officers can make the 'authorised' detention unlawful.[77]

The police may be liable for false imprisonment if other provisions
of PACE are not complied with during detention. For instance, PACE
requires that the detention should be reviewed at periodic intervals, and
consideration given whether continued detention is necessary using a
similar test to that applied when the original detention is authorised.[78]
If the review is not properly carried out, then the detention from the
time of the review may become unlawful.[79]

In addition, if the police fail to follow the provisions enabling them
to detain someone in excess of the statutory time limits (generally 24
hours in the first instance),[80] then the detention becomes unlawful.

74 PACE s37(1) and (10).
75 Ibid s37(2) and (3).
76 McKenzie et al, 'Helping the police with their enquiries: the necessity
principle and voluntary attendance at the police station' [1990] Crim LR
22, and Mackenzie 'Detention in a police station and false imprisonment'
(1992) 142 NLJ 534.
77 Clayton and Tomlinson in 'Civil actions against the police: recent developments in the law' October 1993 Legal Action 15, cite an unreported county
court case, Cannon v Chief Constable of Lincolnshire, 1 March 1993, as an
example.
78 PACE s40.
79 See PACE s40(3)(a) and Hamp v Chief Constable of Cambridgeshire (1991)
23 May, unreported, cited in Mackenzie 'Civil liability for PACE breaches'
NLJ 7 June 1991, p788.
80 PACE ss34 and 41–3.

There is a positive duty to release a detainee or bring him/her before a magistrate within 36 hours of the start of the detention and an action for false imprisonment should succeed if this is not done.[81] Even after the granting of a warrant of extended detention, the regime of reviews should be continued to make the detention lawful. The powers of a custody officer should normally be performed by an officer designated for that purpose, but it seems as though the courts will not strictly enforce this provision and other officers will be able to exercise the powers in his/her place.[82]

Unless a person is released from police custody after being charged, the detention will be unlawful unless one or more of the limited grounds exist for keeping a person at the police station.[83]

Voluntary attendance at police station

Under PACE, someone who attends a police station voluntarily for the purpose of assisting with an investigation, without having been arrested, is entitled to leave at will, unless s/he is then placed under arrest. There is no requirement on the police to tell a person who is attending voluntarily that s/he is free to leave, but the Act does make it clear that if a police officer decides to arrest a person, s/he must be informed immediately.[84] The Act does not explicitly state that a breach of this rule makes the confinement unlawful, but this is almost certainly the case.[85]

Imagine a situation where a person agrees to go to a police station voluntarily to answer some questions. The officer questioning leaves the interview room to check on something that has been said, locking the door in the process so that the person cannot leave. As there has been no proper arrest the confinement is unlawful and the confined person can sue for false imprisonment. Alternatively, after a period of questioning the person decides that enough is enough and decides to leave. An officer stops the person and says, 'You can't go; you're helping us with our enquiries.' Again, in the absence of a proper arrest, the person could sue for false imprisonment.

81 See *R v Slough JJ ex p Stirling* [1987] Crim LR 576, DC and PACE s43.
82 PACE s31(6) and see *Vince v Chief Constable of Dorset Police* [1992] 3 All ER, 98, QBD.
83 PACE s38; and see Wadham, 'Bail from police stations' December 1988 *Legal Action* 24.
84 PACE s29. Cf *R v Lemsatef* [1977] 2 All ER 835 and Code C para 3.15.
85 See PACE s28.

Detention after lawful arrest

When a prisoner has been lawfully committed to custody, a deterioration in the conditions of detention will not give rise to a claim for false imprisonment. In two Court of Appeal cases, the court had, first, refused to strike out an action for false imprisonment by a convicted prisoner held overnight in a strip cell[86] and, second, suggested that an action for false imprisonment might be possible if the conditions of detention became unbearable.[87] However, when these cases were further appealed, the House of Lords ruled that there is no such thing as a person's 'residual liberty' which can be taken away when s/he is otherwise lawfully held in prison.[88] Therefore, if conditions deteriorate, there can be no further deprivation of liberty which could constitute the tort of false imprisonment. The House of Lords went on to say that, if conditions of an otherwise lawful detention are truly intolerable, the law ought to be capable of providing a remedy directly relating to those conditions, without characterising the detention itself as unlawful; Lord Bridge said that this remedy is already provided by the law, as a person in lawful detention is owed a duty of care by those holding him/her in custody and could sue in negligence if there was a breach of this duty (see p137). An action might also lie in assault and battery and/or misfeasance in public office.[89]

Who is liable: police or informant?

If an informant, say a shopkeeper, calls a police officer who then makes an arrest and the arrest amounts to false imprisonment, who is liable, the police officer or the shopkeeper? The law is unclear on this point but it is said that the normal test is, 'Who was "active in promoting and causing" the confinement?'.[90]

It seems that, where the police make their own enquiries after having been called by an informant, and make an arrest on their own authority,

---

86 *Weldon v Home Office* [1990] 3 All ER 672, CA.
87 *R v Deputy Governor of Parkhurst Prison and others ex p Hague* [1990] 3 All ER 687, CA.
88 *R v Deputy Governor of Parkhurst Prison and Others ex p Hague* [1991] 3 WLR 340, HL.
89 See *Racz v Home Office* [1994] 2 WLR 23, HL.
90 *Aitken v Bedwell* (1827) Mood & M 68; see also *Ansell v Thomas* [1974] Crim LR 31, CA.

the informant is not liable, even if the informant signs the charge sheet.[91] Store detectives and private security guards who provide information to the police with a clear intention and expectation that an arrest will follow will not be in a different position from ordinary members of the public if, after providing the information, they leave the police officers to act in the exercise of their own discretion to arrest.[92]

If the informant signs a charge sheet at the police station, that in itself is not evidence that s/he was active in promoting and causing the confinement.[93] However, if a police officer refuses to make an arrest unless the informant accepts responsibility for charging the person, it is the informant who is liable for false imprisonment.[94]

The position is different if the informant merely identifies a person when asked to do so by a police officer.[95] Thus, if someone were picked out from an identification parade, s/he would not have a claim for false imprisonment against the person who identified him/her.

The duration of the confinement

In theory, there is no minimum period of confinement for a claim for false imprisonment to succeed. In practice, the duration is important, as a long period might justify a larger sum of damages, see p146. However, being confined for even a short period can be serious. For example, a person wrongly arrested in a public place in circumstances that attracted a lot of attention, even if released after a few minutes, might suffer more embarrassment, distress and damage to his/her reputation than if s/he were arrested at home but kept for several hours. In one case, the Court of Appeal ordered a retrial of a case in which a judge implied that a 30-minute false imprisonment was a 'technical' false

---

91 *Grinham v Willey* (1859) 4 H&N 496.
92 *Davidson v Chief Constable of the North Wales Police and Another* [1994] 2 All ER 597, CA.
93 *Sewell v National Telephone Co* [1907] 1 KB 557, CA. If the charge sheet also states that the informant 'did give him charge', it may be evidence that the informant was active in promoting and causing the confinement: *Clubb v Wimpey & Co* [1936] 1 All ER 69; the point was not decided by the Court of Appeal when ordering a new trial: [1936] 3 All ER 148.
94 *Hopkins v Crowe* (1836) 4 Ad & E 774; *Austin v Dowling* (1870) LR 5 CP 534.
95 *Gosden v Elphick* (1849) 4 Exch 445.

imprisonment.[96] In addition, an assault and battery can constitute false imprisonment if the person is restrained during its occurrence, and thus give rise to a right to a jury trial.[97]

The police are liable in damages for the whole of the period of confinement until release or until remand in custody by a magistrate.[98]

Knowledge of false imprisonment

It is now clear that someone can bring an action for false imprisonment even though s/he did not know s/he was being unlawfully detained, or they were not harmed by the detention.[99] Thus an unconscious person could be falsely imprisoned. However, in cases where there is no knowledge and no harm caused a person 'can normally expect to recover no more than nominal damages'.[100]

Defences to false imprisonment

The general principle is that the police have a defence to false imprisonment if they can show that they had a lawful excuse or authority for their action. The burden of proof thus lies with the police. The most common defences open to the police are that they were carrying out a lawful arrest or stop and search or that they were lawfully acting on a warrant issued by a court. It is beyond the scope of this work to deal with all the technicalities of what and what is not lawful in all these circumstances, but some general principles can be described.

The police may make an arrest or may carry out a 'stop and search' without a warrant. They can only do this if certain conditions apply.[101]

---

96 *Kay v James* (1989) 21 April, unreported, cited in Clayton and Tomlinson, 'Civil actions against the police: recent developments', May 1990 *Legal Action* 16.

97 *Foley v Metropolitan Police Commissioner* (1989) 14 December, unreported; cited in Clayton and Tomlinson, May 1990 *Legal Action* 16.

98 *Lock v Ashton* (1848) 12 QB 871.

99 *Murray v Ministry of Defence* [1988] 2 All ER 521, HL, approving the dictum, of Atkin LJ in *Merring v Grahame-White Aviation Co* n70 at 53–54; and see Kodwo Bentil 'False imprisonment proceedings for alleged improper arrest and detention of suspect', *Justice of the Peace* 7 January 1989, p6.

100 *Murray v Ministry of Defence* n99 at 529 per Lord Griffiths.

101 See PACE Pts I and III.

Four of the several situations in which the police can arrest a person without a warrant are as follows:[102]

a) the police have reasonable grounds for suspecting that an arrestable offence[103] has been, or is about to be, committed; and they have reasonable grounds for suspecting the person arrested to be guilty of the offence, or for suspecting the person is about to commit the offence;[104]
b) in relation to non-arrestable offences the police have reasonable grounds for suspecting that the offence has been committed, attempted or is in the process of being committed or attempted, and reasonable grounds for suspecting that the person arrested has done any of these acts; and either the service of a summons is impracticable or inappropriate because any of the general arrest conditions are satisfied;[105]
c) the police may arrest without warrant a person committing a breach of the peace, a person who, it is reasonably apprehended, will imminently commit a breach of the peace,[106] or a person who, having committed a breach, is reasonably expected to be about to renew it;
d) the police may arrest without warrant anyone whose conduct is reasonably suspected as likely to cause harassment, alarm or distress (following a warning to stop such conduct).[107]

If 'reasonable grounds to suspect' is raised as a defence by the police, it would be for them to prove the existence of such reasonable grounds. A *mere* suspicion, in the sense of a hunch, would not be sufficient, but the

---

102 In addition, PACE s117 (which allows a police officer to use reasonable force in carrying out functions under the Act) extends to detaining a person to allow a search under the Act to be effected: *Parry v Sharples* (1991) 17 July, CA, Lexis.
103 Arrestable offence is defined by PACE s24(1).
104 Ibid s24(6) and (7).
105 PACE s25(1) and (2). The general arrest conditions relate to failure of the suspected person to provide a satisfactory name or address, or the need to protect others or the person arrested or property, or prevent an unlawful obstruction of the highway: s25(3).
106 A police officer must 'honestly believe on reasonable grounds' that a breach of the peace is imminent for an arrest before the breach takes place to be lawful: *Lewis v Chief Constable of Greater Manchester* (1991) *Independent* 23 October.
107 Public Order Act 1986 s5.

present law on 'reasonable grounds' for that suspicion suggests that the standard the police have to meet is not a high one. Suspicion is a state of conjecture or surmise where proof is lacking[108] and is something much less than knowledge of guilt. If, for example, the police could show that they had received at least some information from a reliable source that the person had committed the offence (even if this later turned out to be incorrect), they may well have a good defence on the basis that they had reasonable grounds to suspect that person.

In *Castorina v Chief Constable of Surrey*[109] police investigated a burglary from a company which appeared to have been committed by someone with inside information. The managing director informed the police that the only person with a grudge against the company was an ex-employee. She was arrested and held for nearly four hours before being released without charge. Her claim for false imprisonment failed, because the police successfully argued to the Court of Appeal that, on this information, they had reasonable cause to suspect that she had committed the burglary and, in these circumstances, it was unnecessary for them to make further inquiries before arresting her.

However, in *James v Chief Constable of South Wales Police*,[110] the Court of Appeal warned that, while it was not the law that reasonable suspicion could not be based solely upon information received from an informant, 'such information should be treated with considerable reserve, and any police officer should hesitate before regarding it, without more, as a basis for reasonable suspicion'.

In *Tomlinson v DPP*[111] it was held that wandering aimlessly and acting strangely in Soho (where drug abuse is commonplace) was not, in itself, reasonable grounds to suspect a person of being in possession of a controlled drug. The question of what amounts to 'reasonable grounds' is a question of law which must be decided by the judge, not the jury[112] (see below p254). The jury's role is to resolve any conflicting evidence as to what happened. The judge then has to rule whether the conduct of the police was reasonable or unreasonable, and to decide what facts are relevant to that question.[113] The same approach is applied where the

108 *Holtham v Commissioner of Police for the Metropolis* (1987) *Times* 28 November, CA.
109 (1988) NLJ 24 June, p180, CA; for a full discussion of the case see Clayton and Tomlinson, 'Arrest and reasonable grounds for suspicion' *LS Gaz* 7 September 1988, p22; see also *Dallison v Cafferty* [1964] 2 All ER 610, CA.
110 (1991) *Daily Telegraph* 3 May, CA per Lord Donaldson MR.
111 May 1992 *Legal Action* 21.
112 *Lister v Perryman* (1870) LR 4 HL 521; *McArdle v Egan* [1933] All ER Rep 611.
113 *Dallison v Cafferty* [1965] 1 QB 348.

court has to decide whether an arresting officer had 'a reasonable belief' that a breach of the peace is likely to occur.[114]

Police officers have a discretion whether to exercise their powers of arrest or not. So even where the police have satisfied the condition precedent for arrest, it is open to the plaintiff to show that the power to arrest was exercised, in a public law sense (see p302), unreasonably[115] and therefore unlawfully. Thus, in one case even though the arresting officer had reasonable grounds to suspect that the person arrested was guilty of an arrestable offence he also knew that the arrested person's victim had accepted an apology and was not pressing charges. The Court of Appeal said it was possible for the plaintiff to argue that, as there was no prospect at all of him being prosecuted, the arrest was unlawful.[116]

A store detective or a private security guard has no special powers of arrest other than the general 'citizen's arrest' power, which can be exercised only where an arrestable offence has in fact been committed.[117] Whether or not there were reasonable grounds to suspect that an offence had been committed by the person arrested, if that person succeeds in showing that no offence was committed, then the arrest will have been unlawful.[118]

Even if an arrest or stop and search can be justified by the police, a claim for false imprisonment may still succeed if it can be shown that the manner in which it was carried out made it unlawful. For example, on arrest, a person must be informed of the fact and of the grounds for the arrest, either at the time of the arrest or as soon as practicable afterwards. If the police fail to do either of these things, the arrest is unlawful[119] and any defence based on the arrest will fail.

In *Abbassy v Metropolitan Police Commissioner*[120] the plaintiff and his wife were stopped while driving by four police officers who considered that the plaintiff had been driving inconsiderately. They were unable to elicit any information concerning the ownership of the car from the plaintiff and he was arrested (and told he was being arrested)

---

114 *Kelly v Chief Constable of Hampshire* (1993) *Independent* 25 March, CA.
115 *Holgate Mohammed v Duke* [1984] AC 437; and *Associated Provincial Picture Houses v Wednesbury Corporation* [1948] 1 KB 223.
116 *Plange v Chief Constable of South Humberside Police* (1992) *Times* 23 March.
117 PACE s24 (4), (5).
118 See, for instance, *R v Self* [1992] 3 All ER 476, CA.
119 PACE s28(1) and (3); for stop and search, see ss1 and 3 and *Pedro v Diss* (1980) 72 Crim App R 193.
120 [1990] 1 All ER 193, CA; and see *Christie v Leachinsky* [1947] AC 573, HL.

for 'unlawful possession'. It was held by the Court of Appeal that the arrest was lawful even though there is no such offence as unlawful possession in relation to a motor car. It was not necessary to specify a particular crime if, by using commonplace language, it was clear to the suspect what type of offence he was being arrested for, so that he had an opportunity to volunteer information which would avoid the arrest.

This case was decided on the law before PACE and it may be that more detailed information should now be given to a suspect to make an arrest lawful, as a police officer must state the ground for the arrest, regardless of whether this is obvious.[121] In *Edwards v DPP*,[122] a case where the officer failed to state one of the general arrest conditions (see above p141) as a reason for the arrest, the Divisional Court said that it:

> had sympathy for police officers in difficult circumstances but it had to be borne in mind that giving the correct information as to the reason for an arrest was a matter of the utmost constitutional significance in a case where a reason can be and is given at the time of the arrest.

However, the Court of Appeal was prepared to take a much more flexible approach in *Parry v Sharples*.[123] Police officers detained a man at gun-point without giving any reasons while his house was searched under the authority of a warrant, but the Court of Appeal said that the 'controlling or restraining', which amounted to a wrongful arrest, was otherwise justified under PACE s117, which allows a police officer to use reasonable force in carrying out his/her duties under the Act.

It is lawful for the police to arrest a person and not provide him/her with the necessary information if it is not reasonably practicable to do so (for instance, if the person is struggling violently). The police still have a duty to inform the person that s/he is under arrest and the ground for the arrest as soon as it becomes practicable.[124] However, in this situation it will not make the original arrest retrospectively unlawful if they fail to do so and the arrest and detention will be lawful up to the time when it would have been practicable to have informed the person.[125] Where it would have been practicable to inform a person of the reason for his/her arrest, but this was not done until some time later, the

121 PACE s28(3) and (4).
122 [1993] COD 378.
123 17 July 1991, CA, Lexis.
124 PACE s28(1) and (3).
125 *DPP v Hawkins* [1988] 1 WLR 1166; 3 All ER 673, DC; and see Reville, 'PACE and entrapment' *LS Gaz* 22 February 1989 p19.

arrest and the detention will be unlawful until those reasons are given.[126]

It appears that the use of undue force in effecting an arrest will not make the arrest unlawful if the arrest was otherwise justified in law,[127] although the use of force may amount to assault.

Confinement after court proceedings

As a general principle, if someone is held after a court has ordered their confinement, there is no claim against the police for false imprisonment.[128] Thus, if a person is arrested under a warrant, s/he has no claim against the police officer who acts in obedience to the warrant.[129] However, the police would not be protected if they did not act in obedience to it, for example, by arresting someone who was not named in the warrant.

Problems may arise if the warrant does not use the correct form of words. While it has been held that an officer is protected in obeying a warrant that was 'invalid or unlawful' because it did not contain the form of words required,[130] it is doubtful whether s/he would be protected by a warrant that had a more substantial defect, such as the omission of the cause of arrest.[131] A police officer must produce the warrant if asked by the person it is intended to arrest and will be liable if s/he fails to do so.

---

126 *Lewis v Chief Constable of South Wales Constabulary* [1991] 1 All ER 206, CA.
127 *Simpson v Chief Constable of South Yorkshire Police* (1991) *Independent* 14 March.
128 For the liability of the judiciary, see *Fray v Blackburn* (1863) 3 B&S 576; *Anderson v Gorrie* [1895] 1 QB 668: judge of superior court of record not liable for judicial acts within his jurisdiction even if malicious; *Sirros v Moore* [1974] 3 All ER 776: judge not liable for judicial acts beyond his jurisdiction made in good faith; *In re McC (a minor)* (1984) *Times* 28 November: N Ireland magistrate liable if acts outside his jurisdiction; *R v Waltham Forest Justices ex p Solanke* [1985] 3 All ER 727, confirmed (1986) *Times* 24 June: effects of Justices of the Peace Act 1979 s52; *Beckett v Walker* [1985] 3 CL 16a: negligent issue of warrant for arrest. See also 'Suing the beaks', *Justice of the Peace* 7 April 1990 p212 and *R v Sheffield Justices ex p Turner* [1991] 1 All ER 858.
129 Constables' Protection Act 1750 s6.
130 *Horsfield v Brown* [1932] 1 KB 355 at 369.
131 See Street on Torts, 8th edition 1988, Butterworths, p88.

Remedies

In theory there are three legal remedies for false imprisonment:

- self-help, ie escape;
- habeas corpus;
- damages.

Escape
In practice the dangers, both physical and legal, of attempting to escape from unlawful custody mean it should not be regarded as a 'remedy' at all. Its practical importance is rather as a defence if charged with a criminal offence, say, assault with intent to resist arrest.[132]

Habeas corpus
Habeas corpus is an emergency remedy. It can be used to bring a false imprisonment to an end but is suitable only for serious cases.[133] Legal aid can be obtained to apply to the High Court but the delays involved in the legal aid application mean that it will not usually be a practical remedy, except in the most lengthy detentions.[134]

The usual remedy is to sue for damages after the event.

Damages
In *Murray v Minister of Defence* Lord Griffiths said:

> The law attaches supreme importance to the liberty of the individual and if he suffers a wrongful interference with that liberty it should remain actionable even without proof of special damage.[135]

Damages for false imprisonment are intended to compensate for loss of liberty, discomfort and inconvenience (provided it is substantial),[136] injury to dignity and loss of reputation. The damage to reputation continues until the police admit the imprisonment was false.[137] It

132 Offences Against the Person Act 1861 s38, as amended.
133 *R v Holmes ex p Sherman* [1981] 2 All ER 612.
134 See Gifford and O'Connor, 'Habeas corpus', August 1979 *LAG Bulletin* 182.
135 [1988] 1 WLR 692 at 704.
136 *Bailey v Bullock* above n61 at 1170 H.
137 *Walter v Alltools Ltd* (1944) 171 LT 371 at 372 per Lawrence LJ, followed in *Hook v Cunard Steamship Co Ltd* [1953] 1 All ER 1021 at 1042 H. Persisting in a false charge may be grounds for awarding aggravated damages: *Warwick v Foulkes* (1844) 12 M&W 507.

may be possible to claim for substantial emotional shock if medical evidence of this can be produced.[138] It will be possible to claim damages for any cash loss, such as loss of earnings.[139] A study calculated the average 'hourly rate' for loss of liberty in decided cases using 1986 as a base year for inflation purposes. It suggested a figure of £251 per hour in cases heard before a judge without a jury and £530 per hour in jury cases.[140] However, it is submitted that it is inappropriate to view the question in terms of an hourly rate, as many factors other than the length of the detention will be reflected in the size of the award. Great caution must be taken in advising on damages. It is dangerous to rely on average figures as they inevitably disguise substantial differences that reflect the very wide disparity in the merits of different cases. This is particularly true of jury cases. As in defamation cases, the jury will receive almost no guidance on the level of damages in false imprisonment and malicious prosecution cases. Thus Purchas LJ, in the Court of Appeal, has noted:

> Parliament has seen fit to leave the assessment of damages to the judgment of the jury rather than the judge . . . these are areas where the question of damages is so utterly subjective to the individual facts involved that I think it would be wrong to attempt to influence by judicial interference consideration of damages by the jury.[141]

In addition, it is normal practice to seek aggravated damages and exemplary damages in cases of false imprisonment by the police. In practice, these might not be awarded if it appears that there is little fault attached to the police or that they have simply made a mistake. If no real loss can be shown, only nominal damages may be awarded (see p192).

Malicious prosecution

> It is a tort maliciously and without reasonable and probable cause to initiate against another judicial proceedings which terminate in favour of that other and which result in damage to reputation, person, freedom or property.[142]

138 *McLoughlin v O'Brien*, above at n63; cf *Wilkinson v Downton* [1897] 2 QB 57.
139 *Childs v Lewis* (1924) 40 TLR 870; *Harnett v Bond* [1925] AC 669, HL.
140 Clayton and Tomlinson, 'Assessing damages in civil actions against the police' *LS Gaz* 25 November 1987, p3397.
141 *Abassy v Commissioner of Police for the Metropolis* n120 at 204 per Purchas LJ.
142 Street on Torts 1993 edn p473.

The right to sue for malicious prosecution is intended to protect people from unwarranted accusations that are brought to the criminal courts. Every year thousands of people are acquitted of the offences of which they were accused; some will say they were framed or fitted up or just prosecuted for no good reason. Yet only a handful succeed in claims for malicious prosecution. Malicious prosecution is probably the most difficult type of police misconduct to prove. There are many protections for the prosecutor which, as Fleming states, reflect society's interest:

> . . . in the efficient enforcement of the criminal law, which requires that . . . prosecutors . . . should be adequately protected against the prejudice which is likely to ensue from termination of the prosecution in favour of the accused. So much weight has been attached to this consideration that the action for malicious prosecution is held on a tighter rein than any other in the law of torts.[143]

Unusually in the law of torts, the *motive* of the alleged tortfeasor is a vital element in proving the plaintiff's case. In practice, it is almost impossible to collect concrete evidence before the case begins, as much depends on what was going on in the mind of the police officer. One study concluded that the threat of suit for malicious prosecution is 'no obstacle to the dishonest prosecutor and no real protection to the innocent who are prosecuted'.[144]

To succeed in a claim for malicious prosecution against the police, it must be shown that:

– damage has been suffered *because*:
– the police prosecuted; *and*
– the criminal case was concluded in the accused's favour; *and*
– reasonable and probable cause were absent in the bringing of the prosecution; *and*
– the police acted maliciously.

Despite this daunting list of elements, some of which are difficult to prove (see below), the tort is some kind of guarantee of civil liberties, however flawed, and may be particularly appropriate where it is being

143 Fleming, *The Law of Torts*, Sweet & Maxwell 8th ed 1993 at p609.
144 Lidstone, Hogg and Sutcliffe, *Prosecutions by private individuals and non-police agencies*, Royal Commission on Criminal Procedure Research Study No 10 HMSO, 1980, p106.

alleged that the police acted as *agents provocateurs* or have manufactured evidence.[145]

Necessary elements

Damage
Unlike most other types of police misconduct (for instance, assault and battery, and false imprisonment), it is necessary, for a case to be successful, to show that actual damage has been suffered. Historically, only three very specific types of damage are relevant. These are: loss of reputation, the risk of loss of 'life, limb or liberty;' and financial loss.[146] They are discussed in more detail below (p155).

Police prosecution
The prosecutor sued must be the person who was 'actively instrumental in putting the law in force.'[147] Usually the police are clearly responsible for bringing the prosecution, and it appears that it will be rare for it to be appropriate to sue a member of the public who has provided information to the police which has led to a prosecution. However, in *Martin v Watson*[148] the House of Lords held that where a member of the public falsely and maliciously provides information to the police indicating that a person was guilty of a criminal offence, then that member of the public can be regarded as a prosecutor in setting the law in motion.

Lord Keith explained the reasoning of the House when he said that where the circumstances were such that the facts relating to the alleged offence could be within the knowledge only of the member of the public, then it became 'virtually impossible' for a police officer to exercise any independent discretion or judgment, and therefore it was not right to say that the police officer was the prosecutor.[149]

In the light of this judgment, practitioners involved in malicious prosecution cases against the police should always consider the possibility that the police will argue that the correct defendant is the person

---

145 Eg, *Sam v Cluney* [1956] Crim LR 271: giving false evidence of gross indecency in a public lavatory. See HC Debs col 2525, 16 February 1956.
146 *Savile v Roberts* (1698) 1 Ld Raym 374 at 378.
147 *Danby v Beardsley* (1880) 43 LT 603.
148 [1995] 3 WLR 318, HL.
149 *Martin v Watson* (supra) at 327.

who informed the police of the alleged offence. If necessary that person should then be added as a defendant to the action.

Under the Prosecution of Offences Act 1985,[150] the police remain the 'prosecutors', even though the Crown Prosecution Service now takes responsibility for prosecutions following charge or summons by the police.[151] One commentator offers the view that if the CPS continues the prosecution, thus endorsing the view of the police, then proving lack of reasonable and probable cause will be 'a mammoth task'.[152] However, it is submitted that this would not be the case if it is later shown that the police had manufactured evidence or fabricated statements.

The criminal case must end in favour of the person suing
The criminal prosecution must have ended in favour of the person suing for malicious prosecution.[153] This can be achieved by a verdict of acquittal, by the conviction being quashed on appeal,[154] by an acquittal on a technicality, such as an error in the indictment,[155] or by the discontinuance of proceedings.[156] It has been argued that the case need not have reached a first court appearance for there to be a 'prosecution'; it will be enough, for instance, if a person has been charged.[157]

A claim can still succeed even if there was a conviction for a less serious offence than the one for which a person is charged.[158] Where a trial results in a person being acquitted of some offences but convicted of others,[159] there may be claims for malicious prosecution in relation to

---

150 Section 15(2).
151 Section 3(2).
152 Street on Torts, 1993 edn, p479.
153 *Parker v Langley* (1713) 10 Mod 145 and 209.
154 *Herniman v Smith* [1938] 1 All ER 1, HL; *Berry v British Transport Commission* [1961] 3 All ER 65, CA.
155 *Jones v Gwynn* (1712) 10 Mod 148 at 214; *Wicks v Fentham* (1791) 4 Term Rep 247.
156 *Watkins v Lee* (1839) 5 M & W 270. However, where the Attorney-General stays proceedings (by nolle prosequi), the position is less clear; See Winfield and Jolowicz on Torts 1994 edn p575.
157 See Sanders, 'Malicious prosecution – further problems,' *LS Gaz* 28 May 1986 p1626.
158 *Boaler v Holder* (1887) 51 JP 277.
159 *Reed v Taylor* (1812) 4 Taunt 616; *Leibo v Buckman Ltd* [1952] 2 All ER 1057, CA.

those offences on which there has been an acquittal. If offences are ordered to 'lie on the file' after the defendant has pleaded guilty to other offences, it is likely that this will be treated as an 'adjournment' of the proceedings rather than a termination, favourable or otherwise. If proceedings have been stayed because they have been held to be an abuse of process (for instance, because of the length of time it has taken to bring the prosecution), then the 'stay' would be more likely to be regarded as a termination in favour of the plaintiff.[160]

Special problems arise if someone is bound over to keep the peace and to be of good behaviour. If s/he is bound over after the hearing of a 'complaint',[161] the case does not end in his/her favour and s/he cannot sue.[162] More commonly, however, bind-overs are agreed to by the defence before the case is heard, in exchange for the prosecution offering no evidence on the charge before the court.

In *Hourihane v Metropolitan Police Commissioner*[163] the police applied to strike out a claim for malicious prosecution where the plaintiff had agreed to a bind-over, the CPS had offered no evidence, and the charges (of disorderly behaviour) were duly dismissed. The Court of Appeal held that it was impossible to draw any inference that proceedings had terminated adversely to a defendant from the mere statement that s/he was bound over to keep the peace. The court said there might be many reasons why a defendant would prefer to agree to be bound over rather than run the risk of conviction. As the issue in the civil proceedings was whether the charges were brought maliciously and without reasonable and probable cause, the existence of a record showing that, following dismissal of the charges, the plaintiffs were bound over could not be a good ground for striking out their claims.

If there is a conviction, a claim for malicious prosecution cannot succeed, even if there is no further right of appeal and even if it can be

---

160 These last two examples are discussed further in Clayton and Tomlinson, *Civil Actions against the police* p293.
161 Under Magistrates' Courts Act 1980 s115.
162 *Everett v Ribbands* [1952] 1 All ER 823, CA; see also *Bynoe v Bank of England* [1900–3] All ER Rep 65.
163 (1995) *Independent* 18 January.

proved that the conviction was obtained by fraud,[164] for example, where the police had planted evidence or fabricated statements. This rule has been justified on the ground that to allow such cases would be to turn the civil case into a retrial of the criminal case, and so create a 'Court of Appeal' where parliament had not intended one.[165] However, as the burden of proof in malicious prosecution actions is so difficult to discharge, this rule is open to the criticism that it is unnecessarily strict. Where a defendant has been given an absolute or conditional discharge in a criminal trial it is clear that the proceedings have not terminated in his/her favour.[166]

The prosecution must lack reasonable and probable cause

As stated above, there are obvious reasons of public policy why the police should not feel inhibited from prosecuting criminals. However, innocent people should not have to suffer criminal trials where their prosecutors acted without good reason. Over the years, judges who feared that individual juries would upset the balance of these competing issues of public policy evolved a principle whereby they reserved to themselves the task of deciding the crucial issue of whether the prosecution was brought without reasonable and probable cause. Other issues of fact are left to the jury, but this question is decided by the judge. The effect of this is to make it difficult for people to bring cases of malicious prosecution except in the most clear-cut of cases.

Most unusually in English law, a negative has to be proved by the plaintiff. S/he has to prove that the police lacked reasonable and probable cause, rather than the police having to prove that they had such cause.[167] As the burden of proof is on the plaintiff, no particulars will be ordered to be given of the defendant's simple denial of lack of reasonable and probable cause.[168]

The difficulty is compounded by the inability of the judges to agree on the meaning of 'reasonable and probable cause'.[169] Perhaps the best explanation, provided by the House of Lords in the case of *Glinski v McIver*, is that it means:

> that there must be cause (that is sufficient grounds . . .) for thinking that the plaintiff was probably guilty of the crime . . . This does not mean that

164 *Basebe v Matthews* (1867) LR 2 CP 684. For remedies for wrongful conviction now available, see p258.
165 Ibid.
166 Powers of Criminal Courts Act 1973 s13.
167 *Stapeley v Annetts* [1969] 3 All ER 1541; [1970] 1 WLR 20, CA.
168 Ibid.
169 *Abbott v Refuge Assurance Co* [1961] 3 All ER 1074 at 1086.

the prosecutor has to believe in the probability of conviction . . . The prosecutor has not got to test the full strength of the defence; he is concerned only with the question of whether there is a case fit to be tried.[170]

In the same case the House of Lords held that the plaintiff had to prove one of two things to show that the police lacked reasonable and probable cause in bringing a prosecution, the first being a subjective test, and the second an objective test, as follows:

1) Did the police actually believe the plaintiff was probably guilty? or
2) Would a reasonable person, looking at the facts honestly believed by the police, conclude that they were sufficient to give the police cause to think the plaintiff was probably guilty?

Thus, there must be *actual* belief and *reasonable* belief in the probable guilt of a person for there to be reasonable and probable cause to prosecute. These tests will be considered in turn:

1) *The actual (subjective) belief of the police in the guilt of the plaintiff* The plaintiff can succeed in showing there was no reasonable and probable cause if s/he can show that the police officers involved did not in fact believe that s/he was probably guilty of the offence, at the time of proceeding with the prosecution. This subjective test is for the jury, not the judge, to decide, but the test should be put to the jury only where there is actual evidence that the police did not believe in the guilt of the plaintiff.[171] In practice it is very difficult to prove exactly what a police officer did or did not believe at the time of preferring charges.

Thus the test may be relevant if, for instance, the police indicated that they accepted a plaintiff's alibi but still proceeded with the prosecution: 'We know you didn't do it, but we're going to nick you anyway'. However, for the question to go to the jury there would also need to be some actual *evidence* (for instance, witness statements or oral evidence of what was said by an officer) to indicate that the police proceeded in this way.

A police officer who is found by a jury not to believe in the probable guilt of a person cannot have reasonable and probable cause to prosecute that person.[172]

170 *Glinski v McIver* [1962] 1 All ER 696 at 714.
171 *Herniman v Smith* [1938] AC 305 HL at 315, per Lord Atkin.
172 *Glinski v McIver* [1962] AC 726 at 753 per Lord Radcliffe.

2) *The reasonable person (objective) test of the probable guilt of the plaintiff (based on the honestly believed facts as found by the police officer)*   This objective test is for the judge alone to decide, if the question of honest belief has not had to be put to the jury or if the jury has found that the police did honestly believe in the guilt of the plaintiff. The judge should enquire whether 'a person of ordinary prudence and caution' would have decided that the plaintiff had probably committed the offence.[173] It is no help to show that the police were mistaken about the facts, provided that it was a reasonable mistake.

If the judge finds that on this test, despite the honest belief of the police, a reasonable person would not have decided that the plaintiff was probably guilty of the offence for which s/he was prosecuted, then the judge must find that there was no reasonable or probable cause for the prosecution.

The police acted maliciously

In order to prove that the police acted maliciously, it must be shown that their motive, or their main motive, was something other than the simple desire to bring the plaintiff to justice.[174] Thus in *White and Another v Metropolitan Police Commissioner*,[175] the police brought the prosecution (for assaulting police officers) in order to cover up their own wrongdoing, namely, unlawfully assaulting Mr and Mrs White. If the police are partly motivated by a desire to bring someone to justice, but also partly by an improper motive, the question is: which was the dominant purpose? If the improper motive was dominant, the claim can still succeed.

However, just because malice can be proved, it does not follow that a lack of reasonable and probable cause is automatically proved.[176] The two issues are separate: it may be that, although the police acted maliciously, they still had reasonable and probable cause, in which case the claim will fail.

For instance, two men are caught together in suspicious circumstances. One is black and one is white. The police have reasonable and probable cause for prosecuting both but only prosecute the black man. If there is clear evidence that the motive was to harass the black man

173 *Hicks v Faulkner* (1881) 8 QBD 167 at 171; and see Street on Torts 1993 edn p477.
174 *Stevens v Midland Counties Railway* (1854) 10 Exch 352.
175 (1982) *Times* 24 April.
176 *Glinski v McIver* [1962] 1 All ER 696.

because of his race, the element of malice will be proved. However, the fact that there was reasonable and probable cause would defeat a claim for malicious prosecution.[177]

On the other hand, a lack of reasonable and probable cause can be evidence that the police acted maliciously.[178] If the police plant stolen goods on a man who is a known criminal, on either the objective or the subjective test described above there is no reasonable and probable cause to believe him guilty. For the same reason, the police must have acted maliciously because, whatever their motive, it could not have been a desire to bring him to justice. Whether there is *evidence* of malice is a matter for the judge to decide. Whether or not, on that evidence, the motive was malicious is a question of fact for the jury to decide.[179]

Damages

To bring an action for malicious prosecution it must be shown that at least one of three types of loss has been suffered:

- loss of reputation;
- the risk of loss of 'life, limb or liberty';
- financial loss.[180]

It is not clear whether, having met one of these conditions, damages are then limited to these types of loss. The modern approach seems to be that they constitute a hurdle but, once over it, damages are not limited to the three heads and may include such things as the humiliation and indignity of having to face a charge and the distress and anxiety felt while awaiting trial.[181]

In respect of loss of liberty, it is enough that the offence for which the plaintiff is prosecuted is one punishable by imprisonment:[182] there need not be actual loss of liberty. Legal costs incurred in defending oneself

---

177 For the disciplinary offence of racially discriminatory behaviour, see Police Discipline Code para 9 (Appendix 2, p324, below).
178 *Brown v Hughes* [1891] 2 QB 718 at 722.
179 *Mitchell v Jenkins* (1833) 5 B & Ad 588; *Hicks v Faulkner* (1878) 8 QBD 167 at 175; *Brown v Hawkes* [1891] 2 QB 718.
180 *Savile v Roberts* (1698) 1 Ld Raym 374; *Berry v British Transport Commission* [1960] 3 All ER 322, QBD per Diplock J.
181 See Gifford 'Civil actions against the police', July 1983 *LAG Bulletin* 85.
182 *Wiffen v Bailey and Romford UDC* [1915] 1 KB 600.

against a malicious prosecution constitute sufficient damage to qualify as financial loss, even where the court grants an allowance towards those costs.[183]

High awards of damages may be expected due to the gravity of the matter, subject, of course, to the circumstances of the particular case and the fact that the jury is given little guidance in deciding damages. Aggravated damages are likely in most cases and a claim for these and exemplary damages should be considered. A 1987 study attempted to rationalise damages awards by studying 70 recent police misconduct cases and submitted that:

> a successful plaintiff in a malicious prosecution case can expect to recover at least £1,000 compensation for the prosecution itself and a much greater sum if prosecution for a serious offence was involved. In addition, a conventional sum of £300 per hour should be awarded for any 'loss of liberty' suffered by the plaintiff, for example, time spent on remand awaiting trial.[184]

Damages for loss of reputation may be reduced through the bad character of the plaintiff and exemplary damages may be reduced by the plaintiff's provocative conduct.[185] The general principles on which damages are awarded are described in chapter 6 below.

Malicious process

Malicious process is a civil wrong, separate from malicious prosecution, which entails instituting a legal process short of prosecution without reasonable and probable cause and with malice.[186] The two most common examples are applications for arrest and search warrants.

The principles concerning 'reasonable and probable cause' and 'malice' are the same as in malicious prosecution, with two main exceptions. First the process (that is, the application for the warrant) does not have to end in favour of the plaintiff. A claim can succeed even though the warrant was issued. Second, the plaintiff does not have to show the particular types of damage necessary in malicious prosecu-

---

184 Clayton and Tomlinson, 'Assessing damages in civil actions against the police', *LS Gaz* 25 November 1987, p3397.

185 *Bishop v Commissioner of Police of the Metropolis* (1990) *LS Gaz* 10 January, p30; (1989) *Times* 5 December, CA.

186 Eg, *Roy v Prior* [1970] 2 All ER 729, HL; see *Beckett v Walker* [1985] 3 CL 16a for a case of negligent issue of a warrant.

tion. Any kind of special damage (cash loss) will be sufficient (see chapter 6 below).

Negligence

Clerk and Lindsell succinctly state that the tort of negligence 'is committed when damage, which is not too remote, is caused by the breach of a duty of care owed by the defendant to the plaintiff'.[187]

If this definition is unpacked, then the following requirements for liability for negligence can be identified:[188]

- a duty of care must be recognised in law as being owed to the class of person to which the plaintiff belongs by the class of person to which the defendant belongs;
- there must be a breach of the duty of care by the defendant (that is, the behaviour of the defendant must, by its carelessness, fail to reach the standard set by the law); and
- there must be a 'causal connection between the defendant's careless conduct and the damage' and forseeability that the careless conduct would cause the damage complained of by the particular plaintiff.

It is clear that a police officer, like anyone else, may be liable in negligence to a person who is injured as a direct result of his/her acts or omissions. However, there are considerable legal problems in establishing these principles in practice. As the major problem in recent years has been establishing that there is a duty of care at all between the police and particular groups of potential and actual plaintiffs, it is this element of the tort that will be concentrated on in this section.

The duty of care

General

It seems that there is no general test which can be applied to a particular situation to determine whether a duty of care is owed. The House of Lords in *Murphy v Brentwood DC*[189] has said that it prefers the view 'that the law should develop novel categories of negligence incrementally and by analogy with established categories, rather than by a massive extension of a prima facie duty of care'.[190]

187 1989 edn p427.
188 Ibid p428.
189 [1991] 1 AC 398.
190 Ibid per Lord Keith at 461, citing with approval the Australian case of *Sutherland Shire Council v Heyman* (1985) 60 ALR 1 at 43–44.

Thus, to prove liability for negligence in an area where liability is not generally established, it is not enough just to show that the harm caused was foreseeable for it to be said that a duty of care was owed to the plaintiff by the defendant.[191] The courts will also look at whether there is a sufficient proximity of relationship between the parties and at whether 'the situation should be one in which the court considers it fair, just and reasonable that the law should impose a duty of a given scope upon one party for the benefit of the other'.[192]

This 'incremental' approach has made it difficult to enunciate general principles by which it can be said that the police owe a duty of care in any particular case. This section describes some of the cases where it has been held that a duty of care does exist, before discussing the manner in which the 'proximity' and 'fairness' factors have been used to restrict the scope of the duty of care in other cases.

Situations where the duty of care is owed (and on what basis)
That a duty of care is owed by the police to certain groups of people while carrying out certain functions seems to be established.

Traffic   A police officer driving a vehicle in the course of his/her duties owes the same duty of care to members of the public as do all other road users. This duty is to 'exercise such care and skill as is reasonable in all the circumstances'.[193] The duty extends even to a criminal who is being pursued.[194] The standard of the duty is discussed below (p163).

In custody   Even before PACE came into force it seems that the police owed a special duty to take care of people in police custody.[195] In one case, a plaintiff received damages for negligence, including exemplary damages, when she was detained by police, who owed her a duty of care, but who failed to obtain treatment for a broken ankle she had suffered before her arrest.[196] It is likely that a duty of care is owed to solicitors who attend police stations and who are subsequently attacked and injured by a client.[197]

191 See, for instance, *Hill v Chief Constable of West Yorkshire* [1989] AC 53, HL per Lord Keith at 60.
192 *Caparo Industries PLC v Dickman* [1990] 2 AC 605, 617 per Lord Bridge.
193 *Gaynor v Allen* [1959] 2 QB 403.
194 See *Marshall v Osmond* [1983] QB 1034, CA.
195 *Bryson v Northumbria Police Authority* [1977] CLY 2042.
196 *Annables v Chief Constable for South Yorkshire* August 1993 *Legal Action* 16; see also *White v Chief Constable of Merseyside*, Current Law Week Vol 2 Issue 42/94 p2.
197 See Samuels, 'Solicitor injured at the police station,' (1992) *SJ* 15 May p461 for a discussion of the law in such a case.

In *Kirkham v Chief Constable of Greater Manchester Police*[198] it was held that the police owed a duty of care to a man who committed suicide while in prison custody. The police knew of the man's suicidal tendencies and should have passed this information on to the prison authorities. There was an established procedure and a special form provided for this purpose. The Court of Appeal held that, even though the negligence of the police concerned a 'pure omission', there could be liability as they had assumed a responsibility towards the man and were therefore under a duty to act or speak in accordance with this duty.

Other situations A police officer who took charge of a dangerous traffic situation, but negligently failed to close a tunnel, and then told a police motorcyclist to ride against the flow of traffic, thus causing an accident, owed a duty of care to that motorcyclist.[199] However, as the plaintiff was a police officer acting under instructions from a superior officer, the duty owed would have been that owed by an employer rather than that owed to other road users.

In *Rigby v Chief Constable of Northamptonshire*[200] a duty of care was owed to the owners of a property damaged by fire when a CS canister was fired into it to flush out an intruder. The police had negligently failed to have fire-fighting equipment on hand. The court held that a duty of care was owed to a very restricted number of people whose property could have foreseeably been damaged by the careless-ness of the police.

The police (and the Crown Prosecution Service) may owe a duty of care to those caused damage by acts or omissions which precede a court process. In *Welsh v Chief Constable of the Merseyside Police*[201] the judge refused to strike out an action for negligence by a plaintiff who claimed the police and the CPS had failed to pass on information to a magistrates' court, which failure led to the plaintiff's arrest and detention. However, at least in the case of the CPS, it appears that such pre-court process liability will only arise if there is assumed, by conduct, a responsibility towards the particular plaintiff.[202]

Proximity of relationship
However, a duty of care is not owed to people with whom the police do not have a sufficient pre-existing relationship. Thus, the police could not

198 [1990] 3 All ER 246, CA, and see Hibbs, 'Police liability to suicide's widow' *LS Gaz* 28 March 1990, p 24.
199 *Knightley v Johns* [1982] 1 WLR 349, CA.
200 [1985] 2 All ER 985.
201 [1993] 1 All ER 692. Only the CPS applied for the action to be struck out.
202 *Elguzouli-Daf v Commissioner of Police of the Metropolis* [1995] 2 WLR 173, CA.

be made a third party in a case of a car accident caused by the failure of traffic lights, even when the failure has been reported to the police. The fact that a police station had received the information about the traffic lights was not sufficient to impose on the police a duty of care to every motorist who might thereafter use the junction.[203]

Similarly, in *Ancell v McDermott*[204] the plaintiff's wife died when her car skidded on a patch of oil left by a previous accident. The police had been aware of the spillage almost immediately but had done nothing about it. The court held no duty of care was owed to road users in general to protect them from hazards created by third parties. Beldam LJ explained why in his view a duty of care should not be owed:

> Such a duty of care would impose upon a police force potential liability of almost unlimited scope. Not only would the class of persons to whom the duty was owed be extensive, but the activities of police officers which might give rise to the existence of such a duty would be widespread. The constable on the beat who failed to notice a danger on the pavement or noticed it but dismissed it as insufficiently serious to warrant his attention, the officer who searched for but failed to find property when he might have done or the officer who misinterpreted a breathalyser reading might all be said to come under liability to anyone who could show that they suffered injury or loss as a result of his failure.[205]

In *Alexandrou v Oxford*[206] the plaintiff sued the police for negligence after his shop was burgled and the stock stolen. There was an alarm connected to the police station which, when set off, activated a recorded 999 call. The police failed to take reasonable action on receipt of the call and, at first instance, the judge held that the plaintiff belonged to a group of people, namely those with intruder alarms, with whom the police had a special relationship, and that the police were negligent in not stopping the burglary. However, the Court of Appeal held that the relevant group of people with whom it should be considered whether there was a special relationship, was in fact all members of the public who give information of a suspected crime against themselves or their property. This group was too wide for there to be a special relationship and therefore there was no duty of care owed by the police to that group.[207]

203 *Clough v Bussan (West Yorkshire Police Authority, third party)* [1990] 1 All
      ER 431, QBD.
204 [1993] 4 All ER 355.
205 Ibid at 365.
206 [1993] 4 All ER 328, CA.
207 Ibid at 338 per Glidewell LJ.

The duty of care becomes even more difficult to establish when the way in which the police have investigated a case is challenged. There seems to be no duty of care to conduct an investigation expeditiously and efficiently owed to a civilian suspect by a police officer investigating a crime, nor owed by a police officer investigating a police disciplinary offence to the officer under investigation.[208]

In a case brought against West Yorkshire Police by the mother of the last victim of the 'Yorkshire Ripper', it was held that the police were not liable to the plaintiff for the failure of officers to apprehend the perpetrator of the offences which, it could be inferred, had been committed by the same man. The House of Lords gave two reasons for this decision. First, the class of people at risk (defined by Lord Keith as 'the female general public') was too wide for a special relationship to exist between that class and the police and therefore there was no duty of care owed by the police to the plaintiff's daughter. This was the case even though it was reasonably foreseeable that harm would be caused to a member of the public if the criminal was not caught. Second, it was held that, even if such a duty did exist, public policy required that the police should not be liable in such circumstances, as they had to be able perform their main function, the suppression of crime, without unnecessary distractions.[209]

Public policy and the duty of care
The 'public policy' defence has now been applied in a number of cases. Although in *Ancell* and *Alexandrou* (above) one reason for the court holding that no duty of care was owed to the plaintiff was the lack of sufficient proximity (see above p158), a 'public policy' defence was also upheld in both cases. *Ancell v McDermott* was a case involving general police duties (dealing with a road accident) rather than the investigation of crime. However, the Court of Appeal extended the public policy defence to this case also. It was held that the possibility of the police facing negligence claims of a potentially unlimited scope 'would . . . extensively hamper the performance of ordinary police duties and create a formidable diversion of police manpower' and this was a good public policy reason for holding that there was no duty of care.[210] In *Alexandrou v Oxford* it was said that it would not be in the public interest to impose such a duty on the police as it would not promote the obser-

208 *Calveley and Others v Chief Constable of Merseyside Police* [1989] 1 All ER 1025, HL.
209 *Hill v Chief Constable of West Yorkshire* [1989] AC 53, HL: see also *Rigby v Chief Constable of Northamptonshire* [1985] 2 All ER 985, QBD.
210 [1993] 4 All ER 355, CA, at 366 per Beldam LJ.

vance of a higher standard of care by the police.[211] The court gave no reasons for this assertion and, as the authors argue below (p163), it is at least possible that it is wrong.

In *Hughes v National Union of Mineworkers*[212] the court held that, as matter of public policy, senior police officers were not generally liable to individual officers if those officers were attacked during strike action by pickets. To hold that there was a duty of care in such circumstances would be detrimental to the control of public order if, in deciding what was an adequate force, a senior officer was in fear of a potential claim in negligence from a subordinate officer.

In *Osman v Ferguson*[213] 'public policy' was the only successful defence raised. The police had failed to arrest and charge a teacher against whom a number of very serious complaints had been made by a former pupil with whom the teacher was obsessed. Eventually the teacher shot and injured the pupil and killed his father. The deceased's family sued the police for negligence. The Court of Appeal held that, although the repeated complaints about the teacher may have been enough to create sufficient proximity for there to be a duty of care, public policy meant that a duty of care enforceable in the courts should not be placed on the police to prevent criminals causing damage to members of the public. Such a duty would not promote a higher standard in police work and would divert resources in defending such claims. The plaintiff argued that the public policy immunity defence should not apply to 'operational' decisions as opposed to 'policy' decisions, but the Court of Appeal considered that such a dividing line was 'utterly artificial and impossible to draw' and, in any event, the court was bound by the judgment in *Hill*, which had not made this distinction.[214]

These cases show that the courts will be extremely reluctant to hold the police liable in negligence for the way in which they handle case investigations and, most probably, for the way in which other duties are performed.[215] Even if there is foreseeability that the negligent act or omission would cause damage to the plaintiff and there is 'sufficient proximity' to establish a duty of care, any plaintiff will probably find a case being struck out as unarguable at an early stage of litigation for public policy reasons.[216] There had been an argument that the more

211 [1993] 4 All ER 328, CA at 340 per Glidewell LJ.
212 [1991] 4 All ER 278, QBD.
213 [1993] 4 All ER 344, CA.
214 *Osman v Ferguson* [1993] 4 All ER 344, CA at 353–354 per McCowan LJ.
215 See Greenfield et al, 'Police liability after Ancell', *SJ* 9 April 1993 p328.
216 The case of *Osman* has been ruled admissible by the European Commission of Human Rights.

'operational' a function is, the more susceptible it would be to a private law action in negligence. This was to be compared with policy decisions which involved the exercise of a discretion which would be actionable only if the police had acted *ultra vires*.[217] However, given the recent case law, it would seem that this distinction has become academic.

The courts argue that operational functions and investigations by the police will be more efficient without the threat of litigation if things go wrong and without the necessity to divert resources to defend cases when they arise. However, there is a counter argument that the police become more efficient, accountable and professional as a *result* of increased civil actions and the pressure of liability in negligence, and that this is exactly what has happened in countries like the United States where there has been an enormous growth in civil actions against the police in the last decade or so.[218]

Breach of the duty of care

Even if it is established that a duty of care is owed to the plaintiff, the nature of the activities of the police often mean that the standard of care expected is not high. For instance, when the police are driving, the danger and urgency of the driving will be taken into account when deciding what standard should be set and whether it has been breached. In *Rigby v Chief Constable of Northamptonshire*[219] the court accepted that in emergency situations a lower standard of care might apply.

There has often been difficulty in proving liability when the police have injured innocent people (sometimes using firearms) when apparently in the execution of their duty. A police officer in the execution of his duty may not:

> ignore entirely the safety of innocent persons, though he is apparently justified to resort to measures, even the use of firearms, which involve

217 See Brennan, 'Police negligence defined', *NLJ* 7 August 1992, p1118 and 14 August, p1169.

218 See, for instance, an article by the director of the US Institute for Liability Management: Gallagher, 'You too could be sued', *Policing* Vol 6 No 1 Spring 1990, 399. See also Her Majesty's Inspectors of Constabulary report on Merseyside Police, 1993, which reported that the force had launched a civil litigation strategy to raise operational standards in response to the growth in civil actions.

219 [1985] 2 All ER 985, 990.

220 Fleming *Law of Torts*, 8th edition 1992 p116–117.

some risk to bystanders but are no more than reasonably necessary to effect his purpose.[220]

Thus, a duty of care is owed to the person injured, but often there will not have been a breach of the standards expected by police officers if they have been 'in the execution of their duty'. The standard of care expected might involve the question of whether officers have been properly selected and trained (for instance, if the case involves firearms), and whether Home Office or force guidelines have been followed.[221]

The PACE Code of Practice C on the treatment of people in police custody covers such matters as the conditions of detention, the treatment of detained persons and medical treatment. While a breach of the code does not of itself render any individual officer liable to a separate civil action, it might be evidence of a lack of the standard that ought properly to be observed in order to discharge the duty of care.[222]

Death

Civil actions against the police arising out of a death are very rare. Although the number of deaths that occur while people are in police custody varies from about 40 to 80 a year, in most of these cases there is no suggestion of any misconduct on the part of the police.[223]

Apart from unlawful killing by police officers, there may be other situations, such as some deaths by poisoning by drugs or alcohol, where the police may have been negligent in the way they cared for the person, and so may be liable in a claim for damages.

Survival of cause of action

There are two matters to be considered if a person dies as a result of police misconduct. First, any cause of action that the deceased person would have had if s/he had not died survives the death and his/her estate is able to sue. Second, certain family members can sue for any

221 See Williams, 'Compensation for accidental shootings by police', *NLJ* 22 February 1991, p231.
222 PACE s67(10)–(11). Breach of the code is usually a disciplinary offence (see p323).
223 See annual reports of the Commissioner of the Police of the Metropolis and HM Inspectors of Constabulary.

loss they have suffered as a result of the death.[224] Under the Law Reform (Miscellaneous Provisions) Act 1934, the estate of a person whose death has been caused by a tortious act can bring proceedings against the wrongdoer, although the estate can neither claim exemplary damages[225] nor make a claim for defamation. Under the Act the estate can sue for reasonable funeral expenses, any special damages the person could have claimed, including loss of earnings from the date of the accident to the date of death, and general damages for pain, suffering and loss of amenity (unless the person died instantly).[226] No claim is available to the estate for the loss of potential income for the time after the person died.[227] Any claim under the 1934 Act is in addition to a claim under the Fatal Accidents Act 1976.

Fatal Accidents Act 1976

The Fatal Accidents Act 1976 allows dependants to claim for loss *they* have suffered against anyone who causes death by their wrongful act, neglect or default, provided the person who died could have made a claim if s/he had survived. In other words, the act, neglect or default must constitute a civil wrong: if the police would have had a good defence to the civil wrong, the dependants' claim for damages resulting from the death also fails.

Who can sue?

Most members of the family of the dead person can sue, including:

- spouse;
- parents or grandparents;
- children or grandchildren;
- siblings, uncles and aunts and all their descendants;
- common-law spouse of two years' standing (lesbian and gay relationships are therefore excluded);
- anyone treated as a child of the family following a marriage;
- anyone treated as a parent.

224 See, for instance, *Kirkham v Chief Constable of the Greater Manchester Police* [1990] 3 All ER 246, CA, where both procedures were pursued.
225 Administration of Justice Act 1982, s4(2), replacing s1(2)(a) of the 1934 Act.
226 Law Reform (Miscellaneous Provisions) Act 1934 s1.
227 Ibid s4(2)(a).

Wrongful act, neglect or default of the police
It has to be shown that the wrongful act, neglect or default of the police caused the death.[228] The problems involved in this where negligence or default are involved have already been considered (see above) and the same principles can be applied in cases involving death.

In some situations, it will be clear that the wrongful act of the police has caused death. Other situations will be less clear. For instance, if a suicide were induced by a wrongful act of the police, a claim can succeed even though the person who died took his/her own life.[229] But there must be a definite link between the wrongful act and the suicide, such as where the police negligently fail to carry out their responsibilities to a person who is known to be clinically depressed and who subsequently kills him/herself.[230] If the police have a good defence to the principal cause of action, eg negligence or assault, the claim for damages arising from the death will also fail.

Damages
Damages are awarded only for:

– bereavement; and
– the loss of reasonable expectation of financial benefit.

Damages for bereavement are a fixed amount, currently £7,500 for causes of action accruing on or after 1 April 1991.[231] They are awarded only to the spouse of the deceased or someone under the age of 18 who never married.

Damages for loss of reasonable expectation of financial benefit can include such things as loss of a parent's financial support, loss of a son's voluntary gifts during a period of employment[232] or loss of free services, where a wife who was killed acted as a housewife.[233] However, if the person who died earned his/her income from a life of crime, the dependants are not allowed to claim for loss of the benefits of crime.[234]

228 Fatal Accidents Act 1976 s1(1) (as amended).
229 *Pigney v Pointers Transport Services Ltd* [1957] 2 All ER 807; *Cavanagh v London Transport Executive* (1956) *Times* 23 October.
230 See, for instance, *Kirkham v Chief Constable of Greater Manchester Police* [1990] 3 All ER 246, CA.
231 Fatal Accidents Act 1976 s1A, inserted by the Administration of Justice Act 1982 s3 as amended by Damages for Bereavement (Variation of Sum) (England and Wales) Order 1990 SI No 2575.
232 *Hetherington v North-Eastern Railway* (1882) 9 QBD 160.
233 *Berry v Humm & Co* [1915] 1 KB 627.
234 *Burns v Edman* [1970] 2 QB 541.

Trespass to land

The right of individuals to be secure in their own homes and free from arbitrary searches is an ancient one that was guaranteed in a series of important constitutional cases in the eighteenth century.[235] Today these rights are principally protected by the law of trespass. Police officers commit trespass if, without permission or lawful authority, they enter or remain on land that the plaintiff possesses (ie, lawfully occupies or owns).

'Enters or remains'

Trespass can be committed by a police officer who merely walks onto land without permission. However, if there is a front garden and the gate is kept unlocked, the law implies that there is permission to walk up the garden path to the house in order to ask for permission.[236] There is no implied permission to do anything else,[237] for instance, to search the garden on the way to the front door. If the police are given permission to enter, then they have a licence to be on the land and are not trespassers. The person who gives the police the licence does not necessarily have to be the occupier, so long as it is someone who has the occupier's authority to do so. Once permission has been granted, it can be expressly revoked and if, after a reasonable interval, the police fail to leave, they become trespassers.[238]

There is no need to show that the police have used force in order to enter or remain, although, if they have done so, it is evidence that they did not have permission and is likely to affect the amount of damages. If the police are deceitful about their identity or the purpose for which they wish to enter, it is likely that they will be trespassers.[239]

If the police enter land with lawful authority (rather than merely with the occupier's consent), and then commit a trespass, either to the person or to goods, then it appears that this wrongdoing may nullify the lawful authority under which they first entered and make them trespassers from that initial moment of entry onwards.[240]

The police can be treated as 'entering' land if they have physical

---

235 *Entick v Carrington* (1765) 19 St Tr 1030; *Wilkes v Wood* (1765) 19 St Tr 1153.
236 *Robson v Hallett* [1967] 2 All ER 407 per Diplock J.
237 *Brunner v Williams* (1977) 73 LGR 266.
238 *Minister of Health v Bellotti* [1944] 1 All ER 238.
239 See Feldman, *The Law relating to Entry, Search and Seizure* (1986, Butterworths) para 2.09–2.10.
240 See *Six Carpenters' Case* (1610) 8 Co.Rep 146a, and Clayton and Tomlinson pp220–222 for a full discussion of this doctrine.

contact with the land, for instance, if a door or window is removed[241] or if a ladder is placed against a wall.[242] In such cases, there is no need to show that they came any further into the home. Additionally, causing a foreign matter to enter the land will be a trespass. This might include a police dog ordered to run on the land.[243]

The land possessed

'Land' has a special meaning. It can include the home and garden; it covers a flat as well as a house, regardless of whether the flat is on the ground floor or the twentieth floor. It also includes anything attached to the land or the structure of the home, such as a door or fitted cupboards. It includes the air-space which is required for the ordinary use of the land.[244]

The plaintiff must 'possess' the land. This is certainly the case if s/he owns the freehold or leasehold or is a tenant. The position of licencees, eg, a lodger, is less clear. It seems that a licensee can sue for trespass if s/he has a right of exclusive possession, for example, of his/her room (for instance, if s/he has the right to bar other people from the room).[245] There may also be difficulties if the person aggrieved lives with someone else who is the owner, for instance, a parent or partner. In such a case, s/he can probably sue if s/he has the owner's authority to exclude strangers. It is also possible that a squatter who has actual exclusive possession of land, but no legal estate or other right in it, may sue for trespass,[246] although the limits of such a principle have not been tested.

Defences to trespass

The police have wide powers to enter premises for specific purposes. These include power to enter to carry out an arrest and to conduct a search, either with or without a warrant.[247] It is not possible here to

241 *Lavender v Betts* [1942] 2 All ER 72.
242 *Westripp v Baldock* [1938] 2 All ER 779; [1939] 1 All ER 279, CA.
243 *Beckwith v Shordike* (1767) 4 Burr 2092.
244 *Kelsen v Imperial Tobacco Co of Great Britain* [1957] 2 QB 334. 'However, flights which interfere with the use and enjoyment of the land beneath, for example by polluting the air, causing excessive noise or vibration, or harassing the occupier by persistent surveillance, may constitute actionable nuisance': Fleming, *The law of torts*, 8th edition 1992, pp46–47.
245 See Street on Torts 9th edition 1993 p74; Fleming *The law of torts* 8th edition 1992 pp43–44.
246 Street supra p75.
247 PACE Pts I and III.

describe them (there are well over 70). However, the important principle is that there are limits to all these powers. So, for example, although the police have power to enter premises to execute a warrant for a person's arrest, they can do so only if they have reasonable grounds for believing him/her to be on the premises.[248] If they do not have reasonable grounds, the entry is unlawful and they can be sued for trespass. If the police do not have a warrant, they can enter premises to arrest someone unlawfully at large, but only if they are actually in pursuit of the person at the time.[249] Likewise if the police obtain a warrant to search premises, they must comply with the provisions of the warrant and the limits set down by statute (for instance, PACE ss15 and 16).[250]

If the police have power to enter in a particular case, they also have power to use reasonable force, if necessary.[251] Obviously, force is not necessary if the occupier would have agreed to the police entering his/her home if given the opportunity. For instance, if a person hears his/her doorbell ring and as s/he goes to answer it, the door is kicked in and a number of police officers with a search warrant enter, s/he has a good claim for trespass because s/he was not given the opportunity to consent.[252]

Mistake is no defence to trespass. The police cannot claim that they are not liable in trespass merely because they intended to enter another person's land, for which they had, for instance, a valid search warrant, but, in fact, entered the plaintiff's land.[253] If, through negligence, the police unintentionally enter a person's land, this is probably also a trespass.[254]

On an increasing number of occasions the police have hired video companies to film a search or invited the media to accompany them on a 'raid'. Such people will not be covered by any search warrant and their presence, without consent, on a person's property would be a trespass.

248 Ibid s17(1) and (2).
249 Ibid s17(1)(d) and *D'Souza v DPP* [1992] 1 WLR 1023, HL.
250 See for instance *R v Reading JJ and Others ex p South West Meats* (1991) *Independent* 13 December, DC and Lexis.
251 PACE s117. See also p64 (chapter 3) on forcible entry techniques.
252 See Report to Police Complaints Board on inquiry by Deputy Commissioner Dear into police operations in Railton Road, Brixton on Wednesday 15 July 1981. Summary of events and main conclusions referred to in Christian *Policing by Coercion* 1983, GLC.
253 *Basely v Clarkson* (1681) 3 Lev 37.
254 *League Against Cruel Sports Ltd v Scott* [1986] QB 240.

Damages

As with false imprisonment and assault, in theory a person can sue for trespass without showing any actual loss,[255] although s/he may receive only nominal damages, see p192. The manner and violence the police use to enter the property is relevant to the level of damages,[256] and may justify awards of aggravated or exemplary damages (see p194). In *R v Reading JJ ex p South West Meats Ltd*[257] (see p172 below) exemplary damages of £22,000 were awarded in addition to compensatory damages of £3,000 for a trespass to land and goods following the unlawful exercise of a search warrant. Special damages are payable to compensate for anything broken or damaged.

Seizure of goods

If the police unlawfully seize something that belongs to a person, for example, while searching him/her in the street or searching his/her home, that person can claim damages and the recovery of the goods. Technically, the claim may be for 'trespass to goods' or 'conversion'. If the person simply wants the goods back, and is not concerned about claiming damages, s/he may apply to recover the property in the magistrates' court under the Police (Property) Act 1897 procedure (see p311).

There is a considerable overlap between trespass to goods and conversion. In many cases, it may be possible to sue either for one or the other or both. However, a claim in conversion is appropriate in order to assert the right to the physical possession of something and in trespass to goods to assert the right to its physical condition. Conversion should therefore be used if the police have seized something and its return is required, and trespass to goods should be used if something has been damaged or altered. The difference between conversion and trespass to goods becomes important in assessing damages (see p175).

Defences to seizure

The police have many powers under various statutes to seize a wide range of specific items or types of evidence of particular offences.[258] In addition, under PACE, they have general powers of seizure in certain

---

255 *Armstrong v Sheppard & Short Ltd* [1959] 2 All ER 651, CA.
256 *Huxley v Berg* (1815) 1 Stark 98.
257 (1992) 4 Admin LR 401, (1991) *Independent* 13 December and Lexis.
258 Coveniently listed in Levenson and Fairweather, *Police Powers* (LAG).

circumstances either with or without a warrant.[259] Under the Act, items that are subject to legal privilege, eg, a solicitor's letter giving legal advice, cannot be seized.[260] Although the powers of seizure are wide, the limits are strict. If the police exceed their powers, the seizure becomes unlawful. So, for example, the police cannot go on 'fishing expeditions' in the hope that something incriminating will turn up. If they seize a large number of documents, they must therefore consider whether each file, book, bundle or separate document is covered by a power of seizure.[261]

The most common defence to a claim will be based on the general statutory power of seizure. This arises where an officer is lawfully[262] on the premises and has reasonable grounds for believing that something has been obtained in consequence of the commission of an offence, or is evidence in relation to any offence, *and*, in either case, it is necessary to seize it in order to prevent its being concealed, lost, altered or destroyed.[263] The police could therefore enter a home on a search warrant for, say, cannabis and instead lawfully seize goods they reasonable suspect to be stolen.

Once something has been lawfully seized, the police are entitled to retain it for as long as is necessary in all the circumstances.[264] Anything seized for the purposes of a criminal investigation can be retained for use as evidence in a trial or for investigation or forensic examination.[265] However, if there is no statutory power to retain it once a person has been convicted, it must be returned to the owner, even if money seized is the result of an illegal contract which formed the basis of the criminal charges.[266] Nor are the police entitled to an order to retain the money on public policy grounds under the Police (Property) Act 1897[267] (see p311).

However, the police should return the original if a photograph or copy would be sufficient.[268] They can also retain anything in order to

259 PACE Pt I.
260 Ibid ss8(1)(d), 9(2)(a), 10, 18(1) and 19(6).
261 *Reynolds v Commissioner of Police of the Metropolis* [1984] 3 All ER 649.
262 It is unclear whether an officer has common law powers of seizure if unlawfully on the premises: see PACE s19(5). Cf *Ghani v Jones* [1969] 3 All ER 1700.
263 PACE s19(1), (2), (3).
264 Ibid s22(1).
265 Ibid s22(2)(a).
266 See, for example, the powers under the Police (Disposal of Sound Equipment) Regulations 1995 SI No 722; and *Chief Constable of West Midlands Police v White* (1992) *Times* 25 March, CA.
267 *Chief Constable of West Midlands Police v White* (above).
268 PACE s22(4).

establish its lawful owner.[269] They cannot retain property solely in anticipation of a court order making a compensation, forfeiture or restitution order against a person if s/he is later convicted of an offence.[270]

The case of *R v Reading JJ ex p South West Meats Ltd*[271] illustrates ways in which the police can exceed or abuse their powers of search and seizure, even with a warrant, and become liable to pay substantial sums in damages as a result. In this case the police sought a search warrant to search the premises of a company after receiving information from a government agency about possible theft charges. The search warrant was granted by the magistrates' court after an officer swore on oath that, pursuant to PACE s8, the documentation required was relevant evidence, did not consist of or include items subject to legal privilege, and that the purpose of the search might be frustrated or seriously prejudiced unless an officer arriving at the premises could secure immediate entry to them. The warrant was granted, but when it was executed the police did not take part in the search but allowed employees of the government agency to carry it out. A large amount of material was taken away, including information covered by legal privilege. A senior executive of the company sought access to some of the material but this was denied, not by the police, but by the government agency who held the documentation. The court found that:

a) There had been no basis for the statement to the magistrates by the police that the purpose of the search might be frustrated without a warrant for immediate entry.

b) The police had allowed the government agency to remove and retain documents that only the police had powers to remove and retain under PACE s16.

c) Large quantities of documents were removed from the premises which obviously did not fall within the terms of the warrant, contrary to PACE s8(2), including a file whose contents were the subject of legal privilege.

d) The delay in allowing the company access to the documents and in returning the documents was far greater than was necessary and in breach of PACE s21.

The court found that the seizure and retention of the documents amounted to trespass and that 'the exercise from start to finish was

269 PACE s22(2)(b).
270 *Malone v Commissioner of Police of the Metropolis* [1979] 1 All ER 256.
271 (1992) 4 Admin LR 401, (1991) *Independent* 13 December, and Lexis.

unlawful'. Although the police could rely on Constables Protection Act 1750 s6[272] in relation to any technical breaches in the granting of the warrant, this did not cover the police where they acted outside the terms of the warrant and statute. The court found that the breaches had been 'a deplorable abuse of power by public officials' and awarded £22,000 exemplary damages in respect of the oppressive, arbitrary, and unconstitutional conduct of the police.

If the police do seize documents while unlawfully executing a warrant, they have no right to retain them and must return them.[273]

In *R v Central Criminal Court ex p AJD Holdings*[274] the court recommended that careful consideration should be given, before applying for a search warrant, to what material it is hoped a search will reveal. Once the warrant was obtained, the officers carrying out the search should be carefully chosen and properly briefed. This advice was given because a breach of the stringent rules in PACE ss15 and 16, albeit the result of an honest mistake, could render the whole execution of the warrant unlawful.

If something is taken from a person while in police custody or detention, on the ground that it might be used for one of the following:

– to cause physical injury to someone;
– to damage property;
– to interfere with evidence;
– to assist an escape,

then it should be returned to him/her on release.[275] If it is not returned, the police can be sued in conversion.

Remedies

In theory, if the police have wrongfully taken goods out of a person's possession, s/he can lawfully resist the seizure and take them back again and can use reasonable force against anyone who resists him/her.[276] In

272 'No action shall be brought against any constable . . . or against any person or persons acting by his order and in his aid, for anything done in obedience to any warrant under the hand or seal of any justice of the peace until demand has been made . . . by the party. . . intending to bring such action.'
273 *R v Chief Constable of Lancashire Constabulary ex p Parker* [1993] 2 All ER 56.
274 (1992) *Times* 24 February.
275 PACE s22(3).
276 *Blades v Higgs* (1861) 10 CB (NS) 713.

practice, however, this right is principally relevant as a defence to, eg, assault or obstruction, rather than as a 'remedy' which could ever be prudently recommended, as there is almost certain to be legal argument about whether the police were entitled to seize the goods. If it turns out they were acting lawfully, the person might be guilty of a number of criminal offences, including assault and obstructing the police in the course of their duty.

The legality of seizure should therefore be tested by an action for damages, or for an order for the return of the property, or both.[277] This is explained in detail at pp311–315.

If the police lawfully seize items, they must supply a record of everything they have taken within a reasonable time of being asked for such a record.[278] They can be asked for the list at the time the items are taken or at any later time. A person can also ask for access to anything that has been seized, for example, so that s/he can inspect it, or for anything that has been seized to be photographed or copied, provided that this would not prejudice police investigations or any later trial.[279]

If documents are unlawfully seized, in addition to suing for their return, it is thought that the owner is entitled to receive any copies that have been made[280] but not to an injunction preventing the use of any information gleaned from them.[281]

Damages

If damages only are sought (and not the return of the property), at least the value of the goods at the time they were seized can be expected. However, compensation can also be awarded for the loss of use of something that is seized. For example, if the police seized a person's car, s/he could recover damages for the loss of its use while in their possession.

If the action is in trespass to goods, the plaintiff is entitled to at least

---

277 Torts (Interference with Goods) Act 1977 s3.
278 PACE s21(1), (2) and Code B para 6.8.
279 PACE s21(3), (4), (6), (8) and Code B para 6.9; see also *Arias v Commissioner of Police of the Metropolis* (1984) *Times* 1 August for the common law right to require the police to deliver up copies of documents that have been lawfully seized.
280 Byatt, 'Seizure and privilege: the solicitor's Hobson's choice' (1984) 81 LS Gaz 1973.
281 *Frank Truman Export Ltd v Metropolitan Police Commissioner* [1977] 3 All ER 431 at 436j.

nominal damages, even if s/he cannot show any real loss[282] (see p192) and, in appropriate cases, there may also be an award of aggravated and exemplary damages[283] (see p194). If the action is in conversion, the claim will fail if actual loss cannot be shown; it is uncertain whether the plaintiff can be awarded aggravated or exemplary damages.

Damage to goods

If the police damage or destroy belongings, for example, while searching a home, there may be a claim for damages. Technically, the claim might be for 'trespass to goods' or 'negligence', although in most cases it is probably simpler to rely only on negligence. The cause of action need not be pleaded, as trespass to goods tends to be more difficult to establish. For example, it has to be shown that the police deliberately damaged something, say, by forcing the locks on drawers. In negligence, however, it has to be shown only that property was damaged through carelessness, for example, where something is accidentally knocked over or scratched.

Defences

As has already been seen, where the police have a power which can be exercised without consent, they can also use reasonable force if necessary to exercise the power.[284] If they have power to search a home, they would also have power to break into a locked cabinet in order to search inside it, if this were both necessary and reasonable. However, this defence could be defeated if, for example, it could be shown that the plaintiff offered to unlock the cabinet, as the use of force would then be unnecessary (and unreasonable).

Damages

If the police damage goods, their owner is entitled to the cost of repair.[285] If the goods are destroyed or damaged beyond repair, or if it would be uneconomic to repair them, then their owner is entitled to the value of their replacement. In addition to damages for repair or replacement, a claim can also be made for the loss of the use of an

---

282 *William Leitch & Co v Leydon* [1931] AC 90 at 106. See, however, Winfield and Jolowicz on Torts 1994 edn pp487–8.
283 *Sears v Lyons* (1818) 2 Stark 317; *Rookes v Barnard* [1964] AC 1129.
284 PACE s117.
285 *The Bernina* (1886) 55 LT 781.

article, eg, if a television is damaged, compensation for the loss of enjoyment while it was repaired or replaced can be claimed.

If the action is in negligence, the claim will fail if actual loss cannot be shown and, it seems, the plaintiff probably cannot be awarded aggravated or exemplary damages.[286]

Misfeasance in public office

Street on Torts describes the tort of misfeasance in public office as 'embryonic' in English law, despite the fact that the leading recent judicial analysis of the tort traces cases back to the eighteenth century.[287] It is true that the tort has not been greatly used and there are no reported cases concerning a successful action against the police. Street goes on to describe misfeasance in public office as follows:

> Where an individual suffers loss or damage consequent upon administrative action which the relevant officer knows to be unlawful that loss or damage is recoverable in tort.[288]

A police officer would qualify as 'the relevant officer' in this definition. It is necessary that damage is caused, as the tort is not actionable without loss (unlike, for instance, false imprisonment or assault). Malice is not an essential ingredient of the tort. It is enough that the defendant knew that the act complained of was unlawful and knew that the act could, and subsequently did, cause loss or damage to the plaintiff.[289] Clayton and Tomlinson argue that a lawful exercise of powers for an improper (ie malicious) motive would also make an officer liable.[290]

In *R v Deputy Governor of Parkhurst Prison ex p Hague*, Lord Bridge said that a prison officer who acts in bad faith by deliberately subjecting a prisoner to a restraint which he knows he has no authority to impose, commits the tort of misfeasance in public office.[291] In *Racz v Home Office*,[292] a case where a prisoner claimed he had been mistreated by prison officers, the Home Office attempted to strike out a claim for misfeasance in public office. It was argued that as the tort necessarily

286 *Cassell & Co Ltd v Broome* [1972] 1 All ER 801 at 828, HL.
287 *Bourgoin SA v Ministry of Agriculture, Fisheries and Food* [1986] 1 QB 716.
288 Street on Torts, Butterworths, 9th edition 1993, p481.
289 *Bourgoin* (above).
290 *Civil Actions against the Police*, 1992, p371.
291 [1992] 1 AC 58 at 164, HL.
292 [1994] 2 WLR 23, HL.

involved officers acting outside their lawful authority, the Home Office, as their employers, could not be vicariously liable for their actions. The House of Lords refused to strike out the claim for misfeasance in public office, holding that it was a matter of fact and degree whether the actions of the prison officers were such as to divest the Home Office of vicarious liability, and this could only be decided at trial.[293]

Many of the situations where it could be said that a police officer is liable for this tort, for instance, unlawful arrest, are covered by other causes of action described in this book (for instance, false imprisonment). If plaintiffs find it impossible to prove all the necessary elements of a more conventional tort such as malicious prosecution or false imprisonment, the courts are not likely to allow instead a claim for misfeasance in public office, which is perhaps better viewed as a residuary cause of action offering protection against executive injustice, applicable where other, more common, causes of action do not apply.[294]

In one case a county court judge refused to strike out a claim against the police for misfeasance in public office where the plaintiff's case was that an officer had refused to intervene to prevent an attack on the plaintiff.[295] The tort may also be available in situations, like *Racz v Home Office*, where a prisoner in lawful custody has been mistreated in breach of prison rules or PACE.

Other causes of action

This section explores some of the torts less frequently used in civil actions against the police, and some torts whose extent is uncertain but which may be extremely useful in the right situations. The causes of action outlined are:

– causing nervous shock;
– harassment and intimidation;
– unlawful strip searches.

Causing nervous shock

There are situations where there is no physical force used, nor threat of physical force nor detention, but where the law provides a remedy for personal injury. The Law Commission has said that there:

293 Ibid at 26–27 per Lord Jauncey.
294 See *McDonagh v Metropolitan Police Commissioner* (1989) *Times* 28 December.
295 *Gray v Metropolitan Police Commissioner* (1991) 1 March unreported, cited in Clayton and Tomlinson op cit 1992 p374.

is probably authority for the proposition that intentional or reckless conduct aimed at the plaintiff and resulting in personal injury can found an action in tort, even though the 'indirectness' of the harm means that there is no action for trespass to the person.[296]

This forms a cause of action in its own right rather than the head of damage known as nervous shock which is recoverable in some cases.[297]

There are situations where a plaintiff will be deliberately and falsely told something that will cause him/her 'physical harm', whether psychiatric illness or otherwise. In a non-police case, *Wilkinson v Downton*,[298] the plaintiff was informed, as a practical joke, that her husband had been badly injured in a road accident. The effect of this news was 'a violent shock to the nervous system producing vomiting and other more serious and permanent physical consequences, at one time threatening her reason and entailing weeks of suffering and incapacity'.[299] She was able to recover damages for the physical harm caused by the defendant's wilful act. It did not matter that the defendant had not intended his comments to be taken seriously, but it is clear that there must be some physical effect of the shock (rather than the shock itself) before a case is actionable. The judge held:

> The defendant has willingly done an act calculated to cause harm to the plaintiff – that is to say, to infringe her legal right to personal safety, and has in fact caused physical harm to her. That proposition without more appears to me to state a good cause of action, there being no justification for the act.

Thus, if a police officer had made a similar claim, or, for instance, had told someone, wrongly and with the intention to cause harm, that a friend or relative had been arrested, and damage had been caused then the person would have a claim against the police. Likewise, if a person in detention was told, say, that an accident had happened to a relative, then there would be a claim in tort if physical harm resulted to the arrested person. In *Janvier v Sweeny*[300] a man called at a woman's house and told her (falsely as it transpired) that he was a detective inspector from Scotland Yard and that she was wanted for corresponding with a German spy. The woman suffered a severe nervous shock and a long period of illness as a result and was able to recover damages despite there being no assault, battery or arrest.

296 Law Commission, *Liability for psychiatric illness*, HMSO 1995 pp2–3.
297 See for instance, *Alcock v Chief Constable of South Yorkshire* [1991] 3 WLR 1057, HL. (See p134.)
298 [1897] 2 QB 57.
299 Ibid per Wright J.
300 [1919] 2 KB 316.

'Harassment' and intimidation

In a family law case the Court of Appeal has held that harassment that does not include the use or threat of force is actionable, under the rule in *Wilkinson v Downton*, where the harassment reaches such a level that impairment of health is caused.[301] Street on Torts states that 'the potential development of a tort of "personal injury by molestation" offers enhanced protection to a range of otherwise remediless victims'.[302] Such victims could include those who are continually harassed on the streets by police officers by acts, such as abusive language, which fell short of lawful, or unlawful, stop and searches, for instance.

In *Khorasandjian v Bush*[303] the Court of Appeal upheld a county court injunction which restrained the defendant from 'harassing' the plaintiff. The case involved an ex-boyfriend who pestered the plaintiff and made unwanted telephone calls. The court held that oral harassment which could not be strictly classified as a threat was actionable in tort if it caused physical or psychiatric illness to the recipient. Some commentators have described the judgment as creating a new tort of harassment,[304] although it is more likely that the court was extending the tort of private nuisance to include protection from harassment.[305]

In *Godwin v Uzoigwe*[306] the Court of Appeal held that a person subjected to intentional unlawful coercion has a cause of action in the tort of intimidation. It is suggested that the tort of intimidation could have applicability in actions against the police where, for instance, the police have used threats to force a person to make a false confession. There is much anecdotal evidence, for example, of police officers threatening alleged prostitutes with action by social services departments to take their children into care unless they confess to charges of soliciting. Similarly, there are allegations that police routinely threaten to expose gay men's sexuality to family or employers unless they confess to importuning charges.[307]

301 *Burnett v George* [1992] 1 FLR 525, CA.
302 9th edition 1993 p31.
303 [1993] 3 WLR 476, CA.
304 Murphy, 'The emergence of harassment as a recognised tort' *NLJ* 25 June 1993; see also HH Judge Fricker, 'Harassment as a Tort' (1992) NLJ 247.
305 Noble, 'Harassment – a recognised tort?' *NLJ* 26 November 1993, p1685.
306 (1992) *Times* 18 June.
307 See, for instance, Baldwin, 'Getting the record straight', *LS Gaz* 3 February 1993 p28; and Baldwin, 'Power and police interviews' *NLJ* 13 August 1993 p1194.

Unlawful strip searches

In the county court case *Bayliss v Secretary of State for the Home Department*[308] visitors to a prison inmate were told they would not be allowed to visit unless they submitted to a strip search. They had to remove their clothes in a side room, each supervised by a prison officer of the same sex. Officers and members of the public passing by were able to see into the room where the search was taking place. Both the plaintiffs were upset by the experience and one suffered symptoms of post-traumatic stress disorder. At trial they were awarded a total of £18,000 between them. It would have been very difficult to prove that the searches were, in themselves, unlawful, given the wide discretion under the prison rules for prison officers to search visitors. However, the judge held that the power to search was subject to an implied limitation that the search must be seemly, and the jury in the case held that the search had been unseemly because of the manner in which it was conducted.

As there had been no false imprisonment, assault or battery involved in the 'unseemly' search, the judge identified a new tort described as 'unlawfully inducing a person to remove their clothes' to avoid the situation where the plaintiffs would have had no private law remedy for the unlawful search. The case was not appealed by the Home Secretary. The plaintiff's lawyers have argued that:

> Although the police have more limited powers of search than prison officers, before this decision it was unclear whether an unlawful search gave rise to a tort and therefore a remedy in damages, unless there was non-consensual touching and therefore an assault. Now the victim could argue that there was a trespass to his or her person on the basis that s/he had been unlawfully induced to remove his or her clothes.[309]

Although no cases against the police based on this cause of action have come to court, the authors understand that a number of cases where the tort has been pleaded have settled with damages being paid to the plaintiff by the police.

---

308 February 1993 *Legal Action* 16.
309 Williams and Deighton, 'Unlawful strip-searching', (1993) SJ 23 April p377. This article also contains the facts relied on here. For arguments that the new tort may be unnecessary, see Clayton and Tomlinson, 'Civil actions against the police' October 1993 *Legal Action* 15, and Tregilas-Davey, 'Unnecessary invention' *LS Gaz* 2 June 1993 p17; and further comment in support of the need for the tort on *Legal Action* letters page December 1993 p24.

CHAPTER 6

Suing the police: pre-action considerations

Bringing a civil action against the police is a specialist area of the law and needs to be done by lawyers who are aware of the special considerations in these cases described in this and the next two chapters. Lawyers who are involved in this area of work need to be especially sensitive to the needs of their clients, who will often have had their confidence in 'authority' and 'the establishment' badly shaken by their experiences. More so than in other casework areas it is essential that a plaintiff should not feel that he or she has handed over control of the case to a professional who is remote and unapproachable and who conducts the case in a way that ignores the plaintiff's ultimate objectives.

This chapter describes the main strategic and procedural issues that the lawyer and client need to consider before proceedings are issued:

– how to arrange for the transfer of legal aid from a solicitor with whom the plaintiff may be dissatisfied;
– the various ways of financing an action;
– the inherent delays in any civil action, how these affect police actions and why they need to be explained to the plaintiff at the outset;
– an outline of damages, including exemplary and aggravated damages, to help practitioners advise clients and the Legal Aid Board on quantum;
– publicity for the case;
– the relationship between a complaint and a civil action against the police;
– suing after the plaintiff has been convicted;
– the role of the jury; and
– the contents of the letter before action.

Change of solicitors

Plaintiffs have traditionally found it difficult to find solicitors prepared to handle a case against the police or capable of handling it proficiently. Some solicitors feel it is not quite proper to be seen 'attacking' the police, or, especially in small communities, may find it socially embarrassing. However, there is a growing number of firms which specialise in civil actions against the police, and some criminal solicitors who also deal efficiently with a number of cases which arise out of their criminal practice. Liberty (NCCL) and some law centres also bring cases. Liberty normally only brings test cases in the hope of establishing new points of law, so the number of cases it handles is small, although it has recently embarked on a *pro bono* programme. Those law centres that undertake this kind of work (by no means all of them) will usually only act for people living or working in their catchment area.

Given the limited number of solicitors with the necessary skills and enthusiasm to bring a civil action against the police, it is not unusual for a potential plaintiff to find him/herself with legal advice that s/he finds unsatisfactory, and to wish to change solicitors. There is a general principle that a person can dismiss their solicitor at any time[1] and appoint another solicitor of his/her choice.[2] If a client feels that a different solicitor from the one that acted in an associated criminal trial is desirable, it is obviously best to make the change before the original solicitor starts the civil case. This kind of change is quite straightforward: the only disadvantage to the client is that the papers concerning the criminal trial will have to be obtained from the first solicitor before advising about the merits of the civil case. Changing solicitors is more difficult if the first firm has started off the civil case with the benefit of legal aid. The Legal Aid Board will have to be convinced that the client should be allowed to transfer legal aid to the new firm and this can be difficult if the original firm proves uncooperative. Clearly the new firm will not be paid under the legal aid scheme until legal aid has been transferred, and it may be difficult for it to advise the client under the green form scheme as it is likely that the original solicitor will already have advised the client under the scheme.

Suing after a criminal trial

Those with a grievance against the police will commonly have been charged with offences themselves. It will usually be wise to wait and see

1 *Court v Berlin* [1897] 2 QB 396 at 400–401.
2 *Watts v Official Solicitor* [1936] 1 All ER 249, CA.

how the criminal trial turns out before making a final decision whether to sue the police, provided limitation peroids allow (see p189). The plaintiff's lawyers will want to see whether new facts emerge at the criminal trial of which the plaintiff is unaware or about which the plaintiff has been unforthcoming. Furthermore, if the police know a civil action might follow, they may fight the criminal trial particularly aggressively. As described earlier (see p150), in claims for malicious prosecution it must be shown that the criminal case ended in favour of the accused plaintiff. In other actions an acquittal may, in practive, very much strengthen a civil case. Detailed research in the USA has shown that civil actions against the police are much less likely to succeed if the court believes that the plaintiff has a 'criminal life-style'.[3] It also seems that even if such cases are successful, damages awards are likely to be lower: either juries feel such people are less 'deserving' or that their evidence is less convincing.

However, there is no general rule that the police cannot be sued for something that arose out of an incident which led to a conviction. A common example is where someone has been arrested for an offence which they committed but the police have used an unreasonable degree of force in making the arrest. S/he has a good case for a claim of assault. This may be the case even though the plaintiff has been convicted of a crime of violence arising out of the same incident: the conviction does not necessarily mean that the police did not assault the plaintiff as claimed.[4] A person who pleads guilty to an offence can still claim for false imprisonment if the requirements of the Police and Criminal Evidence Act 1984 have not been complied with during the arrest and subsequent detention. The claim cannot be struck out simply on the ground that the person had indeed committed the offence for which s/he was arrested since the bare fact of a conviction is not enough to establish that the arrest and detention was necessarily lawful.[5]

In some circumstances a plaintiff will wish to prove that, although s/he was convicted of an offence, s/he did not in fact commit it. Rules of court prescribe the formalities to be followed when attempting to show that a conviction was wrong. If, for instance, the police plead in their defence the fact that the plaintiff has been convicted of an offence, then it is possible for the plaintiff to disprove the offence on the balance of

3 See Cragg, 'Police misconduct litigation in the USA' *LS Gazette* 17 June 1987, p1800.
4 *Simpson v Chief Constable of Yorkshire Police* (1991) *Independent* 14 March; (1991) *Times* 7 March.
5 *Hill v Chief Constable of Yorkshire Police* [1990] 1 All ER 1046, CA.

probabilities in a subsequent civil action.[6] Problems arise, however, if the main purpose of bringing the civil case is to mount a collateral attack on the criminal conviction. In 1981 the House of Lords decided the case of *Hunter v Chief Constable of West Midlands Police*,[7] in which the Birmingham Six sued the police for assault. Their convictions for the 1974 Birmingham pub bombing were obtained almost wholly on the basis of alleged confessions which it was claimed had been induced by a beating from the police. The House of Lords ruled that it would be an abuse of the process of the court to allow a claim where the dominant purpose of the action was not to recover damages, but to establish that the conviction was induced by police violence, and where this issue had already been finally decided in favour of the police (or so it seemed at the time) by another court of competent jurisdiction. Consequently the case was struck out. The House of Lords did say that a civil action would be allowed to proceed where fresh evidence was obtained since the criminal trial which 'entirely changes the aspect of the case'. However, it held that evidence that was available, or could have been obtained with reasonable diligence at the time of the criminal trial was not 'fresh evidence'. The test of evidence that 'entirely changes the aspect of the case' imposes a deliberately high standard that in many cases will be difficult to meet.

A subsequent attempt to extend the principles in *Hunter* to strike out elements of the defence in a civil action against police failed.[8] It was argued that as the plaintiff had been acquitted of causing a breach of the peace, it was not open to the police to argue that his arrest had been lawful. However, the Court of Appeal held that the acquittal may have been because the magistrates had not been satisfied of the breach of the peace to the criminal standard of proof, which was a higher standard than that required in the civil action, and therefore the pleadings were allowed to stand.

Suing after accepting a caution

Clients are sometimes released from a police station after being cautioned for the behaviour for which they have been arrested. Accepting a caution usually involves accepting responsibility for the offence which lead to the arrest, and it may prove difficult subsequently to rebut a

6 See Civil Evidence Act 1968 s11(2)(a) and RSC Order 18 r7A(3).
7 [1982] AC 529.
8 *Nawrot v Chief Constable of Hampshire Police* (1992) *Independent* 7 January.

defence that an arrest was not based on reasonable suspicion. However, people sometimes accept cautions at the police station because they are desperate to leave a hostile environment, or because the police have told them that a charge will be made if the caution is not accepted. While clearly the police will make as much as possible in civil proceedings of the acceptance of the caution, it is submitted that the circumstances in which it was accepted will be relevant to the question of whether it truly represents an admission of guilt.

Financing the case

Legal aid

The types of action described in chapter 5 are all within the scope of the civil legal aid scheme. The fact that criminal legal aid was obtained for the criminal trial does not, of course, mean that civil legal aid will automatically be granted for a damages claim against the police. With the growth of civil actions against the police the Legal Aid Board has become increasingly familiar with this kind of case and often uses a standard form of words in granting legal aid to cover assault, false imprisonment and malicious prosecution.

Advice and assistance under the green form scheme, if the complainant is eligible, can be used to make an application for legal aid. The two hours' worth of work initially available under the scheme to take details and advise can usually be extended by another two hours to make the application. In a straightforward case it may take the board four to six weeks to decide on the application, but it can be quicker where the applicant is on income support (and can quote their income support reference number). However, a delay of several months is not unknown and if there is any problem with limitation periods (see below p189), then an emergency legal aid application should be considered.

To obtain legal aid an applicant must qualify on financial grounds. The Legal Aid Board looks at the applicant's income, capital and financial commitments. For all but the very poor there is likely to be a stiff contribution to pay monthly from income or in a lump sum from capital. Since April 1993 any monthly contribution from income is payable throughout the life of the case.

As well as the means test there are two further hurdles to be cleared before civil legal aid can be granted. First, the applicant must show that there is an issue of fact or law which it is reasonable to submit to the court for decision and that s/he has a reasonably strong case. This is known as the legal merits test.[9] Second, even when the applicant has satisfied the legal merits test, legal aid can be withheld if it appears to the Board that in the particular circumstances of the case it is unreasonable that the applicant should receive legal aid.[10] Examples of where it may be unreasonable to grant legal aid are cited in the *Legal Aid Handbook's* Notes for Guidance. Those which may be relevant in civil actions against the police include cases where the claim is small, and where the estimated costs of proceedings are likely to outweigh the benefit to the client. In practice, legal aid will usually not be granted if the claim is worth less than £1,000 unless there is some special feature to justify it. Therefore, in smaller cases it will be worthwhile when applying for legal aid to note the probability of aggravated and exemplary damages (see below) to enhance the value of the case and to note that the amount of damages is largely left up to a jury, which makes assessing quantum difficult.[11] Additionally, as suing the police is expensive and costs might outweigh the *financial* benefit to the client, it is essential to emphasise the other benefits that will accrue to the client through winning the case (clearing his/her name, obtaining justice, making the police accountable, challenging a common but improper practice or procedure, etc) in the legal aid application.

There are specific problems which arise with legal aid applications when judicial review of the PCA is considered and these are described at p302.

Even where legal aid is granted, there may be a limit placed on how far the case can be taken before the Legal Aid Board will want to review it. A common limitation is for legal aid to be initially granted only for a barrister's opinion on merits and quantum. This written opinion will be sent to the Legal Aid Board, who will then decide whether to continue to fund the action. Often the Board will want counsel to give another opinion before sanctioning legal aid to cover the hearing, as this is the most expensive part of the case.

Refusal or non-availability of legal aid

If legal aid is refused, the refusal letter from the Board will briefly explain the reasons. There is a right of appeal against refusal in many

---

9 See Legal Aid Act 1988 s15(2).
10 Legal Aid Act 1988 s15(3)(a).
11 In fact, claims of false imprisonment of an hour (or maybe less) should pass the £1,000 threshold at 1995 levels (see p147 for some possible quantum figures for false imprisonment).

cases, although legal aid does not cover the appeal procedure. If the case has merit and legal aid was refused only on financial grounds, then it may be worthwhile exploring other options:

- Will a trade union or other organisation pay?
- Can the individual pay for the case with his/her own money?
- Are there lawyers prepared to act without charge?
- Could a claim be made under the criminal injuries compensation scheme (see p307)?
- Could an *ex gratia* payment from the Home Office be claimed (see p273)?

Funding by trade unions and other organisations
Some trade unions will pay the legal costs of bringing a case against the police. This is especially likely if the incident arose out of a trade union activity, such as picketing. Other trade unions, whose members are especially likely to be arrested in the course of their work, will also fund cases. For instance, the National Union of Journalists, whose members are sometimes arrested while covering demonstrations, has helped a number of members in cases against the police. Generally, a client should apply for support through his/her shop steward or branch secretary. If they are unhelpful, s/he should write to the local district office or the general secretary at the union's national headquarters. If a union is unable to help, then consideration should be given to other organisations or individuals who might be interested in helping the case. If there is a lawyer who is able or willing to act without charge, or if the plaintiff is financing the case him or herself (see below) it may be possible to get help from a union or other organisation to indemnify the plaintiff against having to pay the police legal costs if the case is lost.

Can clients fund cases themselves?
It is difficult to advise a paying client at the start of a case of the likely cost, especially since a high number of cases settle. If the case goes to trial, this could be three or four years away, by which time substantial costs will have been incurred which could be far beyond the means of an ordinary person.

It is, of course, important to keep a client informed of costs being incurred on his/her behalf as the case proceeds so that s/he can monitor the situation. The real problem lies with the costs being incurred by the police, which the plaintiff will probably have to pay if s/he loses the case. Often the plaintiff may be the only witness on his/her side. But the police will frequently have many witnesses: the arresting officers, their superior officers, the custody officer, officers who saw what happened at the police station. All these witnesses have to be interviewed, statements have to be taken and cross-checked. In many cases it is safe to assume that the police costs will be much higher than the plaintiff's. This unknown costs risk places a huge burden on any non-legally aided client.

Law centres

Law centres and other 'not for profit' legal agencies are able to act without charge in some cases under the Employed Solicitors Code 1990 paragraph 7. To enable the organisation to recover its legal costs from the police if the case is won, however, the client should be informed that s/he remains liable to pay his/her own legal costs but that s/he will be indemnified by the management committee of the organisation in so far as the costs are not recoverable from any other source.[12] If this procedure is not adopted the police may be able to argue that as the service has been provided free of charge, no costs have been incurred for them to pay.

Other solicitors

Occasionally a solicitor will be prepared to take on a civil action against the police without charge to the plaintiff. It has been suggested that the way to ensure that costs will be paid in such a situation is to advise the client that s/he will be liable for his/her own costs irrespective of the outcome of the proceedings but to agree that the liability need not be discharged until the end of the case. At that stage it would be open to the solicitor to decide not to enforce the right to be paid if some or all of his/her costs were unrecovered from the other party to the proceedings.[13] It is uncertain whether it would be possible to say that costs will not be enforced unless the client can afford to pay.[14]

In 1995 the Lord Chancellor made regulations[15] permitting solicitors to enter into an agreement with clients to act on a conditional fee basis in certain types of case, including personal injury and ECHR cases. It is now possible for lawyers to agree with clients that they will only receive their costs (at an enhanced hourly rate) if the case is won. However, even

---

12 Law Society Employed Solicitors Code 1990 para 7(a)(iii); *British Water-ways Board v Norman* (1993) *Times* 11 November, DC.
13 *British Waterways Board v Norman*; and see Hartley, 'Acting for clients who cannot pay', (1994) LS Gaz 19 January p40.
14 Hartley, op cit.
15 Conditional Fee Agreements Order 1995 SI No 1674 and Regulations SI No 1675.

if it is possible to find a lawyer prepared to act without charge, the risk of paying the other side's costs if the case is lost remains, and will need to be covered by insurance.

Limitation periods

Limitation periods should not usually prove to be a problem provided the client and lawyer act promptly. However, there are different time limits for different types of cases and it is important to be aware of these. An action which consists of, or includes a claim in respect of, personal injuries for negligence, nuisance or any breach of duty (contractual, statutory or otherwise) must be started within three years, either from the date of the incident or from the date of the plaintiff's knowledge that an injury was significant and attributable to the defendant's act or omission.[16] An injury is significant if it would have been reasonable to take proceedings in respect of it. Knowledge includes that which a plaintiff could reasonably be expected to acquire him/herself or with the help of expert advice.[17] Even if the plaintiff is outside the three-year period s/he can still apply to the court to allow a claim out of time in cases involving personal injuries and death.[18] The fact that the plaintiff did not realise that s/he had a legal cause of action may be a reason for extending the time limit.[19]

However, the three-year rule does not apply to claims for injuries arising from complaints of deliberate assault.[20] In this and in other kinds of actions against the police (for instance, false imprisonment, negligence, wrongful interference with goods) the period within which to begin an action is six years from the end of the act that gave rise to the action. Thus in a case of false imprisonment, time would run from release, not arrest.[21] In a case of malicious prosecution the position is less certain but it appears that time begins to run from the date the plaintiff is acquitted or the case is otherwise determined in his favour, whether this is at the original trial or on a subsequent appeal. Practitioners acting for young people should note that for all cases time does not begun run against a minor until s/he reaches the age of 18.[22] However, a note should be made of the expiry of the limitation period

16 Limitation Act 1980 s11.
17 Limitation Act 1980 s14.
18 Limitation Act 1980 s33.
19 *Halford v Brookes* [1991] 3 All ER 559.
20 *Stubbings v Webb* [1993] 2 WLR 120, HL.
21 Limitation Act 1980 s2.
22 Limitation Act 1980 s28.

in all cases. This is especially important in cases where there is a criminal trial to be resolved before a civil action can be considered. Indeed, as a matter of good practice, consideration should be given to opening a civil action file at the first indication that this is a possibility, even if no action is taken till the criminal trial is over.

Avoiding delay

When people start off their case they are often fired with enthusiasm and a sense of outrage about what has happened to them. As the case drags on and they begin to realise just how long the whole process is likely to take they begin to wonder if it is all worthwhile. This feeling that the case is never going to end can seem all the worse if it was started with an unrealistic expectation of how soon the case could be concluded and clients should be warned of the possible delays and the reasons for them at the very start of the case. This is especially important for the growing number of people who have to pay signifi-cant contributions to the legal aid they receive throughout the case.

Because of the inherent delays, once the case has been issued , there is a responsibility for the plaintiff's solicitor to ensure that a potential case is prepared for issue as quickly as possible. In most cases this will mean the case is ready to start within six months of the time of the first interview and only in rare cases should the lapse of time be longer than a year (and only then if the limitation period allows). This time will be spent taking instructions, applying for legal aid, proofing witnesses, instructing experts, obtaining the medical reports and preparing the schedule of special damages that need to be lodged with the claim, instructing counsel and preparing the case for issue.

Almost all the pressure for a speedy hearing of the case must come from the plaintiff's side, and almost all the pressure to delay will come from the defence. There is nothing improper in this; the police are entitled to prepare their case in meticulous detail. It is also quite usual for defendants in any type of civil action to use the maximum amount of time available in the hope of pressing the plaintiff to drop the case or accept a very low settlement. Police solicitors are aware that plaintiffs in civil actions against the police can (and do) become disillusioned enough to drop the case.

A study by the authors of 25 cases showed that the average time from the date of the incident to the conclusion of the trial was three years and nine months (ranging from one year and five months to six years and four months). These figures do not distinguish between High Court cases and those in the county court. High Court cases tend to take longer; for instance, one study reported that in civil jury trials in the High Court (of which actions against the police make up 17%) the average time to the setting down of the trial is over four years.[23] In nine out of the 25 cases in the authors' survey that were settled, the average time from incident to settlement was three years and three months, with total case time ranging from 18 months to over five years.

In May 1995 the time from setting down (see below) to trial in a jury trial at the Central London County Court trial centre (where two courts are set aside for jury trials) was up to ten months.

Publicity

Complaints and especially civil actions against the police can often be high-profile cases in which the media express enormous interest. Such cases are always newsworthy locally, and sometimes nationally. Solicitors need to consider their clients' feelings about publicity and the question should be raised in the first interview, see p3. Newspapers will always want photographs of clients to enhance an article and will want to speak to them personally, even if a press release has been put out. If there has been a conspicuous incident or an acquittal in a criminal trial, the media may already have contacted the client before legal advice is sought. However, in many other cases journalists will only really become interested if there is a settlement for a substantial amount or if the case reaches a full trial. Adverse publicity in itself may persuade the police to offer a generous settlement of the case. Sometimes, however publicity might make them more likely to fight the action.

If a client's reasons for bringing a case were to clear his/her name or to see the police being held accountable in public for their misconduct, then s/he may be extremely keen on publicity. It is possible to publicise the case at a number of stages – when legal aid is granted, when proceedings are commenced, when the result of any police complaint becomes known, when a settlement is accepted or at the end of the trial. All are good opportunities to get the attention of the media. Journalists are bombarded with hundreds of press releases every day, so it is important that it is in an easily accessible format. It may also be important to prepare a press release if the case is lost in order to put across any positive aspects from the client's point of view, to announce a possible appeal or to act as a counterweight to any statement the police are likely to have made to the press.

23 NLJ 11 August 1989 p1102.

The press release should preferably be sent to a named journalist, usually the home affairs or legal correspondent. It should be faxed and then chased up with a telephone call. Local TV and radio should not be forgotten as quick and accessible ways to get coverage. In a few cases where publicity can be shown to be important, such as in a test case or in achieving a settlement the time spent on press work may be allowed on taxation.

As many civil actions against the police are heard before juries, the closer to trial the more caution that should be exercised in speaking publicly about the case so as not to fall foul of the laws of contempt and the laws against perverting the course of justice. Some solicitors make it a rule not to publicise the case at all after it has been set down.

It is equally important to protect clients from unwanted publicity. Some clients, for instance, may find it hugely embarrassing that they have been involved with the police or charged with an offence even if they have subsequently been acquitted.

Types of damages

Many people bring a case against the police as a matter of principle and say that the amount of damages is very much a secondary consideration. Nevertheless, it is always an important issue. The type and level of damages may indicate the court's opinion of the merits of the case and the conduct of the police. The types of damages which a court can award are considered below. The level of damages for particular causes of action is considered in chapter 5.

Nominal damages

Historically, certain legal rights have been considered so important that even a technical breach of them entitles a person to sue without having to prove that they suffered any real detriment. False imprisonment, assault, trespass to land and trespass to goods are actionable *per se* in this way. Once the case has been made out, damages must be awarded, even if no real loss has been suffered. These damages, known as nominal damages, are not intended to compensate, but rather to demonstrate that rights were infringed. They may be as small as £2 but it should be noted that exemplary damages may also be available which could greatly increase the award (see below).[24] When awarding

---

24 However, in *Cumber v Chief Constable of Hampshire Constabulary* (1995) *Times* 28 January it was held that it had to be rare if not unique for an award of exemplary damages not to be coupled with one of compensatory damages.

only nominal damages the court can still order the other side to pay the plaintiff's legal costs,[25] although if s/he has suffered no inconvenience an order as to costs may not be made.[26]

Nominal damages must be distinguished from contemptuous damages, say one penny, which are intended to demonstrate that although the case is made out it should never have been brought to court.

General and special damages (compensatory damages)

Special damages are designed to make good the past financial loss which can be calculated at the date of trial, such as medical bills, repair bills and past loss of earnings. General damages are all the other types of damage suffered, such as the pain, suffering and loss of amenity following an assault, the harm done to the plaintiff's reputation by a malicious prosecution, or future loss of earnings. Damages for post-traumatic stress disorder can be claimed under these headings. General damages are at large (determind by the court); special damages must be specified in detail in the claim and (usually) supported by invoices, etc.

It should be remembered that damages for nervous shock can be recovered where psychiatric illness has been caused, for instance, from witnessing the effects of a defendant's tortious action on another. In *Alcock v Chief Constable of South Yorkshire Police*[27] the limits of liability for damages for nervous shock were examined by the House of Lords. The case involved the Hillsborough football stadium disaster and the plaintiffs, who all had relatives or friends who died in the disaster as a result of the negligence of the police, suffered pyschiatric illness from witnessing the disaster. The court held that as well as the necessity for nervous shock to be a foreseeable result of the negligence, liability also depended on the closeness of the relationship of the plaintiff to the victim and the closeness of the plaintiff to the incident in time and space. If a plaintiff is directly involved in an accident, then foreseeability of physical injury is sufficient to enable him/her to recover damages for nervous shock even though, in the event, no physical harm was suffered.[28]

25 *Beaumont v Gateshead* (1846) 2 CB 494 at 499.
26 *Marzetti v Williams* (1830) 1 B & Ad 415 at 425.
27 [1992] 1 AC 310, HL. See also the Law Commission consultation paper *Liability for psychiatric illness*, HMSO 1995 for a full discussion of the issue.
28 *Page v Smith* [1995] 2 All ER 736, (1995) *Times* 12 May, HL.

In cases where there are serious injuries, future loss of earnings can constitute a very great part of the award. The plaintiff has a duty to mitigate his/her loss. So, for example, retraining for a different type of job might need to be considered. Deductions are also made for certain monies received by the plaintiff, for example, depending on the amount recovered, all or part of certain social security payments will have to be repaid to the DSS. Where a plaintiff is being compensated for loss of reputation, for instance after malicious prosecution and false imprisonment, then damages can be lowered if the plaintiff had little reputation to lose.

Aggravated damages

Aggravated damages may be payable in addition to general or special damages. They are conventionally seen as an extra element of compensation in recognition that the exceptional motives, conduct or manner of the defendant have aggravated the plaintiff's damage by intangible injury to personality (insult, humiliation, degradation, indignation, outrage, distress, hurt feelings, etc).[29]

The fact that the defendant's exceptional behaviour is a precondition to the award of aggravated damages has cast doubt on the purely compensatory nature of aggravated damages and suggests that they also contain a punitive element as well. If this is so, then the restrictions placed on the availability of the entirely punitive exemplary damages (see below) may be to an extent lessened where aggravated damages are available in their stead.[30]

Aggravated damages can be awarded in the following actions involving police misconduct:

false imprisonment[31]
malicious prosecution[32]

---

29 *Rookes v Barnard* [1964] AC 1129; *Cassell v Broome* [1972] AC 1027; 1 All ER 801, HL and see the Law Commission consultation paper no. 132, *Aggravated, Exemplary and Restitutionary Damages* HMSO, 1993 para 1.15 for this definition (at the time of writing the Law Commission's final report has not been published).

30 See Law Commission paper para 2.7.

31 *Warwick v Foulkes* (1884) 12 M&W 507; *Walter v Alltools Ltd* (1944) 171 LT 371 and *White v Metropolitan Police Commissioner* (1982) *Times* 24 April.

32 *Leith v Pope* (1779) 2 Wm Bl 1327 and see, eg, *Marks v Chief Constable of Greater Manchester* (1992) *Times* 28 January, CA.

assault and battery[33]
trespass to land[34]
trespass to goods[35] and
intimidation.[36]

It is generally thought that the need for exceptional conduct by the defendant means that aggravated damages are not available in negligence actions.[37]

Aggravated damages may also be available for the conduct of the police subsequent to the incident giving rise to the civil action. It is clear that they will be available in actions for defamation[38] and the Law Commission reports that:

> The conduct of the defendant at trial has . . . been considered relevant to aggravated damages in cases of malicious prosecution [and] false imprisonment where the persistence by the defendant in damaging allegations about the plaintiff or in attempts to tarnish character can be viewed as analogous to attempts to sully reputation, that is, as a form of defamation.[39]

Given the non-pecuniary and intangible losses that aggravated damages are designed to compensate coupled with the relevance of the defendant's conduct and the possible inclusion of a punitive element, it is difficult to predict the level of an award. In serious cases, aggravated damages (often together with exemplary damages) can be substantial and sometimes can far outstrip the purely compensatory element in an award. It should

33 *Grey v Grant* (1764) 2 Wils 252; *Forde v Skinner* (1830) 4 C&P 239; cutting the hair of a pauper would merit aggravated damages if it were done to take down her pride and not for cleanliness.
34 *Sears v Lyons* (1818) 2 Stark 317; *Williams v Currie* (1854) 1 CB 841.
35 *Owen and Smith (t/a Nuagin Car Services) v Reo Motors (Britain) Ltd* (1934) 151 LT 274, CA.
36 *Godwin v Uzoigwe* (1992) *Times* 18 June.
37 See for instance *AB v South West Water Services Ltd* [1993] QB 507. However, in *Hicks v Chief Constable of South Yorkshire Police* [1992] 2 All ER 65, HL, involving the negligent policing of a football crowd, the House of Lords left open the question whether damages for physical injuries should be increased 'on account of the terrifying circumstances in which they were inflicted'.
38 *Sutcliffe v Pressdram Ltd* [1991] 1 QB 153.
39 Law Commission consultation paper para 3.5, and see *Marks v Chief Constable of Greater Manchester* (n32) and *Warby v Cascorino* (1989) *Times* 27 October.

lastly be noted that a plaintiff's conduct, behaviour and provocation can be taken into account in calculating aggravated damages.[40]

Exemplary damages

The Law Commission[41] has described exemplary damages in the following terms:

> Exemplary (or punitive) damages are awarded by reference to the defendant's conduct and are intended to deter similar conduct in the future (whether by the defendant or others) and to signify condemnation or disapproval. They can therefore serve deterrent, symbolic and retributory functions. In deterring and condemning undesirable behaviour exemplary damages can also serve the distinct purpose of vindicating an individual's rights and the strength of the law.

The Commission went on to say that exemplary damages 'continue to play an important role in the protection of civil liberties . . . [and have] been the basis for significant development in the law concerning police misconduct'.

The availability of exemplary damages is narrower than that of aggravated damages in that they are only available for specific causes of action and only where the actions of the police fall into certain categories (see below). However, unlike aggravated damages, they can be awarded even where there are no aggravating circumstances[42] and at least in principle can be awarded even where no intangible loss (see above) has been suffered.[43]

Categories of action

Since the landmark case of *Rookes v Barnard*, exemplary damages have only been available in three categories of cases, all of which relate to the defendant's conduct.[44] Only one of these categories is usually relevant in

40 *O'Connor v Hewitson* [1979] Crim LR 46; Clayton & Tomlinson 'Civil actions against the police: damages' January 1988 *Legal Action* 18.
41 Law Commission consultation paper paras 1.15 and 3.41.
42 *Holden v Chief Constable of Lancashire* [1987] QB 380.
43 *Cassell v Broome* [1972] AC 1027, HL.
44 *Rookes v Barnard* [1964] AC 1129 at 1226. The other two categories encompass situations where the award of exemplary damages is authorised by statute, and where the wrongful conduct has been calculated to make a profit which may well exceed the compensation payable to the plaintiff. It was held in *Cassell v Broome* [1972] AC 1027, HL that the phrase 'servants of the government' extended to include the police despite the fact that police officers are not the employees of central or local government: *Fisher v Oldham Corporation* [1930] 2 KB 364.

police actions and this is described in that case by Lord Reid as 'oppressive, arbitrary or unconstitutional action by servants of the government'. The terms 'oppressive, arbitrary or unconstitutional action' should be read disjunctively. Thus, where it was held that in itself a wrongful arrest could be an unconstitutional act by the police, it was not necessary also to show that the arrest was oppressive or arbitrary before exemplary damages were available.[45] Exemplary damages have been awarded where the wrongful acts of the police have been compounded by lying to the courts,[46] persisting in a baseless defence[47] and racist behaviour.[48] The 'privatisation' of some police functions (see pp39 and 208) raises questions as to whether exemplary damages will be available against the individuals or bodies that exercise these functions. The conventional view would suggest that this will depend on whether they can properly be described as 'servants of the government'. In *AB v South West Water Services Ltd*[49] it was held that employees of a privatised water company could not be described as government servants when the conduct they were engaged in was 'not an exercise of executive power derived from government, central or local'. It is submitted that it is wrong in principle for the award of exemplary damages to depend on whether the abuse of power in question has been committed by an individual who happens to be a government servant rather than by an employee of a privatised company, and that functions, such as the care and transportation of prisoners, the handling of 999 calls and forensic examinations by scene of crime officers all involve the exercise of executive power.

The 'cause of action' test
The availability of exemplary damages is limited to the particular causes of action listed below. This limitation was described in 1993 in *AB v South West Water Services Ltd*[50] when the Court of Appeal reviewed the decisions in *Cassell v Broome*[51] and *Rookes v Barnard*.[52] The Court of Appeal said that the House of Lords intended to apply a restrictive test to the award of exemplary damages, and therefore they were only

45 *Holden v Chief Constable of Lancashire* [1987] QB 380.
46 *George v Commissioner of Police for the Metropolis* (1984) *Times* 31 March.
47 *Connor v Chief Constable of Cambridgeshire* (1984) *Times* 11 April.
48 *Daly v Commissioner of Police for the Metropolis*, news report, *Times* 18 and 23 July 1980.
49 [1993] QB 507, CA, at 525 per Stuart-Smith LJ.
50 [1993] QB 507.
51 [1972] AC 1027. See for instance Lord Diplock at 1130–1131.
52 [1964] AC 1129.

available in a cause of action in which an award of exemplary damages had already been made before the judgment in *Rookes v Barnard* in 1964. Despite the hesitant nature of the judgment[53] the case was not appealed to the House of Lords. It is submitted that the 'cause of action' test is contrary to the principle of a developing common law and in practive gives rise to some odd results.

The tort of malicious prosecution probably passes the 'cause of action' test. However, the uncertainty arises because although exemplary damages were awarded in pre-1964 cases[54] they were not awarded for 'oppressive, arbitrary or unconstitutional action' committed by a *government servant* (see above) and the question has been raised whether this part of the *Rookes v Barnard* test also has to be satisfied.[55] It is submitted that it would be contrary to principle if a restrictive interpretation were put on the availability of exemplary damages in malicious prosecution actions, given the important punitive role they have had in recent cases. False imprisonment, assault and battery, and trespass to land or goods all satisfy the 'cause of action' test.[56]

Exemplary damages are available for the tort of intimidation[57] and probably in private nuisance.[58] In the *South West Water* case[59] it was held that exemplary damages cannot be awarded in negligence[60] and public nuisance cases, as they would not pass the 'cause of action' test. It also appears that there are no cases of exemplary damages being awarded for the tort of misfeasance in public office (see p176) prior to 1964 and so, somewhat incongruously given the degree to which this tort relies on malicious abuse of power by public officials, it is also excluded by the 'cause of action' test. It has also been held that exemplary damages are not available in race discrimination cases[61] and this will no doubt extend to sex discrimination cases, as both torts only came into existence after 1964.

---

53 See for instance the speech of Bingham MR.
54 *Leith v Pope* (1779) 2 Black W 1327, 96 ER 777; *Chambers v Robinson* (1726) 2 Str 691, 93 ER 787.
55 See Law Commission consultation paper para 3.60.
56 See Law Commission consultation paper para 3.57 and 3.60 for discussion and examples of pre-1964 cases.
57 *Rookes v Barnard* [1964] AC 1129.
58 *Bell v Midland Railway Co* (1861) 10 CB (NS) 287, 142 ER 462.
59 [1993] QB 507, CA (see above).
60 In *Annables v Chief Constable for South Yorkshire* August 1993 *Legal Action* 16, a county court case decided after *AB v South West Water*, the case note states that exemplary damages were awarded in an action against the police for negligence.
61 *Deane v Ealing LBC* [1993] ICR 329.

Discretionary nature of awards

Although society might expect police officers to conduct themselves with higher standards than the rest of the public, generally there is no obligation on the court to award exemplary or aggravated damages in all cases of tortious acts by the police just because they were committed by a police officer.[62] The court retains a discretion whether or not to award exemplary damages.

In a jury trial (which is available in many of the causes of action for which exemplary damages are frequently awarded), while it is up to the jury to decide whether exemplary damages should be awarded, the judge can direct the jury as to the special features of the case, such as absence of aggravating circumstances, which the jury may then take into account when deciding whether to award exemplary damages and, if so, how much.[63] That the police have made an honest mistake, for instance, in wrongfully arresting a person might lead to a finding that there are no circumstances justifying exemplary damages.[64]

The behaviour of the plaintiff can be taken into account when deciding the level of exemplary damages to be awarded to punish the defendant[65] and occasionally it may exclude them altogether in extreme cases.[66] As the purpose of exemplary damages is to punish, they ought not to be awarded against individual officers who have already been punished under criminal law, for example, by a term of imprisonment,[67] although they may still be payable by the chief officer of police (see below p203).

The extent to which, in general, the judge can give guidance to the jury on the level of damages is considered at p210.

It appears that in cases where exemplary damages are awarded it is proper for the judge or jury to award a single sum and not to separate the various parts of the award. It is said that the reason for this is to avoid the risk of double counting, that is, the adding together of compensatory and exemplary damages.[68] However, in practice and apparently especially in police misconduct cases, awards are frequently itemised in terms of general, aggravated and exemplary damages,[69] and

62 *O'Connor v Hewitson* [1979] Crim LR 46.
63 *Holden v Chief Constable of Lancashire*, n42 supra.
64 *Simper v Metropolitan Police Commissioner* [1982] CLY 3124.
65 *Bishop v Commissioner of Police for the Metropolis* (1989) *Times* 5 December; (1990) LS Gaz 10 January p30, CA.
66 *Holden v Chief Constable of Lancashire* [1987] 1 QB 380.
67 *Archer v Brown* [1985] 1 QB 401.
68 *Rookes v Barnard* [1964] AC 1129, 1228.
69 See Law Commmission consultation paper para 3.91 and n367.

it is submitted that this approach helps both the police and the plaintiff identify the weight the judge or jury attached to various aspects of the misconduct pleaded.[70] Indeed, this approach is a guarantee against double counting, as any erroneous double counting would become apparent from the itemisation.

Vicarious liability and exemplary damages

A chief officer of police will usually be vicariously liable for the misconduct of his/her officers and it is usual for the chief constable to pay any exemplary damages awarded. However, if an individual officer is found to be 'on a venture of his own' rather than involved in an improper mode of carrying out an authorised task, then his/her chief officer will not be vicariously liable for the acts committed (see p205). Exemplary damages can still be awarded against the individual officer. It has been suggested[71] that an officer's means should be taken into account when calculating the amount. However, this overlooks the fact that a police *authority*, as distinct from a chief officer, has a very wide discretion to pay 'any damages or costs awarded against a member of a police force maintained by it',[72] and in practice usually does.

Where an officer has already been convicted of a criminal offence relating to the same subject matter as the civil action, thus preventing an award of exemplary damages against the individual officer, (see above) they could still, presumably, be recovered from the chief officer of police unless of course it is held that the chief officer is not vicariously liable because the subordinate officer was engaged on a venture of his/her own.

The relationship between a police complaint and a civil action

In the past some lawyers have felt that an official complaint should be made before suing the police. They felt that this would forestall any criticism from the judge that no complaint had been made.

There now seems to be a general consensus that this is too simplistic. Many lawyers feel that there is little benefit in pursuing an official

---

70 For instance in 1991 a High Court jury awarded £50,000 exemplary damages out of a total of £55,000 against the Chief Constable of Greater Manchester to a woman arrested at a demonstration: January 1992 *Legal Action*, back page.
71 *Makanjuola v Commissioner of Police for the Metropolis* [1992] 3 All ER 617, obiter.
72 Police Act 1964 s48(4).

complaint if there is any possibility of bringing a civil action.[73] When a complaint is made, the case to be made in court is effectively 'given away', and there may be tactical reasons for not wanting to do this at an early stage of the case. Further, the complainant may inadvertently make a mistake or admission in his/her statement to the police. S/he may also identify witnesses, thus enabling the police to interview them. Practitioners also need to be aware of the impact of public interest immunity as it relates to documents created in course of an investigation into a police complaint discussed in chapter 3 at p75–76. In chapter 8 we discuss how discovery in a civil action is affected by public interest immunity. Here we describe the tactical decision a plaintiff has to make at the start of a case.

In its Triennial Review for 1988–91 the Police Complaints Authority noted that the law at that time allowed a police force's legal advisers a right to see the investigating officer's report, and any statements made to him/her but denied this right to complainant who was suing the police:

> It is our view that this gives the police an advantage over the plaintiff which is not insubstantial – and which results in plaintiff/complainants refusing to co-operate with the complaints procedures until after their civil claim for damages has been heard or settled. This is a serious matter . . . '[74]

The practical consequence of this was that in most cases advisers had to consider very carefully whether they should advise their client to co-operate with the investigation of a complaint before the conclusion of any civil action. In many cases the unlikelihood of a satisfactory outcome from the complaint and the information it would put at the disposal of the police was enough to discourage plaintiffs from pursuing both courses of action at the same time.

However, in *R v Chief Constable of West Midlands ex p Wiley*,[75] the House of Lords held that public interest immunity does not attach to police complaints documents as a class. Lord Woolf noted that in *Neilson v Laugharne*,[76] Oliver LJ had asked whether a liability to disclose documents in civil proceedings would adversely affect the legislative purpose of the police complaints system, and had concluded

---

73 See eg, Harrison, 'Police complaints: pitfalls for the unwary litigant' NLJ 13 December 1985, p1239; and Harrison and Cragg, 'Suing the police: should plaintiffs also make a complaint?' June 1991 *Legal Action 22*.
74 Chapter 4.
75 [1995] 1 AC 274, HL.
76 [1981] QB 736.

that it would because police officers, witnesses and complainants themselves would not make statements to investigating officers if they thought they might be used in open court. However, the only evidence for this had been a single affidavit from a deputy chief constable. That was held to be insufficient evidence on which to establish a new class of public interest immunity.

Solicitors acting for plaintiffs in civil actions against the police have had to change the way they consider the police complaints procedure in the light of *Wiley*. All documents having probative value created in the course of a complaints investigation will potentially be open to discovery and use in court. Undoubtedly, some investigating officers are extremely thorough in their work, leave no stone unturned and the fruits of their labour may be of great use to a plaintiff, but this will not always be the case and solicitors will have to judge the usefulness of pursuing a complaint in each individual case.

There will, however, be nothing to stop the police using the complaint documents, including the complainant's statement, in the preparation of pleadings or directly as the basis for cross-examination, contrary to the case law prior to *Wiley* when this was prohibited.[77] Some investigating officers already accept written statements prepared by a complainant plaintiff's solicitor in a form so as to satisfy Criminal Justice Act 1967 s9 (the form in which written evidence at summary trials is usually presented) and there will be pressure to extend this practice. Where possible other witness statements can be prepared in the same way. Minimal extra work should be generated, as statements would already need to be prepared for the civil proceedings. One effect of *Wiley* may be that legal aid in civil actions will be extended to cover the preparation of the police complaint into the same incident.

One possible tactic will be to postpone co-operation with the complaints procedure (eg, in allowing the plaintiff to be interviewed) beyond preparing a s9 statement until the exchange of witness statements stage in the civil action[78] (see p242), in order to avoid the police having the benefit of the plaintiff's statement at an earlier point in the proceedings. In some cases it may be appropriate to prepare very detailed particulars of claim in the civil action and invite the investigating officers to take this as the basis of the complaint in lieu of a statement. In other cases it is appropriate to keep the particulars in a

---

77 An ill-prepared complaint, submitted, for example, before a complainant has sought legal advice, may therefore prove to be a major problem in any subsequent litigation.

78 RSC Order 38 r2A; CCR Order 20 r12A.

case as short and concise as practicable so as not to give too much away to the lawyers acting for the police. Tactics will differ from case to case depending on how much it is thought the plaintiff has to lose or gain from full co-operation with the complaints procedure.

The PCA has the power to dispense with an investigation if it believes that the complainant is refusing or failing to make a statement (see p67). It can exercise this power where it is not reasonably practicable to complete a satisfactory inquiry within a reasonable period, and in the circumstances the complaints procedure should be dispensed with.[79] Where the complainant has chosen to wait until the exchange of witness statements stage of the civil proceedings before s/he furnishes the investigating officer with a statement, the PCA may feel justified in exercising its power to dispense with the need for an investigation into the complaint. If this happens then the courts, through an application for judicial review, may be called upon to decide if this is a lawful use of the PCA's powers.

The impact of the decision in *Wiley* in relation to police complaints and civil actions is likely to be an increase in the number of serious complaints pursued and a parallel increase in the number of complaints supervised by the PCA. Fewer guilty officers should, in theory at least, escape punishment. There is also likely to be greater scrutiny of the role of the investigating officer and the PCA's supervisory function now that the complaints file will be available in civil actions.

Whom to sue

The principle of vicarious liability (which holds employers jointly liable with employees for their employees' wrongful acts committed in the course of their employment) has been statutorily extended to include the police service. Thus, the chief officer of police[80] is liable for wrongful acts committed by police officers, including special constables[81] 'under his direction and control in the performance or purported performance of their functions'.[82] It is not necessary to know the names or identities of the particular officers complained about. The chief officer of police can therefore be sued and in practice s/he should normally be sued alone. While it is possible to sue the individual officers

79 Dispensation Regs 1985 reg 3(3).
80 Police Act 1964 ss 48(3) and 62 and Sch 8; and see *Sheikh v Chief Constable of Greater Manchester* [1989] 2 All ER 684.
81 Police Act 1964 s18 and Sch 2.
82 Ibid s48.

either alone or with the chief officer, there is usually no advantage and there will frequently be serious disadvantages.[83] Where individual officers and the chief officer have been sued together, it is common for the chief officer to want to settle out of court but for the individual officers to hold out for a full hearing in court in the hope of clearing their names. This situation only causes greater delay and a greater costs risk.

A greater sum of damages cannot be won by suing individuals in addition to the chief officer. The only difference is that the damages are apportioned between them. Police authorities have a wide discretion to pay any damages and costs awarded against individual officers[84] in proceedings for a tort committed by them and in practice usually do so. The power extends to any sum required in connection with the settlement of any claim that has or might have given rise to tort proceedings, and as to any costs incurred and not recovered in any such proceedings.

There is, however, an advantage in suing the chief officer and the individual officers if there is a possibility that the chief officer might deny liability because, for example, the officers were arguably not acting in the performance or purported performance of their functions. In such circumstances the case might be lost against the chief officer but still succeed against the individual. In practice, it is possible (subject to limitation periods) to wait and see if the chief officer denies liability on this ground and then to join the individual officer(s) to the action if necessary.

It is very unusual for a chief officer not to take responsibility for the actions of an officer, but in one case it was held that the Metropolitan Police Commissioner could not be held liable for an officer who allegedly demanded sexual favours in return for not reporting a suspect's immigration 'irregularities'.[85] Advisers should be watchful for cases where it appears that a 'rogue officer' may be acting on 'a squalid adventure of his own'.[86]

In *Racz v Home Office*,[87] the House of Lords overturned a Court of

---

83 See Harrison 'Suing the police: choosing the defendant' May 1987 *Legal Action* 20.

84 Police Act 1964 s48(4) ie, against members of the police force maintained by them, any constable [which includes an officer of any rank] for the time being required to serve with that force by virtue of s14, or any special constable appointed for that area.

85 *Makanjuola v Commissioner of Police for the Metropolis* [1992] 3 All ER 617.

86 Ibid.

87 [1994] 2 WLR 23.

Appeal decision that the very nature of the tort of misfeasance in public office (see p176) was such that in law the Home Office could not be vicariously liable for prison officers who would be necessarily acting outside the scope of their authority or maliciously when the tort was committed. Lord Jauncey said that the nature of the tort was not decisive as to vicarious liability and refused to strike out the part of the plaintiff's claim that alleged misfeasance in public office. He said that it is likely to be a question of fact and degree whether the prison officers were engaged in a misguided and unauthorised method of performing their authorised duties (for which the Home Office would be vicariously liable) or were engaged in what was tantamount to an unlawful frolic of their own. It is submitted that the court would take a similar approach when considering the vicarious liability of a chief constable for misfeasance in public office by one of his/her officers.

If individual officers are not joined as defendants, this enables the plaintiff to apply for them to be excluded from the courtroom until their evidence is given. However, if they are parties to the action, they have the right to hear *all* the evidence.

Special problems may arise if it is wished to sue an officer who is a member of one police force but who was under the 'direction and control' of another at the time of the incident. This situation may occur in 'mutual aid' exercises such as the 1984–85 miners' strike. In such cases the officers are treated as being under the control of the chief officer to whose aid they have been sent.[88]

Police officers who are seconded to undertake 'central services' are treated as remaining members of their original police force for certain purposes of the Police Act 1964. However, the Home Secretary is liable for torts committed by such officers in the performance or purported performance of their functions.[89] 'Central services' includes such things as duties at police training colleges, forensic science laboratories and staff officers to the Inspectors of Constabulary.[90]

Cadets

A police cadet is not a constable or a member of a police force but is treated as being a person undergoing training with a view to becoming a

88 Police Act 1964 s14(3).
89 Police Act 1964 s43(3B), inserted by Police Officers (Central Services) Act 1989 s1.
90 Police Act 1964 ss41 and 43.

member of a police force. For the purposes of vicarious liability the police authority is treated as the cadet's employer and thus is the body which should be sued, instead of the chief officer.[91] In the case of a Metropolitan police cadet, the Receiver for the Metropolitan Police District should be sued.[92]

Independent police forces

Ministry of Defence police
The Ministry of Defence police force (which is quite separate and distinct from the military police) has a wide variety of responsibilities covering UK military, naval and air force installations, vehicles, vessels and aircraft, bases of visiting forces, dockyards and ordnance companies. The police force was put on a statutory basis in 1987[93] and consists of special constables who are nevertheless under the direction and control of its chief constable.[94] Members of the MOD police are civil servants in the employment of the Crown; any civil proceedings may be brought against the individual officer or the Ministry of Defence,[95] although it will usually be preferable to sue the Ministry alone. The force has agreed a complaints procedure with the PCA, see p79; it has a statutory discipline system[96] and is periodically inspected by HM Inspectorate of Constabulary.

Atomic Energy Authority Constabulary
The United Kingdom Atomic Energy Authority (UKAEA) maintains the Atomic Energy Authority Constabulary (AEAC). The AEAC has a chief constable who is responsible for the operational control, recruitment, supervision and general efficiency of the constabulary; however, he has no special statutory status. All the members of the AEAC (including the

---

91 Ibid s17(5). Legal proceedings are brought against the local government officer representing the police committee: ibid s2(7) and Local Government Act 1972 Sch 29 para 4.
92 Police Act 1964 s17(4) and Metropolitan Police (Receiver) Act 1861 s1.
93 Ministry of Defence Police Act 1987 s1(1).
94 Ibid s1(3).
95 Crown Proceedings Act 1947 s2(1).
96 Ministry of Defence Police Act 1987 s4; Ministry of Defence Police (Representation at Disciplinary Proceedings) Regulations 1988 SI No 1099; for an account of a MOD police disciplinary tribunal and a MOD police board of inquiry, see *Police Review* 8 July 1994, 26 August 1994 and 2 September 1994.

chief constable) are sworn in as special constables[97] on the nomination of the UKAEA and are employees of the UKAEA. Accordingly any civil proceedings may be brought against the individual officer or the UKAEA in its vicarious capacity in accordance with the usual common law principles, although it will usually be preferable to sue the UKAEA alone.

British Transport Police

The British Transport Police are organised in accordance with a statutory scheme.[98] On the application of the British Railways Board any two justices may appoint a person to act as a constable throughout England and Wales.[99] Any person so appointed has all the powers, protection and privileges of a constable in respect of the exercise of his/her duties,[100] but may not act as a constable unless in uniform or provided with an authority to act as such.[101] The police authority of any area is not liable for any expense of, or responsible for any acts or defaults of, such constables or for anything connected with or consequent upon their appointment.[102] Members of the British Transport Police are employees of the British Railways Board, which may be joined as a defendant in its vicarious capacity in accordance with the usual common law principles, although it will usually be preferable to sue the Board alone.

Civil actions concerning officers in other independent police forces may similarly usually be brought against the employing body or the individual or both, subject to any local or private Act of Parliament governing the force.

Special constables

A chief officer of police is liable for the wrongful acts of special constables under his/her control (see p203). However, while regular

97 Special Constables Act 1923 s3; Atomic Energy Authority Act 1954 Sch 3; Ministry of Defence Police Act 1987 s7; although they are only special constables, members of the AEAC have exceptional statutory powers to carry firearms which give them a legal status similar to members of the armed services: Atomic Energy Authority (Special Constables) Act 1976 s1.
98 Transport Act 1962 s69(1); British Transport Police Force Scheme 1963 (Amendment) Order 1992 SI No 364.
99 British Transport Commission Act 1949 s52(1) as amended by Railways Act 1993 Sch 10 para 1(2).
100 Ibid s53(2)(b); Transport Police (Jurisdiction) Act 1994 s1.
101 British Transport Commission Act 1949 s53(2)(e).
102 Ibid s53(2)(d).

police officers can exercise the powers of a constable throughout England and Wales, a special constable can only exercise his/her powers in the police area to which s/he is appointed.[103]

Civilian employees
There has been a significant move in recent years towards the civilianisation of functions formerly carried out by police officers. There are approximately 42,000 civilian staff carrying out a range of duties, including those of control room staff, front desk staff, scene of crimes officers and the handling and transportation of prisoners. Civilian staff employed by police authorities are under the direction and control of the chief officer of police,[104] but the employing police authority nevertheless remains vicariously liable for their wrongful acts. An action may therefore be brought against either the individual or the police authority, although it will usually be preferable to proceed only against the authority.

Trial by jury

In cases of false imprisonment and malicious prosecution there is a right to have the case decided by a jury. This is so whether the case is in the High Court or in the county court. The only exception is where the trial requires a prolonged examination of documents or accounts or any scientific or local investigation which cannot conveniently be made with a jury.[105] In *Taylor v Anderton*[106] it was held that a jury trial would not be convenient under the Supreme Court Act 1981 s69(1) (and was therefore refused) because of the large amount of detailed documentation that had been produced by the police in their defence to wide-ranging allegations made by the plaintiff. The case concerned allegations asserting 'a far-reaching plot to destroy the plaintiff as a means of destroying Mr John Stalker' (a former deputy chief constable of Greater Manchester) with whom the plaintiff was associated. It is submitted, however, that cases involving serious allegations going to the good faith and constitutionality of the actions of the police such as this, are the very cases where a jury trial would be most appropriate. The case was, however, extremely unusual amongst police misconduct cases in that

103 Police Act 1964 s19(2).
104 Police Act 1964 s10, as amended by PMCA 1994 s10 and Local Government Act 1972 s101.
105 County Courts Act 1984 s66(3) and Supreme Court Act 1981 s69(1).
106 [1995] 1 WLR 447, CA.

the documentation involved came to tens of thousands of pages,[107] and it is further submitted that if jury trial is to be denied as inconvenient, such a course of action should only be considered in cases of this magnitude. The Court of Appeal in that case also said that the judge at first instance had erred by taking into account when deciding the question of mode of trial the fact that the plaintiff was legally aided. A plaintiff was not entitled to better treatment simply because s/he is privately funded.

If the case concerns assault, death, trespass, seizure of goods or damage to goods, negligence, misfeasance in public office, etc, the judge has a discretion to order a jury trial.[108] Judges are often reluctant to allow juries in such cases, probably because jury trials tend to take longer and involve the court in extra expense. However, where there is a straight conflict of evidence about what happened and the case turns upon whether the plaintiff or the police is telling the truth, the judge should be asked to allow a jury to decide. When an application is made the judge will balance the importance of the trial and the risk of damage to the plaintiff's honour and integrity against the increased cost (especially to the police if the plaintiff is on legal aid) in deciding whether to differ from the norm of such cases being heard by a judge alone. Applications are rarely successful but, in a personal injury case not involving the police, the Court of Appeal commented that, where 'personal injuries resulted from conduct on the part of those who were deliberately abusing their authority', this might place a case in an exceptional category meriting a jury trial.[109]

In *Racz v Home Office*[110] it was argued that as elements of the tort of misfeasance in public office were similar to those in some of the torts for which there is a right to trial by jury, the court should exercise its discretion to allow a jury trial. However, the House of Lords rejected this argument, saying that it could see no logical connection between the various torts for which jury trial is still an entitlement.

Usually there are considerable advantages in having a jury trial. There is a common view amongst lawyers that judges are more likely than juries to accept the police version of events uncritically. Some also assume that juries are more likely than judges to have personal experience of the kind of police practices being complained about. Results of a

107 Ibid at 453.
108 See *Ward v James* [1965] 1 All ER 563, CA at 576: in a personal injury claim for negligence it was held there must be exceptional circumstances.
109 *H v Ministry of Defence* [1991] 2 WLR 1192 CA at 1199.
110 [1994] 2 WLR 23 at 29 per Lord Jauncey.

study published in 1987 showed that on average damages awarded by a jury in false imprisonment cases were nearly 50% higher than damages awarded by judges.[111] However, it should also be borne in mind that one of the highest awards in court, £51,000 in 1982, was made by a judge sitting without a jury.[112] Furthermore, a judge sitting alone might be preferable if, for example, there was a technical breach of the plaintiff's rights which a jury might not value highly or where a jury might disapprove of a plaintiff's way of life or beliefs and there is a risk they might, albeit unfairly, reflect their opinion in the size of the award.

Plaintiffs' lawyers should be aware that where there is a right to jury trial, the police defendants can exercise this right also, and might well do so in the situations described. There is nothing the plaintiff can do about this.

Judges sitting alone give reasons for their decisions; juries on the other hand do not. Where there has been an unfounded allegation against the plaintiff's character, a judge sitting alone should not reduce the damages awarded simply because the judgment contains an explicit vindication. The principles to be applied by a judge in assessing damages are the same as those to be applied by a jury.[113] However, under the Courts and Legal Services Act 1990 s8 and RSC Order 59 r11(4), the Court of Appeal has the power not only to order a new trial where the damages awarded by a jury are excessive or inadequate but can instead substitute for the sum awarded by the jury such sum as appears to it to be proper.

In *Rantzen v Mirror Group Newspapers*[114] the Court of Appeal considered this power in relation to a libel case where the same statute and court rules apply and felt that over time 'proper' awards substituted by the Court of Appeal would begin to set down a norm to which litigants will refer. In the same case, it was felt that the practice of the trial judge of not giving guidance to the jury on damages should continue, as damages for defamation were intended, at least in part, as a vindication of the plaintiff in public. Juries should, however, be invited to consider what could be bought with any award that they are minded to make, and to ensure that any award is proportionate to the

111 Clayton and Tomlinson 'Assessing damages in civil actions against the police' *LS Gaz* 25 November 1987, p3397.
112 *White v Metropolitan Police Commissioner* (1982) *Times* 24 April, QBD.
113 *Associated Newspapers Ltd v Dingle* [1964] AC 371, overruling *Hook v Cunard Steamship Co Ltd* [1953] 1 All ER 1021.
114 (1993) NLJ April 9, p507. See Milmo 'Libel damages and European human rights' (1993) NLJ, April 16, p550 for an argument that the Court of Appeal interpreted its powers too widely in this case.

damage the plaintiff has suffered. It is submitted that the same principles can be applied to jury trials involving false imprisonment and malicious prosecution.

In *Lewis v Chief Constable of Greater Manchester*,[115] where the plaintiff was detained at a police station over a weekend in his night clothes, the Court of Appeal decided that an award of £17,500 for false imprisonment, on the facts of the case, could not be supported and substituted an award of £5,000. In *Cumber v Chief Constable of Hampshire Constabulary*[116] the Court of Appeal held that a jury that had awarded £50 exemplary damages but no compensatory damages to a 15-year old girl detained wrongly for over four hours was perverse and substituted its own award of £350 compensatory damages.

Letter before action

The first step in bringing legal proceedings and informing the police of the substance of the case against them is the letter before action. In the Metropolitan police area the letter should be sent to the force's solicitors at New Scotland Yard. In other parts of the country it should be sent to the clerk to the relevant police authority unless it is known that particular solicitors are instructed to accept service generally. A copy of the letter should also be sent to the Legal Aid Board when applying for legal aid. Legal aid can be applied for at the same time as the letter is sent, as the Board do not, as a matter of practice, seem to need to see any reply to the letter before legal aid is granted. This is probably because the police will almost always deny liability initially.

The letter before action should set out the case against the police in very brief terms. There is little point in engaging in correspondence of any length with the police legal advisers before issuing proceedings. However, on those matters where the burden of proof in a trial will be on the police (eg, the lawfulness of arrest or detention) a full explanation should be sought in the letter before action. The usual blanket denial from the police will not provide such an explanation.

The police will not automatically treat the letter before action as a complaint; however, they will want to know whether the plaintiff wishes to have it treated as a complaint and if so whether s/he is willing to co-operate in its investigation.[117] It will therefore be helpful to make these points clear at the outset (see p200).

115 (1991) *Independent* 23 October.
116 (1995) *Times* 28 January.
117 GCO para 4.30.

CHAPTER 7

Bringing the action – from issue of proceedings to summons for directions

This chapter aims to provide the practitioner with the information to commence a civil action against the police and to take the case to the directions stage in both the High Court and the county court, highlighting the tactics and pitfalls.

Which court?

Many lawyers believe that, other considerations being equal, it is preferable to bring a case in the High Court rather than the county court, as the procedures can be used more effectively by a plaintiff's solicitor, it exerts a psychological advantage on the defendant, the quality of judicial decision-making is superior and the county courts are perceived as having difficulty coping administratively with their caseload.[1] However, the choice is less acute since the financial limits for county court actions were raised on 1 July 1991. Since then, plaintiffs have been governed by new provisions when deciding in which court to commence an action and where the case will finally be heard.

A case including a claim for personal injuries with a value of less than £50,000 must be commenced in the county court. This includes personal injuries to the plaintiff or any other person, and includes disease, impairment of physical or mental condition, and death.

There is an argument that the provision includes civil actions against the police where personal injuries have been suffered, but for the reasons explained below it is submitted that this is not the case. These arguments were succesfully employed in *Elsworth v Commissioner of Police for the Metropolis*[2] where Keene J overturned the decision of a master

---

1 See, for instance, discussion in Hendy, Day and Buchan, *Personal Injury Practice*, LAG 2nd edn 1994 pp98–99.
2 (1994) 2 November, QBD, unreported. Analysis in the following paragraphs relies on counsel's arguments in the case which were accepted by the court.

that he was bound to transfer the case to the county court because, as it was a 'personal injuries' claim worth less than £50,000, it should under the revised rules have been commenced in the county court.

The Civil Justice Review, published in 1988 by the Lord Chancellor's Department,[3] recommended the present changes in the allocation of business between the High Court and the county court. It is clear from the review that in discussing the allocation of personal injury cases, only conventional negligence and breach of statutory duty cases were under consideration. There is no mention in the review of battery, malicious prosecution or false imprisonment cases, nor indeed of any civil actions against the police which give rise to personal injuries.

Changes in the rules of court (requiring an indorsement on a High Court writ that the value of a case is in excess of £50,000 in 'an action for personal injuries'[4]) and the High Court and County Courts Order 1991 (section 5 of which states that proceedings including a claim for damages in respect of personal injuries should be started in the county court unless the value is more than £50,000) were introduced under Courts and Legal Services Act 1990 s1. The Lord Chancellor stated in the House of Lords, on the second reading of the Bill, that the purpose of s1 was to enable his department:

> to make flexible arrangements as between the two courts about what should be done. As I said earlier, I intend that the allocation will be on the basis recommended by the Civil Justice Review.[5]

It can be argued that in expressly following the recommendations of the Civil Justice Review, parliament had no intention that the reorganisation of the allocation of court business should affect civil actions against the police.[6]

Thus, it is submitted, most civil actions against the police should be treated as if the rules for personal injury cases do not apply. In such non-PI cases there is a greater freedom to chose in which court to commence proceedings. This view is now supported by the practice of the Action Department of the High Court, which does not require the 'over

3 Cm 394, 1988.
4 RSC Order 6 r2(1)(f).
5 Hansard, HL, Vol 514 Col 619.
6 Courts can now examine parliamentary materials, especially statements made about the intention behind a bill by its promoter, in interpreting an Act and statutory instruments where there meaning is ambiguous: *Pepper v Hart* [1993] AC 593, HL.

£50,000' indorsement in actions against the police for assault and battery, malicious prosecution and false imprisonment.

However, when deciding in which court a non-personal injury case (as defined above) will be heard, there is, in effect, a presumption that cases with a value of less than £25,000 will be heard in the county court and those with a value of more than £50,000 will be heard in the High Court. This is not a rigid rule and, in deciding whether to hear or transfer a case, the court must have regard to certain matters, including:[7]

a) the financial substance of the case
b) whether the action is otherwise important and, in particular, whether it raises questions of general public interest to persons who are not parties;
c) the complexity of the facts, legal remedies or procedures involved; and
d) whether transfer is likely to result in a speedier trial of the action.

The High Court has directed, *inter alia*, that claims for 'malicious prosecution and false imprisonment' and 'claims against the police', may be regarded as important and therefore suitable for trial in the High Court.[8] This direction does not indicate any particular level of value before a claim becomes 'suitable' for the High Court and this further supports the argument above that the 'personal injury claim' rules do not apply to most civil actions against the police.

If a case is commenced in the High Court, these arguments can be used at the summons for directions stage, and when the case is set down if the judge in charge of the jury list is minded to transfer the case to the county court for trial. In practice, cases with an expected value below £25,000 are likely to be transferred,[9] unless there are any unusual factors about the case which can be emphasised, for instance, the publicity surrounding a case, or if it occurred during a 'public order' incident.

7 High Court and County Courts Jurisdiction Order 1991 art 7(5).
8 *Practice Direction* [1991] 3 All ER 349, QBD.
9 Clayton and Tomlinson report that 'save in the most exceptional cases, the practice of the judge in charge of the jury list in London is to transfer . . . actions to the county court for trial:' January 1994 *Legal Action* 20. Practitioners interviewed by the authors in May 1995 felt that the regime, at that time, was not quite so harsh.

The procedure for transferring cases

Cases can be transferred from the High Court to the county court by the court acting on its own initiative or on the application of any party[10] if it is thought that the criteria set out above are not satisfied and therefore the case is not suitable for trial in the High Court. This is often done when directions are given or the case is set down. Where the court proposes to transfer a case, notice must be given to the parties, who may within 14 days file an objection to the transfer. Costs in cases transferred between the courts are at the discretion of the court of final determination and the costs of the whole proceedings are taxed in that court.[11] If, in the opinion of the court, the case was wrongly commenced in the High Court, the circumstances which led to this can be taken into account by that court when determining the level of costs.[12]

A county court can transfer proceedings to the High Court where it is satisfied that the action should be heard by the High Court.[13]

Pre-commencement applications

In both the High Court and the county court it is possible, in some cases, to obtain pre-action discovery of documents and inspection of property. In relation to documents, pre-action discovery is only available where the action contemplated is one in respect of personal injuries or death and the party against whom discovery is sought is 'likely to be party' to any subsequent litigation.[14] An order for pre-commencement inspection of property is available in all cases.[15]

In a case against the police this procedure may be useful, for example, where it is thought that police documents may reveal whether a client has a cause of action but there is no entitlement to the documents and the police refuse to release them without a court order. The documents should be requested in writing from the police before any application to the court is made. The application must be made by way of originating summons in the High Court or originating

10 County Courts Act 1984 ss40 and 42 (as substituted by Courts and Legal Services Act 1990 s2(1) and (3)).
11 Supreme Court Act 1981 s45 (as amended) and County Courts Act 1984 s45 (as amended).
12 Supreme Court Act 1981 s51(8).
13 County Courts Act s 42(1).
14 RSC Order 24 r7A; CCR Order 13 r7.
15 RSC Order 29 r7A.

application in the county court with an affidavit in support. Any grant of legal aid should specifically cover such an application.

Commencing proceedings

In practice the police rarely pay damages where proceedings have not been issued. Therefore there is little point in engaging in correspondence with the police after the reply to the letter before action has been received. Every effort should be made to commence proceedings as soon as practicable, unless, of course, the reply undermines the client's case to such an extent that it is clear there is no reasonable prospect of success.

Instructing counsel

Once the decision to sue has been made, counsel will usually need to be instructed. Counsel will often be required by the Legal Aid Board to give a written opinion on the merits and quantum in the case before legal aid is extended to cover the commencement of proceedings. Given the difficulties in calculating quantum, advice on which court to start proceedings in should be sought. Although in general personal injury cases it is often not the practice to have a conference with counsel before the action is pleaded, in civil actions against the police more thought should be given as to whether to do so. The conference should be justifiable for the purposes of legal aid. Actions against the police will almost invariably involve hotly disputed issues of fact in which the plaintiff's credibility is at stake. Clients who have suffered at the hands of the police are commonly distrustful of establishment figures and will often want to meet the barrister to put their minds at rest about him/her. An early conference can give the barrister an indication at least about what kind of witness the plaintiff will make, which can be important if difficult decisions about whether to settle the case need to be made later on in the litigation.

Issue and service of a writ in the High Court

The writ is a straightforward document to complete. Proceedings are commenced in the High Court by lodging or posting the endorsed writ and a copy (and a copy for the defendant) after paying the court fee (£100 at the time of publication). The endorsement is a concise statement of the nature of the claim[16] containing the essential details of the

16 RSC Order 6 r2.

cause of action and the damages claimed. The statement of claim can be lodged with the court either at the same time as the writ or within 14 days of the receipt of the acknowledgement of service from the police (see below). A statement of special damages and a medical report should be lodged with the writ (see below), but the lack of these should not prevent the writ being issued.

Although the writ can be served in person on the chief officer of police, in practice the solicitors acting for the police will accept service on his/her behalf. It will be usual to serve the writ by post.[17] Unless an extension is obtained from the court, the writ must be served within four months of issue.[18]

Issue and service in the county court

In the county court there needs to be a full 'particulars of claim' (see below) before the court can issue a summons, rather than only the short endorsement required on the High Court writ. The request for a default summons is completed by the plaintiff's solicitor and is a straightforward document. The fee and copies for the court and the defendant, and a stamped addressed envelope should be provided to the court staff. The court will post the summons and particulars of claim to the defendant and inform the plaintiff's solicitors that this has been done. The same rules concerning medical reports and statements of special damage in personal injury cases apply as in the High Court. Proceedings can be commenced in any county court.

Pleadings

The pleadings in a civil case are the documents which set out the matters that each side will argue in court. Pleadings enable both sides to see the case they will have to meet at trial, and show the court the issues between the parties. Although it is often possible to amend pleadings, if a matter is excluded from the pleadings, the party wishing to raise it at trial may be prevented from doing so. The usual pleadings in a civil action against the police are the statement of claim (in the High Court) or particulars of claim (in the county court), a defence, and sometimes a reply. There are often requests for 'further and better particulars' of these pleadings.

The most appropriate person to draft the pleadings will usually be

17 RSC Order 10 r1(2).
18 RSC Order 6 r8(1).

the advocate who will eventually have to argue the matters contained in them at court.

Statement of claim in the High Court and particulars of claim in the county court.

In the High Court the plaintiff must serve a statement of claim on the defendant at any time before the expiry of 14 days from the date the defendant gives notice of intention to defend, unless the statement of claim is already endorsed on the writ.[19] In the county court the particulars of claim must be provided to the court when the summons is issued and will be served with the summons.[20]

The main rules on drafting pleadings, applicable to High Court and county court alike, are to be found in RSC Order 18. The statement of claim or the particulars of claim must contain only the material facts on which the plaintiff's case will rely and not the evidence by which those facts will be proved,[21] or the law on which the claim is based. The relevant matters should be stated briefly, succinctly and in strict chronological order.[22]

In actions against the police, the burden of proof on some issues falls on the plaintiff and on other issues (such as that of reasonable grounds for suspicion in false imprisonment cases) on the defendant. Thus, for instance, in false imprisonment cases it may be sufficient simply to relate the facts of the arrest and detention and that they were unlawful; the police then have to prove the lawfulness of those actions in their defence.

Where the actual officers complained about are not to be sued personally but the defendant is to be the chief officer of the police force involved (see p203), then the vicarious liability of the chief officer should be established in the pleadings by stating that the defendant is the chief officer for the area concerned and that the officers referred to in the pleadings 'were at all material times Constables acting under his direction and control and in the performance or purported performance of their police functions' (see appendix 3.2).[23]

The effect of any document or the gist of any conversation should be briefly stated unless the words actually used are material, as may be the case in an action against the police, for instance, for false imprisonment

19　RSC Order 18 r1.
20　CCR Order 3 r3.
21　RSC Order 18 r7.
22　See White Book Vol. 1 para 18/7/6.
23　Cf Police Act 1964 s48(1).

where what is said to the plaintiff at the time of arrest may be important and should be quoted verbatim.

If any party wishes to adduce evidence that a person has been convicted of a criminal offence, then the court, conviction, date and issue to which the conviction is relevant must be pleaded in the High Court.[24] There is no necessity to do so in the county court, but it is considered desirable in practice.[25]

The factors which might be cited in support of a claim for aggravated or exemplary damages are discussed at p194 (and see appendix 3.2). A statement specifically claiming exemplary damages (if these are appropriate, see p196), together with supporting facts, must be included in the body of the statement of claim and not just in the prayer.[26] In practice the facts relied on for a claim of aggravated damages should also be specifically pleaded.[27] In the county court, where a plaintiff claims exemplary or aggravated damages the particulars of claim must contain a statement to that effect and state the facts relied on in support of the claim.[28] Particulars of general damages (see p193) need not be given.

A claim for interest must be specifically pleaded both in the body of the claim and in the prayer; otherwise the Court will not award the plaintiff any interest.[29]

The elements of the various torts for which claims may be made are set out in chapter 5. It is important for each of the elements to be pleaded in the statement of claim or particulars of claim. In actions for assault and battery, the intentional nature of the acts of the police should be pleaded. In actions for false imprisonment, as the burden of proof is on the police to prove that a detention is lawful, then, strictly speaking, the plaintiff need only state that s/he has been unlawfully detained. However, in practice it may be desirable (and shorten the pleadings stage of the proceedings) to set out more fully the nature of the unlawfulness alleged to allow the police to address all the relevant allegations in their defence. If malice is material (for instance, in cases of malicious prosecution or misfeasance in public office), the particulars of the facts on which the plaintiff relies should be expressly alleged.[30]

24 Civil Evidence Act 1968 s11 and RSC Order 18 r7A.
25 CCR Order 20 r11 and Green Book (County Court Practice) notes thereto.
26 RSC Order 18 r8.
27 White Book Vol. 1 para 18/12/16.
28 CCR Order 6 r1B.
29 RSC Order 18 r8(4); CCR Order 6 r1A; *Ward v Chief Constable for Avon and Somerset* (1985) 129 SJ 606; and see White Book Vol 1 para 18/8/9.
30 RSC Order 18 r12.

In cases involving a claim for personal injuries, a medical report substantiating all the personal injuries alleged and a statement of special damages (giving full details of expenses and losses already incurred and an estimate of any future expenses and losses, including loss of earnings and of pension rights) should be served with the statement of claim or particulars of claim.[31] If they are not so served then the court can specify the time limit within which they are to be provided.[32]

In the county court, plaintiffs must provide a statement of value in the particulars of claim, otherwise the action will be presumed to fall within the jurisdiction of the district judge which is £5,000.[33] Failure to provide a statement can prevent the trial proceeding and lead to a wasted costs order against the plaintiff's lawyers.

Acknowledgement of service and defence

In the High Court the defendant has 14 days to complete the standard form acknowledgement of service that is served with the writ.[34] The defence itself must be served within 14 days of the service of statement of claim, or 28 days if the statement was served with the writ.[35] In the county court there is a standard form on which the defendant can admit the claim, otherwise a defence has to be filed with the court within 14 days of the service of the summons.[36]

The police will often request an extension to allow them to prepare a full defence to the claim. In many cases such a request will be reasonable, as a number of officers may have to be interviewed and statements taken, documents will have to be gathered and counsel instructed to settle the defence. To allow an extension of time of, say, three or four weeks for the defence to be served is realistic, but care must be taken to enforce time limits by an application to court if the defence is not forthcoming after the first agreement of an extension.

The police are under a duty to raise in their defence any matter which makes the plaintiff's case unsustainable, or which would take the plaintiff by surprise if not pleaded, or which raises issues of fact not arising out of the plaintiff's claim.[37]

If the police intend to rely, for instance, on a warrant to justify what

31 RSC Order 18 r12(1A); CCR Order 6 r1(5).
32 RSC Order 18 r12(1B); CCR Order 6 r1(6).
33 CCR Order 6 r1(1A).
34 RSC Order 12 r5.
35 RSC Order 18 r2.
36 CCR Order 9 r2(6).
37 RSC Order 18 r8(1).

would otherwise be an unlawful act, then this must be pleaded with precision, stating the date, general nature of the document and the name of the person who signed or issued it.[38] In chapter 5, examples of possible defences to the torts described are set out. If the police fail to plead a defence afforded them by the Limitation Act 1980 (see p189), they will be deemed to have waived any benefit under the Act, unless leave to amend is granted.[39]

It is not enough for the police merely to deny every element of the plaintiff's claim for false imprisonment if in fact they wish to argue, for instance, that a detention was lawful. If they do so the court may well not allow the defence of lawfulness to be raised at the trial. Rather the police should 'confess' (ie, admit) the detention and 'avoid' the effect of the confession by pleading, for instance, the powers of arrest that justify the detention.[40]

The police are likely to deny anything that can be denied, for example, anything that will need to be proved by the plaintiff, and are likely to give a full account of any arrest and detention in order to defend a claim for false imprisonment. A copy of the defence should be sent to the plaintiff with a covering letter explaining the nature of the defence raised by the police and explaining that the forthright nature of the defence is to be expected, if this has not been done already. The plaintiff should then be interviewed in person to obtain his/her views on the defence and a statement drawn up expressing those views.

Reply

A reply is served if the plaintiff wishes to respond to any matters raised in the defence. A reply is not compulsory and if one is not served, it is assumed that the defence raised is denied.[41] If the police have set out in their defence that they intend to rely on the conviction of the plaintiff, then, if the plaintiff intends to deny the conviction or allege that it was erroneous, this must be pleaded[42] and the reply will often be the most appropriate time to do this.

In some cases full particulars of a false imprisonment will not have been set out in the claim (see above p219) and the defence may then raise matters when stating that the arrest was lawful. If the plaintiff wishes to raise new facts not already pleaded, in response to the defence raised,

38 White Book Vol 1 1995 para 18/12/11.
39 See O'Hare and Hill *Civil Litigation*, 6th edition 1993, Longman.
40 See White Book Vol 1 1995 para 18/8/2.
41 RSC Order 18 r14.
42 RSC Order 18 r7A.

then this can be done using a reply. For instance, if in the claim the plaintiff simply states that s/he was unlawfully detained resulting in false imprisonment and the police admit the detention but state in their defence that powers under PACE were being exercised, the plaintiff may then need to serve a reply if s/he wishes to claim, for example, that no reasons for the arrest were provided, as required by PACE.

A reply should be filed within 14 days of the receipt of the defence,[43] unless an extension has been agreed.

Further and better particulars of the plaintiff's or the defendant's case
The purpose of the right to obtain further and better particulars is to ensure that the litigation between the parties is conducted fairly, openly and without surprises and so as to minimise costs.[44] Therefore, it may be appropriate to ask for further and better particulars to clarify the case to be met and the evidence that needs to be prepared to meet it.[45] The court has the power to order particulars of any claim or defence to be served on the other parties.[46] In *Mercer v Chief Constable of the Lancashire Constabulary*[47] the Court of Appeal urged district judges to take a proactive approach to this task:

> . . . however unilluminating the pleadings, the district judge at any hearing for directions can and should metaphorically take the case by the scruff of the neck and shake it with a view to finding out what are the real issues between the parties and, on the basis of that information, ensuring that neither party is taken by surprise or need have additional evidence available to deal with a possible ambush. If, for example . . . the plaintiff is alleging that, if he was lawfully arrested, he was detained in other than a designated police station (s35 of PACE) or that, despite the fact that he was awake and his detention continued for a sufficient time to call for its review under s40, he was given no opportunity of making representations, he should be required to say so.[48]

The Master of the Rolls explained how the defence pleaded by the police was inadequate to deal with the claim by the plaintiff that he was wrongfully arrested and detained in a police station for a specified time, and what should be required by way of defence:

> The chief constable by way of defence has pleaded in the case of Mr Holden that the arrest was lawful by reason of the constable's reasonable suspicions

43 RSC Order 18 r3(4).
44 See White Book Vol. 1 1995 para 18/12/1.
45 RSC Order 18 r7A.
46 RSC Order 18 r12(3).
47 [1991] 2 All ER 504, CA.
48 Ibid at 511 per Lord Donaldson MR.

and that at an unspecified time during his detention inquiries revealed that the engine had been bought by his employer. The defence continues: 'By reason of the premises the plaintiff's arrest and detention were lawful.' This pleading is defective, or at least cries out for a request for further and better particulars, in that it does not say when this information came to the notice of the police and whether it is alleged, as it would have to be if the plaintiff was not to succeed, that he was released with all reasonable promptness thereafter.[49]

In another case for damages for false imprisonment where the police justified the arrest of the plaintiff on the ground that there was reasonable and probable cause for suspecting that a felony had been committed, and that the plaintiff had committed it, the police were ordered to give particulars of the alleged felony and also of the reasonable and probable cause for suspicion.[50] This approach was confirmed by the Court of Appeal in *Stapeley v Annetts*[51] on the basis that the burden of proof to show reasonable and probable cause is clearly on the police in a false imprisonment case (see p219).

However, in a malicious prosecution case, if the police simply deny acting without reasonable or probable cause, the plaintiff is not entitled to particulars of the grounds on which s/he has been prosecuted,[52] as the burden is on the plaintiff to prove that there was no reasonable and probable cause. Only if the police put forward a positive claim that they had reasonable and probable cause for the prosecution would the plaintiff be entitled to seek particulars of what that cause might have been.[53]

In practice, a party will serve a request for further and better particulars on his/her opponent. If the particulars are given, 'the request or order shall be incorporated with the particulars, each item of the particulars following immediately after the corresponding item of the request'.[54] It will be necessary to apply to the court if a party refuses to provide the particulars, or claims that his/her opponent is not entitled to the particulars. If the pleadings of the police are clearly defective, consideration should be given to not requesting further and better particulars when it appears that they will be unlikely to raise a defence at trial.

49 Ibid at 510.
50 *Green v Garbutt* (1912) 28 TLR 575, CA, and see White Book Vol. 1 1995 para 18/12/7.
51 [1970] 1 WLR 20, CA.
52 *Stapeley v Annetts* [1970] 1 WLR 20, CA.
53 Ibid at 22.
54 RSC Order 18 r12(7).

Summary judgment, questions of law and striking out

Throughout the pre-trial proceedings there are a number of possible procedural applications in the plaintiff's armoury which may become appropriate at various stages as the case develops. If there is a timely summons for directions or pre-trial review, it may be appropriate to apply for these orders at that point in the case. Otherwise, the procedure for applying in the county court is usually on a standard form returnable to the district judge. In the High Court a summons for directions will usually need to be issued returnable to a master or a judge depending on the time and complexity of the application.

Summary judgment

Consideration should be given to applying for summary judgment in cases where no proper defence has been put forward by the police.[55] However, this procedure is not available in cases where there is a claim for malicious prosecution or false imprisonment[56] and so it will not be applicable in many civil actions against the police. There is, however, a danger, if such an application is unsuccessful, of giving away too much of the plaintiff's case at an early stage and therefore the procedure must be used with caution.

Questions of law

In the High Court an application can be made, by summons or by motion, to determine questions of law and construction without the need for a full hearing.[57] The procedure is only available if it appears to the court that the result of the application will finally determine the entire case or, for instance, determine liability, leaving only the question of damages to be decided. This procedure is appropriate if it is felt that a question of law is the only matter preventing the police from making a suitable settlement of the case.

Striking out

The court may at any stage of the proceedings order to be struck out any pleading on the ground that it:

a) discloses no reasonable cause of action or defence;
b) is scandalous, frivolous or vexatious;
c) may prejudice, embarrass or delay the fair trial of the action; or

55 RSC Order 14 r1(1); CCR Order 9 r14.
56 RSC Order 14 r1(2); CCR Order 9 r14(1)(c).
57 RSC Order 14A rr1 and 2.

d) is otherwise an abuse of the process of the Court.[58]

The plaintiff should consider making an application to strike out if the defence received from the police breaches any of these principles. The powers exerciseable by the court should only be used in plain and obvious cases where a claim or defence is 'obviously unsustainable'.[59] The mere fact that a case or a defence is weak is not grounds for striking it out. In actions against the police the present law on the liability of the police in negligence cases (see p161) has led to a number of claims in negligence being struck out[60] on the basis that there is no reasonable cause of action. In a claim for breach of confidence when police 'reasonably' circulated a photograph taken in custody of a known troublemaker to local shopkeepers, the action was struck out on the basis that the police were bound to succeed with a defence that their actions had been 'in the public interest'.[61]

A claim by a plaintiff for assault against the police will not be struck out simply on the basis that s/he has been convicted of crimes of violence, even where those crimes arose out of the same incident and a police officer was the victim. The fact of such convictions does not necessarily carry the conclusion that the plaintiff was not assaulted by the police.[62]

Directions

Directions following the close of pleadings are the way in which the court provides a timetable for the case to which the parties are expected to keep. There are slightly different procedures in the county court and in the High Court.

County court

In the vast majority of cases in the county court the directions stage has become automatic with a standard set of directions issued at the close

58 RSC Order 18 r19.
59 *Attorney-General of Duchy of Lancaster v London & North Western Railway Co* [1892] 3 Ch 274 CA, and see White Book Vol. 1 1995 para 18/19/7.
60 See for instance *Clough v Bussan* [1990] 1 All ER 431; *Hill v Chief Constable of West Yorkshire* [1989] AC 53; *Hughes v NUM* [1991] 4 All ER 278; and see White Book Vol. 1 1995 para 18/19/18.
61 *Hellewell v Chief Constable of Derbyshire* (1995) LS Gaz 15 February p35.
62 *Simpson v Chief Constable of South Yorkshire Police* (1991) *Independent* 14 March, CA.

of pleadings. It should be said immediately, though, that many civil actions against the police are the exception to this rule as there is a specific exclusion from automatic directions in actions where there is trial by jury (which includes cases of malicious prosecution and false imprisonment). In these cases a pre-trial review still needs to be held to determine the directions for the case. However, as non-jury trial civil actions (eg assault cases) are covered by automatic directions, and because many of the automatic directions will be desirable in jury cases in any event, the standard procedure is described first.

Automatic directions

Close of pleadings is deemed to be 14 days after the delivery of a defence[63] and automatic directions take effect thereafter.[64] The directions are summarised as follows:[65]

a) There shall be discovery of documents within 28 days, and inspection within 7 days.
b) Except with leave of the Court or where all parties agree:
  i)   no expert evidence may be adduced at the trial unless the substance of that evidence has been disclosed to the other parties in the form of a written report within 10 weeks; and
  ii) the number of expert witnesses of any kind shall be limited to two (except in an action for personal injuries where the usual limit is two medical experts and one expert of any other kind);[66] and
  iii) any party who intends to place reliance at trial on any other oral evidence shall, within 10 weeks, serve on the other parties written statements of all such oral evidence at the trial which he intends to adduce.[67]
c) Photographs and sketch plans and in an action for personal injuries the contents of any police accident report book shall be receivable in evidence at the trial and shall be agreed if possible.
d) Unless a day has already been fixed, the plaintiff shall within 6 months request the proper officer to fix a day for the hearing.

---

63 CCR Order 17 r11(10).
64 CCR Order 17 r11(3).
65 Ibid (a)–(d).
66 See CCR Order 17 r11(7).
67 See p242 for further discussion of exchange of witness statements.

Other directions can be given where appropriate on the application of any party or on the court's own motion.[68] Suggestions for directions when it is intended to use notes of evidence, etc from criminal trials or coroner's inquests in the action are given below at p230.

Included in the automatic directions rule is the provision that if no request is made for the case to be fixed within 15 months of the close of pleadings, then the application will be automatically struck out. Fifteen months should be sufficient to have a case ready to be fixed, but if extension of time is required, the application should be made to the court. Automatic striking out will then only apply nine months after the expiry of the time limit granted by the court at such hearing.[69] Automatic striking out should be avoided at all costs by the plaintiff's solicitor as restoring an application after striking out, although possible, is difficult.[70]

Directions in jury trials
Automatic directions do not apply in actions for false imprisonment and malicious prosecution.[71] Cases which include one or both of these torts as well as others such as assault or negligence will also be outside the scope of automatic directions.

The procedure for cases where there are no automatic directions is that a pre-trial review has to be held.[72] A date should be fixed by the court for the pre-trial review without the need for an application, but because many courts are used to automatic directions applying in the vast majority of cases this is often not done. Therefore, it is good practice for the plaintiff's solicitor to apply for a pre-trial review as soon as the defence is received. This can be done by letter to the court or by standard application. If it has been decided at this point that a jury trial will be requested (see p208 for a discussion of the pros and cons), then, as this must be applied for on notice, it is appropriate to include the request for jury trial in the same application. In the county court there is no time restriction on applying for jury trial, but if the plaintiff applies for a jury trial within 10 days of the date set for the trial, then the court may postpone the trial.[73]

68 CCR Order 17 r11(4).
69 CCR Order 17 r11(9).
70 See *Rastin v British Steel PLC* [1994] 1 WLR 732, CA, which sets down the principles upon which a county court judge should exercise discretion to reinstate a case that has been automatically struck out.
71 County Courts Act 1984 s66(3); CCR Order 17 r11(1)(h).
72 CCR Order 17 r1.
73 CCR Order 13 r10.

The application may, therefore, read as follows:

The Plaintiff applies for:

1. A pre-trial review as this is an action covered by CCR Order 17 r 11(1)(h) and therefore automatic directions do not apply; and

2. Trial by jury in this action which is listed in section 66(3) of the County Courts Act 1984.

Negotiations can then be started with the police solicitors for suitable directions. Often these will be very similar to the automatic directions but the following points should be noted:

a) The directions should include provision for jury trial.

b) The exchange of witness statements is compulsory.

c) The automatic striking out provision does not apply and a direction such as the following would be appropriate to ensure that the case is set down speedily and without delay: 'The action be set down for trial on the first open date after 14 days upon the filing of a Certificate of Readiness by either party with a written estimate as to the length of trial after giving the other party not less than seven days notice in writing of the intention to set down and of the estimate and time'.[74]

d) Liberty to apply should be included as a direction and it is usual for the costs of the pre-trial review to be 'in the cause'.

e) See below p230 for directions where it is sought to use notes of evidence, etc in the action from criminal trials or coroner's inquests.

It may be possible to agree suitable directions with the police solicitors, who will then often not wish to attend the pre-trial review. It is possible for the plaintiff's solicitors also not to attend court but to send by post the proposed directions and the defendant's agreement. However, it is not unknown for the court to lose the correspondence (and for the proceedings to be struck out because of the non-appearance of the plaintiff)[75] or for the district judge to refuse one or more of the agreed directions[76] and to adjourn the case, thus causing delay. It is therefore better practice to attend the pre-trial review even where directions have

74 Otherwise the police have been known to take months to state that they are ready.

75 Order 17 r5.

76 Under CCR Order 17(1) the District Judge's duty is to 'give all such directions as appear necessary for securing the just, expeditious and economical disposal of the action'.

been agreed in advance, and especially if a request for a jury trial is an infrequent event in a particular court.

High Court

In the High Court there must be a summons for directions in all cases begun by writ[77] unless the action includes a claim for damages for personal injuries, in which case automatic directions will apply.[78] An action for personal injuries includes any impairment of a person's physical or mental condition and includes a claim in respect of a person's death.[79] Thus, automatic directions will cover many civil actions against the police, for example where personal injuries (including post-traumatic stress disorder) have been caused by assault, negligence or other torts. Unlike the county court, there is not a different procedure where the action is to be tried by a jury.

Automatic directions

Automatic directions take effect upon the close of pleadings.[80] The substance of the automatic directions which will be relevant to the vast majority of civil actions against the police is as follows:[81]

a) There shall be discovery of documents within 14 days of close of pleadings and inspection seven days thereafter.

b) Where any party intends to place reliance at the trial on expert evidence, a written report of the substance of the evidence shall be disclosed to the other parties within 14 weeks, which shall be agreed if possible.

c) Witness statements of any other oral evidence it is intended to adduce at trial shall be served with 14 weeks.

d) If the expert reports are not agreed, the parties are entitled to call up to two medical experts and one other expert to give evidence at the trial

e) Photographs, a sketch plan and the contents of any police accident report book shall be receivable as evidence at the trial and shall be agreed if possible.

f) The action shall be tried at the trial centre for the place in which the

77 RSC Order 25 r1.

78 RSC Order 25 r8.

79 RSC Order 1 r4.

80 Deemed to be 14 days after the service of a reply if there is one and otherwise 14 days after the service of the defence (or defence to counterclaim if there is one) – RSC Order 18 r20.

81 For the full list see RSC Order 25 r8(1)(a)–(g).

action is proceeding or at such other trial centre as the parties may agree in writing.

g) The action shall be tried by judge alone, is classified as a case of substance or difficulty (category B) and shall be set down within six months

Although these directions will be appropriate in many actions against the police, it will be noticed immediately that a direction that the action be tried by judge alone is included. There is scope in the rules for a party to apply to the court for 'further or different' directions, and clearly this should be exercised if trial by jury is to be requested.[82] Such an application would be made in the same way as the summons for directions in non-personal injuries cases.

If reference is to be made in the trial to notes of evidence, depositions and transcripts from a previous criminal trial, then, rather than subpoena the person who took down the evidence to produce his/her note or transcript in the civil proceedings, the following direction is commonly requested:

> That the notes of evidence or depositions or transcript of the evidence taken in the proceedings before . . . concerning matters arising in the action (duly certified by. . . or agreed between the parties) be admissible at the trial for the same purposes and to the same extent as the contents thereof would have been if duly proved by the person who took down the same without calling such person and without proving the original or copy.[83]

A similar direction may be requested in relation to coroners' depositions or notes of evidence (which can be used for the purposes of cross-examination only) to obviate the need to call the coroner to prove his or her notes.[84]

Summons for directions
In cases where automatic directions do not apply in the High Court (eg, malicious prosecution and/or false imprisonment cases where there is no claim for personal injuries), then a summons for directions must be taken out within 28 days of the close of pleadings.[85]

---

82 RSC Order 25 r8(3).
83 White Book Vol. 1 1995 para 25/3/4.
84 Ibid. para 25/3/3.
85 RSC Order 25 r1(1). For the procedure and forms to be used see White Book Vol. 1 1995 para 25/1/2. See above p226 for when pleadings are deemed to be closed.

The directions sought should be set out in the summons and consideration should be given to including directions along the lines of the automatic directions listed above with suitable variations and additions (see p226). The court has jurisdiction to make orders and directions of its own motion.[86] Exchange of witness statements will usually be ordered unless there are reasons to the contrary,[87] although it may be possible to agree a longer time limit for exchange if this is desirable, and a time estimate for the trial should be included.

A statement of value must be lodged with the court and served on the other parties by the plaintiff at least one day before the hearing of the summons for directions.[88] Failure to do so will mean the action is transferred to the county court.

The plaintiff should apply for trial by jury before the mode of trial is fixed at the summons for direction,[89] but the judge has a discretion to allow an application after this time.[90] The Court of Appeal has upheld a judge's decision to allow an application for a jury trial after the summons for directions as the case was of 'public concern' and decided that the costs factor was not important as the case was only to last two days.[91]

Once the summons for directions has been issued, it should be sent to the solicitors acting for the police, who should be invited to agree the directions. A consent order can be drawn up, but given the court's powers to act on its own motion, it is advisable to attend the hearing of the summons in any event.

---

86 RSC Order 25 r3.
87 White Book Vol. 1 1995 para 25/3/2A.
88 RSC Order 25 r6(2A).
89 Supreme Court Act 1981 s69(2) and RSC Order 33 r4.
90 Supreme Court Act 1981 s69(3).
91 *Cropper v Chief Constable of South Yorkshire Police* [1989] 1 WLR 333, CA.

CHAPTER 8

The civil action – from discovery to trial

This chapter deals with the difficult question of discovery in a civil action against the police, and explains the major privileges from disclosure together with public interest immunity. It also covers the preparation of witness statements, issues of settlement and payments in (together with the possibility of making a statement in open court after settlement), preparations for trial and the trial procedure itself, with special emphasis on the role of the jury.

Discovery and inspection

Procedure in the High Court and county court

Discovery is the process whereby the existence of relevant documents is disclosed by one party in an action for the benefit of his/her opponent. Inspection involves production of the actual document (or a copy of it). Some documents must be disclosed, that is, their existence must be revealed, but need not (or in some cases must not) be produced for inspection. In High Court actions begun by writ[1] and in almost all county court actions (except those involving trial by jury),[2] there is provision for automatic discovery. In other cases it is necessary to seek discovery by application to the court. Even where there is automatic discovery, applications for discovery of specific documents may still be needed.

In the High Court, an order for automatic discovery requires the parties, within 14 days of the close of pleadings, to serve on each other a list of all relevant documents which are or have been in their possession, custody or power.[3] There will be automatic discovery in all police cases in the High Court begun by writ.

1 RSC Order 24 r2.
2 CCR Order 17 r11.
3 RSC Order 24 r2.

In the county court, there is an exclusion from automatic discovery for cases where there is a right to a jury trial (eg, false imprisonment and malicious prosecution),[4] but in other cases against the police there is usually automatic discovery in cases commenced after 1 October 1990 and discovery should take place within 14 days of the close of pleadings.[5]

It is clearly important for solicitors to inform their clients as soon as possible of the need to preserve all documents that may be relevant, whether they assist the client's case or not. As discovery also has to be given of documents created after the action has commenced,[6] no new non-privileged documents should be generated without legal advice. A discovered document can be used for other purposes only after it has been read to or by the court, or referred to in court – unless the court orders otherwise on the application of the owner of the document.

Plaintiff's documents

In most cases against the police the plaintiff will have very few documents to disclose (and most of these are likely to be copies of documents, such as the custody record, received from the police). The other common kind of documents that will need to be disclosed are those relating to special damages for loss of earnings such as wage slips, employers' letters and benefit details in situations where personal injuries have been caused by the police. Lastly, it will be necessary to disclose medical records which are relevant to the injury that gave rise to the claim. Where there is a claim that a plaintiff has suffered an injury which has caused permanent loss of earnings and loss of earning capacity, all his/her medical records should be listed.[7]

The list of documents should be prepared and can be served as soon as pleadings have closed. An alternative practice is to let the police solicitors know that the plaintiff's list is ready and that the plaintiff is ready to exchange lists. Both these approaches progress the case while putting pressure on the police to produce their list, which will generally be much longer than the plaintiff's. Procrastination by the plaintiff at this stage encourages the police in the belief that this is a case where,

---

4 CCR Order 17 r11(1)(h).
5 CCR Order 17 r11(3)(a).
6 See White Book Vol 1 1995 para 24/1/2.
7 *Dunn v British Coal Corporation* [1993] PIQR 275, CA. The court said (at p282) that if the records reveal an unrelated but embarassing condition to the defendant, disclosure could be limited to the defendant's medical advisers.

after time, the plaintiff will lose interest.[8] In both the county court and the High Court the list of documents should be served on the defendant and a copy lodged with the court.

What is discoverable?

Almost all documents which are held by the police and which are relevant to an action are discoverable. The general principle was set out by the Court of Appeal in *Thorpe v Chief Constable of Greater Manchester Police*.[9]

> Any document must be disclosed which it is reasonable to suppose contains information which may enable the party applying for discovery either to advance his own case or to damage that of his adversary or which may lead him to a train of enquiry which may have either of these two consequences. Discovery is thus not necessarily limited to documents which would be admissible in evidence.

The kinds of documents that the police may have are described in chapter 2 (see p29). It is the general practice for the police to disclose most documents relevant to the case, including official records such as notebooks and the search register. In addition, because of the decision in *Ex p Wiley* (see p239) documents made pursuant to any police complaint must also be disclosed. Solicitors are under a duty to explain to their clients the responsibilities of discovery and to take steps to ensure that documents are preserved.[10] However, even with the best will in the world, mistakes can occur and the lawyers acting for the police may be dependent on their clients handing over all the documentation that they have which relates to the case. One lawyer who advises the police has said 'Officers should be educated in the tactical importance of disclosing all relevant documents [to their lawyers] early in the proceedings. Late disclosure suggests weakness and lack of organisation'.[11] It is good practice to ask specifically for copies of all the types of documents listed in chapter 2, if they may be relevant, to ensure that nothing is overlooked. 'Documents' which should be on the list prepared include photographs, films, computer tapes and tape recordings. A liberal approach is taken as to what constitutes a relevant document.[12]

---

8 For detailed information on completing the list of documents see, for instance, Hendy, Day and Buchan, *Personal Injury Practice* LAG 1994 pp181–182.
9 [1989] 2 All ER 827, CA at 829 per Dillon LJ.
10 See White Book Vol 1 1995 para 24/2/3.
11 'Damage control', news report in *Police Review* 21 April 1995.
12 *Compagnie Financière v Peruvian Guano* (1882) 11 QBD 55, CA.

Documents concerning previous misconduct

Plaintiffs will be anxious to discover any documents that link the defendant police officers with previous incidents of police misconduct, whether similar in kind, or not. The police, on the other hand, will want to keep as much of this information as possible out of the litigation. The extent to which such information is relevant and therefore must be included in the list of documents has, not surprisingly, been the subject of litigation.

In *DPP v P*,[13] the House of Lords explained the basis on which similar fact evidence should be admissible in criminal cases. The principles of admissibility of evidence of similar facts are in general the same in civil cases.[14] Lord Mackay LC said that although in many cases the similarity between previous crimes and the one for which a person is presently accused should be 'striking' before evidence of the former can be admitted, there may be other circumstances where the probative force of evidence outweighs the prejudice to the client and therefore evidence that may be less than striking should be admitted.

As already stated in this section, the test at the discovery stage is lower than that for admissibility at trial. In *Steel v Commissioner of Police for the Metropolis*,[15] Beldam LJ stated that, 'At the stage of specific discovery it would in my view be premature to have regard to the concept of "prejudice"'. It would be up to the trial judge, then, to carry out the balancing between probative value and prejudice described by Lord Mackay.

Two Court of Appeal decisions, already referred to, in actions against the police illustrate how these principles can be applied. In *Thorpe v Chief Constable of Greater Manchester* it was held that adjudications of guilt against an officer in disciplinary proceedings sought for the purposes of following a 'similar facts' line of argument which did not reveal a system of conduct or which provided material to be used solely for the purposes of cross-examination as to the credibility of the witness, would not be allowed as they were not probative of anything.[16]

In *Steel v Commissioner of Police for the Metropolis*[17] two brothers brought actions for malicious prosecution and false imprisonment. They had been convicted of serious offences and alleged that a police

13 [1991] 2 AC 447.
14 *Thorpe v Chief Constable of Greater Mancester* (n9 above) per Dillon LJ at p830.
15 (1993) 18 February, CA, Lexis.
16 [1989] 2 All ER 827, CA.
17 (1993) 18 February, CA, Lexis.

officer had fabricated confessions. In quashing their convictions the Court of Appeal concluded that the officer (D/S Day) could not be believed. In the civil action the plaintiffs sought discovery of documents concerning corruption and fabrication of evidence by the officer in previous, but largely unrelated, cases. The police argued that the evidence of previous misconduct at best showed a propensity to mis-behaviour, could therefore only go to credit and was not discoverable. Beldam LJ said

> I consider the significance of the misconduct alleged went beyond mere propensity. All similar fact evidence relating to misconduct on other occasions could be stigmatised as showing a propensity to misbehave in that fashion, but the allegations in the present case, if accepted show that on other occasions D/S Day was prepared to pervert the course of justice in a manner which made it more probable that he did so on the occasion in question.
>
> In my view conduct of this kind is so contrary to the expected standard of behaviour of an investigating officer that, if proved, it is capable of rendering it more probable that the plaintiff's alleged confession was not made.

Thus it seems that documents concerning police misconduct in other cases must show more than a mere propensity in an officer to misbehave to be relevant for the purposes of discovery but do not need to show a 'striking similarity' between the previous misconduct and the present case. It will be a question of degree in each case whether the documents sought will be discoverable. Even if the evidence is disclosed to the plaintiff it is still open to the trial judge to hold that the prejudicial effect of the evidence outweighs its probative value and rule it inad-missible.

Any certificates of convictions in the criminal courts are admissible under Civil Evidence Act 1968 s11 and are therefore discoverable.

Enforcing discovery
If the police fail to serve a list of documents within the time limits set by automatic discovery or ordered in the pre-trial review, an application to the court to strike out their defence because of this failure may be effective in obtaining the list promptly. Given the delay in the hearing of such an application, it should be made as soon as possible after the time limit has lapsed.

If there is any suspicion that the police list is incomplete, the court can be asked to order the police to list their documents or to swear that any specific document or class of document is not or has not been in their possession, custody or power.[18] Reference should be made to the list of documents in chapter 2 (see p29). Another useful check is to make sure that all the documents *referred to* in the documentation the police have disclosed, are also included in the documentation received. If there is doubt about whether the discovery made by the police is as full as it should be, then counsel's advice could be sought. Plaintiffs' solicitors should be aware that disputes over discovery can take up months (and sometimes years) and this stage of the case needs to be pursued as vigorously as possible.

Although the obligation to make discovery is a wide one (see above p234), the general obligation is subject to an important proviso that the court:

> shall in any case refuse to make . . . an order if and so far as it is of the opinion that discovery is not *necessary* either for disposing fairly of the cause or matter or for saving costs.[19]

Thus, even where the documents for which discovery or inspection[20] is claimed are relevant, the court can refuse to make an order if it is not necessary for the purposes described in the rules.[21]

Documents exempt from production

There are a number of grounds on which the police (or the plaintiff) may or must refuse to disclose a document which is relevant and material to the determination of issues involved in civil proceedings. If a privilege or an immunity is claimed in respect of a document, then it must still be identified in the list of documents but it need not actually be produced (see below) unless a court orders that the document is not exempt from production. Those documents for which immunity or privilege is claimed should be listed separately in the list of documents.

Legal professional privilege
Legal professional privilege can be claimed for documents where communications are made for the purpose of giving or receiving legal advice. The courts will look at the dominant purpose for which the document was prepared in cases where it appears that there was more

18 RSC Order 24 r3; CCR Order 14 r2.
19 RSC Order 24 r8.
20 RSC Order 24 r13.
21 Per Lord Woolf in *R v Chief Constable of West Midlands Police ex p Wiley* [1995] 1 AC 274, at 288.

than one purpose.[22] Legal professional immunity can be waived expressly or impliedly.

Public interest immunity

A party may refuse to disclose documents from the list of documents in 'the public interest that harm shall not be done to the nation or the public service by disclosure of certain documents'.[23] This principle has become known as public interest immunity. A claim to public interest immunity can only be justified if the public interest in preserving the confidentiality of a document outweighs the public interest in securing justice.

There are two kinds of public interest immunity. The first will apply to a class of documents, widely or narrowly drawn, for which the court holds that immunity attaches to all documents generated within that class. The test to be applied before a class immunity exists has been said to involve asking whether the withholding of a document because it belongs to a particular class is really 'necessary for the proper functioning of the public service'.[24] The other kind applies to the contents of a particular document or part of a document.

Since 1962, when the Lord Chancellor announced two important changes in practice, claims of immunity in actions against the police have been the exception rather than the rule:

> the first [change] is that privilege will not be claimed in proceedings for malicious prosecution, wrongful arrest and other proceedings against the police where the justification for the prosecution, arrest or other police action is an issue in the proceedings, unless the disclosure of the statement would reveal the identity of a police informer. The second modification relates to the manner of claiming privilege for statements made to the police. The claim of privilege will still be made on the ground of public interest, but it is proposed that in future the claim should be made without a Minister's certificate or affidavit and that the court should be left to decide, having regard to the principles laid down in the cases, whether the statements should be produced.[25]

However, for many years 'class' public interest immunity was thought to attach to all documents generated during a police complaints investigation on the basis, *inter alia*, that this was necessary for witnesses to be confident that statements made by them would not be disclosed in civil

22 *Waugh v British Railways Board* [1980] AC 521, HL.
23 *Conway v Rimmer* [1968] 1 All ER 874, HL at 880 per Lord Reid.
24 Ibid at 942.
25 Viscount Kilmuir, HL Debs cols 1191–1192, 8 March 1962.

proceedings.[26] However, as has previously been described, in *R v Chief Constable of West Midlands Police ex p Wiley*[27] the House of Lords has now held that the 'class' immunity extending generally to the documents generated by an investigation of a complaint against the police (see p76) was never justified.

The PCA in *Ex p Wiley* argued that public interest immunity class protection for the report of the investigating officer would need to be retained, as this provides the PCA with 'an assessment of the quality and credibility of witnesses and with a recommendation'.[28] Lord Woolf had 'considerable reservations as to whether it would be possible to justify a class claim to immunity as opposed to a contents immunity in respect of some reports' and left this matter open.[29] However, the view of the PCA has now been upheld in *Taylor v Anderton* in the Court of Appeal,[30] where the court held that investigating officers' reports formed a class which was entitled to public interest immunity. The Master of the Rolls said that:

> I have no difficulty in accepting the need for investigating officers to feel free to report on professional colleagues or members of the public without the apprehension that their opinions might become known to such persons. I can readily accept that the prospect of disclosure in other than unusual circumstances would have an undesirable and inhibiting effect on their reports.[31]

Even if class immunity has been established, a document may still be discoverable if the public interest in disclosure outweighed the public interest in withholding the document.[32] In *Taylor v Anderton* the Court of Appeal said that it would not always be right for the judge to read a document to see where the balance of public interest lies, but did not specify in what circumstances it would not be appropriate.[33] It had been thought that once a litigant asserts class immunity, then, save in exceptional circumstances, it is the litigant's duty to continue to assert the immunity.[34] However, Lord Woolf in *Wiley* said that the duty was

26 *Neilson v Laugharne* [1981] QB 736.
27 [1995] 1 AC 274, HL.
28 Ibid at p300.
29 Ibid at p306.
30 [1995] 1 WLR 447, CA.
31 Ibid at p465 per Sir Thomas Bingham MR.
32 *R v Chief Constable of West Midlands Police ex p Wiley* [1995] 1 AC 274 and followed by the Court of Appeal in *Taylor v Anderton*, supra at 465.
33 *Taylor v Anderton*, supra at 466.
34 *Makanjuola v Commissioner of Police of the Metropolis* [1992] 3 All ER 617, CA per Bingham LJ.

not as strong as this and that in a police case, for instance, chief constables could agree amongst themselves that in a particular case class immunity would not be claimed where the administration of justice outweighs the interest against disclosure.

Investigating officers often prepare an index to the documents submitted to the PCA with their report, and there is no reason why the plaintiff should not have discovery of this index in order to see what documents the investigating officer thought it relevant for the PCA to see.

It is also clear that even if class immunity does not apply to most kinds of documentation that are possessed by the police or the PCA, contents immunity can still apply to a particular document.[35] Such documents might include material relating to police policy on operational matters. However, even where contents immunity is claimed in these cases, it will still be possible in some cases to argue that the public interest in disclosure outweighs the reasons for withholding the document, and even if it is not it may be possible to obtain part of the document or necessary information without seeing the document itself.[36] As Lord Woolf said in the judgment in Ex p Wiley, the whole tenor of which was that documents should only be withheld where absolutely necessary:

> There is usually a spectrum of action which can be taken if the parties are sensible which will mean that any prejudice due to non-disclosure of documents is reduced to a minimum.

It will be interesting to see if pre-*Wiley* cases that concerned documentation other than that produced in the course of a complaints investigation will be followed. In one case it has been held that a police report of a criminal investigation submitted to the DPP was subject to public interest immunity in a subsequent civil action against the police,[37] and two police officers injured during 'riot training' were denied access to the police public order manual on the grounds that it contained information that would be useful to 'factions hostile to the police'.[38] In another case, Alison Halford, an assistant chief constable, was denied access to police discipline files in her Employment Appeal Tribunal claim against her chief constable as well as complaints files on the basis that they were covered by class immunity.[39] It is submitted

35 *Wiley* [1995] 1 AC 274 at 282.
36 Ibid at 307.
37 *Evans v Chief Constable of Surrey* [1988] QB 588.
38 *Goodwin v Chief Constable of Lancashire* (1992) *Times* 3 November, and transcript.
39 *Halford v Sharples* [1992] 3 All ER 624.

that, in the light of the decision in *Wiley*, all these cases might have been decided differently and the documentation sought should have been disclosed.

However, there is some evidence of a retrenchment by the judiciary. Explicitly following the sentiments expressed by the Master of the Rolls in the case of *Taylor* (see p239), the High Court in *O'Sullivan v Metropolitan Police Commissioner* (1995) *Times* 3 July decided that a pro forma created by the police to enable a summary of a case to be provided to the Crown Prosecution Service was subject to class immunity. The judge said that although the report was 'plainly a relevant document which is prima facie discoverable' (transcript, p3):

'. . . there is a clear distinction between the primary documents generated in an investigation into criminal conduct, such as witness statements, entries in police officers' notebooks, forensic reports and the like, and secondary documentation comprising a report based on that primary material directed to the CPS'. (transcript, p12)

Thus, although the case concerned one type of document the implication here is that class immunity can (and perhaps should) apply to all 'secondary documentation'.

It is submitted that this approach is too restrictive and contravenes at least the spirit of the judgment in *Wiley* (see especially Lord Templeman's speech). There is surely no reason why contents immunity should not be applied to a specific document or part of a document, if necessary. This case has not been pursued to the Court of Appeal.

Privilege against self-incrimination

The heads of claim in a civil action against the police may well, in effect, allege that a criminal offence has been committed. The most common example of this will be assault. People in civil proceedings alleged to have committed a criminal offence are granted, by the common law, a privilege against self-incrimination if there is reasonable likelihood that they will be charged as a result of disclosing the information. Thus a police officer could refuse to disclose information to the plaintiff which indicates that a criminal offence has been committed by him/her. But it is submitted that a Chief Constable when sued for actions committed by his officers cannot claim the privilege in relation to documents which incriminate those officers. It seems as though it will not be enough for the plaintiff's solicitors to give an undertaking (or be subject to an injunction) that the information they receive on discovery will not be disclosed to any other person.[40] It

40 *United Norwest Co-operatives Ltd v Johnstone* (1994) *Times* 24 February.

seems that a letter from the Crown Prosecution Service confirming that it will not seek to gain access to the material disclosed will remove the possibility of a charge and the defendant will then not need, nor be able, to invoke the privilege of self-incrimination.[41]

In many civil actions against the police, the CPS will have already considered whether to prefer charges against police officers, either as part of the complaints and discipline machinery (see chapter 4) or otherwise, and, in the vast majority of cases, will have decided not to prosecute. In such cases, it is submitted, a claim of privilege against self-incrimination should not succeed.

Exchange of witness statements

Law and procedure
In all cases (jury and non-jury) exchange of witness statements is now compulsory.[42] Witness statements contain the oral evidence which the party intends to adduce on any issues of fact to be decided at the trial.[43] They are different from pleadings in that pleadings contain only the facts and do not include evidence.

The requirement to exchange witness statements has a number of implications in an action against the police. In many cases the plaintiff will already know what the police and their witnesses are going to say. The police cannot now seek public interest immunity for witness statements taken during the investigation of a complaint (see p239). The police will also have to disclose copies of statements taken in the course of a criminal investigation. Of course, the plaintiff may also have given a statement for the purposes of the police complaint or during the criminal investigation but there may be circumstances (for instance, where the plaintiff was charged but then the prosecution was subsequently dropped) where no statement has ever been give prior to the civil action.

There is a very real need to ensure that all witnesses are properly interviewed and proofs of evidence prepared at the start of the case to ensure that the exchange of witness statement rules can be complied with and to avoid the danger that evidence is excluded at trial. Clients and their witnesses need to be made aware that their evidence will be made available to the police at an early stage in the case. However, the

41 *AT & T Istel Ltd v Tully* [1993] AC 45, HL.
42 RSC Order 38 r2A and CCR Order 20 r12A.
43 Ibid.

contents of an exchanged witness statement remain confidential until the trial of the case unless the privilege is waived.

The aim of the exchange of witness statements is to effect a fair and speedy trial of the issues and to save costs.[44] It is thought that when all parties 'have their cards on the table' there will be a greater incentive to settle the case.[45] Thus when the witness statements are received from the police they should be carefully studied for areas of agreement and potential cross-examination.

In the High Court the court must direct at the summons for directions that there be simultaneous exchange of witness statements within 14 weeks from the date of the order (or such other period as the court shall direct). Where automatic directions apply, the period is set at 14 weeks after the close of pleadings.[46] In the county court this period is 10 weeks.[47] If the police have not served all their witness statements by the due date, consideration should be given to applying to court to debar them from calling any witness whose statement has not been served. The police must then produce any statements promptly.

At trial, if a witness is not called by the party who has served his/her statement, no other party may use the statement of the witness in evidence.[48] However, if it is feared that a witness whose statement is served by the police will not be called at the trial, but the plaintiff wishes to adduce the statement of the witness, a Civil Evidence Act 1968 notice should be served on the police.[49]

The statement will form the evidence-in-chief of the witness at the trial and in non-jury trials the witness will not usually be permitted to add to the statement before being subjected to cross-examination.[50] Following a practice direction issued in the High Court which stated that every witness statement shall stand as the evidence-in-chief unless otherwise ordered,[51] the position is uncertain in jury trials. However, it is submitted that in jury trials it is important that the jury members hear the evidence of the witness in person to enable them to decide on the credibility of witnesses and on questions of fact.[52]

44 RSC Order 38 r2A(1) and CCR Order 20 r12A.
45 See White Book Vol 1 1995 para 38/2A/2.
46 RSC Order 38 r2A(2).
47 CCR Order 20 r12A(2).
48 RSC Order 38 r2A(6); CCR Order 20 r12A(6).
49 Civil Evidence Act 1968 s4; *Youell v Bland Welch (No 3)* [1991] 1 WLR 122.
50 RSC Order 38 r12A(7); CCR Order 20 r12A (7).
51 *Practice Note (civil litigation: case management)* [1995] 1 WLR 262; [1995] 1 All ER 385.
52 See *Mercer v Chief Constable of Lancashire Constabulary* [1991] 2 All ER 504.

Practice

When drafting witness statements it is important to include all matters that the witness will give evidence upon, as it will be unusual for the court to allow the witness to adduce evidence which is not in his/her statement.[53] Statements of all witnesses to be called must be exchanged, as it will be unusual for the court to allow a witness whose statement has not been exchanged to give evidence at court.[54] As the written statement is equivalent to oral evidence it must contain only material facts that are within the witness's own knowledge and must exclude hearsay and opinion; it must contain 'the truth, the whole truth and nothing but the truth'.[55]

By the time witness statements come to be exchanged, the plaintiff's version of events may already have been presented in several forms. The plaintiff's statement in a police complaint, the letter before action, the claim itself and maybe the medical evidence also (see p000) will all need to be carefully examined to ensure that there are no discrepancies between the contents of these documents and the witness statement. Instructions should also have been taken on the defence of the police and the results of the discovery process before the witness statement is completed.

It is not unusual for counsel to be instructed to draft the witness statement, and some solicitors also find that this is a good time to have a conference with counsel to review the evidence and to seek advice for the purposes of removing any limitation placed on the legal aid certificate.

The notes to the White Book indicate the form which the statement should take. Essentially the statement should be set out as a well-prepared proof would be, starting with the plaintiff's name, address and description, explaining his/her relationship to the proceedings and setting out the evidence chronologically in numbered paragraphs.[56] The statement should be signed and dated (but not sworn) and state that the contents are true to the best of the witness's knowledge and belief.[57]

The police may be able to satisfy wholly or in part the requirements to exchange witness statements by service of statements prepared for the purposes of criminal proceedings.[58]

---

53 Ibid.
54 RSC Order 38 r12A(10); CCR Order 20 r12A(10).
55 See White Book Vol 1 1995 para 38/2A/7.
56 Ibid Para 38/2A/8.
57 RSC Order 38 r2A(4); CCR Order 20 r12A(4).
58 *Mercer v Chief Constable of Lancashire Constabulary* [1991] 2 All ER 504, 506 CA.

Payments into court and offers of settlement

Specific concerns in civil actions against the police

Police solicitors have developed skills in making payments into court and offers of settlement which put pressure on plaintiffs and their advisers to settle a case before it reaches full trial. In very many cases the plaintiff is not interested so much in the financial aspect of the case but in vindicating him/herself in court and making the police accountable for their actions. Very often, then, clients are reluctant to accept a settlement. However, in legal aid cases an offer of settlement or a payment in will have ramifications for the continuation of legal aid (see below). Damages in police cases are often decided by a jury which is given few guidelines on quantum. Therefore, offers of settlement and payments in to court give plaintiffs particular problems in deciding what is a reasonable offer which should be accepted.

Payments into court

A payment into court by the police is an offer to settle the matter and if it is accepted the case is concluded. A payment in can be made at any time after the service of the writ or summons[59] but it is more usual for the police to wait at least until the close of pleadings before making a payment in. The police effect the payment in by giving notice to the plaintiff who, in the High Court, must acknowledge receipt within three days.[60] In the county court the court sends notice to the plaintiff and no acknowledgement is necessary. The plaintiff then has 21 days from the date of the payment in to accept it. If the plaintiff does so, s/he will also be entitled to have his/her costs taxed and paid.[61] If a plaintiff fails to accept a payment, and at trial receives damages of less or the same amount (inclusive of interest) as the amount paid in, the police will usually be entitled to their costs from the date of the payment in. The fact that a payment in has been made cannot be revealed to the trial judge or jury until the question of costs comes to be decided at the end of the case.[62]

Although the judge will retain a discretion not to award the defendant costs, this is rarely exercised in the plaintiff's favour. However, in one case against the police where the jury awarded the plaintiff less than the police had paid into court the judge held nevertheless that

59 RSC Order 22 r1(1); CCR Order 11 r1(1).
60 RSC Order 22 r1(2).
61 RSC Order 62 rr5(4) and 29(1); CCR Order 11 r3(5).
62 RSC Order 22 r7; CCR Order 11 r7.

where a defendant had been guilty of disgraceful conduct the court would be very slow to allow it costs in any case. The judge held that the case was about more than money, that the plaintiff was entitled to be vindicated by a jury's verdict and that the conduct of the officers had been oppressive and abusive of their powers. He therefore ordered the police to pay the plaintiff's costs despite the payment in.[63]

Having made an initial payment in, the police can increase the payment in as the case proceeds by giving notice in the same manner described above.[64] It is possible for a payment in to be made or increased within 21 days of the trial and even after the trial itself has started.[65]

A plaintiff accepts a payment in by giving notice to the court officer and the defendant within 21 days of receipt, and in any event before the start of the trial (three days before in the county court), or if payment in is made or increased after the start of the trial, within two days (14 days in the county court), and in any event before the judge begins the summing up.[66] Late acceptance of a payment in is possible but only with leave of the court to give the defendant the opportunity to make an application for costs.[67]

Settlements

The police will make any offers of settlement by letter to the plaintiff's solicitors. There is no penalty if the offer is not accepted but the offer must be referred to the Legal Aid Board (see below). The client must be carefully advised on whether a settlement is reasonable. This can be extremely difficult in civil actions against the police where the amount of guidance given to the jury in deciding the level of damages is minimal. It is likely that the police have counsel's advice about the higher and lower limits of damages if the case goes to trial and any offer of settlement will be made with this advice in mind. When a settlement is accepted, any court order that is then drawn up should include specific mention of the plaintiff's right to make a statement in open court, if it is intended to exercise it.

63 *Wilson and Farbridge v Patterson and Others* (1985) 10 December, HC, unreported; see also *Smiths Ltd v Middleton (No 2)* [1986] 1 WLR 598.
64 RSC Order 22 r1(3); CCR Order 11 r1(4).
65 See RSC Order 22 r3(2) and White Book Vol 1 1995 para 22/3/1; CCR Order 11 r3; for the effect that such a payment in has.
66 RSC Order 22 r3; CCR Order 11 r3.
67 CCR Order 11 r5(3).

Legal aid and offers of settlement or payment in

It is important to warn all clients that the grant of legal aid is not the same as the grant of the right to take the case through to trial. Solicitors are under a duty to report to the Legal Aid Board when their legally aided client refuses to accept a reasonable offer of settlement or payment into court.[68] To find that legal aid has been withdrawn following such a report can be a great shock to a client for whom it was important to pursue the case to trial and to see the police officers involved in court. It can also leave a client feeling very bitter towards his/her solicitor.

If the plaintiff is advised to reject an offer from the police, it is prudent to obtain counsel's advice as to why the offer is not sufficient and to submit this to the legal aid area office with a request for specific permission to proceed with the case.

Statements in open court

A plaintiff who accepts a settlement or a payment into court in a case involving malicious prosecution or false imprisonment can seek leave to read a statement in open court. This gives a plaintiff a chance to 'have his/her day in court' and to seek some publicity without having to take the case all the way to trial.[69] When this rule was first introduced it was held that the statement could not refer to any related actions, for instance, assault or negligence,[70] but this position has now been reversed by an amendment to the rules.[71] Although there is no such rule in the county court, in appropriate cases it is submitted that leave can be given to make a statement in open court under the County Courts Act 1984 s76, whereby the county court can adopt the general principles of practice of the High Court,[72] and it is not uncommon for this to happen.

There is a slightly different procedure in the High Court depending on whether the case has been settled or if a payment in has been accepted. If the case has settled a summons for directions returnable before the master must be issued to set the case down for trial and to expedite the proceedings. Copies of the statement should be lodged for

68 Civil Legal Aid (General) Regulations 1989 reg 70(1)(a).
69 RSC Order 82 r5 and see notes to the White Book Vol 1 1995 p1400–1401.
70 *Smith v Commissioner of Police for the Metropolis* [1991] 1 All ER 714.
71 RSC Order 82 r5(3).
72 See Clayton and Tomlinson, 'Civil actions against the police: practice and procedure', January 1994 *Legal Action* 20.

the judge to consider for approval before the listed court date when the statement will be read.[73] When a payment in has been accepted, it is not necessary to set the matter down for trial but a summons must be issued returnable before a judge in chambers seeking leave to make a statement in open court in terms approved by the judge. If leave is granted, the statement can be read out in open court thereafter.[74]

The police will have the right to be heard at any application for leave and to object to a proposed statement, as it affects them as well as the plaintiff.[75] In exercising discretion to allow a statement in open court following the acceptance of a payment in, the judge should be slow to refuse a plaintiff leave to make an appropriate statement and the judge may assess whether the sum paid in is substantial enough to merit a statement.[76] The judge can also assess the strengths and weaknesses of the plaintiff's case in deciding whether to grant leave.[77] The police are not entitled to insist that such a statement indicates that the payment in is without any admission of liability.[78] There is an example of a 'statement in open court' at appendix 3.6. Solicitors have rights of audience in the higher courts to read out a statement in open court.

A press release should be issued announcing that a statement is to be read in court and the text of the statement can be distributed to the press after the event.

Reviewing the case

In a case to be argued by counsel, it is desirable for the barrister to assess the available evidence when all the interlocutory matters are complete but before the trial is in prospect. In a legally aided case, it may well be a condition of legal aid that counsel's opinion is obtained on the evidence at this point, before legal aid is extended to cover the trial. For an excellent analysis of the factors to consider when reviewing the case see Hendy, Day and Buchan, *Personal Injury Practice.*[79]

---

73 RSC Order 82 r5(2) and White Book 1995 Vol 1 para 82/5/4 for fuller details.
74 See RSC Order 82 r5(1) and notes in the White Book 1995 Vol 1 para 82/5/2.
75 *Wolesley v Assoicated Newspapers Ltd* [1934] 1 KB 448, CA.
76 *Jones v Lohrer* (1984) 20 February, unreported, per Balcombe J, cited with approval in *Honeyford v Commission for Racial Equality* (1991) *Independent* 13 May and Lexis by Drake J.
77 *Honeyford v CRE* above n76.
78 Ibid.
79 LAG, 2nd edn 1994, chapter 15.

Preparations for trial

Duty to conduct cases economically

A practice direction from the High Court[80] indicates the impatience that judges have with long-drawn-out trials. The court has said that 'failure by practitioners to conduct cases economically will be visited by appropriate orders for costs, including wasted costs orders'. It is likely that the spirit of the practice direction at least will apply in the county court. Lawyers for both sides should bear the terms of the practice direction in mind as the trial approaches:

– Parties should use their best endeavours to agree which are the issues in the case, and to reduce or eliminate the expert issues,
– Paginated, legible, indexed, chronological bundles in ring binders must be lodged at least two clear days before the trial,
– A pre-trial review should be held in cases likely to last more than ten days;
– A skeleton argument 'concisely summarising the party's submissions' must be lodged at least three clear days before the hearing of an action,
– Each party must lodge a completed pre-trial checklist at least two months before the date of a trial. The questionnaire seeks information about the state of preparation of the case, presumably in an attempt to prevent issues arising at the last minute.

The solicitor must state whether alternative dispute resolution (ADR), such as mediation, has been discussed with the client, whether ADR might assist, and whether ADR has been explored with the other party. Mediation or without prejudice negotiations may achieve creative settlements which would not normally be ordered by the court, as, for example, where the complainant particularly wishes to maintain his/her anonymity or seeks vindication in the form of an apology. However, it is not appropriate where, for example, the object is to establish a constitutional principle.

Setting down the case for trial

County court – automatic directions
As already mentioned (see above p227), cases where automatic directions apply must be set down within six months of close of pleadings. If a case is not set down within 15 months of the close of pleadings, the

claim can be automatically struck out. A case is set down by writing to the court with a time estimate (upon which counsel should be consulted) and the agreement of the police if possible. The court should give not less than 21 days' notice when fixing a date for the hearing.[81]

County court – no automatic directions

Automatic directions do not apply in many police actions (see p226). The case cannot be struck out automatically for failure to set down. At p228, a suggested direction is listed for dealing with the question of setting down, whereby the case should be listed before a judge and jury after filing a certificate of readiness by either party after giving notice of the intention to set down to the other party. If such a direction has not been given by the court and the police fail to agree to set down the case, then an application will need to be made to the court to do so.

High Court

If automatic directions apply, the case should be set down within six months of the close of pleadings.[82] Otherwise setting down depends on the order made for directions (see p226). For the plaintiff, setting down the case as soon as possible is desirable.

A practice direction sets out what the court expects in jury trial cases.[83] Parties must comply with an order to set down the case. The practice direction says that cases are likely to 'come on for trial almost immediately after they are set down'[84] and if the parties need more time to prepare the case, an application should be made to the judge in charge of the jury list. Any further interlocutory applications will normally be heard by this judge, who will 'exercise full control over the pre-trial conduct of the action'.[85] Any party in default of an order to set down could find the action struck out.

To set down a case, two copies of a bundle containing the writ, the pleadings, legal aid details, time estimate and interlocutory orders, the list into which the case should be included must be lodged together with a fee of £50, and a statement of value.[86] All details of the parties' solicitors must be endorsed on a backsheet.[87] The defendant should

---

81 CCR Order 17 r11(10).
82 RSC Order 25 r8(1)(f).
83 *Practice Direction (Jury List: Setting Down)* [1995] 1 WLR 364, QBD.
84 Ibid.
85 Ibid.
86 RSC Order 34 r3(1).
87 Ibid.

be informed that the case has been set down within 24 hours.[88]

An application to fix the date for trial should be made within 28 days of setting down in London and within seven days outside London.

Updating evidence

Once the case has been set down a number of things need to be considered as the trial approaches.

The client and witnesses need to be aware as soon as possible of the trial date and need to be reminded to check through their witness statement a number of times before the trial.

Experts' reports should not be more than a year old at most, and should be agreed if possible. If the reports cannot be agreed, then the plaintiff's expert should be sent a copy of the police's expert report. The plaintiff's expert is likely to have to give oral evidence if the reports are not agreed.

Plans, photographs and videos should be exchanged and are usually agreed. If they are not agreed, then it will be necessary to call the maker to give evidence to prove them.

A check should be made that witness summonses (in the county court)[89] or subpoenas (in the High Court)[90] will not be necessary. Sometimes co-operative witnesses will need these, for example, to be relieved from work, to be able to attend court.

An updated schedule of special damages should be served on the police at least 28 days before the trial. The police have to indicate their agreement or otherwise to each item on the schedule at least 14 days before the trial.

Briefing counsel and pre-trial conference

A full trial brief should be prepared and sent to counsel, preferably some weeks before the trial. To provide for the eventuality that the counsel who has drafted the pleadings is not available for the trial, the brief should be prepared with the assumption that counsel will know nothing about the case. A pre-trial conference should be arranged with the client to go through the trial procedure, check the preparedness of witnesses (including the client), discuss the contents of the trial bundle, and any possible last minute settlement.

88 RSC Order 34 r8(1).
89 CCR Order 20 r12.
90 RSC Order 38.

Bundles

Bundles of documents must be prepared and agreed if possible. In the High Court the defendant should indicate to the plaintiff at least 14 days before the date fixed for the trial which documents the police wish to have included in the bundle.[91] At least two clear days before the trial the plaintiff must lodge with the court two bundles consisting of the witness statements, those documents central to the plaintiff's and defendant's case, and disclosed experts' reports (indicating whether agreed). A skeleton argument should be lodged in all cases.[92]

In the county court the police have to inform the plaintiff of the documents they wish to have in the bundle 14 days before the date fixed for trial, and at least seven days before the trial date the plaintiff must lodge two bundles consisting of pleadings, further and better particulars, replies to interrogatories, witness statements, disclosed experts reports (indicating whether agreed) and legal aid documents.[93]

A special bundle of documents needs to be prepared for the jury. There are no notes for guidance about what should go in these bundles, but it is usual to keep the bundles as simple as possible. If the witnesses are to give oral evidence, then the witness statements should be excluded. The pleadings, agreed medical reports and maps and photographs and essential police documentation, such as the custody record, should be included.

The court hearing

Supporters at the hearing

Many plaintiffs find it helpful and reassuring to have friends and relatives to support them at the hearing itself. This will often improve the plaintiff's performance as a witness in court. A large number of people attending the hearing may also make the judge aware that the case is one of public interest and this may help to restrain hostile remarks or a prejudicial summing up.

The hearing

In estimating the length of a trial, it is a useful rule of thumb that a jury trial will take twice as long as a trial before a judge alone.[94] The brief

91 RSC Order 34 r10.
92 *Practice Note* [1995] 1 All ER 385.
93 CCR Order 17 r12.
94 Perhaps even more so now that witness statements stand as evidence in chief in non-jury cases (see p242).

order of proceedings is usually as follows.[95] In jury trials, before the jury is empanelled, applications can be made, for example, on admissibility of documents or exclusion of witnesses from the court. The jury (if any) is then empanelled. In the High Court there can be between nine and 12 jurors although normally there are 12; in the county court there must be eight,[96] unless the plaintiff and the police agree to proceed with an incomplete jury.[97] In the civil courts the plaintiff can only object to a juror 'for cause', that is for a specific reason that might make the jury biased, such as that the juror is a relative of one of the police officers involved. There is no general principle that a jury must be racially balanced.[98]

Witnesses who are also parties to the action or expert witnesses cannot be excluded from the courtroom. However, non-expert witnesses who are not parties can be excluded until they give evidence and the advocate should consider in advance whether to make an application at the start of the hearing. This is particularly relevant where proceedings have been brought only against a chief officer of police, as the officers involved in the incident can be excluded.

The plaintiff's advocate makes an opening speech and calls witnesses who can subsequently be cross-examined by the defendant. Even if the burden of proof falls largely on the defendant, it is usual for the plaintiff to begin if there are damages to be proved. If the plaintiff fails to appear at the trial, then his/her lawyers are permitted to proceed with the trial if the burden of proof is entirely on the police (for instance, to prove the lawfulness of an arrest where the facts of the arrest are admitted).[99]

At the conclusion of the plaintiff's case, if it is heard by a judge alone, the defendant may submit that there is no case against him/her that calls for an answer. However, the defendant must first elect not to call any evidence[100] and thus, if the application is unsuccessful, the police are disallowed from continuing with any defence to the plaintiff's claim. In a jury trial the judge has a discretion whether to insist that the defendant so elects[101] and, in practice, the defendant's evidence is heard

95 For a fuller discussion see Clayton and Tomlinson, *Suing the Police*, Longmans 1989 p74–83.
96 County Courts Act 1984 s67.
97 Juries Act 1974 s17(5).
98 *R v Ford* [1989] 3 WLR 762, CA. The Lord Chancellor has expressed strong opposition to the idea.
99 *Whelan v Commissioner of Police of the Metropolis* (1991) Independent, 7 October, CA.
100 *Alexander v Rayson* [1936] 1 KB 169, *Storey v Storey* [1960] 3 All ER 279.
101 *Young v Rank* [1950] 2 KB 510.

before a submission of no case to go to the jury is heard.[102]

Assuming the case proceeds, the usual practice is for the defendant's advocate to make a speech opening the case for the defence. In the High Court the defence is entitled to make this speech[103] but in the county court, if a speech is made at this point, the defence cannot, as of right, make a closing speech. Whether or not a second address is allowed is at the discretion of the judge. The practice in the local county court should be ascertained before the case begins and, if necessary, an application for permission to make a closing speech should be made at an early stage of the case.

The admissibility of certain kinds of evidence which are frequently of importance in civil actions against the police has been discussed at various points in this book. To summarise, the admissibility of:

- spent convictions under the Rehabilitation of Offenders Act 1974 is discussed at p22 (chapter 2);
- the fact of a conviction is discussed at pp24 and 219 (chapters 2 and 7);
- similar fact evidence is discussed at p235 (chapter 8);
- evidence in previous criminal proceedings is discussed at p23 (chapter 2);
- documentation from the police complaints and discipline procedures is discussed at pp10, 76 and 200 (chapters 1, 3 and 6).

The role of the jury in the verdict of the court

As has already been described, claims for damages for malicious prosecution and false imprisonment are among the very few types of action in the civil courts for which there is a right to trial by jury. As it is so unusual, the role of the jury in deciding the case and awarding damages is described here in some detail.

The role of the jury in cases against the police is not, as it is in a criminal case, to hear all the evidence and then decide who wins the case. In civil cases, the jury has a much more limited task. The function of the civil jury is to provide answers to questions relating to disputed matters of fact. The answers to these questions provide information that the judge requires in deciding the case. In other words, where there is conflicting evidence, it is for the jury to decide what, in fact, happened. But when this has been established, it is for the judge to

102 *Payne v Harrison* [1961] 2 QB 403.
103 See Common Law Procedure Act 1854 s18.

rule, for instance, whether the defendant's actions were reasonable or not (as often has to be decided in false imprisonment or malicious prosecution cases).[104]

Indeed, it is for the judge to decide whether the evidence on a particular matter raises issues of fact to be left to the jury.[105] For instance, if there is no real conflict of evidence, there may be no findings of fact for the jury to reach. Alternatively, either party might argue that if the opponent's case is taken at its highest it could not satisfy the burden of proof on a vital element of a tort or defence. For instance, the plaintiff may have failed to show that there was lack of reasonable or probable cause for a prosecution, or the police may have failed to show that there were reasonable grounds to suspect the plaintiff. In such cases the party can apply to the judge for a ruling that there is no case to go before the jury.

In most cases of malicious prosecution, the central matter to be decided is whether there was reasonable and probable cause for the plaintiff's prosecution (see above p152). This, however, is a matter of law which is reserved for the judge, and the jury will be left to decide those matters of fact which are in dispute and are central to the issue of liability (for instance, whether police evidence has been fabricated). However, if the judge decides there is evidence that the police did not honestly believe that the plaintiff was guilty of an offence, it is for the jury to decide whether this was in fact the case (see p153). It is for the jury to decide if the prosecution has been brought maliciously (see p154).

In false imprisonment cases the question whether an officer had reasonable grounds to suspect the plaintiff is one for the judge to decide.[106] The jury's role is in deciding disputed questions of fact. For instance, there may be a dispute on the evidence whether the police informed the plaintiff of the reason for his/her arrest (see p143). Failure to follow other provisions of PACE can make a detention unlawful and whether in fact these failures occurred will be decided by the jury. In the rare cases where there is evidence to suggest it, the jury will be asked to decide whether the officer had an honest belief or suspicion even where reasonable grounds have been made out.

---

104 *Dallison v Caffery* [1965] 1 QB 348, CA at 372 per Diplock LJ.
105 Ibid.
106 Ibid; and for more recent affirmation of this see *Kelly v Chief Constable of Hampshire* (1993) *Independent* 25 March, and *Staton v Chief Constable of Northamptonshire Police*, (1993) 21 January, CA, Lexis, per Ralph Gibson LJ.

Lord Denning summed up the position in false imprisonment and malicious prosecution cases in the case of *Dallison v Caffery*:[107]

> It is for the judge to decide what facts given in evidence are relevant to the question of whether the defendant acted reasonably. It is thus for him to decide, in the event of a conflict of evidence, what finding of fact is relevant and requisite to enable him to answer that question. But a jury is entitled to base findings of fact only on the evidence called before it and, as in any other jury trial, it is for the judge in an action for false imprisonment or malicious prosecution to decide whether the evidence on a relevant matter does raise any issue of fact fit to be left to a jury. If there is no real conflict of evidence, there is no issue of fact calling for determination by the jury. This applies not only to issues of facts as to what happened, on which the judge has to base his determination whether the defendant acted reasonably, but also to the issue of fact whether the defendant acted honestly, which, if there is sufficient evidence to raise the issue, is one for the jury.

The questions which the jury has to decide, after the evidence has been heard, should be drawn up in writing by the parties and agreed if possible, although ultimately it is for the judge to decide which questions s/he wants the jury to answer. All the questions should be drafted in such a way as to allow the jury to answer 'yes' or 'no'. It may also be wise to give the jury the questions in two sections if the burden of proof is not all on one party.[108] The questions will be put after the closing speeches and the judge's summing up. In a simple case alleging assault and false imprisonment the questions might be:

a) Was the plaintiff assaulted?
b) If the answer to question (a) is yes, what sum do you award by way of damages?
c) Was the plaintiff wrongfully arrested?
d) If the answer to question (c) is yes, what sum do you award by way of damages?[109]

A jury's verdict on the questions before it need not be unanimous, so long as a reasonable time for consideration has elapsed, given the nature and complexity of the case.[110] A verdict of 10:2 or 11:1 in the High Court or 7:1 in the county court can then be accepted. In addition the

107 [1965] 1 QB 348, CA at 372.
108 See, on this point and in general, Nolan, 'The jury in the county court' *LS Gaz* 24 February 1988, p19.
109 Questions taken from the case of *Parry v Sharples*, (1991) 17 July, CA, Lexis.
110 Juries Act 1974 s17.

parties can agree (usually before the jury retires) to accept a simple majority verdict (eg 7:5); this will avoid the need for a rehearing.

If the case ends in the plaintiff's favour, it is the jury's task to decide the level of damages to be awarded. As previously mentioned, while the jury is directed on the basis upon which damages are to be awarded, no figures should be suggested to it either by the judge or the advocates. The jury should not even be told what limit there is on the pleadings on the damages claimed.[111] The role of the jury in awarding damages and the few restraints placed on the jury by statute and the Court of Appeal are fully discussed at p208.

Costs

The usual rules on costs apply in civil actions against the police and if a plaintiff wins his/her case, then it can be expected that the police will be ordered to pay the plaintiff's costs. However, there may be occasions where an action has been pursued in the High Court because of the level of damages that it has been estimated the jury will award. If in fact the jury had awarded a very low amount, in these circumstances the judge previously had the power to limit the costs awarded to the county court scale.[112] This power has now been removed,[113] as it is now virtually impossible to commence a low-value action in the High Court without it being transferred to the county court (see p214). Perversely low (or high) awards of damages by juries can now be rectified by the Court of Appeal.[114]

111 See *Cole v Chief Constable of Merseyside* (1993) 11 March, CA unreported cited in Clayton and Tomlinson, 'Civil actions against the police: practice and procedure' January 1994 *Legal Action* 20.
112 County Courts Act 1984, s19.
113 Courts and Legal Services Act 1990 Sch 20 (repealing County Courts Act 1984 s19).
114 Courts and Legal Services Act 1990 s8.

CHAPTER 9

Other remedies

Wrongful convictions

Every year people are convicted for offences they did not commit. The cases of the Birmingham Six and the Guildford Four spring to mind. The organisation Justice has suggested that, on average, at least 15 people a year are wrongly convicted on indictment and sentenced to more than four year's imprisonment and 'the figure could be much higher'. As sentences of four years or more represent only 1.3% of all convictions in the Crown Court, it has been estimated that there may be at least a thousand wrongful convictions every year in the Crown Court alone, to say nothing of those convicted in the magistrates' court. Of course, an innocent person may find him/herself wrongly convicted for any number of reasons, police misconduct being only one.

Whatever the reason for the wrongful conviction, the usual course is to appeal to the superior courts directly after conviction.[1] The grounds and procedure are briefly set out below. However the remainder of this section is concerned with references to the Court of Appeal by the Home Secretary (which may be made long after conviction), references to the Court of Appeal by the proposed Criminal Cases Review Commission, free pardons and statutory and ex gratia payments of compensation for miscarriages of justice.

Appeals against conviction

The decisions of a magistrates' court can be challenged by way of an appeal to the Crown Court,[2] or by way of case stated[3] or judicial

1 Criminal Appeal Act 1968 s18.
2 Magistrates' Courts Act 1980 s108.
3 Ibid s111.

review.[4] In police misconduct cases, which will almost invariably involve disputed evidence, the usual route would be by way of appeal to the Crown Court. The decision of the Crown Court rehearing a case on appeal from the magistrates can be challenged by way of case stated to the High Court[5] or by way of appeal to the Court of Appeal. Only an appeal to the Court of Appeal is described here.

A person convicted of an offence on indictment can currently appeal to the Court of Appeal against the conviction

- on any ground which involves a question of law alone; and
- with the leave of the Court of Appeal, on any ground which involves a question of fact alone, or a question of mixed law and fact, or on any other ground which appears to the Court of Appeal to be a sufficient ground of appeal.

Leave is not required if the trial judge certifies that the case is fit for appeal on a question of fact or mixed law and fact.[6] However, the Criminal Appeal Act 1995, when it comes into effect, will provide that such appeals lie only:

a) with the leave of the Court of Appeal or
b) if the trial judge certifies the case is fit for appeal.[7]

The Court of Appeal must currently allow an appeal against conviction if it thinks that:

- the conviction should be set aside on the ground that under all the circumstances of the case it is unsafe or unsatisfactory; or
- the judgment of the court of trial should be set aside on the grounds of a wrong decision on any question of law; or
- there was a material irregularity in the course of the trial.

However, the last point is subject to a proviso that even if the court thinks that the point raised in the appeal might be decided in favour of the appellant, it may still dismiss the appeal if it thinks that no

---

4 RSC Ord 53, see p302 and, eg, *R v Bolton Magistrates' Court ex p Scally and Others* [1991] Crim LR 550: applications for certiorari to quash conviction not limited to proceedings vitiated by fraud.
5 Supreme Court Act 1981 s28.
6 Criminal Appeal Act 1968 s1.
7 Section 1, from a date to be appointed.

miscarriage of justice has actually occurred.[8] A successful appeal operates to quash the conviction and, unless there is to be a retrial, as a direction to record a verdict of acquittal. Once the Criminal Appeal Act 1995 comes into force, these tests are to be replaced by a single question: is the conviction unsafe?[9] (See p265.)

If the appeal fails, there is a further right of appeal to the House of Lords, but only if the appeal raises an important point of law. If leave is refused, the ordinary legal remedies are at an end. The next stage is to petition the Home Secretary. The Home Secretary can be petitioned to exercise one of his/her discretionary remedies where a person has been convicted on indictment, or been tried on indictment and found not guilty by reason of insanity, or been found by a jury to be under a disability and to have done the act or made the omission charged against him/her. The discretionary remedies are:

a) to refer the whole of the case to the Court of Appeal as if it were a fresh appeal against sentence or conviction[10] or
b) to recommend the royal prerogative of mercy to grant either a free pardon[11] or a remission of sentence.

The Home Secretary generally only intervenes if there is fresh evidence or some other new matter of substance (see below). S/he first considers whether a case is appropriate for reference to the Court of Appeal. Only if it is not will it be considered for the royal prerogative of mercy.[12] Petitions seeking either a reference to the Court of Appeal or a pardon may be presented on behalf of victims of miscarriages of justice who have since died.[13]

Ideally an effective petition needs the assistance of a lawyer, but only green form advice and assistance is available. It must be stressed that the

8 Criminal Appeal Act 1968 s2.
9 Section 2, from a date to be appointed.
10 Criminal Appeal Act 1968 s17(1)(a); the Home Secretary may also refer a case if s/he desires the assistance of the court on any point arising in the case, eg, as to whether, if evidence were to be tendered in an appeal the court would be required to receive it: Ibid s17(1)(b), see, eg, *Re McMahon* (1978) 68 Cr App R 18.
11 A conditional pardon, to commute a death sentence to life imprisonment, is now only relevant in the Isle of Man and in Jersey.
12 Home Office Memorandum (HO Memo) 23 June 1982, para 4, reproduced in *Miscarriages of Justice*, Sixth Report of the Home Affairs Committee (HAC) 1981/82 HC 421, HMSO.
13 *R v Maguire and Others* [1992] 1 QB 936; *R v Secretary of State for Home Department ex p Bentley* [1993] 4 All ER 442.

experience of many prisoners has been that with both of these procedures the rules appear to be stacked against the convicted person and are more concerned with upholding the inviolability of the jury's verdict than in securing justice. Statistically, the chances of success are slim: each year approximately 750 petitions are submitted of which usually fewer than 10 are referred to Court of Appeal and fewer than 15 non-traffic cases result in a pardon. It remains to be seen what effect the Criminal Appeal Act 1995 will have.

The Police Complaints Authority will draw evidence of miscarriages of justice that it discovers in the course of its investigations to the attention of the Home Secretary (or the CPS) of its own volition, see p81.

References to the Court of Appeal

Currently cases can only be referred by the Home Secretary. However, when the Criminal Appeal Act 1995 comes into force, this power will switch to a new body, the Criminal Cases Review Commission, see p266.[14]

Until the 1995 Act comes into effect only cases that were tried before a jury in the Crown Court can be referred to the Court of Appeal under this procedure. The Home Secretary has power to refer the case 'if he thinks fit'.[15] However, successive Home Secretaries have 'held firmly to the principle that it would be wrong for them to intervene in a case on the basis of information which the courts have considered, whatever their own assessment of that information may be.'[16] It is therefore crucial that there should be fresh evidence or other new matters of substance and in order to establish whether such evidence or new matters exist, there will be an internal Home Office investigation which may involve calling upon the police to make further inquiries, see p270.

Historically:

the Secretary of State does not normally exercise his power to refer a case to the Court of Appeal unless there is some new evidence or other consideration of substance which has not been before the Court (and which was not

14 1995 Act ss3 and 9, from a date to be appointed.
15 Criminal Appeal Act 1968 s17.
16 HO Memo para 4.

previously available to be brought before the Court) and which appears to cast doubt on the safety of the conviction.[17]

Sir John May's conclusion upon his inquiry into the case of the Maguires[18] commented that this policy 'is a limiting one and has resulted in the responsible officials within the Home Office taking a substantially restricted view of cases . . . '. In 1994 the policy was considered in *R v Secretary of State for Home Department ex p Hickey (No 2)*,[19] which held that it was too narrow. The correct approach is to ask whether the new material could reasonably cause the Court of Appeal to regard the verdict as unsafe. If it could, then the Home Secretary should refer the case for hearing as an appeal without more ado. Specifically it is not for the Home Secretary himself to determine whether the conviction is unsafe. He should only ask himself if the Court of Appeal, rather than he himself, could reasonably conclude that the conviction was unsafe. Obviously this is likely to result in many more cases being referred.

Before *Ex p Hickey* the Home Secretary would routinely issue a terse letter stating his decision and reasons but as a matter of policy would not disclose the new material revealed as result of his/her inquiries except in the briefest summary form. The court in *Hickey* held that if the Home Secretary's inquiries reveal fresh material unknown to the petitioner, fairness requires that this should be disclosed so that he may have an opportunity to make further representations, before a decision is made on the petition.

The proper test to be applied in deciding the level of disclosure, the court held, is to ask what would be sufficient to enable the petitioner to present his/her best case effectively. That can only be done if s/he adequately appreciates the nature and extent of the evidence elicited by the Home Secretary's inquiries. While each case must be considered on its own merits, expert reports should 'almost without exception' be disclosed verbatim and statements of civilian witness should be disclosed verbatim unless they were given on at least a tacit understanding of confidence or disclosure would risk the safety of witnesses. As there would only be a negligible risk of intimidation to police or prison

17 *R v Secretary of State for the Home Department ex p Hickey and Others (No 2)* [1995] 1 All ER 490, QBD.
18 The Guildford and Woolwich pub bombing case: see *R v Maguire* [1992] 2 All ER 433, CA, which held that the defendants had been victims of a serious miscarriage of justice.
19 [1995] 1 All ER 490 at 501; for commentary see Thomson, 'In the interests of justice' March 1995 *Legal Action* 8.

TABLE 12

References to Court of Appeal under Criminal Appeal Act 1968 s17(1)(a) in respect of convictions, 1988–94

Year	Cases (defendants)		Outcome of appeal			
			Allowed		*Dismissed*	
1988	2[a]	(2)	–	(6)	1	(1)
1989	3	(6)	3	(20)	NIL	
1990	7	(20)	7	(12)	NIL	
1991	10	(12)	10[b]	(8)	NIL	
1992	8	(11)	5	(5)	3	(3)
1993	8	(9)[c]	4	(2)	2	(2)
1994	9	(12)[d]	1		NIL	

(a) 1 case later abandoned
(b) court ordered a re-trial in one case: defendant later acquitted
(c) 2 cases outstanding
(d) 8 cases outstanding

Source: HC Written Answer, 9 March 1995.

officer witnesses, these provisos do not apply and statements concerning such individuals should normally be disclosed verbatim.

It has been the Home Secretary's practice to consider whether there was a reasonable explanation why the 'fresh evidence' was not produced at the original trial.[20] This raised concerns that evidence that was available to the defence at the time of the trial but which lawyers decided not to call for tactical reasons, which might or might not have been sound at the time, would be excluded.[21] In 1983 the government responded that:

> the Home Secretary will in future be prepared to exercise his power of reference more readily; and the Lord Chief Justice, who has been consulted about this reply, sees room for the Court to be more ready to exercise its own powers to receive evidence . . . Petitions are not currently rejected simply and solely because the evidence presented could have been placed before the courts.'[22]

Although the issue was not directly in question in *Ex p Hickey*, it appears

20 Anticipating the requirement on the Court of Appeal under the Criminal Appeal Act 1968 s23(2)(b), see HO Memo para 6.
21 HAC, *Miscarriages of Justice* (n12 above) para 2.8.
22 *Miscarriages of Justice: the Government Reply to Sixth Report of the Home Affairs Committee* April 1983, Cmnd 8856, HMSO, paras 10–11.

that the Home Secretary should not concern himself at all with asking whether it was reasonable not to call evidence at the original trial. A case should be referred 'without more ado' provided 'only and always there indeed exists substantial new evidence or other considerations in the case and that he will not, therefore, be inviting the court merely to re-examine essentially the selfsame case as it will have already rejected . . .'[23]

Rehearings before the Court of Appeal

The Court of Appeal's power to hear fresh evidence is no greater in a case that has come before the court on a reference by the Home Secretary than it would be in an ordinary appeal.[24] Similarly, the fact that a case has come before the court on a reference from the Home Secretary makes no difference to the court's substantive powers,[25] although if considerable time has passed between the first appeal and the reference appeal, it may be impracticable to order a retrial.[26]

The fact that the Home Secretary's letter of reference may be framed in narrow terms should not usually cause difficulties. The power is to 'refer the whole case', and the case is then to be treated for all purposes as an appeal to the Court of Appeal by the convicted person. The general principle is that once a reference has been made, *any* matter of law or fact or mixed law and fact may be raised by the appellant even if it was not included in the reference.[27] However, if an appellant seeks to raise matters that are not only unconnected with the matters in the letter of reference but also have already been unsuccessfully relied upon in a previous appeal or application for leave to appeal against conviction, the court will give weight to the previous judgment of the Court of Appeal and will be slow to differ, unless there is some cogent argument that had not been advanced at the earlier appeal and which, if it had been properly developed, would have resulted in the appeal being allowed.[28]

23 [1995] 1 All ER 490 at 496C per Simon Brown LJ.
24 *R v Conway* (1979) 70 Cr App R 4.
25 *Stafford and Luvaglio v DPP* [1974] AC 878.
26 See R Buxton 'Miscarriages of justice and the Court of Appeal' (1993) 109 LQR 66.
27 *R v Chard* [1984] AC 279, [1983] 3 WLR 835, [1983] 3 All ER 637, HL.
28 Ibid, obiter, per Lord Diplock.

Reform of criminal appeals and establishment of a Criminal Cases Review Authority

After years of criticism of the practice of the Court of Appeal and the Home Office, the Royal Commission on Criminal Justice[29] recommended that an independent criminal cases review body should be created which would take over the Home Secretary's function of investigating miscarriages of justice cases and making references to the Court of Appeal. The Criminal Appeal Act 1995 received royal assent in July 1995 and (from a date to be announced) will amend the powers of the Court of Appeal to allow a greater number of cases to be considered and establish a Criminal Cases Review Commission, with some powers modelled on the PCA.

The main provisions of the Act are summarised below.

Grounds for allowing an appeal

The Act provides that the Court of Appeal must allow an appeal against conviction if it thinks that the conviction is unsafe (and must dismiss such an appeal in any other case).[30] The former tests of a conviction being unsafe or unsatisfactory (see p259), based on a wrong decision of any question or law or that there was a material irregularity in the course of the trial, will be abolished, on the assumption that in genuine miscarriage of justice cases the second and third limbs of the test will be subsumed within the broad catch-all term 'unsafe', and that the current formula allows many guilty persons to escape their just deserts.[31] The proviso that the court may dismiss the appeal if no miscarriage of justice had actually occurred will also be abolished. The new test will also apply to appeals against verdicts and findings where the appellant is under a mental disability.

Fresh evidence

The power of the Court of Appeal to receive evidence is amended by requiring it to ask whether the evidence is capable of belief (rather than having to receive it if 'likely to be credible' as previously), whether it may afford a ground for allowing the appeal, whether it would have been admissible in the original trial, and whether there is a reasonable explanation for failing to adduce it then.[32] The type of evidence that

29 Report, Cm 2263, 1993; hereafter 'Royal Commission'.
30 Section 2.
31 See Royal Commission chapter 10 paras 27–34 and HC Committee 21 March 1995 col 25 and 27.
32 1995 Act s4, amending Criminal Appeal Act 1968 s23(2); see Royal Commission chapter 10 para 60.

may be received has therefore been broadened, and in particular it need no longer be 'fresh'.

Criminal Cases Review Commission

A Criminal Cases Review Commission is established by the Act. It is to consist of at least 11 commissioners, including a mix of lawyers, people with experience of the criminal justice system and lay people. It is not expected to take up its functions until at least 12 months after the royal assent.

References to Court of Appeal.

The Commission will have power at any time to refer the conviction or sentence in a case tried on indictment to the Court of Appeal, and any such reference will be treated for all purposes as an appeal by the defendant concerned.[33] However, a conviction may not be referred unless:

– the Commission considers there is a real possibility the conviction would not be upheld if a reference was made; and
– it thinks so because of an argument or evidence not previously raised at trial or on appeal; and
– an appeal against conviction has been lost, or leave to appeal has been refused.[34]

These requirements may be waived in exceptional circumstances. A reference may be made either after an application has been made by or on behalf of the accused to whom it relates or without any application having been made, eg, possibly after the intervention of the PCA or some other body.[35] In considering whether to make a reference, the Commission must have regard to any application or representations made to it.

Similar provisions apply to references concerning verdicts or findings against persons under mental disabilities.

In considering whether to make a reference to the Court of Appeal, the Commission may ask the Court for its opinion on any point. Where

33 1995 Act s9.
34 Ibid s13.
35 The Home Office discussion paper 'Criminal Appeals and the Establishment of a Criminal Cases Review Authority', 1994, para 68, noted that legislation would be needed to allocate investigation responsibilities, which might otherwise be duplicated, between the PCA and the Commission; however, the Act makes no such provision.

the Commission makes a reference to the Court of Appeal, it must give the court a statement of its reason for making the reference and send a copy to any person who is likely to be a party to the resulting appeal, eg, the appellant and the CPS. Similarly, it must give reasons to an applicant if it decides not to make a reference.

Where a reference is treated as an appeal against conviction, verdict, finding or sentence, the appeal may be on any ground relating to that matter, whether or not the ground is related to any reason given by the Commission for making the reference. Thus new evidence or arguments can be introduced.

Similar provisions are introduced for cases tried in the magistrates' courts to be re-heard on appeal in the Crown Court, and for the Crown Court to grant bail in appropriate cases.[36] The Home Office currently receives about 100 petitions a year in respect of summary convictions; hitherto there has been no power to refer such cases to the courts for a further appeal, the only remedy being to grant a free pardon.

The power of the Home Secretary to refer cases to the Court of Appeal will be abolished when the Act comes into force.[37]

Investigations by the Commission
The Commission will be able to appoint an investigating officer to make inquiries for the purpose of assisting it with its functions. In the great majority of cases the investigating officer will in practice be a police officer, although where the original investigation that led to the prosecution was brought by some other public body such as Customs and Excise or a local authority, the investigating officer may be drawn from such a body.[38] In the case of police investigations, the investigating officer may be drawn from a force other than the force that conducted the original investigation.

The reliance on the use of serving police officers to investigate cases which will often raise issues of police misconduct in the original criminal investigation has attracted much criticism, and unfavourable parallels with the police complaints system have naturally been drawn. The success of the new scheme is likely to be largely judged by the effectiveness of the Commission in directing and supervising vigorous, probing and imaginative investigations.

The investigating officer will be under a duty to undertake such inquiries as the Commission may reasonably direct, and the Commis-

36 1995 Act s11.
37 Section 3.
38 Section 19.

sion has wide powers to supervise those inquiries as it considers appropriate.[39] However there is no requirement that the Commission must supervise all investigations and it remains to be seen what criteria the Commissioners will use to decide which cases should be supervised and which should not. The Commission will also have wide powers to take any steps which it considers appropriate to assist it in the exercise of its functions, including undertaking inquiries and obtaining statements, opinions or reports, or arranging for others to do so.[40]

The practical and financial difficulties that petitioners have faced in the past in obtaining forensic scientific and other expert reports have been a major obstacle in launching miscarriage of justice cases. It remains to be seen how liberally the Commission will obtain such reports and what criteria it will apply before authorising the use of funds on them. The explanatory and financial memorandum to the Bill said that it was difficult to predict the extent to which the Commission will seek reports from independent experts, but the costs of this were estimated at approximately £100,000 a year. If predictions of an initial workload of approximately 1,500 cases a year prove to be correct, this would allow only an average of £67 per case.

Reports: disclosure and confidentiality
When the inquiries have been completed, the investigating officer must prepare a report of his/her findings and submit it to the Commission and his/her chief officer. The Commission will also receive any statements, opinions and reports required by the investigating officer.[41] The disclosure of information otherwise by a member or employee of the Commission or by an investigating officer is, subject to exceptions, a criminal offence.[42] However, information may be disclosed for the purposes of any criminal, disciplinary or civil proceedings.[43] It is submitted that any statements or expert opinions (including forensic science reports) obtained by the Commission should not attract public interest immunity as a class, by analogy with *R v Chief Constable of West Midlands Police ex p Wiley*.[44] However, the analogy with the police complaints procedure should not be taken too far; the objects of the two investigations and the nature of investigating officers' reports will be quite different. It is therefore submitted that if the investigating officer's

39 Section 20.
40 Section 21.
41 Section 20(7).
42 Section 23.
43 Section 24.
44 [1995] 1 AC 274; see pp201–203.

inquiries reveal fresh material unknown to the potential appellant, including the investigating officer's report, this should be disclosed to the potential appellant in order that s/he may have the opportunity to make further representations, just as s/he might do before.[45] It is submitted that it would be wrong to extend public interest immunity to investigating officers' reports as a class by analogy with police complaints investigating officers' reports,[46] as the need to allow the appellant to make informed new submissions will be crucial to the fairness of the process; the government originally proposed (before *Ex p Hickey*) that the Commission itself should determine in the circumstances of each case what information it would be appropriate to provide to applicants about the progress of enquiries and about the decision taken at their conclusion, with a view to them being open and fair while preserving necessary confidentiality.[47]

Appeals and judicial review

There will be no right of appeal against the substance of a decision by the Commission, although there will be no bar to making fresh representations. The Royal Commission recommended that judicial review should not lie against decisions of the Commission, but this recommendation has not been followed in the Act.

The royal prerogative

Free pardon

Free pardons are usually considered only for cases that are not appropriate for referral to the Court of Appeal, for example, because the new evidence is inadmissible in court or because of the lapse of time since the original trial. The appellant must satisfy the Home Secretary that there are not just doubts about his/her guilt but convincing reasons for believing that s/he is innocent.[48] This is a reversal of the burden of proof required in criminal trials and consequently is an onerous test for appellants to meet. Furthermore, pardons are restricted to cases where someone's name can be completely cleared, that is, to those who are morally as well as 'technically' innocent.

The effect of a free pardon depends on the terms of the pardon itself. A pardon may contain a form of words such as:

45 *R v Secretary of State for Home Department ex p Hickey and Others (No 2)* [1995] 1 All ER 490; see p262 above.
46 *Taylor v Anderton* [1995] 1 WLR 447.
47 *Criminal Appeals and the Establishment of a Criminal Cases Review Authority: a discussion paper*, Home Office, 1994.
48 Waller, *Miscarriages of Justice*, Justice 1989, para 5.5.

Now know ye that We in consideration of some circumstances humbly represented to Us, are Graciously pleased to extend Our Grace and Mercy unto X and to grant him Our Free Pardon in respect of the said conviction, thereby pardoning, remitting and releasing unto him all pains, penalties and punishments whatsoever that from the said conviction may ensue.

The effect of such a pardon relieves the person pardoned, so far as possible, of all the 'pains, penalties and punishments' that flowed from the conviction, but it does not operate as an acquittal or to expunge the conviction itself.[49] Where a person has been pardoned, measures are taken to ensure that the conviction is not held against him/her in future proceedings, at least without the pardon being mentioned.[50] However, as the conviction still stands, it is possible to appeal to the Court of Appeal and for the accused to be acquitted.[51]

TABLE 13
Free pardons on grounds affecting original conviction (other than road traffic offences) 1989–94

Year	Free pardons
1989	15
1990	17
1991	14
1992	4
1993	5
1994	3

Source: HC Written Answers, 9 March 1995.

Remission of sentence

Most remissions of sentence have nothing to do with the merits of the original conviction. They were used as a reward for helping the prison authorities or as a means of releasing a dying prisoner. Remissions of sentence were always rare and have now become obsolete: there have been none since 1982.

Internal Home Office investigation

Petitions are considered by means of internal Home Office investigations. In 1982, the Home Office described the process:

49 *R v Foster* [1984] 3 WLR 401, CA.
50 Lord Eldon, HL Debs col 104, 21 November 1983.
51 *R v Foster*; see Wolfgarten and Khan, 'Free pardon' *SJ* 28 February 1986, p157.

The initial consideration will normally entail establishing two key facts: whether usual avenues of appeal have been exhausted, and whether the arguments put forward constitute new evidence (ie evidence that has not been considered by the courts). In order to establish the latter the [Home Office] will normally examine the Court of Appeal's papers (which normally include a copy of the trial judge's summing up) or call for a report from the police on the evidence produced at the trial. Where a formal complaint has been made about the conduct of police officers involved in the case it is also normal practice to seek a copy of the report of the police officer appointed to investigate it . . .

Where there is new evidence in the case it will also be necessary to consider whether supplementary enquiries need to be made to elicit further information. In making this assessment Home Office staff scrutinise documents such as police complaints reports and court transcripts which are immediately available. But as these were compiled for specific purposes distinct from that of examining the facts of the case as a whole in relation to conviction, it is frequently necessary to make further enquiries, often of the police, from this different standpoint . . .

In exceptional cases it will be necessary to call for a systematic further enquiry into the circumstances of the case, often by a senior officer of an 'outside' police force. Very occasionally there have been public enquiries by independent figures of legal standing . . . [52]

The investigation by the Home Office staff is conducted in writing. They will interview witnesses only in exceptional circumstances and will never interview prisoners. The organisation Justice has criticised the investigation process because reinvestigations by the same police force that investigated the original offence 'seem more often an attempt to shore up the case against the defendant than a disinterested examination of the complaints.'[53]

Compensation

There are two systems of compensation for wrongful conviction: a statutory scheme and a discretionary scheme. The statutory scheme was introduced by the Criminal Justice Act 1988 [54] and partly supersedes the previous, discretionary scheme. However, the discretionary scheme remains in force and may be appropriate where there has been injustice due to serious default on the part of the police or some other public authority.

---

52 HO Memo paras 20–22, HAC *Miscarriages of Justice* (n12 above).
53 Waller op cit para 5.1.
54 The statutory scheme was introduced in compliance with the International Covenant on Civil and Political Rights Art 14 para 6.

TABLE 14
Compensation for miscarriages of justice, 1989–94

Year	Compensation £ millions
1989–90	0.285
1990–91	0.839
1991–92	1.719
1992–93	0.532
1993–94	1.506
part year ending 31.12.94	1.363

Note: the figures include interim payments in cases in which the final amount has yet to be determined and also a grand total of £565,733 paid in ex gratia awards.

Source: HC Written Answers, 9 March 1995.

Statutory scheme

The Home Secretary must pay compensation to a person convicted of a criminal offence if that conviction is subsequently reversed or the person is pardoned on the ground that a new or newly discovered fact shows beyond reasonable doubt that there has been a miscarriage of justice.[55] In this context 'reversed' refers to a conviction having been quashed on an appeal out of time or on a reference by the Home Secretary under the Criminal Appeal Act 1968 s17.[56] Compensation is not payable simply because a conventional appeal within time has been successful.

Compensation is paid to the person who has suffered punishment as a result of conviction or, if s/he is dead, to his/her personal representatives. A person is treated as having 'suffered punishment as a result of conviction' when sentence is passed. It seems that there is no requirement that the accused spent time in custody. However compensation is not payable if the non-disclosure of the unknown fact was wholly or partly attributable to the person convicted.

55 Criminal Justice Act 1988 s133(1). The test of 'beyond reasonable doubt' is less stringent than that in the International Covenant on Civil and Political Rights (n54 above), which requires that the evidence shows 'conclusively' that there has been a miscarriage of justice; however an attempt to delete the test from the legislation altogether was unsuccessful: Hansard HL Vol 499, col 1631, 22 July 1988.
56 Or on a reference from the Criminal Cases Review Commission: Criminal Appeal Act 1995 Sch 2 para 16(4) from a date to be appointed.

The requirement to show that there is a new or newly discovered fact applies whether the conviction was reversed or whether the person was pardoned. A legal ruling, such as that a bye-law is invalid or that a judge made an error of law in admitting inadmissible evidence, does not constitute a new or newly discovered fact.[57]

An application for compensation must be made to the Home Secretary and s/he decides whether the applicant is entitled. The amount of compensation is assessed by an assessor appointed by him/her.[58] Although the Act is silent on the point, it appears that it is the practice of assessors to calculate the level of compensation in accordance with the general principles in civil claims for damages.

The sums paid in compensation for miscarriages of justice are set out in table 14.

Discretionary scheme
The Home Secretary also pays compensation to people who do not fall within the statutory scheme but who have spent a period in custody following a wrongful conviction or charge, where s/he is satisfied that it has resulted from serious default on the part of a member of a police force or of some other public authority.

The Home Secretary also considers cases outside these categories in exceptional circumstances that justify compensation:

> In particular, facts may emerge at trial, or on appeal within time, that completely exonerate the accused person. I am prepared, in principle, to pay compensation to people who have spent a period in custody or have been imprisoned in cases such as this. I will not, however, be prepared to pay compensation simply because at the trial or on appeal the prosecution was unable to sustain the burden of proof beyond reasonable doubt in relation to the specific charge that was brought.[59]

The element of public default may vary but, in the past, has included such things as the police or prosecution failing to inform defence solicitors of the existence of certain witness statements, police identification parades not being fairly conducted and improper handling of forensic exhibits.

In *R v Secretary of State for Home Department ex p Bateman and Howse*[60] the applicants alleged they had wrongfully spent periods in

57 *R v Secretary of State for Home Department ex p Bateman and Howse* [1994] Admin LR 175.
58 Criminal Justice Act 1988 s133(4) and Sch 12.
59 HC Written Answers cols 691–692, 29 November 1985.
60 [1994] Admin LR 175, CA.

custody, the one because a judge had wrongly admitted inadmissible evidence and the other because either a parliamentary draftsman or a minister had been responsible for invalid bye-laws. It was held that it was open to the Home Secretary to conclude that in both cases the periods spent in custody did not result from serious default on the part of a member of a police force or some other public authority.[61] Nor was it irrational for him to decide that such cases did not fall within the category of exceptional circumstances that would justify compensation.

It has been the practice since 1957 for the amount of compensation paid under the discretionary scheme to be fixed by an assessor, who applies principles analogous to those on which claims for damages arising from civil wrongs are settled. Although successive Home Secretaries had always accepted the assessor's advice, they had not been bound to do so. In 1985, the Home Secretary announced that in future he would regard such assessments as binding upon him.

Assessment of compensation

In applications under both the statutory and the discretionary schemes, claims should be considered under the following heads at least.

Pecuniary loss

- Loss of earnings as a result of the charge or conviction.
- Loss of future earning capacity.
- Legal costs incurred.
- Additional expense incurred in consequence of detention, including expenses incurred by the family.

Non-pecuniary loss

- Damage to character or reputation.
- Hardship, including mental suffering, injury to feelings and inconvenience.

> When making his assessment the assessor will take into account any expenses legal or otherwise incurred by the claimant in establishing his innocence or pursuing the claim for compensation. In submitting his observations, a solicitor should state, as well as any other expenses incurred by the claimant, what his own costs are, to enable them to be included in the assessment.

61 [1994] Admin LR 175 at 183, although Bingham MR added 'I say no more than that it was open to him so to conclude. It is not a question whether I, as a member of this court, agree with him or not'.

In considering the circumstances leading to the wrongful conviction or charge the assessor will have regard, where appropriate, to the extent to which the situation might be attributable to any action, or failure to act by the police or other public authority or which might have been contributed to by the accused person's own conduct. The amount offered will accordingly take account of this factor, but will not include any element analogous to exemplary or punitive damages.[62]

It seems that people with no previous convictions receive higher sums than those who have been convicted before.

Pressure and publicity

The Home Office itself has said, 'In practice [our] decision to act may depend on the amount of pressure that is brought to bear on the Home Secretary by people of influence.'[63]

How to go about mobilising support for a case will depend on the particular circumstances, but the obvious people to contact are the person's solicitor and MP and the organisation Justice (see appendix 14 for address). Justice is a group of lawyers which takes up individual cases and has written a number of reports on the problem.[64]

European Convention on Human Rights

The European Convention on Human Rights is an international treaty which provides basic guarantees of a number of fundamental human rights. It is not a part of ordinary English law, but, most unusually for an international treaty, it allows individuals as well as states to complain about violations. It can also be used by English courts to help them in construing English statutes.[65]

The convention requires the states which ratify it to guarantee the rights it contains to everyone within their jurisdiction,[66] and everyone whose rights are violated 'shall have an effective remedy before a national authority, notwithstanding that the violation has been committed by persons acting in an official capacity'.[67] States are therefore under a duty to ensure that their laws comply with the convention and it

62 HC Written Answers cols 328–330, 29 July 1976.
63 HAC *Miscarriages of Justice* (n12) p(vi), para 10.
64 Waller, op cit.
65 *Waddington v Miah* [1974] 2 All ER 377: *R v Sec State Home Dept ex p Brind and Others* [1991] 1 AC 696, (1991) *Times* 8 February, HL.
66 Article 1.
67 Article 13.

is no defence to a complaint that the violation was lawful under domestic law. It has, therefore, been suggested that the provisions in the PACE concerning intimate body searches could be struck down as a violation of article 3 of the convention which prohibits torture and inhuman or degrading treatment.[68]

Similarly, it has been suggested that a number of measures introduced by the Criminal Justice and Public Order Act 1994 may breach the Convention: abolition of the 'right to silence' in criminal investigations may contravene article 6 (fair trial and presumption of innocence); the provisions concerning aggravated trespass, trespassory assembly and raves may contravene articles 10 and 11 (freedom of expression and peaceful assembly) amongst others; and the designation of stop and search areas may contravene article 5 (liberty and security of the person).[69]

The convention does not cover the whole field of human rights and notably omits most economic and social rights that might prove politically contentious. The following articles are among the most relevant to police conduct.

ARTICLE 2

1. Everyone's right to life shall be protected by law. No one shall be deprived of his life intentionally save in the execution of a sentence of a court following his conviction of a crime for which this penalty is provided by law.
2. Deprivation of life shall not be regarded as inflicted in contravention of this Article when it results from the use of force which is no more than absolutely necessary:

a) in defence of any person from unlawful violence;
b) in order to effect a lawful arrest or to prevent the escape of a person lawfully detained;
c) in action lawfully taken for the purpose of quelling a riot or insurrection.

ARTICLE 3

No one shall be subjected to torture or to inhuman or degrading treatment or punishment.

68 See, eg, Levenson and Fairweather *Police Powers: a practitioner's guide* LAG, 1990, p247.
69 Hamilton, Leach and Wadham, 'Criminal Justice and Public Order Act 1994 and the European Convention on Human Rights', April 1995 *Legal Action* 14; Gilchrist, 'Crime Reporter' (commentary on *Saunders v UK* and *Murray v UK* (Application No 1873/91) and article 6) *SJ* 14 October 1994 p1047.

ARTICLE 5

1. Everyone has the right to liberty and security of person. No one shall be deprived of his liberty save in the following cases and in accordance with a procedure prescribed by law:

a) the lawful detention of a person after conviction by a competent court;
b) the lawful arrest or detention of a person for non-compliance with the lawful order of a court or in order to secure the fulfilment of any obligation prescribed by law;
c) the lawful arrest or detention of a person effected for the purpose of bringing him before the competent legal authority on reasonable suspicion of having committed an offence or when it is reasonably considered necessary to prevent his committing an offence or fleeing after having done so;
d) the detention of a minor by lawful order for the purpose of educational supervision or his lawful detention for the purpose of bringing him before the competent legal authority;
e) the lawful detention of persons for the prevention of the spreading of infectious diseases, of persons of unsound mind, alcoholics or drug addicts or vagrants;
f) the lawful arrest or detention of a person to prevent his effecting an unauthorised entry into the country or of a person against whom action is being taken with a view to deportation or extradition.

2. Everyone who is arrested shall be informed promptly, in a language which he understands, of the reasons for his arrest and of any charge against him.
3. Everyone arrested or detained in accordance with the provisions of paragraph 1(c) of this Article shall be brought promptly before a judge or other officer authorised by law to exercise judicial power and shall be entitled to trial within a reasonable time or to release pending trial. Release may be conditioned by guarantees to appear for trial.
4. Everyone who is deprived of his liberty by arrest or detention shall be entitled to take proceedings by which the lawfulness of his detention shall be decided speedily by a court and his release ordered if the detention is not lawful.
5. Everyone who has been the victim of arrest or detention in contravention of the provisions of this Article shall have an enforceable right to compensation.

ARTICLE 6

1. In the determination of his civil rights and obligations or of any criminal charge against him, everyone is entitled to a fair and public hearing within a reasonable time by an independent and impartial tribunal established by law. Judgment shall be pronounced publicly but the press and public may be excluded from all or part of the trial in the interest of morals, public order or national security in a democratic society, where the interests of juveniles or the protection of the private life of the parties so require, or to the extent

strictly necessary in the opinion of the court in special circumstances where publicity would prejudice the interests of justice.

2. Everyone charged with a criminal offence shall be presumed innocent until proved guilty according to law.

3. Everyone charged with a criminal offence has the following minimum rights:

a) to be informed promptly, in a language which he understands and in detail, of the nature and cause of the accusation against him;
b) to have adequate time and facilities for the preparation of his defence;
c) to defend himself in person or through legal assistance of his own choosing or, if he has not sufficient means to pay for legal assistance, to be given it free when the interests of justice so require;
d) to examine or have examined witnesses against him and to obtain the attendance and examination of witnesses on his behalf under the same conditions as witnesses against him;
e) to have the free assistance of an interpreter if he cannot understand or speak the language used in court.

ARTICLE 7

1. No one shall be held guilty of any criminal offence on account of any act or omission which did not constitute a criminal offence under national or international law at the time when it was committed. Nor shall a heavier penalty be imposed than the one that was applicable at the time the criminal offence was committed.

2. This Article shall not prejudice the trial and punishment of any person for any act or omission which at the time when it was committed, was criminal according to the general principles of law recognised by civilised nations.

ARTICLE 8

1. Everyone has the right to respect for his private and family life, his home and his correspondence.

2. There shall be no interference by a public authority with the exercise of this right except such as is in accordance with the law and is necessary in a democratic society in the interests of national security, public safety or the economic well-being of the country, for the prevention of disorder or crime, for the protection of health or morals, or for the protection of the rights and freedom of others.

ARTICLE 11

1. Everyone has the right to freedom of peaceful assembly and to freedom of association with others, including the right to form and to join trade unions for the protection of his interests.

2. No restrictions shall be placed on the exercise of these rights other than

such as are prescribed by law and are necessary in a democratic society in the interests of national security or public safety for the prevention of disorder or crime, for the protection of health or morals or for the protection of the rights and freedoms of others. This Article shall not prevent the imposition of lawful restriction on the exercise of these rights by members of the armed forces, of the police or of the administration of the State.

ARTICLE 13

Everyone whose rights and freedoms as set forth in this Convention are violated shall have an effective remedy before a national authority notwithstanding that the violation has been committed by persons acting in an official capacity.

ARTICLE 14

The enjoyment of the rights and freedoms set forth in this Convention shall be secured without discrimination on any ground such as sex, race, colour, language, religion, political or other opinion, national or social origin, association with a national minority, property, birth or other status.

First Protocol to the Convention 1952

ARTICLE 1

Every natural or legal person is entitled to the peaceful enjoyment of his possessions. No one shall be deprived of his possessions except in the public interest and subject to the conditions provided for by law and by the general principles of international law.

The preceding provisions shall not, however, in any way impair the right of a State to enforce such laws as it deems necessary to control the use of property in accordance with the general interest or to secure the payment of taxes or other contributions or penalties.

References in the convention to 'law', 'lawful arrest or detention', 'lawful order', 'authorised by law' etc do not simply refer to the domestic law of the state but are also 'a reference to the rule of law, or the principle of legality, which is common to democratic societies and the heritage of member states of the Council of Europe'.[70] Thus, telephone tapping by the Post Office on behalf of an English police force was held to be a violation of article 8, even though it was in accordance with English law.[71]

70 *Silver* Report No 5947/72 European Court of Human Rights para 281.
71 *Malone* Report No 8691/79 European Court of Human Rights para 121.

Where the convention allows restrictions to the rights and freedoms it guarantees, these must not be applied for any purpose other than those for which they have been prescribed.[72] And even these restrictions must be in accordance with the general principle of proportionality, ie, there will be a breach of the convention when it is clearly established that there is no reasonable relationship of proportionality between the means employed and the aim sought to be realised.[73]

Institutions

The Convention and its institutions are creatures of the Council of Europe (not the European Union). Complaints of violations are currently handled by three bodies:

- the *European Commission of Human Rights*, which receives initial complaints, rules on their admissibility, makes an investigation and prepares reports;
- the *Committee of Ministers*, which decides on the merits of cases not referred to the court and supervises the execution of the judgments of the court; and
- the *European Court of Human Rights*, which makes authoritative decisions as to whether or not the Convention has been violated, and on costs and compensation.

Making an application[74]

Who can bring a complaint?

A complaint can be brought by any 'person, non-governmental organisation or group of individuals'.[75] The nationality of the complainant is irrelevant; it is sufficient for him/her to be within the jurisdiction of a state that has ratified the Convention. There is no age limit: a complaint can be brought by a child. However, the person, organisation or group of individuals must themselves be the victims of a violation, either directly or indirectly. The family of a person who died in the course

---

72 Article 18.
73 *Belgian Linguistic Case*, Series A, No 6, European Court of Human Rights, 23 July 1968; see also *Handyside Case*, Series A, No 24, European Court of Human Rights, 7 December 1976.
74 In this section the authors have drawn on L J Clements, *European Human Rights: Taking a case under the Convention*, Sweet and Maxwell, 1994, an invaluable practical guide.
75 Article 25.

of a violent arrest, for example, would be indirect victims of a violation. Companies, trade unions, friendly societies and unincorporated associations may all bring complaints provided they have themselves been victims, but local authorities may not, although individual politicians or political parties may do so.

Anonymity and confidentiality

Anonymous complaints, ie, those that do not reveal the identity of the complainant to the Commission, will not be accepted. However, if a complainant fears that his/her safety may be jeopardised by making a complaint, a request can be made to the Commission for undertakings or other protective measures to be given by the state.[76]

A complainant can request that his/her name be kept confidential, although it will have to be disclosed to the state. The request should be made in the initial letter of complaint (see below) and the complainant should thereafter be referred to by initial letters.

Exhaustion of domestic remedies

Complaints can only be considered by the Commission after all effective domestic remedies have been exhausted.[77] If it is quite obvious that there is no possibility of effectively pursuing an appeal, the Commission may deem that domestic remedies have been exhausted, although counsel's opinion to this effect is usually necessary.

The availability of a domestic remedy will not afford a state a defence unless it can fully rectify the violation. Thus compensatory damages paid to a prisoner held for an excessively long period on remand have been held to be an inadequate remedy.[78] However damages for physical abuse or mistreatment are generally an adequate remedy, unless the violation takes the form of an officially approved administrative practice.[79]

Judicial review (see p302) may constitute an effective remedy, but not if the relief is insufficient to meet the violation in all respects.[80] Ex gratia payments and free pardons (see pp269–275) do not constitute effective remedies.[81]

76 Commission Rules, r36.
77 Article 26.
78 DR 56/62.
79 DR 20/184.
80 *Agosi v UK*, 9 EHRR 1.
81 DR 42/171.

Time limits
The complaint must be made within six months from the date on which
the final domestic decision was taken.[82] If there is a deemed exhaustion
of remedies and thus no 'final effective domestic decision', time runs
from the date of the incident constituting the violation. Cases should be
brought promptly as the time limit is strictly enforced. However, the
time limit is not applicable in the case of a continuing breach such as
where domestic legislation constitutes a violation of the Convention.

There is an obvious risk of falling foul of the time limit rules because
an applicant has over-zealously sought to observe the exhaustion of
domestic remedy rules. Conversely, one may fall foul of the requirement
to exhaust domestic remedies out of a fear of missing a time limit. If
this appears to be a risk, applicants should submit one or more
'holding' applications to the Commission, explaining the difficulty
and that attempts are being made to exhaust domestic remedies. The
advice should, therefore, be to apply to Strasbourg 'early and often'.

Legal aid
English legal aid (including advice and assistance under the green form
scheme) is not available for any part of the case.

The Commission and the court can grant its own form of legal aid,
but only after the Commission has sent the complaint to the respondent
government and that government has replied with written representations or the deadline for such representations has passed. If legal aid is
granted, it can retrospectively cover the cost of preparing the original
application, as well as subsequent work in preparing the case and for
representation at any hearing.

Legal aid is subject to a financial means test, but an applicant will
qualify if s/he would qualify for English legal aid, and may qualify even
if s/he would not qualify under the English system. The applicant's
means form must be endorsed by the Benefits Agency, Legal Aid
Assessment Office, Albert Edward House, No 3 The Pavilions, Ash-
ton-on-Ribble, Preston, PR2 2PA, telephone 01772 562940.

The rates of payment, which are calculated on a unit-cost basis, not
an hourly rate, are modest in the extreme, amounting to little more than
token contributions towards the real cost. However, actual out-of-
pocket expenses such as travel and accommodation costs can, with
prior approval, also be met.

82 Article 26.

Contingency fees

The government has brought in arrangements for 'no win, no fee' contingency fees in human rights cases. If an applicant does win, legal fees could be uplifted by up to 100%.[83]

Costs

If a complaint is upheld by the court, it can order the whole or part of the complainant's costs to be met by the respondent government. These should be calculated on a conventional hourly rate basis and presented in the usual form.

Complaints

Complaints about violations of the Convention should be sent to the Commission in Strasbourg (see appendix 14). The complaint can initially be made in the form of a simple letter stating:

- the complainant's name, age, address, nationality and occupation;
- the name and address of any person or organisation representing the complainant;
- the name of the government against whom the complaint is made (ie, the United Kingdom);
- the object of the application and the articles of the Convention which it is alleged have been violated;
- a statement of the facts of the case;
- the reasons why the facts of the case amount to a denial of rights under the Convention;
- details of the steps taken to exhaust domestic remedies demonstrating that the six month time limit has been met.

On receipt of an initial letter the Commission will send out an application form. The formal application form must then be submitted within six weeks. This should contain an explanation of the legal reasoning that supports the applicant's case and should marshal all the arguments the applicant seeks to advance. In practice, the Commission is often prepared to grant extensions of time beyond the six weeks for good reason and provided the extension is sought in advance.

While it is not strictly necessary to have a lawyer in order to make a complaint, and an application to the Commission can be made in person, in practice it is crucial to the chances of success to be legally

83 Conditional Fee Agreements Order 1995 SI No 1674.

represented. Before the court applicants must usually be represented by a qualified lawyer.

Procedure

The current two-stage procedure described below is to be abolished,[84] in an attempt to speed up the time taken for cases to reach the court and arrive at a final determination. However, the timing of implementation is unclear, being dependent on ratification by all member states of the Council of Europe and a one-year delay thereafter. Once implemented, cases will go direct to an enlarged court.

Procedure before the Commission

On receipt of a complaint it is registered and a provisional file is opened; a member of the Commission will be appointed to act as *rapporteur*, to report on its admissibility and the procedure to be adopted. Applications which are anonymous, manifestly ill-founded or an abuse of process will be rejected as inadmissible.[85] The report is considered by the Commission, which may summarily declare the complaint inadmissible. Provided it does not do so, it may ask for further information or send the report to the government for its comments and response. The government's response is then copied to the complainant for his/her comments and response. The Commission then gives a final decision on admissibility after either a committee meeting (usually only held for hopeless cases), a chambers hearing held before seven members of the Commission, or a full session held before all 22 members of the Commission.

If it finds the complaint admissible the Commission will investigate the facts jointly with the complainant and the government, assess the merits of the case and attempt a 'friendly settlement'. If this is successful, it issues a short report. If no friendly settlement can be achieved, the Commission prepares a secret report expressing an advisory opinion which is sent to the government and to the Committee of Ministers. If the Commission's opinion is that there has been a violation, the government may comply with that decision. If it does not do so the Commission or the government (but not the complainant) can refer the case to the court. When a case is referred to the court, a copy of the Commission's final report is released to the complainant.

84 Protocol No 11, 1993.
85 Convention Article 27.

Procedure before the court

The Commission participates in the case before the Court by assisting and informing; in theory the complainant is not a party, although for all practical purposes s/he is treated and is able to participate as if s/he were.[86] Once the court has been constituted (usually as a chamber of nine judges), the state, the Commission and the complainant have a further opportunity to make further written submissions, known as 'memorials', particularly commenting upon how the violation breaches individual provisions of the Convention. Claims for costs and compensation should also be submitted at this stage.

Third party interventions in the form of amicus curiae briefs may be permitted, and can strengthen a case if submitted by a respected lawyer (possibly an academic lawyer) or by an organisation having particular knowledge or expertise in the issues raised by the complaint.[87]

Oral hearings are often concluded in half a day, with oral submissions from representatives of the Commission, the state and the complainant being limited to about 45 minutes. While oral evidence can be admitted, the procedure is not well suited to resolving disputes of fact, which in practice will usually have been settled earlier in the process.

The current procedure does not provide a speedy remedy. Cases that are declared admissible usually take several years to be dealt with by the Commission, with additional delays of several more years if the case goes to the Court.

Inquests

The families and friends of people who have died in controversial circumstances have attempted to use coroners' inquests to establish what happened. These attempts have met with varying degrees of success. Although inquests into deaths in police custody or at the hands of the police have sometimes seemed to families ineffective as a means of establishing the truth, they are often the only means available, and this section explains how to make the most of a limited procedure.

Coroners' inquests have very limited objectives. They are directed solely to ascertaining:

86 Court Rules r1.
87 Court Rules r37(2).

- who the deceased was;
- how, when and where the deceased died; and
- the details necessary to make out a death certificate.[88]

'How' someone dies is decided by discovering 'by what means' s/he has died; it will rarely include an examination of the broader circumstances surrounding the death.[89] An inquest is not usually an appropriate forum for establishing why someone died or who was responsible. Indeed, no verdict can be 'framed in such a way as to appear to determine the question of (a) criminal liability on the part of a named person, or (b) civil liability'.[90] This rule is said to be necessary because a person accused of a crime, or a civil wrong, is provided with certain safeguards when appearing as a defendant at trial, many of which are not provided at an inquest.

However, the jury at an inquest can still return a range of verdicts, including lawful killing, unlawful killing or an open verdict but without naming an individual as being responsible.[91] Further, there is nothing to stop the coroner and the jury exploring facts bearing on criminal or civil liability during the inquest itself provided that the verdict itself is not framed in such a way as to determine liability.

Initial considerations

Legal aid
Other parties at an inquest where the deceased has died in police custody are likely to be represented by lawyers and naturally the deceased's family will also wish to have legal representation. However, legal aid is not available. The green form scheme for legal advice and assistance can pay, or at least go towards paying, for preparation of the case, if there is a relative who is financially eligible, but it will not cover the cost of representation. The cost of a contentious inquest can be high, with legal fees often in the thousands of pounds.

It may be possible, however, to obtain a green form extension for a family member to be accompanied by a 'McKenzie friend' to the inquest; that is, someone to help and advise at the hearing, but not actually to represent the family. In addition, if legal aid has already been

88 Coroners Rules 1984 SI No 552 r36.
89 *R v HM Coroner for North Humberside and Scunthorpe ex p Jamieson* [1994] 3 WLR 82, CA.
90 Coroners Rules 1984 r42.
91 Ibid. r42, Sch 4, form 22 note 4.

granted for a civil action, it is possible for this to be extended to cover the taking of notes and even asking questions at the inquest.

Some law centres may represent families without charge in inquests, but this will depend on the policies and resources of the local centre. In addition, the organisation Inquest, which was set up in 1981 to monitor inquests and provide advice on deaths in custody and other controversial circumstances, may be able to help. In 1994, Inquest handled some 240 new cases.[92] Even where there has been a referral to a solicitor, Inquest continues working on the case to keep legal costs down and to advise on further action if the coroner's verdict is unsatisfactory.

First steps
It is important to be aware of the initial steps that a representative should take on behalf of a deceased's family when an inquest is to be held. They can be briefly described as follows:

a) contact the coroner's officer (usually a seconded police officer) and make sure s/he is aware of the family's interest in the inquest;

b) ascertain the date of the post mortem (see below), and if the relatives wish to instruct a doctor or a forensic pathologist to attend the post mortem, this should be arranged;

c) request a list of witnesses whom the coroner intends to call. If the relatives have other witnesses that they believe should be called, this information should be submitted to the coroner together with any relevant documentation s/he may not have seen;

d) although there is no right to advance disclosure for the relatives (see below), it is worthwhile writing to all the relevant parties (including the coroner) and requesting the information. The prison service, for example, has agreed to release all relevant documentation to the family so long as the coroner does not object.[93]

Jurisdiction
An inquest must be held where a coroner is informed that the body of a person is lying within his/her district and there is reason to suspect that the deceased:

a) has died a violent or unnatural death; or

b) has died a death of which the cause is unknown; or

92 Inquest Annual Report 1994. See appendix 14 for address.
93 See Grealis and Coles, 'Inquests: redressing the balance' (1994) SJ 321.

c) has died in prison (or in a place or circumstances that otherwise require an inquest).[94]

The jurisdiction referred to is a geographical area, usually comprising a county or part of a county. The coroner's duty arises because of the presence of the body in his/her district, irrespective of where the death occurred.[95] There is no general discretion, outside the above criteria, for a coroner to hold an inquest, for instance, if s/he feels it is in the public interest that one should be held.[96] The term 'unnatural death' is to be given its ordinary meaning. Therefore, it has been held that a person who dies of a prolonged asthmatic attack, but whose life may have been saved if an ambulance had arrived in time has not died an 'unnatural death' which would necessitate an inquest.[97]

The term 'prison' is not defined, and there is doubt whether it would include a police station for the purposes of a coroner's inquest. However, Home Office guidance states that it is 'desirable for an inquest to be held, with a jury, in all cases of deaths occurring in any form of legal custody, even though the death may have occurred in hospital or elsewhere and even though it may have been due to natural causes'.[98] In practice, in 1994, for example, there was no inquest held in only two out of 36 deaths in police custody (outside the Metropolitan police area).[99] However, both these deaths appear from the statistics to relate to death from natural causes.

Post mortem examination and toxicology reports

Coroners have a general power to order a post mortem or a 'special examination' (such as a toxicology report).[100] The jury has the right to insist on a post mortem if a majority does not believe that the cause of death has been explained satisfactorily.[101] The family may wish to have an independent post mortem, whether or not one has already been held. This is usually arranged by agreement with the coroner. If possible, a green form extension should be sought to pay for this; otherwise it must

---

94 Coroners Act 1988 s8(1).
95 Ibid.
96 *R v Poplar Coroner ex p Thomas* (1992) *Times* 23 December, CA.
97 Ibid.
98 Home Office Circular 109/1982, 20 December 1982.
99 Home Office Statistical Bulletin, Issue 13/95.
100 Coroners Act 1988 s20.
101 Coroners Act 1988 s21(4).

be at the family's expense. If a coroner refuses to allow an independent post mortem for insufficient reasons, s/he can be compelled to consent by court order.[102]

Obviously, there will usually be no need to order an independent post mortem if the report of the coroner's pathologist is consistent with the families' allegations and the report is not likely to be challenged by, for example, the police. The difficulty usually lies in knowing the contents of the report at a sufficiently early stage, as some pathologists are so busy that their reports are frequently delayed. Coroner's pathologists will usually share information with a family's own pathologist in quite an open manner, certainly more openly than they would with the family. It can, therefore, be helpful to appoint a pathologist very early on, at least to discuss the case, perhaps informally, with the coroner's pathologist, in order to obtain an early indication of whether or not a second post mortem is needed.

If a second post mortem is necessary, it is usually desirable that this should take place as soon as possible after death. While the importance of this varies depending upon the nature of the cause of death (which may, of course, be uncertain), expert medical advice as to the need for an urgent post mortem should be sought at the earliest possible stage.

Testing for drugs or alcohol

If the deceased may have been under the influence of drugs or alcohol, a toxicology report will usually be necessary even if there is not to be a second post mortem. Check with the coroner whether s/he has ordered a toxicology report and, if so, whether this is for standard or for full screening. Standard screening is sufficient to identify the majority of drugs in common circulation, but full screening is more comprehensive and more expensive (say £750). To be effective, blood or other samples for a toxicology analysis need to be taken within two to three days of the alcohol or drugs being ingested. The hospital should therefore be requested to take samples immediately and to preserve them, even if it is initially unclear whether a toxicology report will be required.

When selecting an independent pathologist, consider the nature of the alleged cause of death and take medical advice, eg, from another pathologist or from a friendly consultant in the appropriate specialism, as to the pathologist's expertise and experience in that field. Many pathologists, for example, have little experience in trauma.

102 *R v HM Coroner for Greater London (Southern District) ex p Ridley* [1985] 1 WLR 1347.

Juries

The coroner must sit with a jury, if, among other situations, it appears to him/her that the death occurred:

- in prison;
- in circumstances the continuation or possible recurrence of which is prejudicial to the health or safety of the public or any section of the public; or
- while the deceased was in police custody, or resulted from an injury inflicted by a police officer in the purported execution of his duty.[103]

A coroner has a discretion to summon a jury in any other case where it appears 'that there is any reason to do so'. There is no discretion *not* to summon a jury if it appears to the coroner that one or more of these factors applies.[104]

A coroner's jury consists of between seven and 11 people. The old practice of having the jury selected by the coroner's officer was abolished from 1 January 1984 and now the jury is selected in the same way as a crown court jury.[105] The family of the deceased has no right to challenge individual members of the jury, but the procedures for summoning the jury are mandatory and if they are not followed then this failure can be challenged by way of judicial review.[106]

The right to examine witnesses

The following, among others, are entitled to examine any witness at the inquest, either in person or through a barrister or solicitor:

- a parent, child, spouse or personal representative of the deceased;
- the beneficiary under an insurance policy issued on the life of the deceased;
- anyone whose act or omission may have caused or contributed to the death (or his/her agent or servant);
- a chief officer of police;

103 Coroners Act 1988 s8(3).
104 *R v Poplar Coroner ex p Chaudhury* (1992) *Times* 20 October, CA (an application for leave to apply for judicial review).
105 Coroners' Juries Act 1983.
106 *R v Merseyside Coroner ex p Carr* [1993] 4 All ER 65, DC.

– any other person who, in the opinion of the coroner, is a properly interested person.[107]

In a case concerning the inquest of Colin Roach, who died of gunshot wounds at Stoke Newington police station, the coroner applied to the High Court for a declaration that the Hackney Black People's Association was not a 'properly interested person'. It was decided that 'normally to be an interested person you must be connected in some way either with the deceased or the circumstances leading up to his death'. The association, although concerned with police/black relations, did not qualify. However, it was further decided that the rules do not contain an exhaustive list of those who can be permitted to examine witnesses and that a coroner has 'a residual discretion which may only need to be exercised to allow certain questioning if he considers for good reason that it is appropriate to do so'.[108] Shortly afterwards, the same coroner permitted the Tower House Residents' Association to examine witnesses at the inquest of one of its residents who died in police custody.[109] In the inquest into the death of Blair Peach at the hands of police officers during an anti National Front demonstration in 1980, the Anti-Nazi League, of which he was a member, was represented.

Even if a 'properly interested person' is given the right to examine witnesses, it is important to bear in mind that the nature of the proceedings is quite unlike an ordinary adversarial court, where two parties argue out their case against one another. Coroners and their juries are charged with inquiring into deaths and in theory there are no 'parties' to the case. Inquests are said to be 'inquisitorial'.[110] The right to examine witnesses and to be represented by a lawyer does not confer the right to present a case or to call witnesses. These are matters for the coroner alone.

107 Coroners Rules 1984 r20.
108 *R v Inner London North Coroner ex p Chambers* (1993) *Times* 30 April.
109 *Re Roper* (1983) 5 July, unreported, St Pancras Coroner's Court, see Ward 'Coroners' inquests' February 1984 *Legal Action* 16.
110 For practical advice on representing a deceased's family at an inquest see Mullins, 'Appearing at an inquest' (1994) SJ 336; and Owen, 'Surviving Inquests' (1991) SJ 1168.

Disclosure of documents

At the beginning of the inquest, the coroner should announce what documentary evidence it is proposed to admit from living persons.[111] This does not apply to documents left by the deceased. The Police Complaints Authority will disclose, on the coroner's request, such documents as s/he may require for the proper conduct of the inquest.[112] On payment of a fee the coroner must supply to a 'properly interested person' a copy of any report of a post mortem or special examination, notes of evidence or any document put in evidence at the inquest. Alternatively, the coroner can allow such a person to inspect such documents without payment of a fee.[113]

There is no requirement on a coroner to disclose witness statements taken by the police. In the Blair Peach case, the High Court refused to order the disclosure of such statements to the family on the ground that they were the property of the police and 'could not, without breach of confidence or trust' be shown to anyone other than the coroner.[114] Since that case, the Court of Appeal has indicated that statements taken during the investigation of a disciplinary matter are admissible in criminal and disciplinary proceedings,[115] and has decided that statements taken during the investigation of a criminal matter can be disclosed in a civil action,[116] and the House of Lords has held that the fruits of the investigation of a police complaint can be disclosed in a civil action.[117] It may, therefore, now be in doubt whether the courts would uphold a coroner's refusal to show such statements to the family of the deceased or to a properly interested person.

In a civil case, such as a claim under the Fatal Accidents Act 1976 (see chapter 5), the depositions or witnesses' statements are not admissible as evidence, although they can be used for the purposes of cross-examination.[118] Depositions are admissible in criminal proceedings, but only, it seems, if the accused was present when the witness gave evidence and had an opportunity to conduct a cross-examination.[119]

111 Coroners Rules 1984 r37(3).
112 PCA Triennial Review 1985–1988 para 2.8.
113 Coroners Rules 1984 r57.
114 *R v Hammersmith Coroner ex p Peach* [1980] Crim LR 168, DC.
115 *Neilson v Laugharne* [1981] 1 All ER 829 at 837 and 839.
116 *Peach v Commissioner of Police for the Metropolis* [1986] 2 All ER 129, CA.
117 *R v Chief Constable of West Midlands Police, ex p Wiley* [1995] 1 AC 274.
118 *Barnett v Cohen* [1921] 2 KB 461; *Re Pollock, Pollock v Pollock* [1941] 1 All ER 360 at 362.
119 *R v Cowle* (1907) 71 JP 152; *R v Black* (1910) 74 JP 71.

Witnesses

The coroner must examine, on oath, anyone who wishes to give relevant evidence and everyone 'having knowledge of the facts whom he thinks it expedient to examine'. Provided someone's evidence is relevant,[120] s/he is entitled to be examined, even if not called as a witness: s/he can simply attend and ask to be heard. However, only the coroner can summon witnesses. In *R v HM Coroner for West Yorkshire (Eastern District) ex p Clements*[121] the deceased had hanged himself in a police station's 'cooler cell' and the family wished to call a witness (who had unsuccessfully tried to hang himself in the same police station a year earlier) to show that the police should have been on notice that suicide attempts were not unlikely in that cell. The Divisional Court held that a coroner's discretion based on expediency under the Coroners Act 1988 s11(2) to exclude evidence extended to refusing to hear witnesses who were not closely relevant to the cause of death, especially where the evidence would add considerable length to the inquest.

Witnesses are usually examined first by the coroner, then by anyone else entitled to examine witnesses and lastly by their own lawyer, if they are represented.[122]

Verdict

The coroner (or jury if there is one) must complete a document, known as an inquisition, which records who the deceased was, and how, when and where s/he died. The part that records 'how' the person died is known as the verdict. The Coroners Rules[123] suggest the following forms of verdict:

a) – died from natural causes;
   – died from the industrial disease of . . . ;
   – died from dependence on drugs/non-dependent abuse of drugs;
   – died from want of attention at birth.
   (In any of the above cases, but in no other, it is suggested that the following words may, where appropriate, be added:
   'and the cause of death was aggravated by lack of care/self-neglect'.)
b) In any other case except murder, manslaughter, infanticide or stillbirth, it is suggested that one of the following forms be adopted:
   – killed himself [whilst the balance of his mind was disturbed];
   – died as a result of an attempted/self-induced abortion;

120 Coroners Act 1887 s4(1).
121 (1993) *Independent* 20 August.
122 Coroners Rules 1984 r21.
123 Coroners Rules 1984 Sch 4.

- died as a result of an accident/misadventure;
Execution of sentence of death:
- was killed lawfully.
Open verdict, namely, the evidence did not fully or further disclose the means whereby the cause of death arose.

  c) In the case of murder, manslaughter or infanticide it is suggested that the following form be adopted:
- was killed unlawfully.

It has been held that, despite the above suggestions in the rules, a verdict of 'lack of care' can usually only be returned in conjunction with other verdicts. Seeking to establish a verdict of 'lack of care' in conjunction with other verdicts,[124] like suicide or accidental death, is attractive in cases where the deceased has been in police custody and his/her family feel that the police could or should have done more to prevent their relative committing suicide, or dying as a result of intoxication, illness or injury in the police station. However, the scope of the verdict has been uncertain and the Court of Appeal, in *R v HM Coroner for North Humberside ex p Jamieson*,[125] has now laid down guidelines on when the verdict will be appropriate. These can be summarised as follows:[126]

a) Although a verdict of 'lack of care' is often sought as a stepping stone to a claim in common law for negligence, the two terms are not connected. 'Lack of care' should be replaced in inquests by the term 'neglect'.

b) 'Neglect' in inquests means 'a gross failure by others to provide adequate nourishment or liquid, or provide or procure basic medical attention or shelter or warmth for someone in a dependent position (because of youth, age, illness or incarceration) who cannot provide it for himself.'

c) 'Neglect' can rarely, if ever, be an appropriate verdict on its own, although it will be appropriate in some cases to say that neglect 'contributed to' (usually rather than 'aggravated') death by another cause (say, for instance, drug abuse).

---

124 Verdicts are discussed in various articles: see, for instance, Brayne, 'Confusion on the rock' [1988] 41 LSG 25 (The Gibraltar Three inquest), Coleman and Scraton, 'Unanswered questions' November 1990 *Legal Action* 8; (the Hillsborough inquest); Hesse and Hill, 'Doing it to death' October 1989 *Legal Action* 9 (inquests and black people); and Jennings, 'The death of an Irish inquest' (1990) NLJ 634 (inquest into the killing of three unarmed IRA suspects).
125 [1994] 3 WLR 82, CA.
126 Ibid at 100–101; and see Hinchcliffe 'Lack of care' (1994) SJ 656, 1 July.

d) If it is established that the deceased committed suicide, that must be the verdict. On certain facts it could possibly be correct to hold that neglect contributed to suicide, but not simply on the ground that the deceased was (even carelessly) afforded an opportunity to take his/her own life. There would have to be gross neglect (such as a police officer observing a prisoner about to put a noose round his/her neck, but failing to intervene) before this finding would be appropriate.

e) 'Neglect' should never form part of the verdict unless a clear and direct cause or connection is established between the conduct so described and the cause of death.

In the case of unlawful killing, it is uncertain whether it is sufficient for a jury to return such a verdict on the basis that the conduct of a group of police officers 'in aggregate' led to the death. In *R v West London Coroner's Court ex p Gray*[127] the court held that the death has to be attributable to a particular officer (but, of course, on no account can this officer be named in the verdict as this may appear to be determining a question of civil or criminal liability). However, in *R v Greater London Coroner ex p Diesa Koto*[128] it was held that, even though it would be impossible to attribute the death to acts of any single prison officer, an unlawful killing verdict was possible because there was no reason why the ordinary principles of joint enterprise should not apply to an inquest as they did in a criminal trial.

The standard of proof for a verdict of unlawful killing is beyond reasonable doubt. A stringent standard of proof is also required in cases of suicide, but in relation to other verdicts, apart from an open verdict, proof on the balance of probabilities will suffice.[129] In deciding whether to withdraw a verdict from the jury on the basis that no reasonable jury could hold that the necessary standard of proof could be established, the coroner must not just look at the medical evidence but must take account of all the other evidence (such as eye-witness statements) as well.[130] It will be a breach of natural justice if the coroner refuses to allow counsel's submissions as to what verdicts ought or ought not, as a matter of law, to be left to the jury 'unless it was merely a colourable attempt to persuade the jury of a certain version of the facts'.[131]

127 [1987] 2 WLR 1020.
128 (1993) *Independent* 21 September.
129 Ibid.
130 *Ex p Diesa Koto*, see n128.
131 *R v East Berkshire Coroner ex p Buckley* (1992) *Times* 1 December.

Challenging the decision of the inquest[132]

Following the inquest, if the family is dissatisfied with the verdict, consideration should be given to a possible challenge in the High Court. There are two main ways of doing this and, although they may be pursued together if appropriate,[133] the courts appear to prefer applicants to proceed by the former, if possible.[134]

Coroners Act order

The first is a statutory remedy provided by Coroners Act 1988 s13. The High Court can quash an inquisition of an inquest and order a new inquest to be held where this is in the interests of justice due to 'fraud, rejection of evidence, irregularity of proceedings, insufficiency of enquiry, the discovery of new facts or evidence or otherwise'.[135] The fiat of the Attorney-General and leave of the court are necessary in these proceedings.

Judicial review

The second is by way of judicial review (see in general below p303). Examples of the possible decisions that may be reviewable include the refusal to summon a jury,[136] misdirections as to the burden of proof[137] and refusal to release documents.[138] Other examples have already appeared in the text of this section to illustrate points of law.

Applications for legal aid can be made for both these remedies.

Inquiries

Official inquiries into policing matters can be ordered only by the Home Secretary. These may be held in public or private, and by convention are usually conducted by a senior judge. Police authorities and the Home Secretary can order chief officers to submit a written report to them on any policing matter they specify, but police authorities have no power to

132 See in general Samuels, 'Challenging the decision of the coroner's inquest' (1989) 133 SJ 892 14 July, and Gordon 'Judicially Reviewing the powers of Coroners' [1987] LS Gaz 1322 6 May.
133 *Re Rapier, Deceased* [1986] 3 WLR 830.
134 *R v West Berkshire Coroner ex p Thomas* (1991) *Times* 25 April, DC.
135 Coroners Act 1988 s13(1) and (2).
136 *R v Inner London North District Coroner ex p Linnane* [1989] 2 All ER 254.
137 *R v Wolverhampton Coroner ex p McCurbin* [1990] 2 All ER 759, CA and *ex p Gray* (n127).
138 *R v HM Coroner for Hammersmith ex p Peach* [1980] 2 WLR 496.

order an inquiry. This lack of accountability has occasionally caused local or national organisations, including local authorities, to set up their own unofficial public inquiries.

Official inquiries

Under the Police Act 1964, the Home Secretary has power to order a local inquiry into any matter connected with the policing of any area. This power has been used only rarely: to inquire into the Red Lion Square disorders in 1974 when Kevin Gately died[139] and into the Brixton disorders in 1981.[140] Both inquiries were conducted by Lord Scarman. Before 1964, inquiries were held into a wide range of matters, including cases of serious misconduct involving individual officers.[141] The two inquires conducted since 1964 both involved public disorder. The refusal of inquiries into the deaths of Blair Peach, Jimmy Kelly and Liddle Towers suggest that, as a matter of policy, inquiries into acts of individual misconduct are most unlikely in future. Even calls for inquiries into serious outbreaks of public disorders, such as those in Lewisham in 1977, Southall in 1979 and Bristol in 1980, have been refused. All these occurred after 1976 when the Police Complaints Board was introduced as an independent element in the investigation of police complaints.

It has been suggested that, as the complaints system has been improved, the circumstances in which an inquiry will be ordered have narrowed, so that now an inquiry can be expected only when a disorder amounts to an operational defeat for the police.[142] Indeed, the Home Office has set out some of the criteria it takes into account in response to a request from Hackney Community Defence Association for a local inquiry into policing in Hackney under Police Act 1964 s32, following a series of high-profile police misconduct cases, many of which involved allegations of officers planting drugs on innocent people. The Home Office stated that, in their view, the CPS, the PCA and disciplinary procedures were the appropriate way to deal with the problems, and went on to say that

---

139 Cmnd 5919.
140 Cmnd 8427.
141 Eg, the Thursoe case (Cmnd 718), the Challoner case (Cmnd 2735) and the Sheffield 'rhino whip' case (Cmnd 2176).
142 Jefferson and Grimshaw, *Controlling the constable*, Muller/Cobden Trust, 1984, pp127–132.

Successive Home Secretaries have taken the view that such inquiries should be reserved for the most extreme circumstances, for example where the whole efficiency of a police force is called into question; or where there has been serious public disorder. These amount to circumstances where other ways of enquiring into police behaviour would be inadequate.[143]

It seems that the procedure on the inquiry is largely left to the person conducting it. However, witnesses may be summonsed and evidence can be taken on oath.[144] In the Brixton inquiry, oral evidence was taken at public hearings and then written submissions were considered. A final hearing was held at the end of the inquiry, when represented parties, including a number of community groups, and counsel for the inquiry made closing addresses.[145] The costs of legal representation can be met from police funds if the Home Secretary agrees,[146] and were met in the Brixton inquiry for all represented parties.[147] During the Brixton inquiry, the Attorney-General issued a general immunity from prosecution for everyone giving evidence.[148] If the report of an inquiry is not published in full, the findings and the conclusions must be published in summary form, so far as this appears consistent with the public interest.[149]

After the release of the Guildford Four in October 1989 an inquiry was set up under Sir John May, a retired Court of Appeal judge, under the Tribunals and Inquiries Act 1971 to look into the events leading to and deriving from the trials of the Guildford Four and the Maguire family.[150]

Following the release of the Birmingham Six, the Home Secretary set up a Royal Commission under Lord Runciman, to look into many aspects of the criminal justice system. The commission decided not to make its proceedings open to the public, but invited written submissions from interested groups and organisations. The commission's report proposed wide-ranging changes to the criminal justice system (some of which have been enacted in the Criminal Justice and Public Order Act

143 Letter from Home Office to HCDA dated 1 March 1994.
144 Police Act 1964 s32(3) and Local Government Act 1972 s250.
145 *The Scarman Report*, Pelican Books, 1982, para 1.8.
146 Police Act 1964 s32(5).
147 *The Scarman Report* op cit n145, Appendix A paras 15–17.
148 Ibid Appendix A para 6.
149 Police Act 1964 s32(4).
150 See Return to an address of the honourable the House of Commons dated 12 July 1990 for the inquiry into the circumstances surrounding the convictions arising out of the bomb attacks in Guildford and Woolwich in 1974 – Interim report on the Maguire case 1990, HC 556.

1994) and recommended that an independent body be established to investigate possible miscarriages of justice.[151] This lead to the Criminal Appeal Act 1995 (see p265).

Reports from chief officers of police

Police authorities can require their chief officers to submit a written report to them on such policing matters, and in such form, as they specify.[152] However, this power is qualified. If it appears to the chief officer that such a report would contain information which in the public interest ought not to be disclosed, or is not needed for the discharge of the functions of the police authority, s/he can request the authority to refer the requirement to the Home Secretary. The authority's request is then of no effect unless confirmed by the Home Secretary.[153] Subject to this, a police authority may arrange for or require the chief officer to arrange for, a report to be published.[154] These provisions appy only outside the Metropolitan Police area (although they do apply to the City of London Police).[155]

The Home Secretary can require any chief constable or the Commissioner of Police of the City of London to submit a report on any aspect of the policing of his/her area.[156] The Home Secretary can also require reports from the Commissioner of the Metropolitan Police in his/her capacity as the police authority for the area.[157] Those reports have not usually been published, but there have been exceptions, such as the publication in 1974 of the report on the alleged involvement of police officers in the death of Kenneth Lennon.[158] A statutory power to arrange publication now appears in Police Act 1964 s30(1B), inserted by PMCA 1994.

In addition, all chief officers submit published annual reports to their own authorities and to the Home Secretary.

151 The Royal Commission on Criminal Justice Report Cm 2263, London, HMSO 1993.
152 Police Act 1964 s12(2) and (2A), as amended by PMCA 1994.
153 Police Act 1964 s12(3).
154 Police Act 1964 s12(3A), as amended by PMCA 1994.
155 Ibid s12(4).
156 Ibid s30(1), (1A) and (3).
157 Metropolitan Police Act 1929 s1; see HC Written Answers 15 July 1985, col 18.
158 Report to the Home Secretary from the Commissioner of Police for the Metropolis on . . . the case of Kenneth Joseph Lennon 1974, HC 351.

Unofficial inquiries

The relative lack of public accountability and the fact that it is so difficult to get a public inquiry into policing matters have led to a number of unofficial inquiries being set up. Lord Gifford QC at the first meeting of the enquiry into the disturbances at Broadwater Farm in 1985 set out some reasons for holding an enquiry:

> When there is a conflict in society it is always the powerful institutions which find it easy to put out a version of the events which . . . is reported by the mass media as if there were no other truth.
>   Those without power have no such voice. Our task is to listen to the powerless as well as the powerful. To listen to the ordinary people of this community and the organisations which represent them. And having listened to everyone, to produce recommendations for change.[159]

Inquiries have been set up by local authorities, trade unions, community groups and civil liberties groups. Funding can sometimes be obtained from these bodies as well.[160] It is possible to set up an inquiry as a charitable function if the inquiry is attached to a charitable trust.[161]

An inquiry will usually follow broadly similar procedures to official inquiries. For the sake of being as impartial as possible, an independent board of inquiry is often set up which is a mixture of local representatives and respected people from outside. Frequently, a lawyer chairs the inquiry. It is very unusual for the police to recognise or participate in these inquiries and this can hamper the ability of the inquiry to hear all points of view on an incident.

It is important for the inquiry to be set up as soon as possible after the events it is to investigate as memories can quickly fade. It is equally important to set fairly strict terms of reference for the inquiry as well as deciding a budget, a timescale and methods of investigation. Many inquiries have published reports and these often include a description of how the inquiry was set up, how it operated in practice and the problems that had to be dealt with. Reports which have appeared include:

159 Report of the independent inquiry into disturbances of October 1985 at the Broadwater Farm Estate, Tottenham (chaired by Lord Gifford QC) 1986, p5.
160 See *Policing in Hackney 1945–1984*, Karia Press 1988 p140 and Broadwater Farm Inquiry (above) p12.
161 See Kaye *Unsafe and Unsatisfactory? Report of the Independent Inquiry into the working practices of the West Midlands Serious Crime Squad*, Civil Liberties Trust 1991.

- *Under heavy manners: Report of the Labour movement inquiry into police brutality and the position of black youth in Islington* held on 23 July 1977, Islington 18 Defence Committee.
- *Blood on the streets* Bethnal Green and Stepney Trades Council, 1978.
- *Unofficial committee of inquiry report: Southall 23 April 1979* NCCL, 1980.
- *Slumbering volcano? Report of an enquiry into the origins of the eruption in St Paul's, Bristol on 2 April 1980* Bristol TUC, 1981.
- *Final Report of the Lambeth Council Working Party into Community/Police Relations in Lambeth* Borough of Lambeth, 1981.
- *Unofficial committee of inquiry: the death of Blair Peach* NCCL, 1981.
- *Report of the Moss Side inquiry panel to the leader of the Greater Manchester Council* (chaired by Mr Benet Hytner QC) Greater Manchester Council, 1981.
- *Political policing in Wales* Welsh Campaign for Civil and Political Liberties, 1984.
- *Report of the independent inquiry into disturbances of October, 1985 at the Broadwater Farm Estate, Tottenham* (chaired by Lord Gifford QC) Broadwater Farm Inquiry, 1986 and *Broadwater Farm Revisited: second report of the independent inquiry*, Karia Press, 1989.
- *Policing in Hackney 1945–1984: a report commissioned by the Roach Family Support Committee*, Karia Press, 1989.
- Emmerson and Shamash *A Case to Answer? A report on the policing of the News International demonstration at Wapping on 24 January 1987* Haldane Society of Socialist Lawyers, 1987.
- *Unsafe and Unsatisfactory? Report of the independent inquiry into the working practices of the West Midlands Police Serious Crime Squad* Civil Liberties Trust, 1991.

Judicial review

Judicial review is the process by which the High Court supervises the lawfulness of the actions and decisions of inferior courts and tribunals, public bodies and individuals who carry out public duties and functions. It can, therefore, be used to supervise the activities of chief officers of police, police authorities, custody officers[162] and even individual police officers in appropriate cases. Judicial review is also available against other bodies, officials and tribunals that have an impact on a person's

162 See eg. *R v Cambridge Chief Constable ex p M* [1991] 2 All ER 777.

access to legal remedies for police misconduct. The county courts and magistrates' courts are subject to judicial review, usually in relation to jurisdictional and procedural matters.[163] Judicial review can also be used to review the decisions or refusals to act of the PCA, the Criminal Injuries Compensation Board and coroners.

Judicial review is not usually considered appropriate by the court where there is another effective remedy, such as an appeal to a tribunal or a statutory compaints procedure – save in exceptional circumstances[164] where there is great urgency and interim relief (such as an injunction) is required, or where the case concerns important questions of law which it is clear that the alternative remedy could not cope with. Where there is no other effective right of appeal against a decision, advisers should always consider the possibility of an application for judicial review.

The powers of the court are limited. It can usually take action on a decision or a refusal to act only where one of the following applies:

- a decision is illegal in that there was no power for it to be made (*ultra vires*);
- there has been misinterpretation of the meaning of a power or duty and the way it has been applied in a particular case (error of law);
- the decision is so unreasonable as to be perverse (often called *Wednesbury* unreasonableness);[165]
- relevant factors have not been taken into account or irrelevant factors have been taken into account in the decision-making process;
- proceedings have been conducted unfairly (breach of natural justice).

Where the decision-making process has been shown to be at fault, the court can:

- quash a decision, by an order of certiorari, with the effect that the person or body has to reconsider the decision (eg if the PCA wrongly decides to use its powers to dispense with an investigation, see pp67–69);
- order a person or body to carry out its public duty by an order of

163 See, for some examples, Fordham 'Well kept secret?' (1994) 91/14 LS G a2 13 April p17.
164 *R v Chief Constable of Merseyside Police ex p Calveley* [1986] QB 424, CA.
165 After the case of *Associated Provincial Picture Houses Ltd v Wednesbury Corporation* [1948] 1 KB 223, CA.

mandamus (eg, compel a chief officer to provide copies of seized documents);
- order a person not to act in an unlawful way by an order of prohibition (eg, to prevent an inferior court from hearing a case over which it has no jurisdiction);
- grant an injunction (eg, to prevent the continuation of an unlawful road block);
- make a declaration of the rights of the parties;[166] or
- award damages (but only where a private law civil wrong can be proved as well as the public law grounds for judicial review).[167]

In practice, the court has been reluctant to interfere when the police have a discretion as to how they should act. This is especially true where the powers or duties are broadly expressed, such as the general duty to enforce the law. In 1972, a Mr Blackburn sought an order of mandamus to compel the Metropolitan Police Commissioner to enforce the Obscene Publications Act 1958, and in particular to comply with the duty to bring obscene articles before the courts. The Court of Appeal refused the application, saying it would interfere only in extreme cases where the commissioner was not carrying out his duty to enforce the law. The commissioner had to balance competing demands on the resources available and he was doing what he could.[168]

The Court of Appeal again demonstrated its reluctance to substitute its judgment for that of the police in 1981 when the Central Electricity Generating Board sought an order of mandamus to force a chief constable to remove demonstrators from the site of a proposed nuclear power station. The demonstrators were peaceful and non-violent throughout. Although the police had power to enter the site and eject the demonstrators, it was for them to decide how to exercise that power and, if they concluded that there was no breach of the peace, the court would not make an order of mandamus against them.[169]

---

166 See *Vince v Chief Constable* of *Dorset Police* [1992] 3 All ER 98 (although this case was brought in private law, it is submitted that the subject matter (statutory interpretation of the duties of chief constables to appoint custody officers) could just as well have formed the basis for a judicial review application).

167 See for instance *R v Reading Justices ex p South West Meats Ltd* (1991) *Independent* 13 December.

168 *R v Commissioner of Police for the Metropolis ex p Blackburn (No 3)* [1973] 1 All ER 324, CA. See also *R v Oxford ex p Levey* (1987) 151 LG Rev 371, CA.

169 *R v Chief Constable of Devon and Cornwall ex p CEGB* [1981] 3 All ER 826.

There are a number of cases where judicial review of decisions made by the police has been successful. These usually involve powers or duties that are more specifically defined. For example, the limits of the police's statutory power to enter, search and seize have been the subject of judicial review.[170] A decision to caution a person at the police station in breach of Home Office guidelines has been quashed.[171] It is possible to challenge a decision of the police to prosecute an offender rather than to administer a caution where to do so is clearly in breach of guidelines formulated in the public interest.[172] A decision by the police to refuse solicitors access to their clients at a magistrates' court after 10 am was held to be unlawful.[173] A probationary constable has successfully challenged the decision of his chief constable to dismiss him without a disciplinary hearing.[174]

Procedure[175]

Applications for judicial review are dealt with in two stages. First, an application must be made to the court for leave to apply; once this has been granted, the application itself is made. The initial procedure is relatively simple, requiring only one form which sets out the details of the decision to be challenged and the grounds to be relied upon,[176] and an affidavit setting out the facts.[177] However, legal aid is available in judicial review proceedings and, if granted, counsel is often instructed to settle the grounds and sometimes the affidavit as well. It is usual to apply for emergency legal aid, given the strict time limits for making an application for leave.

The application for leave is usually made *ex parte* with no need to inform the other side unless interim relief such as an injunction or a stay is sought. Consequently, there is a duty for the applicant to disclose fully and frankly all relevant facts, even if these do not support his/her

170 See for example *R v Chief Constable of Lancashire Constabulary ex p Parker* [1993] 2 All ER 56.
171 *R v Commissioner of Police for the Metropolis ex p P* (1995) *Times* 24 May.
172 *R v Chief Constable of the Kent Constabulary ex p L* [1993] 1 All ER 756.
173 *R v Chief Constable of South Wales ex p Merrick* [1994] 1 WLR 663.
174 *R v Chief Constable of West Midlands Police ex p Carroll* (1994) 7 Admin LR 45, CA.
175 A number of practitioners' texts deal with procedure in detail: see, for instance, the Public Law Project's *The applicant's guide to judicial review* (Sweet & Maxwell, 1995).
176 RSC Appendix A Form 86A.
177 RSC Order 53 r3.

case. An applicant can ask the judge to consider the matter solely on the papers submitted. If leave is refused at this stage, the application can be renewed, as of right, within ten days, using another straightforward form,[178] for an oral hearing of the application for leave.

Even if legal aid is refused or the applicant would not quality financially, consideration should still be given to applying for leave. The cost of lodging the application is low – only £20 in 1995 – and the likelihood that the other side will not attend the hearing means that there is little risk of having to pay substantial costs to the other party if the application is unsuccessful. If leave is granted, this will act as a lever on the other side to reconsider its position and maybe to reach a settlement on the issue before the full hearing takes place. In addition, the chances of legal aid being granted will be greatly improved, for those financially eligible, once a judge has granted leave for the application to proceed.

At the leave stage, the court has to determine two questions. The first is to ensure that the applicant has standing to make the application, that is, a 'sufficient interest'[179] in the case. Generally speaking, an applicant with a personal interest in the matter will have standing, but judges are now more likely to accept that a community organisation or pressure group can qualify under this test. Much will depend on how involved the group is with the subject matter of the particular application.[180] The second question is whether, on the merits, the application is fit for further investigation at a full hearing with both sides present. To this extent, the leave stage acts as a filter to eliminate pointless or hopeless applicatons. Leave should be granted if, on a quick perusal, an arguable case has been presented,[181] although in practice there is great disparity between the rates of grant of leave applications between different judges.[182]

The application for leave must be brought promptly and, at the very latest, within three months of the date when the grounds for the application first arose,[183] unless the court considers that there are good reasons for extending the time limit.[184] However, even if a person

---

178 Form 86B.
179 RSC Order 53 r3(7).
180 See *R v Inspectorate of Pollution ex p Greenpeace (No 2)* [1994] 4 All ER 329; *R v Secretary of State for Foreign and Commonwealth Affairs ex p World Development Movement* [1995] 1 WLR 386.
181 *IRC v National Federation of Self-Employed and Small Businesses Ltd* [1981] 2 All ER 93, HL at 106.
182 Sunkin et al. *Judicial Review in Perspective* Public Law Project, 1993.
183 RSC Order 53 r4(1).
184 Ibid.

is within the three-month time limit, the application can still be struck out if the delay which has ensued would substantially prejudice the other side, or any other person.[185]

If an order of prohibition or certiorari is being sought, the court can order that the grant of leave should operate as a 'stay' to stop the matter which is being complained about, until the issue is decided at the hearing on the application for judicial review.[186] Alternatively, an interim injunction can be granted.

If leave is granted, then a notice of motion has to be served on the respondent,[187] who then has 56 days to file an affidavit in response to the applicant's case.[188] Unless expedition is ordered, a full hearing of the application will usually take place, currently, on average, about ten months thereafter. In judicial review cases discovery is very unusual (although it is available)[189] and witnesses are almost never called at the full hearing, where argument concentrates on the extent of the legal powers and duties involved as opposed to the facts of the case.

Criminal Injuries Compensation

The Criminal Injuries Compensation scheme was set up to make discretionary payments to victims of crimes of violence. A person assaulted by the police is as much the victim of a crime as of a civil wrong. A victim of a police crime of violence is therefore as free as the next person to make a claim.

A claim for damages in the civil courts is almost always preferable to a claim under the scheme. Court procedures are designed to allow all the evidence to be probed and tested and for all the issues to be throughly explored. The procedures under the scheme do not anticipate that the 'criminal' will participate and deny the crime, yet this seems to happen in claims alleging police violence. Furthermore, as will be seen below, the level of compensation awarded can be lower than that in the courts.

The only real advantage of the scheme is that it is cheap and simple. however, it is usually appropriate only if a person does not qualify for legal aid and cannot afford a lawyer and there is absolutely no other

185 Supreme Court Act 1981 s31(6).
186 RSC Order 53 r3(10).
187 RSC Order 53 r5.
188 RSC Order 53 r6.
189 RSC Order 53 r8.

means of funding a civil action. In theory, the scheme can be used for claims arising out of crimes of violence that result in death. The procedure for such claims is not described here, since they are rare (see p164), and their complexity makes them suitable only for civil claims in the courts.

The scheme[190]

Under the 1990 scheme in force at time of publication (but see p311), discretionary payments of compensation can be paid for any personal injury directly attributable to a crime of violence.[191] If no crime was committed, for example, because the police officer who caused the injury was acting in self defence, no compensation is payable.[192] Claims must generally be made within three years of the incident giving rise to the injury. However, in exceptional cases, the board will allow a claim after this time limit has expired.[193] In practice, applications should be made as soon as possible after an incident, while the facts are still fresh in the minds of witnesses and before evidence is lost or destroyed.

Currently, the amount of compensation is assessed on the same basis as common law damages, with three important exceptions:

- no compensation will be paid if the amount payable (after deduction of social security benefits) would be less than the minimum award of £750;[194]
- No compensation is paid for exemplary or punitive damages (see chapter 6);
- compensation for loss of earnings will not be more than one a half times the gross average industrial earnings at the date of assessment.

190 Copies of the scheme ('1990 Scheme'), which explain how it operates and how compensation is assessed and paid, are available from the CICA, see appendix 14.
191 1990 Scheme para 4. Compensation can also be paid for personal injuries directly attributable to the apprehension or attempted apprehension of an offender or suspected offender or to the prevention or attempted prevention of an offence or to the giving of help to any constable who is engaged in any such activity.
192 CICB Guide para 2; *R v CICB ex p Comerford* (1980) 19 June, unreported, DC, cited in *CICB 17th annual report* 1981, Cmnd 8401, para 20.
193 1990 Scheme para 22; CICB Guide paras 41–44.
194 1990 Scheme para 5; CICB Guide paras 8–10.

The basic rule is that compensation is paid for the injury. It is not paid for the loss of or damage to clothing or any property, unless it was relied on by the victim as a physical aid.[195] The value of any compensation awarded by a court (civil or criminal) or any out-of-court settlement for personal injuries will be deducted from compensation awarded by the CICB; the complainant must agree to repay any damages, compensation or out-of-court settlement s/he later receives. The amount of compensation can be reduced or completely withheld if:

– the complainant fails to take all reasonable steps to inform the police or any other appropriate authority of the circumstances of the injury within a reasonable time, or if s/he fails to co-operate with them in attempting to bring the offender to justice. It is no excuse to say that the police knew of the offence because it was they who committed it. Nor is it usually any excuse to say that a failure to report an offence or co-operate in its investigation was because of a fear of reprisals.[196] This probably means that a complainant must co-operate in the investigation of a police complaint if one has been made (see p67);
– the complainant fails to give all reasonable help to the CICB or any other authority in connection with the claim;
– it is inappropriate to make a full award or any award having regard to:
  a) the conduct of the complainant before, during or after the incident, or
  b) the character of the complainant as shown by his or her criminal convictions or unlawful conduct.[197] The CICB can take account of convictions which are entirely unconnected with the incident in which the complainant was injured; however, any attempt at reform will be taken into account.[198]

How to apply

Application must be made on a form which asks questions about the incident, injuries and medical treatment. The name of the police station to which the matter was reported must be stated – it need not be the same one as that at which the officer involved in the incident is

195 1990 Scheme para 17.
196 1990 Scheme para 6; CICB Guide para 27.
197 1990 Scheme para 6c.
198 CICB Guide para 37.

stationed. Application forms are available from the CICB (see appendix 14).

The initial decision on an application is taken by a single member of the board or by a member of the board's staff. Where an award is made, the complainant is usually given a breakdown of the assessment of compensation. Where an award is refused or reduced, reasons for the decision are given. The board does not act like insurance companies or police solicitors, that is, it does not offer only the lowest figure it thinks the complainant might be persuaded to accept. It aims to offer a sum based on a fair assessment of what a court would award for the injuries (less the deductions explained on p308).

If there is to be a criminal case against the complainant or, exceptionally, against a police officer, the initial assessment will generally be delayed until the result is known. The board is not bound by the result of the court case but will take it into account.

Hearings

If the complainant is not satisfied with the original decision, s/he may apply for an oral hearing which, if granted, will be held before at least two members of the board (not including the member who made the original decision). The application for a hearing must usually be made within three months of the original decision. Applications must be made on a form supplied by the board and should be supported by reasons, together with any additional evidence.

It is for the complainant to make out his/her case. Witnesses may be called, examined and cross-examined either by the complainant or by a member of staff of the board. Procedure at hearings is informal and any relevant hearsay, written or opinion evidence may be taken into account, whether or not the author gives oral evidence. The complainant can bring a friend or legal adviser to assist him/her.

The complainant (or the board) can call anyone as a witness to a hearing; however, if they decline to attend, they cannot be compelled to do so. In practice, it would reflect very poorly on the police if they refused to attend and it seems that generally they agree to.

Police statements

Whether or not a person attends as a witness, the complainant is always given any witness statements which are in the board's possession, and which are also to be given to members of the board. There is a 'long-standing arrangement' between the board and the Association of Chief Police Officers that any statements received from the police will not be disclosed before the day of the hearing.[199] They are, therefore, supplied to the complainant on the day. An adjournment may be granted to allow them to be studied, but they will be collected up after the hearing.[200] Indeed it has been held that the board would be entitled, should it so decide, to take the view that the arrangement with the police is to supply statements to the board and the board alone. It is submitted that in a case that concerned evidence disputed by police witnesses such an approach, and indeed the practice of only allowing applicants to examine police statements on the day of the hearing (when those witnesses may have had the opportunity to examine them at their leisure) would be unlawful and subject to a successful challenge by way of judicial review (see p302).

Proposals for change

There have been a number of attempts to alter the criminal injuries compensation scheme. The scheme was established in 1964, not by Act of Parliament, but by exercising the royal prerogative to make *ex gratia* payments. The scheme was codified in statute in 1988[201] but the relevant provisions were not brought into force and the non-statutory scheme continued to operate. The Home Secretary subsequently announced that the old scheme would be replaced by a new non-statutory Criminal Injuries Compensation Tariff Scheme, again created in the exercise of the royal prerogative. In April 1995 the House of Lords declared the new scheme unlawful.[202] At the time of writing a Criminal Injuries Compensation Bill has been introduced in an attempt to put the tariff scheme on a statutory footing. Compensation will be reduced in most cases and far fewer applicants will be entitled. The intention is to cut the cost of the scheme to the taxpayer by half by the year 2000.

The Police (Property) Act 1897

The Police (Property) Act 1897 provides a procedure under which application can be made to the magistrates' court for the return of property that is being held by the police. The main purpose of the Act is to protect the police against civil claims in the event of them 'returning'

199 *CICB 23rd annual report 1987*, CM 265, para. 54.
200 *R v Chief Constable of Cheshire and CICB ex p Berry* (unreported), cited in CICB 22nd annual report 1986, Cm 42, para 42.
201 Criminal Justice Act 1988 ss108–117 and Schs 6 and 7.
202 *R v Secretary of State for the Home Department ex p Fire Brigades Union and Others* [1995] 2 All ER 244.

goods to someone who later turns out not to be the real owner. The procedure may not be appropriate if there is likely to be disagreement about the applicant's right to the goods, as magistrates are not obliged to make an order and, in practice, probably will not make an order if there is a complicated point of law or fact at issue.[203] The procedure may be appropriate, however, in other cases, for example, where it is felt that a particular police officer is acting unreasonably in refusing to return goods. PACE retains a specific power for an application under this procedure where propery has been seized by the police.[204]

The magistrates have the power to order goods to be delivered to the person who appears to be the owner of the goods or, if the owner cannot be ascertained, to make such order in respect of the property as seems fit.[205] It appears that magistrates have the power to refuse to make an order under the Act where it is clear that it is contrary to public policy to do so.[206] But the Court of Appeal has held that magistrates were not acting unlawfully by refusing an application from the police under the Act in relation to proceeds from the unlicensed sale of alcohol even where the owner of the proceeds had pleaded guilty to the offences.[207]

The advantages of the procedure over a civil claim in the county court or High Court is that it is simple, quick and cheap. The disadvantages are that compensation will not be awarded and the court does not have to make an order. It is, therefore, a suitable procedure if all that is wanted is the return of the goods. If a client wants compensation or wants to draw public attention to the manner in which the goods were seized, s/he should sue in the civil courts.

The property

The procedure can be used to recover any property that 'has come into the possession of the police in connection with any criminal charge.'[208] This definition should cover almost all cases where the police have seized goods, but it may not apply, say, to lost property. It is not

203 *Raymond Lyons & Co v Metropolitan Police Commissioner* [1975] 1 All ER ER 335 at 338 e–g, per Lord Widgery CJ.
204 PACE 22(5).
205 Police (Property) Act 1897 s 1(1).
206 Magistrates' Courts Act 1980 s64.
207 *Chief Constable of West Midlands Police v White* (1992) *Times* 25 March, CA.
208 Police (Property) Act 1897 s1(1) as amended by Statute Law (Repeals) Act 1989 Sch 1 Pt 1 Group 2. For extensions to other property see Criminal Damage Act 1971 s6(3) and Powers of Criminal Courts Act 1973 s43.

necessary that anyone should have been charged or arrested for the suspected offence, or even that an offence has been committed.[209] It appears that property can include money.[210]

If the goods are used or intended for use for the purposes of crime, the court can order them to be forfeited. In such a case, their owner can apply to have them back if s/he did not consent to their being used, or did not know and had no reason to suspect that they would be used for a criminal purpose. If, say, a friend borrowed some tools which were later forfeited as being used for a burglary, their owner could use the Act to get them back if s/he honestly believed that the friend had wanted to use them to put up shelves at home.[211]

Making an application

Either the police or anyone who claims the goods can apply. In a straightforward case, the owner will simply be claiming his/her own property, but it may happen that the police apply for an order to allow them to dispose of the goods to someone else. The Act is commonly used, for example, where the police seek to return a stolen car but are unsure who is the lawful owner. In such cases, there is no requirement that everyone claiming ownership has to be notified of the application, although in practice either the police or the court would usually attempt to do so.[212]

If a criminal case has been heard in the magistrate's court, it is usual to deal with any application for an order at the end of the hearing. If there has been a trial at the Crown Court or if there has been no trial at all, applications are dealt with in separate magistrates' court proceedings, usually started by complaint and summons, whereby the court gives notice of the complaint and summonses the police to appear before the magistrates.[213] It will generally be good practice to write to the police first, asking for the return of the property. If the police refuse or fail to return the goods, a letter can be sent to the magistrates' court applying for a summons, (see example p315).

209 *R (Curtis) v Justices of Louth* [1916] 2 IR 616.
210 *Chief Constable of West Midlands Police v White* (1992) *Times* 25 March, CA.
211 Powers of Criminal Courts Act 1973 s43.
212 Vale, 'Police (Property) Act 1897' (1977) 127 NLJ 832.
213 Magistrates' Courts Act 1980 s51; *see R v Uxbridge Justices ex p Commissioner of Police of the Metropolis* [1981] 3 All ER 129, per Lord Denning MR.

Effect of an order

The court can make an order only in favour of the person who appears to be the owner of the goods. The making or an order does not immediately give any greater right to them than existed before the order. So, if someone else has a better claim to them, s/he can bring civil proceedings against the person in possession of the goods for their recovery. However, s/he must do so within six months of the order being made. After that time, s/he cannot bring a civil claim,[214] and, it seems, the goods become the property of the person who recovered them from the police.[215]

If the magistrates simply make no order when an application is made (that is, decline to make an order in favour of the person applying or anyone else), there is nothing to stop the applicant suing the police in the civil courts for the return of the property or for damages for conversion.[216] As no order will have been made by the magistrates, the six month time limit for commencing the action does not apply.[217]

Disposal of the goods by the police

The police are generally entitled to dispose of goods after 12 months if no order is made under the Act.[218] It is therefore wise to apply for an order as soon as possible, although there is no time limit as such in the Act. The goods are usually disposed of by sale, unless they are already money, or are unsuitable for sale, for example if they are perishable.

Costs

If the application for an order is started by making a complaint, there is no court fee. The court has a discretion to order legal costs[219] and it seems that such costs can be expected if an order is obtained and the police opposed it, but not if they did not contest it.[220]

214 Powers of Criminal Courts Act 1973 s43.
215 *Irving v National Provincial Bank* [1962] 2 QB 73, per Willmer J.
216 *Rashid v Chief Constable of Northumbria Police* (1990) 17 December, CA, Lexis.
217 Ibid.
218 Police (Disposal of Property) Regs 1975 SI No 1474.
219 Magistrates' Courts Act 1980 s64.
220 *R v Uxbridge JJ* (n213).

Interpleader

Interpleader[221] proceedings may be used as an alternative to the Police (Property) Act 1897, where money, goods or chattels are claimed by two or more rival claimants. The West Midlands police use this procedure in preference to the 1897 Act.[222]

Application for summons

The Chief Clerk
The Magistrates' Court
Tendale   30 September 1995

Dear Sir

Ms Mary Tawny
246 Azalea Street, Tendale

We act on behalf of Ms Mary Tawny who wishes to apply under the Police (Property) Act 1897 s1 for the return of two antique silver candlesticks belonging to her and held by the Tendale Constabulary.

The candlesticks were taken from our client's car by PC Lincoln of Tendale Magna police station on 16 June 1995 when she was stopped for an alleged motoring offence. It was alleged at the time that the police were looking for stolen property similar to the property seized but our client has not been charged with any offence in connection with the candlesticks.

We requested the return of the property to our client by letters to the police solicitors dated 1 September and 22 September 1995 but to date the candlesticks have not been returned. We believe the property is still in the possession of PC Lincoln.

We should be grateful if you would treat this letter as an application for the issue and service of a summons against the Chief Constable of the Tendale Constabulary.

Thank you for your help in this matter.

Yours faithfully,

---

221 RSC Order 17; CCR Order 33.
222 Franklin, 'The Interpleader Procedure', *Police Review* 7 December 1984; 'Law and Police', *Police Review* 17 February 1994.

Appendices

Police complaints deadline targets

A joint statement of intent by the Police Complaints Authority, Crown Prosecution Service and Association of Chief Police Officers

Introduction

1. One of the most frequently voiced criticisms of the police complaints system is the length of time taken to complete investigations and the procedures laid down in the Police and Criminal Evidence Act, 1984 (the Act) to bring cases to a conclusion. In his introduction to the Police Complaints Authority's Annual Report 1990 the Chairman, His Honour Judge Francis Petre, wrote:

'Delay seems to be endemic at all levels of legal and quasi-legal procedures. I am determined to leave here with a very real improvement in the time-scale. To this end I have initiated meetings with high level representatives of all those bodies who are, by statute, involved in the processing of complaints. Those who attended, whose experience in this field far exceeds my own, have been very positive in their response. The meeting has considered some thirty practical points for improvement. This pragmatic approach seems better than mere expressions of good intentions. All agreed that satisfaction with the system not only involved thoroughness, which is generally achieved already, but also a timely outcome. Needless delay defeats the objects of the exercise and causes dismay amongst complainants on the one hand and needless anxiety and injustice to police officers, against whom complaints are made, on the other hand. If real progress can be made in this field during my Chairmanship I will not have wasted my time.

2. The meetings referred to above were discussions between the following or their representatives:

Police Complaints Authority
The Association of Chief Police Officers
The Director of Public Prosecutions
The Home Office

HM Inspectorate of Constabulary were also present and support this joint venture.

Aim

3. The aim of this paper is to record the main decisions reached and to make a statement of intent on behalf of all those involved in the complaints process with a view to reducing to the minimum the time taken to deal with complaints consistent with fair and thorough investigations.

4. The paper is only concerned with matters which can be adopted now – within the existing legislation.

Informal resolution

5. There is almost unanimous agreement that the informal resolution procedure is working well. One of the principal features responsible for its success is that it is quick, especially when considered against the full complaints procedure, which is the subject of this paper. Every encouragement should therefore be given to the informal resolution procedure within the limitations laid down in the Act.

The investigation

6. It is impossible to lay down a time-scale for investigations into complaints because every case involves a different set of circumstances. Some are simple and straightforward, others are extremely complex. Nevertheless, in accordance with agreements made at these meetings all police forces have, since 1 January 1992, used 120 days as the target within which reports should be completed from the time the investigation becomes 'live'.

7. If it is apparent at the outset of an investigation, or if it becomes clear during the course of it, that the investigation cannot be completed within 120 days, the Deputy/Assistant Chief Constable responsible for complaints and discipline in unsupervised cases, or the supervising member of the Authority in supervised cases, will be consulted and a new completion date agreed.

Supervision of investigations by the Authority

8. The Authority recognise:

    a. the need to be sparing in requests for further information unless it is critical;

    b. the need to strike a balance between thoroughness and the disadvantages of unnecessary detail and delay; and

    c. the advantages in issuing an appropriate statement with caveats explaining any deficiencies in a report which could take a long time to resolve, for example, 'The investigation is satisfactory. However, witness A has not been seen . . . and a statement may have to be taken from him later'.

Investigating officers' reports

9. There is scope for reducing the length of investigating officers' reports. The Director of Public Prosecutions will give guidance on this subject to chief officers through the Association of Chief Police Officers.

10. Quicker turn round and a higher standard of reports are achieved if investigations are undertaken by the staff of complaints and discipline departments in headquarters rather than being passed to officers serving on divisions.

Director of Public Prosecution's consideration of reports

11. The Director of Public Prosecutions is conscious of the need to ensure that all cases are considered speedily by the Crown Prosecution Service. The target is to deal with all but the more serious and complex cases within 28 days of receipt of the investigating officer's final report. Where it is thought necessary to seek counsel's advice, the Crown Prosecution Service will normally ask for such advice to be provided within 21 days of counsel receiving instructions.

Police Complaints Authority's consideration of reports

12. The Authority's target is to complete consideration of the disciplinary aspects of cases and to send final letters to complainants within an average of 28 days of receipt of the Deputy/Assistant Chief Constable's memorandum.

Disciplinary hearings

13. In the interests of all concerned, police forces are committed to ensuring that a disciplinary hearing is arranged as soon as possible once a charge has been brought, and in all cases within six months, unless the circumstances are wholly exceptional. The target within which hearings should be arranged is four months. While every effort will be made to meet the accused officer's wishes, a hearing will not be unreasonably delayed because of the inability of a particular 'friend' or counsel to attend.

Sub judice

14. Sub judice is a complex subject on which the Home Office have issued guidance. Each case must be considered on its merits but investigating officers will need to be aware that the sub judice rule applies only to those circumstances of complaint which form a part of legal proceedings. Separate issues may not need to await the outcome of those proceedings.

Progress reports

15. Forces operate various means of keeping complainants and police officers informed of the progress of an investigation, but the police service is now looking at ways of developing a common approach.

Conclusion

16. Each of the parties to this statement is committed to the elimination of unnecessary delay at each stage of the procedure.

The Police Discipline Code

1. *Discreditable conduct*, which offence is committed where a member of a police force acts in a disorderly manner or any manner prejudicial to discipline or reasonably likely to bring discredit on the reputation of the force or of the police service.

2. *Misconduct towards a member of a police force*, which offence is committed where—
a) the conduct of a member of a police force towards another such member is oppressive or abusive, or
b) a member of a police force assaults another such member.

3. *Disobedience to orders*, which offence is committed where a member of a police force, without good and sufficient cause—
a) disobeys or neglects to carry out any lawful order, written or otherwise;
b) fails to comply with any requirement of a code of practice for the time being in force under section 60 or 66 of the Act of 1984; or
c) contravenes any provision of the Police Regulations containing restrictions on the private lives of members of police forces, or requiring him to notify the chief officer of police that he, or a relation included in his family, has a business interest within the meaning of those Regulations.

4. *Neglect of duty*, which offence is committed where a member of a police force, without good and sufficient cause—
a) neglects or omits to attend to or carry out with due promptitude and digligence anything which it is his duty as a member of a police force to attend to or to carry out, or
b) fails to work his beat in accordance with orders, or leaves the place of duty to which he has been ordered, or having left his place of duty for an authorised purpose fails to return thereto without undue delay, or
c) is absent without leave from, or is late for, any duty, or
d) fails properly to account for, or to make a prompt and true return of, any money or property received by him in the course of his duty.

5. *Falsehood or prevarication*, which offence is committed where a member of a police force—
a) knowingly or through neglect makes any false, misleading or inaccurate oral or written statement or entry in any record or document made, kept or required for police purposes, or
b) either wilfully and without proper authority or through lack of due care

destroys or mutilates any record or document made, kept or required for police purposes, or

c) without good and sufficient cause alters or erases or adds to any entry in such a record or document, or

d) has knowingly or through neglect made any false, misleading or inaccurate statement in connection with his appointment to the police force.

6. *Improper disclosure of information*, which offence is committed where a member of a police force—

a) without proper authority communicates to any person, any information which he has in his possession as a member of a police force, or

b) makes any anonymous communication to any police authority, or any member of a police force, or

c) without proper authority, makes representations to the police authority or the council or any county or district comprised in the police area with regard to any matter concerning the force or

d) canvases any member of that authority or of such a council with regard to any such matter.

For the purposes of this paragraph the Isles of Scilly shall be treated as if they were a county.

7. *Corrupt or improper practice*, which offence is committed where a member of a police force—

a) in his capacity as a member of the force and without the consent of the chief officer of police or the police authority, directly or indirectly solicits or accepts any gratuity, present or subscription, or

b) places himself under a pecuniary obligation to any person in such a manner as might affect his properly carrying out his duties as a member of the force, or

c) improperly uses, or attempts so to use, his position as a member of the force for his private advantage, or

d) in his capactiy as a member of the force and without the consent of the chief officer of police, writes, signs or gives a testimonial of character or other recommendation with the object of obtaining employment for any person or of supporting an application for the grant of a licence of any kind.

8. *Abuse of authority*, which offence is committed where a member of a police force treats any person with whom he may be brought into contact in the execution of his duty in an oppressive manner and, without prejudice to the foregoing, in particular where he—

a) without good and sufficient cause conducts a search, or requires a person to submit to any test or procedure, or makes an arrest; or

b) uses any unnecessary violence towards any prisoner or any other person with whom he may be brought into contact in the execution of his duty, or improperly threatens any such person with violence; or

c) is abusive or uncivil to any member of the public.

9. *Racially discriminatory behaviour*, which offence is committed (without prejudice to the commission of any other offence) where a member of a police force—

a) while on duty, on the grounds of another person's colour, race, nationality or ethnic or national origins, acts towards that other person in any such way as is mentioned in paragraph 8 (abuse of authority); or

b) in any other way, on any of those grounds, treats improperly a person with whom he may be brought into contact while on duty.

10. *Neglect of health*, which offence is committed where a member of a police force, without good and sufficient cause, neglects to carry out any instructions of a medical officer appointed by the police authority or, while absent from duty on account of sickness, commits any act or adopts any conduct calculated to retard his return to duty.

11. *Improper dress or untidiness*, which offence is committed where without good and sufficient cause a member of a police force while on duty, or while off duty but wearing uniform in a public place, is improperly dressed or is untidy in his appearance.

12. *Damage to police property*, which offence is committed where a member of a police force—
a) wilfully or through lack of due care causes any waste, loss or damge to any police property, or
b) fails to report as soon as is reasonably practicable any loss of or damage to any such property issued to, or used by him, or entrusted to his care.

13. *Drunkenness*, which offence is committed where a member of a police force renders himself unfit through drink for duties which he is or will be required to perform or which he may reasonably forsee having to perform.

14. *Drinking on duty or soliciting drink*, which offence is committed where a member of a police force, while on duty—
a) without proper authority, drinks, or receives from any other person, any intoxicating liquor, or
b) demands, or endeavours to persuade any other person to give him, or to purchase or obtain for him, any intoxicating liquor.

15. *Entering licensed premises*, which offence is committed where a member of a police force –
a) while on duty, or
b) while off duty but wearing uniform, without good and sufficient cause, enters any premises in respect of which a licence or permit has been granted in pursuance of the law relating to liquor licensing or betting and gaming or regulating places of entertainment.

16. *Criminal conduct*, which offence is committed where a member of a police force has been found guilty by a court of law of a criminal offence.

17. *Being an accessory to a disciplinary offence*, which offence is committed where a member of a police force incites, connives at or is knowingly an accessory to any offence against discipline.

Litigation precedents

3.1 Letter before action

Clerk to the Wessex Police Authority
Town Hall
Casterbridge

24 July 1995

Dear Sirs,

RE: Mr Clym Yeobright

We act for the above named, who was arrested on 25 September 1993, charged with the offence of being drunk and disorderly on 26 September 1995 and was subsequently acquitted of this charge at Casterbridge Magistrates' Court on 19 February 1994.

Our client was detained for approximately six hours following his arrest. It is for the police to justify both the arrest and the following detention, failing which Mr Yeobright will have a good claim against the Chief Constable for false imprisonment.

During the arrest our client was struck on the right side of his jaw, handcuffed, kicked and thrown onto the floor of a police van.

We are also instructed that the written statements and allegations made on oath on which our client's prosecution was based were fabricated and false, and that therefore the prosecution caused to be brought was malicious and without reasonable and probable cause.

Unless we receive, within 14 days, information satisfactory to our client justifying his arrest and detention, or suitable proposals for compensation we will have no alternative but to commence proceedings, without further notice, against the Chief Constable for damages, including aggravated and compensatory damages for false imprisonment, assault and malicious prosecution.

We are also instructed to ask you to treat this letter as our client's official complaint in this matter under Part IX of the Police and Criminal Evidence Act 1984. Any communication concerning this complaint should be sent to us.

Yours faithfully

Eustacia Vye & Co

3.2 Particulars of claim

IN THE BUDMOUTH COUNTY COURT

BETWEEN:

CLYM YEOBRIGHT

Plaintiff

and

CHIEF CONSTABLE OF WESSEX POLICE

Defendant

PARTICULARS OF CLAIM

---

1. The Defendant is and was at all material times the chief officer of police for the Wessex police area and the police officers hereinafter referred to were at all material times constables acting under his direction and control and in the performance or purported performance of their police functions within the meaning of the Police Act 1964.

2. On or about 25th September 1993 the Plaintiff was assaulted by two officers of the Defendant's police force.

PARTICULARS OF ASSAULT

(i)   at approximately 11 pm on 25th September 1993 the plaintiff was on the balcony of the sixth floor of Egdon Heath House on the Anglebury Estate, Mistover MV9. He was standing there with his brother and two others when he was grabbed on the right shoulder by an officer of the Defendant's force and spun around.

(ii) as the Plaintiff turned around the officer struck him on the right side of his jaw. He fell to the ground. Another officer then bent his arm behind his back and handcuffed him.

(iii) the Plaintiff was lifted up by the handcuffs with the officer pressing one arm on the plaintiff's right elbow while his left arm and side were pressed against the balcony wall.

(iv) the officers then dragged the Plaintiff by the handcuffs and threw him into the corner of the lift. When the Plaintiff tried to stand up, the officers kicked his legs so that he fell on his back. The officers continued to kick him in the back inside the lift.

(v) the Plaintiff was carried from the lift in a horizontal position, face down, with one officer holding him by the handcuffs and the other by the legs. He was thrown onto the floor of a marked Sherpa van number 3771.

(vi) while in the van the plaintiff tried to get up on to the seats but the bigger officer of the two was pushing him down. This officer continuously addressed the Plaintiff as 'you black bastard'.

3. The said assaults were unlawful and constituted trespass to the Plaintiff's person either in every respect or as involving the use of excessive and unreasonable force.

4. Further, on or about 25 September 1993 at about 11 pm the Plaintiff was faslely imprisoned by officers of the Defendant's police force at Egdon Heath House on the Anglebury Estate and taken in a police van to Blooms-End police station where he was further detained and falsely imprisoned until he was released on bail at about 5 am on 26 September 1993.

PARTICULARS OF FALSE IMPRISONMENT

(i) the particulars set out in paragraph 2 above are repeated.

(ii) the said officers detained the Plaintiff at Egdon Heath House at about 11pm. He was then taken to Blooms-End police station, arriving at about 11.10 pm. He was put straight into a cell and not informed of the reasons for his arrest.

(iii) after about 6 hours the same two officers took the Plaintiff out of the cell. The Plaintiff was very frightened and angry. The officers laughed at him and charged him with being drunk and disorderly. He was released at about 6 am.

5. The said arrest and detention were unlawful, not being founded upon reasonable suspicion of the commission by the plaintiff of an arrestable offence, or other lawful authority.

6. Further or alternatively, the said arrest was unlawful in that the plaintiff was not informed of the reason for his arrest.

7. If, which is denied, the said arrest was lawful, the Plaintiff was held in police custody for an unreasonably long period.

8. Further, police officers acting under the direction and control of the

Defendant caused the Plaintiff to be, without reasonable cause, and maliciously, prosecuted for the offence of being drunk and disorderly.

PARTICULARS OF MALICIOUS PROSECUTION

(i) At a time unknown to the Plaintiff but prior to his being charged by the officers who had arrested him, the officers fabricated in a written statement an account of events giving rise to the arrest of the plaintiff in which they falsely alleged that they had witnessed the Plaintiff in the commission of the elements that constitute the offence of being drunk and disorderly.

(ii) The said statements were made in the full knowledge that the contents were false and that by reason thereof the Plaintiff would be wrongly prosecuted for the said offence.

(iii) At about 6 am on 26 September 1993 the said officers maliciously caused the Plaintiff to be charged with the offence of being drunk and disorderly.

(iv) The Plaintiff was tried at Casterbridge Magistrates' Court on 19 February 1994 when the said prosecution was determined in his favour by the charge against him being dismissed after the stipendiary magistrate had heard oral evidence from both the said officers and the Plaintiff.

(v) During the course of the trial the said officers repeated on oath the false allegations particularised at paragraph 8 (i) hereabove.

9. As a result the Plaintiff suffered distress, personal injury, injury to his feelings, loss of liberty, loss of reputation, loss and damage.

PARTICULARS

The plaintiff was imprisoned from 11 pm on 25 September 1993 until 6 am on 26 September 1993. He felt acute distress and humiliation during his arrest and imprisonment. He suffered the distress and anxiety of facing a wrongful prosecution and a possible wrongful conviction. He had to attend court on a number of occasions in order to establish his innocence.

PARTICULARS OF INJURY

(i) Severe shock.

(ii) The plaintiff suffered acute dizziness at the time of the assault. He had a 4cm laceration to his left cheek and extensive bruising over an area of 6cm × 3cm around the said laceration. Both his upper and lower lips were swollen. There were red marks completely around his neck, bruising on the right shoulder, abrasion over the left superior anterior iliac spine (the bony prominence at the front of the left side of the pelvis), and red marks around both wrists.

(iii) the injuries took 3 weeks to resolve fully.

10. The aforesaid treatment of the Plaintiff was a gross affront to his personal dignity and integrity for which aggravated damages should be awarded.

11. The Plaintiff will rely on the arbitrary and unconstitutional nature of the said conduct by servants of the Crown in support of his claim for exemplary damages.

12. Further, the Plaintiff claims interest on the amount found to be due to him at such rate and for such periods as the Court thinks fit pursuant to section 69 of the County Courts Act 1984.

AND THE PLAINTIFF CLAIMS:
1. Damages, including aggravated and exemplary damages in excess of £5,000.
2. Special damages of £100 (see attached Schedule).
3. The aforesaid interest pursuant to section 69 of the County Courts Act 1984.
4. Costs.

DIGGORY VENN

Dated 4 September 1995

Eustacia Vye & Co
16 Rainbarrow Road
Mistover
Solicitors for the Plaintiff who will accept service
at this address

To the District Judge

And to the Defendant

3.3 Defence

IN THE BUDMOUTH COUNTY COURT

BETWEEN:

CLYM YEOBRIGHT

Plaintiff

and

CHIEF CONSTABLE OF WESSEX POLICE

Defendant

DEFENCE

---

1. The Defendant admits paragraph 1 of the Particulars of Claim.

2. The Defendant denies that any officer assaulted the Plaintiff in each and every allegation contained within paragraph 2 of the Particulars of Claim or at all.

3. Further the Defendant denies any officer made any threats or was abusive as alleged in paragraph 2 (vi) or at all.

4. Following the Plaintiff's lawful arrest, the Plaintiff struggled and it was necessary to apply some force to restrain him. PC Wildeve and PC Nunsuch handcuffed the Plaintiff, but at no stage was any more than reasonable force used in all the circumstances. The Plaintiff is put to strict proof of all allegations of assault in paragraph 2 of the Particulars of Claim.

5. As to paragraph 4 of the Particulars of Claim, the Defendant admits and avers that on the 25th September 1993 at approximately 11 pm the Plaintiff was lawfully arrested by PC Wildeve at Egdon Heath House, Anglebury Estate, Mistover, MV9 upon the honestly held and reasonably founded suspicion that the Defendant had committed the offence of being drunk and disorderly contrary to section 91(1) of the Criminal Justice Act 1967, for which the officer could lawfully arrest the Plaintiff without warrant.

PARTICULARS

(i) PC Wildeve and PC Nunsuch, acting on information received, went to the 5th floor of Egdon Heath House. They heard shouting coming from the floor above. The Plaintiff was seen together with two others, and the officers saw the Plaintiff throw a beer can down to the ground.

(ii) The officers went up to the 6th floor where the Plaintiff shouted 'come on we're all drunk'.

(iii)   PC Wildeve approached the Plaintiff and asked him what he was doing and specifically asked him why he threw the beer can over the balcony. The Plaintiff replied, 'I was mucking about trying to hit my mate.'

(iv)   The officer noticed that the Plaintiff's eyes were glazed, his breath smelt of intoxicating liquor and he was unsteady on his feet. The Plaintiff had in his hand a can of Tennents Extra Strong lager, and in all the circumstances the officers formed the view that he was drunk.

(v)   When PC Wildeve suggested that the Plaintiff should go home the Plaintiff started shouting, 'I pay me taxes, I can stay where I want.' The Plaintiff would not keep quiet and started shouting to people on the ground. PC Wildeve took hold of the Plaintiff and told him that he was arrested for being drunk and disorderly.

6.   As to paragraph 4(ii) of the Particulars of Claim, the Defendant admits that the Plaintiff was taken to Blooms End Police Station where he arrived at approximately 11.10 pm. The Defendant denies that the Plaintiff was put straightaway into a cell and was not informed of the reasons for his arrest. The Plaintiff was put through the booking-in procedure, which took some 10 minutes before he was put into a cell at 11.20 pm. During the booking-in procedure an account of the reason for his arrest and the details of his arrest were given by the arresting officer to the custody officer. The Defendant denies the remainder of paragraph 4 (ii) of the Particulars of Claim.

7.   The Plaintiff's lawful detention was authorised by the custody officer in order that he could sober up and then be charged.

8.   The Defendant denies paragraph 4(iii) of the Particulars of Claim. The Defendant avers that the Plaintiff was released on bail at 5.51 am having been charged with the offence for which he had been arrested, after a total period of detention of 6 hours and fifty-one minutes.

9.   Save that the Defendant admits that the prosecution was brought on the evidence of PCs Wildeve and Nonsuch, and that the prosecution was continued by the Crown Prosecution Service, and save as to paragraph 8(iv) which is admitted, the Defendant denies paragraph 8 of the Particulars of Claim, to include any allegation of malicious prosecution.

10.   The Defendant denies paragraph 9 of the Particulars of Claim and puts the Plaintiff to strict proof of each allegation contained therein. Further the Defendant avers that if, which is not admitted, the Plaintiff suffered any injury, that the Plaintiff was the author of his own misfortune, by unlawfully resisting his lawful arrest.

11.   The Defendant denies paragraphs 10 and 11 of the Particulars of Claim. In the premises the Defendant denies that the Plaintiff is entitled to any award of damages, whether compensatory, aggravated or exemplary.

ughtyou.

12. If, which is denied, the Defendant is held liable to the Plaintiff for any sum arising out of the matters complained of in the Particulars of Claim, the Defendant denies that the Plaintiff could be entitled to any award of interest for the alleged false imprisonment and malicious prosecution, which is in any event denied.

TIMOTHY FAIRWAY

DATED 4 November 1995
Messrs Cantle & Co. Solicitors for the Defendant whose address for service is 1 Chalk Newton Street, Alderworth AW10 ODY.
To the District Judge and to the Plaintiff

3.4 Further and better particulars

IN THE BUDMOUTH COUNTY COURT

BETWEEN:

CLYM YEOBRIGHT

Plaintiff

and

CHIEF CONSTABLE OF WESSEX POLICE

Defendant

FURTHER AND BETTER PARTICULARS OF
THE PARTICULARS OF CLAIM

UNDER PARAGRAPH 2(i)
OF: 'He was standing there with his brother and two others when he was grabbed on the right shoulder by an officer of the Defendant's force and spun around.'

Request 1
Identify by name, rank, number or otherwise which officer is referred to.

Reply
The Plaintiff is only able to identify the officer by his appearance. He was the taller of the two officers and had short dark-blond hair.

UNDER PARAGRAPH 2(iii)
OF: 'the Plaintiff was lifted up by the handcuffs with the officer pressing one arm on the Plaintiff's right elbow . . .'

Request 2
State precisely how the Plaintiff was lifted up by the handcuffs, to particularise whether the handcuffs were held or whether he was being lifted up by his arms; further identify as above which officer is referred to.

Reply
   The phrase 'The Plaintiff was lifted up by the handcuffs' carries its
ordinary meaning and as such is sufficiently pleaded. The second, shorter
dark-haired officer is referred to. However, for the sake of efficiency the officer
had one hand on the Plaintiff's arm and the other hand on the handcuffs
pulling them upwards.

DATED 10 January 1996
Eustacia Vye and Co
Solicitors for the Plaintiff whose address for service is: 16 Rainbarrow Road,
Mistover

3.5 Lists of documents

IN THE BUDMOUTH COUNTY COURT

BETWEEN:

CLYM YEOBRIGHT

Plaintiff

and

CHIEF CONSTABLE OF WESSEX POLICE

Defendant

PLAINTIFF'S LIST OF DOCUMENTS

The following is a list of the documents relating to the matters in question in
this action which are or have been in the possession, custody or power of the
above-named Plaintiff and which is served in compliance with RSC Order 24,
rule 2.

1. The Plaintiff has in his possession, custody or power the documents relating
   to the matters in question in this action enumerated in Schedule 1 hereto.

2. The Plaintiff objects to produce the documents enumerated in Part 2 of the
   said Schedule 1 on the ground that they are by their very nature privileged
   from production as appears from the description thereof.

3. The Plaintiff has had, but does not have now, in his possession, custody or
   power the documents relating to the matters in question in this action
   enumerated in Schedule 2 hereto.

4. The documents in the said Schedule 2 were last in the Plaintiff's possession,
   custody or power on the dates they were posted to their respective addresses.

5. Neither the Plaintiff nor his Solicitor nor any other person on his behalf, has

now, or ever had, in their possession, custody or power any document whatever relating to any matter in question in this action, other than the documents enumerated in Schedules 1 and 2 hereto.

SCHEDULE 1 – PART 1

DESCRIPTION OF DOCUMENT	DATE
1. Pleadings common to both parties	Various
2. Correspondence from and copy correspondence to Defendant and his servants and his solicitors	Various
3. Medical report from Dr Angel Clare	28 February 1994
4. Copy custody record Clym Yeobright	27 September 1993
5. Copy telephone message	27 September 1993
6. Memorandum of magistrates' court conviction	19 February 1994

SCHEDULE 1 – PART 2

DESCRIPTION OF DOCUMENT	DATE
Correspondence and reports passing between the Plaintiff and his solicitors, notes, reports and memoranda prepared by or on behalf of the Plaintiff and his solicitors, instructions and briefs to Counsel, Counsel's Opinions, drafts and notes, and all other correspondence and documents brought into existence in contemplation of or for the purpose of bringing this action.	Various

SCHEDULE 2

The original of the copy documents referred to at no. 2 in Part 1 of Schedule 1 hereto	Various

Dated 10 December 1995

NOTICE TO INSPECT

Take notice that the documents in the above list, other than those listed in Part 2 of Schedule 1 and Schedule 2 may be inspected at the office of the Solicitors of the above named Defendant by appointment

IN THE BUDMOUTH COUNTY COURT

BETWEEN:

CLYM YEOBRIGHT

Plaintiff

and

CHIEF CONSTABLE OF WESSEX POLICE

Defendant

DEFENDANT'S LIST OF DOCUMENTS

The following is a list of the documents relating to the matters in question in this action which are or have been in the possession, custody or power of the above-named Defendant and which is served in compliance with RSC Order 24, rule 2.

1. The Defendant has in his possession, custody or power the documents relating to the matters in question in this action enumerated in Schedule 1 hereto.

2. The Defendant objects to produce the documents enumerated in Part 2 of the said Schedule 1 on the ground that those numbered 1 are privileged from inspection as appears from the entry in the said schedule; those at 2, were made for the purpose of an enquiry pursuant to Part IX PACE 1984 and their production would be against the public interest and in relation to those at 3 their production would also be against the public interest.

3. The Defendant has had, but does not have now, in his possession, custody or power the documents relating to the matters in question in this action enumerated in Schedule 2 hereto.

4. The documents in he said Schedule 2 were last in the Defendant's possession, custody or power on the dates they were posted to their respective addresses.

5. Neither the Defendant nor his Solicitor nor any other person on his behalf, has now, or ever had, in their possession, custody or power any document of any whatever relating to any matter in question in this action, other than the documents enumerated in Schedules 1 and 2 hereto.

SCHEDULE 1 – PART 1

DESCRIPTION OF DOCUMENT	DATE
1. Original and copy correspondence between the Plaintiff's and the Defendant's Solicitors	22 March 1995 to 25 November 1995

2. Copy pre-action correspondence between
   the Plaintiff's Solicitors and the
   Defendant's Solicitors' Department Various

3. Copy Custody Record No. 2975 of Clym
   Yeobright 25 September 1993

4. Copy IRB of PC 531 'PT' Jude Wildeve 25 September 1993

5. Copy IRB of PC 143 'PT' Christian Nunsuch 25 September 1993

6. Copy Duty State for 'PT' 25 September 1993

7. Copy Form of previous convictions of Clym
   Yeobright

8. Copy Form of notification of complaint re:
   Clym Yeobright 27 September 1993

9. Copy telephone message 27 September 1993

10. Copy Court Clerk's notes in respect of
    hearing at Casterbridge Magistrate' Court 19 February 1994

11. Pleadings and other documents common
    to both parties Various

SCHEDULE 1 – PART II

1. Confidential professional communications and documents of a confidential
   nature consisting of communications between the Defendant's Solicitors and
   the Defendant, Instructions to Counsel, Counsel's Advice and statements
   made to the Defendant's Solicitors for the purpose of substantiating the
   defence against the claims herein.

2. Investigating officer's report made pursuant to Part IX PACE 1984.

3. Form of initial reports and communications with the Crown Prosecution
   Service re: prosecution of Clym Yeobright.

SCHEDULE 2

DESCRIPTION OF DOCUMENTS	DATE
1. Original Record No. 4321 of Clym Yeobright	25 September 1993
2. Original IRB of PC 531 'PT' Jude Wildeve	25 September 1993

3. Original IRB of PC 143 'PT' Christian Nunsuch   25 September 1993

4. Original duty State for 'PT'   25 September 1993

5. Original Form of notification of complaint   27 September 1993

6. Copy telephone message   27 September 1993

Dated 15 December 1995

NOTICE TO INSPECT

Take notice that the documents in the above list, other than those listed in Part 2 of Schedule 1 and Schedule 2 may be inspected at the office of the Solicitors of the above named Plaintiff by appointment.

3.6 Plaintiff's statement in open court

IN THE BUDMOUTH COUNTY COURT

BETWEEN:

CLYM YEOBRIGHT

Plaintiff

and

CHIEF CONSTABLE OF WESSEX POLICE

Defendant

PLAINTIFF'S STATEMENT IN OPEN COURT

---

1. The Plaintiff in this action, Mr Clym Yeobright, is now aged 25 years. At the time of the relevant events in September 1993, he was aged 23 years.

2. The Defendant is the Chief Constable for the Wessex Police and, as such, he is responsible in law for the police officers whose actions are the subject of this claim. Those officers, PC Wildeve and PC Nonsuch, were based at Blooms-End police station, and their actions were in the purported performance of their police functions under the Defendant's direction and control.

3. The Plaintiff's claim against the Defendant is for damages for false imprisonment, assault and battery, and malicious prosecution; in other words that he was wrongfully arrested and unlawfully detained at a police station; assaulted and injured in the course of arrest; and charged and prosecuted in relation to a criminal offence, of which he was innocent, on the basis of evidence fabricated by the arresting police officers. The Plaintiff's claim is

for damages, including aggravated damages to compensate him for the anxiety, distress and humiliation he suffered, and exemplary damages to reflect the arbitrary and unconstitutional nature of the misconduct on the part of the police officers responsible.

4. The events which give rise to these proceedings occurred as follows *[details inserted from the Particulars of Claim on pp327–330]*

5. The Plaintiff has maintained from the outset, as he has in these civil proceedings, that PC Wildeve and PC Nonsuch concocted and fabricated the allegations against him, hoping and intending that he would thereby be wrongfully convicted of a criminal offence of which they knew him to be innocent. In support of his claim for aggravated and exemplary damages, he points in particular to the failure of the Defendant to apologise for or acknowledge the alleged misconduct of his officers. Indeed, by his pleadings in this action, the Defendant has repeated the allegations made by his officers against the Plaintiff and he continues to deny liability. Nevertheless he has paid to the Plaintiff the sum of £7,500.

The ACPO Public Order Manual

This unpublished manual contains guidance to chief officers of police on crowd control and dealing with riots and other situations of actual or potential public disorder. Extracts from the manual were placed in the House of Commons Library after being read into court during the Orgreave 'riot' trials and these extracts were subsequently reprinted as appendix C in *Shooting in the Dark: Riot Police in Britain* by Gerry Northam (Faber & Faber 1988). The Association of Chief Police Officers has declined permission for those extracts to be reprinted in this book. Malcolm George, Secretary of the ACPO Public Order Sub-Committee, stated in a letter to the publishers, '. . . the Association of Chief Police Officers still nevertheless regard the Public Order Manual as being protected from general circulation. The civil courts have respected non-disclosure on the basis that to do so would not be in the public interest, as it may disadvantage the police in handling public disorder and expose police personnel to unnecessary danger.'

The extracts describe the use of long and short shields to protect police officers from injury and to form groups or 'serials' used to clear a hostile crowd from a specified area such as a street or square while providing cover for unarmed arrest groups. The extracts also describe the use of mounted police for crowd control and rapid crowd dispersal.

The manoeuvres described in the manual can be summarised as follows:

Para	Manoeuvre	Summary description
Long shields		
7	1	A show of force
10	2	The unit shield cordon
11	3	The shield cordon base-line
12	4	The individual shield cordon
16	5	The advancing cordon
17	6	The long shielded wedge
18	7	The free-running line
Short shields		
3	1	Tactical manoeuvres

Group 2 – Protection of four-man arrest group

–	2	Arrest squads of 4 officers operating outside the cover of long shield cordons
–	3	Arrest squads of 2 officers, allowing one officer to operate without a shield
–	4	Arrest squads of 4 officers operating in wedge formations
–	5	Baton charge intended to disperse a crowd
–	6	Team carrying short round shields and batons deployed into a crowd
–	7	Teams carrying short shields deployed into a crowd

Mounted police

Group 4 – Crowd dispersal

–	10	Mounted police advance on the crowd signalling that they do not intend to stop
–	11	Mounted police advance on the crowd signalling that they do not intend to stop – *at a canter*
–	12	Rapid advance of mounted police combined with foot police

Guidelines for the police on the issue and use of firearms

From the report of the Home Office working party on the police use of firearms, 3 February 1987

Principles governing issue
Firearms are to be issued only where there is reason to believe that a police officer may have to face a person who is armed or otherwise so dangerous that he could not safely be restrained without the use of firearms; they may also be issued for protection purposes or for the destruction of dangerous animals.

Principles governing use
1. Firearms are to be fired by police officers only as a last resort when conventional methods have been tried and failed, or must, from the nature of the circumstances obtaining, be unlikely to succeed if tried. They may be fired, for example, when it is apparent that a police officer cannot achieve the lawful purpose of preventing loss, or further loss, of life by any other means.
[There is no para. 2.]

Authority to issue
3. Authority to issue firearms should be given by an officer of ACPO rank, save where a delay in getting in touch with such an officer could result in loss of life or serious injury, in which case a Chief Superintendent or Superintendent may authorize issue. In such circumstances an officer of ACPO rank should be informed as soon as possible. Special arrangements may apply where firearms are issued regularly for protection purposes, but these should be authorized by an officer of ACPO rank in the first instance.

Conditions of issue and use
4. The ACPO *Manual of Guidance on the Police Use of Firearms* is the single authoritative source of guidance on tactical and operational matters relating to the use of firearms by the police.
5. Firearms should be issued only to officers who have been trained and authorized in a particular class of weapon. Officers authorized to use firearms must attend regular refresher courses and those failing to do so or to reach the qualifying standard will lose their authorization and must not thereafter be issued with firearms. Authorized firearms officers must hold an authorization card showing the type(s) of weapon that may be issued to them. The author-

ization card must be produced before a weapon is issued and must always be carried when the officer is armed. The cardholder's signature in the issue register should be verified against the signature on the officer's warrant card. The card should be issued without alteration and should have an expiry date.
6. Records of issue and operational use must be maintained. All occasions on which shots are fired by police officers other than to destroy animals must be thoroughly investigated by a senior officer and a full written report prepared.

Briefing
7. In any armed operation briefing by senior officers is of paramount importance and must include both authorized firearms officers and non-firearms personnel involved in the operation. Senior officers must stress the objective of the operation including specifically the individual responsibility of authorized firearms officers. Particular attention must be paid to the possible presence of innocent parties.

Use of minimum force
8. Nothing in these guide-lines affects the principle, to which Section 3 of the Criminal Law Act 1967 gives effect, that only such force as is reasonable in the circumstances may be used. The degree of force justified will vary according to the circumstances of each case. Responsibility for firing a weapon rests with the individual officer and a decision to do so may have to be justified in legal proceedings.

Warning
9. If it is reasonable to do so an oral warning is to be given before opening fire.
10. Urgent steps are to be taken to ensure that early medical attention is provided for any casualties.

Summary
11. A brief summary of the most important points for an individual officer is attached. It is suggested that this summary be placed on the reverse side of each authorization card so that officers will have it with them whenever they are armed.

Authorized firearms officers guidelines on use of minimum force

The Law
Section 3 of the Criminal Law Act 1967 reads:

A person may use such force as is reasonable in the circumstances in the preventing of crime, or in the effecting or assisting in the lawful arrest of offenders or suspected offenders or of persons unlawfully at large.

Strict reminder
A firearm is to be fired only as a last resort. Other methods must have been tried and failed, or must – because of the circumstances – be unlikely to succeed if tried. For example, a firearm may be fired when it is apparent that the police

cannot achieve their lawful purpose of preventing loss, or further loss, of life by any other means. If it is reasonable to do so an oral warning is to be given before opening fire.

Individual responsibility
The responsibility for the use of the firearm is an *individual* decision which may have to be justified in legal proceedings.
REMEMBER THE LAW. REMEMBER YOUR TRAINING.

Police Act 1964 s48

Liability for wrongful acts of constables

48. (1) The chief officer of police for any police area shall be liable in respect of torts committed by constables under his direction and control in the performance or purported performance of their functions in like manner as a master is liable in respect of torts committed by his servants in the course of their employment, and accordingly shall in respect of any such tort be treated for all purposes as a joint tortfeasor.

(2) There shall be paid out of the police fund –

(a) any damages or costs awarded against the chief officer of police in any proceedings brought against him by virtue of this section and any costs incurred by him in any such proceedings so far as not recovered by him in the proceedings; and

(b) any sum required in connection with the settlement of any claim made against the chief officer of police by virtue of this section, if the settlement is approved by the police authority.

(3) Any proceedings in respect of a claim made by virtue of this section shall be brought against the chief officer of police for the time being or, in the case of a vacancy in that office, against the person for the time being performing the functions of the chief officer of police; and references in the foregoing provisions of this section to the chief officer of police shall be construed accordingly.

(4) A police authority may, in such cases and to such extent as they think fit, pay any damages or costs awarded against a member of the police force maintained by them, or any constable for the time being required to serve with that force by virtue of section 14 of this Act, or any special constable appointed for their area, in proceedings for a tort committed by him, any costs incurred and not recovered by him in any such proceedings, and any sum required in connection with the settlement of any claim that has or might have given rise to such proceedings; and any sum required for making a payment under this subsection shall be paid out of the police fund.

Police and Criminal Evidence Act 1984

PART IX

POLICE COMPLAINTS AND DISCIPLINE

The Police Complaints Authority

Establishment of the Police Complaints Authority

83. – (1) There shall be an authority to be known as 'the Police Complaints Authority' and in this part of this Act referred to as 'the Authority.'

(2) Schedule 4 to this Act shall have effect in relation to the Authority.

(3) The Police Complaints Board is hereby abolished.

Handling of complaints etc

Preliminary

84. – (1) Where a complaint is submitted to the chief officer of police for a police area, it shall be his duty to take any steps that appear to him to be desirable for the purpose of obtaining or preserving evidence relating to the conduct complained of.

(2) After performing the duties imposed on him by subsection (1) above, the chief officer shall determine whether he is the appropriate authority in relation to the officer against whom the complaint was made.

(3) If he determines that he is not the appropriate authority, it shall be his duty–

  (a) to send the complaint or, if it was made orally, particulars of it, to the appropriate authority; and
  (b) to give notice that he has done so to the person by or on whose behalf the complaint was made.

(4) In this part of this Act–

  'complaint' means any complaint about the conduct of a police officer which is submitted–

  (a) by a member of the public; or

(b) on behalf of a member of the public and with his written consent;

'the appropriate authority' means–

(a) in relation to an officer of the metropolitan police, the Commissioner of Police of the Metropolis; and
(b) in relation to an officer of any other police force–

    (i) if he is a senior officer, the police authority for the force's area; and
    (ii) if he is not a senior officer, the chief officer of the force;

'senior officer' means an officer holding a rank above the rank of superintendent;

'disciplinary proceedings' means proceedings identified as such by regulations under section 33 of the Police Act 1964.

(5) Nothing in this Part of this Act has effect in relation to a complaint in so far as it relates to the direction or control of a police force by the chief officer or the person performing the functions of the chief officer.

(6) If any conduct to which a complaint wholly or partly relates is or has been the subject of criminal or disciplinary proceedings, none of the provisions of this Part of this Act which relate to the recording and investigation of complaints have effect in relation to the complaint in so far as it relates to that conduct.

Investigation of complaints: standard procedure

85. – (1) If a chief officer determines that he is the appropriate authority in relation to an officer about whose conduct a complaint has been made and who is not a senior officer, he shall record it.

(2) After doing so he shall consider whether the complaint is suitable for informal resolution and may appoint an officer from his force to assist him.

(3) If it appears to the chief officer that the complaint is not suitable for informal resolution, he shall appoint an officer from his force or some other force to investigate it formally.

(4) If it appears to him that it is suitable for informal resolution, he shall seek to resolve it informally and may appoint an officer from his force to do so on his behalf.

(5) If it appears to the chief officer, after attempts have been made to resolve a complaint informally–

(a) that informal resolution of the complaint is impossible; or
(b) that the complaint is for any other reason not suitable for informal resolution,

he shall appoint an officer from his force or some other force to investigate it formally.

(6) An officer may not be appointed to investigate a complaint formally if

he has previously been appointed to act in relation to it under subsection (4) above.

(7) If a chief officer requests the chief officer of some other force to provide an officer of his force for appointment under subsection (3) or (5) above, that chief officer shall provide an officer to be so appointed.

(8) [*Repealed by the Police and Magistrates' Court Act 1994 ss 44, 93, Sch 5, Pt II, para 25, Sch 9, Pt I.*]

(9) Unless the investigation is supervised by the Authority under section 89 below, the investigating officer shall submit his report on the investigation to the chief officer.

(10) A complaint is not suitable for informal resolution unless–

  (a) the member of the public concerned gives his consent; and
  (b) the chief officer is satisfied that the conduct complained of, even if proved, would not justify criminal or disciplinary proceedings.

Investigation of complaints against senior officers

86. – (1) Where a complaint about the conduct of a senior officer–

  (a) is submitted to the appropriate authority; or
  (b) is sent to the appropriate authority under section 84(3) above,

it shall be the appropriate authority's duty to record it and, subject to subsection (2) below, to investigate it.

(2) The appropriate authority may deal with the complaint according to the appropriate authority's discretion, if satisfied that the conduct complained of, even if proved, would not justify criminal or disciplinary proceedings.

(3) In any other case the appropriate authority shall appoint an officer from the appropriate authority's force or from some other force to investigate the complaint.

(4) A chief officer shall provide an officer to be appointed, if a request is made to him for one to be appointed undersubsection (3) above.

(5) No officer may be appointed unless he is of at least the rank of the officer against whom the complaint is made.

(6) Unless an investigation under this section is supervised by the Authority under section 89 below, the investigating officer shall submit his report on it to the appropriate authority.

References of complaints to Authority

87. – (1) The appropriate authority–

  (a) shall refer to the Authority–

    (i) any complaint alleging that the conduct complained of resulted in the death of or serious injury to some other person; and
    (ii) any complaint of a description specified for the purposes of this section in regulations made by the Secretary of State; and

(b) may refer to the Authority any complaint which is not required to be referred to them.

(2) The Authority may require the submission to them for consideration of any complaint not referred to them by the appropriate authority; and it shall be the appropriate authority's duty to comply with any such requirement not later than the end of a period specified in regulations made by the Secretary of State.

(3) Where a complaint falls to be referred to the Authority under subsection (1)(a) above, it shall be the appropriate authority's duty to refer it to them not later than the end of a period specified in such regulations.

(4) In this Part of this Act 'serious injury' means a fracture, damage to an internal organ, impairment of bodily function, a deep cut or a deep laceration.

References of other matters to Authority

88. – The appropriate authority may refer to the Authority any matter which –

(a) appears to the appropriate authority to indicate that an officer may have committed a criminal offence or behaved in a manner which would justify disciplinary proceedings; and

(b) is not the subject of a complaint,

if it appears to the appropriate authority that it ought to be referred by reason—

(i) of its gravity; or
(ii) of exceptional circumstances.

Supervision of investigations by Authority

89. – (1) The Authority shall supervise the investigation—

(a) of any complaint alleging that the conduct of a police officer resulted in the death of or serious injury to some other person; and

(b) of any other descriptions of complaint specified for the purposes of this section in regulations made by the Secretary of State.

(2) The Authority shall supervise the investigation—

(a) of any complaint the investigation of which they are not required to supervise under subsection (1) above; and

(b) of any matter referred to them under section 88 above,

if they consider that it is desirable in the public interest that they should supervise that investigation

(3) Where the Authority have made a determination under this section, it shall be their duty to notify it to the appropriate authority.

(4) Where an investigation is to be supervised by the Authority they may require—

(a) that no appointment shall be made under section 85(3) or 86(3) above unless they have given notice to the appropriate authority that they approve the officer whom that authority propose to appoint or;

(b) if such an appointment has already been made and the Authority are not satisfied with the officer appointed, that—

  (i) the appropriate authority shall, as soon as is reasonably practicable, select another officer and notify the Authority that they propose to appoint him; and

  (ii) the appointment shall not be made unless the Authority give notice to the appropriate authority that they approve that officer.

(5) It shall be the duty of the Secretary of State by regulations to provide that the Authority shall have power, subject to any restrictions or conditions specified in the regulations, to impose requirements as to a particular investigation additional to any requirements imposed by virtue of subsection (4) above; and it shall be the duty of a police officer to comply with any requirement imposed on him by virtue of the regulations.

(6) At the end of an investigation which the Authority have supervised the investigating officer—

  (a) shall submit a report on the investigation to the Authority; and

  (b) shall send a copy to the appropriate authority.

(7) After considering a report submitted to them under subsection (6) above, the Authority shall submit an appropriate statement to the appropriate authority.

(8) If it is practicable to do so, the Authority, when submitting the appropriate statement under subsection (7) above, shall send a copy to the officer whose conduct has been investigated.

(9) If—

  (a) the investigation related to a complaint; and

  (b) it is practicable to do so,

the Authority shall also send a copy of the appropriate statement to the person by or on behalf of whom the complaint was made.

(10) In subsection (7) above 'appropriate statement' means a statement—

  (a) whether the investigation was or was not conducted to the Authority's satisfaction;

  (b) specifying any respect in which it was not so conducted; and

  (c) dealing with any such other matters as the Secretary of State may be regulations provide.

(11) The power to issue an appropriate statement includes power to issue separate statements in respect of the disciplinary and criminal aspects of an investigation.

(12) No disciplinary proceedings shall be brought before the appropriate statement is submitted to the appropriate authority.

(13) Subject to subsection (14) below, neither the appropriate authority nor the Director of Public Prosecutions shall bring criminal proceedings before the appropriate statement is submitted to the appropriate authority.

(14) The restriction imposed by subsection (13) above does not apply if it appears to the Director that there are exceptional circumstances which make it undesirable to wait for the submission of the appropriate statement.

Steps to be taken after investigation – general

90. – (1) It shall be the duty of the appropriate authority, on receiving–

(a) a report concerning the conduct of a senior officer which is submitted to them under section 86(6) above; or

(b) a copy of a report concerning the conduct of a senior officer which is sent to them under section 89(6) above,

to send a copy of the report to the Director of Public Prosecutions unless the report satisfies them that no criminal offence has been committed.

(2) Nothing in the following provisions of this section or in sections 91 to 94 below has effect in relation to senior officers.

(3) On receiving–

(a) a report concerning the conduct of an officer who is not a senior officer which is submitted to him under section 85(9) above; or

(b) a copy of a report concerning the conduct of such an officer which is sent to him under section 89(6) above

it shall be the duty of a chief officer of police–

(i) to determine whether the report indicates that a criminal offence may have been committed by a member of the police force for his area.

(4) If the chief officer–

(a) determines that the report does indicate that a criminal offence may have been committed by a member of the police force for his area,

he shall send a copy of the report to the Director of Public Prosecutions.

(5) In such cases as may be prescribed by regulations made by the Secretary of State, after the Director has dealt with the question of criminal proceedings, the chief officer shall send the Authority a memorandum, signed by him and stating whether he has brought (or proposes to bring) disciplinary proceedings in respect of the conduct which was the subject of the investigation and, if not, giving his reasons.

(6) *[Repealed by the Police and Magistrates' Court Act 1994 ss 35, 93, Sch 9, Pt I.]*

(7) In such cases as may be prescribed by regulations made by the Secretary of State, if the chief officer considers that the report does not indicate that a criminal offence may have been committed by a member of the police force for his area, he shall send the Authority a memorandum to that effect, signed by him and stating whether he has brought (or proposes to bring) disciplinary proceedings in respect of the conduct which was the subject of the investigation and, if not, giving his reasons.

(8) [*Repealed by the Police and Magistrates' Court Act 1994 ss 35, 93, Sch 9, Pt I.*]

(9) Where the investigation–

(a) related to conduct which was the subject of a complaint; and
(b) was not supervised by the Authority.

then, if the chief officer is required by virtue of regulations under subsection (5) or (7) above to send the Authority a memorandum, he shall at the same time send them a copy of the complaint, or of the record of the complaint, and a copy of the report of the investigation.

(10) Subject to secton 93(6) below–

(a) if a chief officer's memorandum states that he proposes to bring disciplinary proceedings, it shall be his duty to bring and proceed with them; and
(b) if such a memorandum states that he has brought such proceedings, it shall be his duty to proceed with them.

Steps to be taken where accused has admitted charges

91. [*Repealed by the Police and Magistrates' Court Act 1994 ss44, 93, Sch 5, Pt II, para 28, Sch 9, Pt I.*]

Powers of Authority to direct reference of reports etc to Director of Public Prosecutions

92. [*Repealed by the Police and Magistrates' Court Act 1994 ss37(b), 93, Sch 9, Pt I.*]

Powers of Authority as to disciplinary charges

93. – (1) Where a memorandum under section 90 above states that a chief officer of police has not brought disciplinary proceedings or does not propose to do so, the Authority may recommend him to bring such proceedings.

(2) Subject to subsection (6) below, a chief officer may not discontinue disciplinary proceedings that he has brought in accordance with a recommendation under subsection (1) above.

(3) If after the Authority has made a recommendation under this section and consulted the chief officer he is still unwilling to bring disciplinary proceedings, they may direct him to do so.

(4) Where the Authority gives a chief officer a direction under this section, they shall furnish him with a written statement of thier reasons for doing so.

(5) Subject to subsection (6) below, it shall be the duty of a chief officer to comply with such a direction.

(6) The Authority may withdraw a direction given under this section.

(7) A chief officer shall—

(a) advise the Authority of what action he has taken in response to a recommendation or direction under this section, and

(b) furnish the Authority with such other information as they may reasonably require for the purpose of discharging their functions under this section.

Disciplinary tribunals

94. [*Repealed by the Police and Magistrates' Court Act 1994 ss37(c), 93, Sch 9, Pt I.*]

Information as to the manner of dealing with complaints etc

95. Every police authority in carrying out their duty with respect to the maintenance of an efficient and effective police force, and inspectors of constabulary in carrying out their duties with respect to the efficiency and effectiveness of any police force, shall keep themselves informed as to the working of sections 84 to 93 above in relation to the force.

Constabularies maintained by authorities other than police authorities

96. – (1) An agreement for the establishment in relation to any body of constables maintained by an authority other than a police authority of procedures corresponding or similar to any of those established by or by virtue of this Part of this Act may, with the approval of the Secretary of State, be made between the Authority and the authority maintaining the body of constables.

(2) Where no such procedures are in force in relation to any body of constables, the Secretary of State may by order establish such procedures.

(3) An Agreement under this section may at any time be varied or terminated with the approval of the Secretary of State.

(4) Before making an order under this section the Secretary of State shall consult–

(a) the Authority; and
(b) the authority maintaining the body of constables to whom the order would relate.

(5) The power to make orders under this section shall be exercisable by statutory instrument; and any statutory instrument containing such an order shall be subject to annulment in pursuance of a resolution of either House of Parliament.

(6) Nothing in any other enactment shall prevent an authority who maintain a body of constables from carrying into effect procedures established by virtue of this section.

(7) No such procedures shall have effect in relation to anything done by a constable outside England and Wales.

Reports

97. (1) The Authority shall, at the request of the Secretary of State, report to him on such matters relating generally to their functions as the Secretary of State may specify, and the Authority may for that purpose carry out research into any such matters.

(2) The Authority may make a report to the Secretary of State on any matters coming to their notice under this Part of this Act to which they consider that his attention should be drawn by reason of their gravity or of other exceptional circumstances; and the Authority shall send a copy of any such report to the police authority and to the chief officer of police of any police force which appears to the Authority to be concerned or, if the report concerns any such body of constables as is mentioned in section 96 above, to the authority maintaining it and the officer having the direction and the control of it.

(3) As soon as practicable after the end of each calendar year the Authority shall make to the Secretary of State a report on the discharge of their functions during that year.

(4) [*Repealed by the Police and Magistrates Court Act 1994 ss37(d), 93, Sch 9, Pt I.*]

(5) The Secretary of State shall lay before Parliament a copy of every report received by him under this section and shall cause every such report to be publshed.

(6) The Authority shall send to every police authority–

(a) a copy of every report made by the Authority under subsection (3) above; and

(b) any statistical or other general information which relates to the year dealt with by the report and to the area of that authority and which the Authority consider should be brought to the police authority's attention in connection with their functions under section 95 above.

Restriction on disclosure of information

98. – (1) No information received by the Authority in connection with any of their functions under sections 84 to 97 above or regulations made by virtue of section 99 below shall be disclosed by any person who is or has been a member, officer or servant of the Authority except–

(a) to the Secretary of State or to a member, officer or servant of the Authority or, so far as may be necessary for the proper discharge of the functions of the Authority, to other persons;

(b) for the purposes of any criminal, civil or disciplinary proceedings; or

(c) in the form of a summary or other general statement made by the Authority which does not identify the person from whom the information was received or any person to whom it relates.

(2) Any person who discloses information in contravention of this section shall be guilty of an offence and liable on summary conviction to a fine of an amount not exceeding level 5 on the standard scale . . .

Regulations

99. (1) The Secretary of State may make regulations as to the procedure to be followed under this Part of this Act.

(2) It shall be the duty of the Secretary of State to provide by regulations—

    (a) that, subject to such exceptions as may be specified by the regulations, a chief officer of police shall furnish, in accordance with such procedure as may be so specified, a copy of, or of the record of, a complaint against a member of the police force for his area—

        (i) to the person by or on behalf of whom the complaint was made; and

        (ii) to the officer against whom it was made;

    (b) procedures for the informal resolutoin of complaints of such descriptions as may be specified in the regulations, and for giving the person who made the complaint a record of the outcome of any such procedure if he applies for one within such period as the regulations may provide;

    (c) procedures for giving a police officer against whom a complaint is made which falls to be resolved informally an opportunity to comment orally or in writing on the complaint;

    (d) for cases in which any provision of this Part of this Act is not to apply where a complaint, other than a complaint which falls to be resolved by an informal procedure, is withdrawn or the complainant indicates that he does not wish any further steps to be taken;

    (e) for enabling the Authority to dispense with any requirement of this Part of this Act;

    (f) for enabling the Authority to relinquish the supervision of the investigation of any complaint or other matter;

    (g) for the time within which the Authority are to give a notification under section 89(3) above;

    (h) that the Authority shall be supplied with such information or documents of such description as may be specified in the regulations at such time or in such circumstances as may be so specified;

    (j) that any action or decision of the Authority which they take in consequence of their receipt of a memorandum under section 90 above shall be notified if it is an action or decision of a description specified in the regulations, to the person concerned and that, in connection with such a notification, the Authority shall have power to furnish him with any relevant information;

    (k) that chief officers of police shall have power to delegate any functions conferred on them by or by virtue of the foregoing provisions of this Part of this Act.

Regulations – supplementary

100. (1) Regulations under this Part of this Act may make different provision for different circumstances and may authorise the Secretary of State to make provision for any purposes specified in the regulations.

(2) Before making regulations under this Part of this Act, the Secretary of State shall furnish a draft of the regulations to the Police Advisory Board for England and Wales and take into consideration any representations made by that Board.

(3) Any power to make regulations under this Part of this Act shall be exercisable by statutory instrument.

(4) Subject to subsection (5) below, regulations under this Part of this Act shall be subject to annulment in pursuance of a resolution of either House of Parliament.

(5) Regulations to which this subsection applies shall not be made unless a draft of them has been approved by resolution of each House of Parliament.

(6) Subsection (5) above applies to regulations made by virtue–

(a) (aa) of section 90(5) or (7) above;
(b) of section 99(2)(b), (e) or (ea) above.

Discipline regulations

101. *[Repealed by the Police and Magistrates' Courts Act 1994 ss37(e), 93, Sch 9, Pt I.]*

Representation at disciplinary proceedings

102. – (1) A police officer of the rank of superintendent or below may not be dismissed, required to resign or reduced in rank by a decision taken in proceedings under regulations made in accordance with section 33(3)(a) of the Police Act 1964 unless he has been given an opportunity to elect to be legally represented at any hearing held in the course of those proceedings.

(2) Where an officer makes an election to which subsection (1) above refers, he may be represented at the hearing, at his option, either by counsel or by a solicitor.

(3) Except in a case where an officer of the rank of superintendent or below has been given an opportunity to elect to be legally represented and has so elected, he may be represented at the hearing only by another member of a police force.

(4) Regulations under section 33 of the Police Act 1964 shall specify

(a) a procedure for notifying an officer of the effect of subsections (1) to (3) above,
(b) when he is to be notified of the effect of those subsections (1) to (3) above,
(c) when he is to give notice whether he wishes to be legally represented at the hearing.

(5) If an officer–

(a) fails without reasonable cause to give notice in accordance with the regulations that he wishes to be legally represented; or
(b) gives notice in accordance with the regulations that he does not wish to be legally represented, he may be dismissed, required to resign or reduced in rank without his being legally represented.

(6) If an offficer has given notice in accordance with the regulations that he wishes to be legally represented, the case against him may be presented by counsel or a solicitor whether or not he is actually so represented.

103 *[Repealed by the Police and Magistrates' Court Act 1994 s 93, Sch 9, Pt I.]*
General

Restrictions on subsequent proceedings

104. – (1)*[Repealed by the Police and Magistrates' Court Act 1994 ss 37(f), 93 Sch 9, Pt I]*

(2)*[Repealed by the Police and Magistrates' Court Act 1994 ss 37(f), 93 Sch 9, Pt I]*

(3) Subject to subsection (4) below, no statement made by any person for the purpose of the informal resolution of a complaint shall be admissible in any subsequent criminal, civil or disciplinary proceedings.

(4) A statement is not rendered inadmissible by subsection (3) above if it consists of or includes an admission relating to a matter which does not fall to be resolved informally.

Guidelines concerning discipline, complaints etc

105. – (1) The Secretary of State may issue guidance to police and authorities, to chief officers of police and to other police officers concerning the discharge of thier functions–

  (a) under this Part of this Act; and
  (b) under regulations made under section 33 of the Police Act 1964 in relation to the matters mentioned in subsection (2)(e) of that section

and police authorities and police officers shall have regard to any such guidance in the discharge of their functions.

(2) Guidance may not be issued under subsection (1) above in relation to the handling of a particular case.

(3) A failure on the part of a police authority or a police officer to have regard to any guidance issued under subsection (1) above shall be admissible in evidence on any appeal from a decision taken in proceedings under regulations made in accordance with subsection (3) of section 33 of the Police Act 1964.

(4) In discharging their functions under section 93 above the Authority shall have regard to any guidance given to them by the Secretary of State with respect to such matters as are for the time being the subject of guidance under subsection (1) above, and shall have regard in particular, but without prejudice to the generality of this subsection, to any such guidance as to the principles to be applied in cases that involve any question of criminal proceedings.

(5) The report of the Authority under section 97(3) above shall contain a statement of any guidance given to the Authority under subsection (4) above during the year to which the report relates.

Police (Complaints) (General) Regulations 1985 (SI 1985 No 520)[1]

Citation and operation

1. – (1) These Regulations may be cited as the Police (Complaints) (General) Regulations 1985 and shall come into operation on 29 April 1985.

(2) The Police (Complaints) (General) Regulations 1977 and the Police (Copies of Complaints) Regulations 1977 are hereby revoked.

Interpretation

2. – (1) In these Regulations the following expressions have the meanings respectively assigned to them, that is to say:
'the Act of 1984' means the Police and Criminal Evidence Act 1984;
'the appropriate authority' has the meaning assigned to it by section 84 (4) of the Act of 1984;
'the Authority' means the Police Complaints Authority established under section 83 (1) of the Act of 1984;
'complaint' means a complaint to which Part IX of the Act of 1984 applies and 'copy of a complaint', in the case of a complaint made orally, shall include a copy of the record of the complaint;
'complainant' means the person by whom, or on whose behalf, a complaint is submitted.

(2) In these Regulations, unless the context otherwise requires, any reference to a paragraph shall be construed as a reference to a paragraph in the same Regulations.

Police Complaints Authority to forward complaints

3. – (1) Subject to paragraph (2), where the Authority have received a complaint against a member of a police force, they shall transmit it to the appropriate authority unless they are satisfied that to do so would be contrary to the complainant's wishes or, in all the circumstances, unnecessary.

(2) Notwithstanding that the complainant may not wish his complaint to be so transmitted, the Authority may, where they are satisfied that the public interest so requires, transmit a complaint received by them to the appropriate authority.

---

1 Cited throughout this work as the Complaints General Regs; made 28 March 1985 under PACE 1984 ss89(10)(c) and 99; came into operation 29 April 1985.

Notification of supervision, etc

4. – (1) Subject to paragraphs (2) and (3), where under section 89 of the Act of 1984 the Authority determine to supervise an investigation they shall notify their determination to the appropriate authority not later than the end of the seventh day after the day on which the complaint or matter in question is received by them.

(2) Where the Authority have requested further information to assist them in deciding whether to make such a determination the notification referred to in paragraph (1) shall be given not later than the end of the seventh day after the day on which they receive such information.

(3) Where an investigation is delayed pending the outcome of criminal proceedings relating to the complaint or matter to be investigated the notification referred to in paragraph (1) shall be given not later than the end of the seventh day after the day on which the Authority receive notification of the outcome of those proceedings.

Supply of information to Authority – general

5. The appropriate authority shall supply the Authority with such information and documents as they may reasonably require relating to a complaint or matter referred to them under section 87 or 88 of the Act of 1984, whether or not such complaint or matter is the subject of an investigation supervised by the Authority, for the purpose of enabling the Authority to fulfil their functions under the said Act.

Information as to consultation with Director of Public Prosecutions

6. The investigating officer shall keep the Authority informed as to the nature and eventual outcome of any consultation which he proposes to conduct with the Director of Public Prosecutions relating to an investigation which is being supervised by the Authority.

Appropriate statements

7. The appropriate statement submitted to the appropriate authority under section 89 (7) of the Act of 1984 may, in addition to the matters required to be dealt with by paragraphs (*a*) and (*b*) of subsection (10) of that section, specify any respects in which the Authority consider that their satisfaction with the conduct of the investigation ought to be recorded, and may deal with any such other matters relating to the investigation or the supervision thereof as the Authority consider should –

  (*a*) be brought to the attention of the appropriate authority, the complainant or the officer under investigation; or
  (*b*) be dealt with in the public interest.

Functions of authority as to disciplinary charges

8. – (1) Where a memorandum is sent to the Authority under section 90 of the Act of 1984 the Authority shall deal with the case under section 93 of that Act without undue delay and shall, as soon as practicable, take such decisions as appear to them appropriate for the purposes thereof.

(2) Where the chief officer concerned has not preferred disciplinary charges or does not propose to do so and the Authority accept his decision they shall –

(a) so inform the chief officer forthwith, and

(b) subject to paragraph (4), notify the complainant of the decision and of their acceptance thereof,

and may furnish the complainant with such relevant information in explanation thereof, if any, as appears to them appropriate.

(3) Where the chief officer concerned withdraws a disciplinary charge with the leave of the Authority given in pursuance of section 93 (6) of the Act of 1984, the Authority shall, subject to paragraph (4), notify the complainant that the charge has been withdrawn with their leave and furnish him with such relevant information in explanation of the withdrawal as appears to them appropriate.

(4) The Authority shall be relieved of the duty of notifying the complainant as mentioned in paragraph (2) (b) or (3) if compliance therewith appears to them to be not reasonably practicable.

(5) Where the chief officer concerned has, under Regulation 15 of the Police (Discipline) Regulations 1985, delegated the duty of deciding under regulation 8 of those Regulations whether a member of a police force should be charged with a disciplinary offence, the references in paragraphs (2) and (3) to the chief officer concerned shall be taken as references to the officer to whom the duty is delegated.

Copies of complaints

9. – (1) Subject to paragraph (2), a copy of the complaint shall be supplied to –

(a) the complainant, or

(b) the officer against whom the complaint was made, where either of them so requests in writing.

(2) The appropriate authority may, by notice in writing to the person who made the request, refuse to supply a copy of the complaint under paragraph (1) if of the opinion that compliance with the request –

(a) might prejudice any criminal investigation or proceedings pending at the time the request is made, or

(b) would be contrary to the public interest and the Secretary of State agrees the request should not be complied with;

and where such notice is given no further request may be made under paragraph (1) within the period of 6 months beginning with the date of the notice, without prejudice, however, to further such requests being made subsequently.

Time limits

10. – (1) Where a complaint is required to be referred to the Authority by the appropriate authority under secton 87 (1) (a) (i) of the Act of 1984 notification of the complaint shall be given to the Authority not later than the end of the day following the day on which it first becomes clear to the appropriate authority that the complaint is one to which that sub-paragraph applies.

(2) Where, under section 87 (2) of the act of 1984, the Authority require a complaint to be submitted to them by the appropriate authority for consideration, the appropriate authority shall so submit the complaint not later than the

end of the day following the day on which they received notification of the requirement.

Withdrawn complaints

11. – (1) The provisions of Part IX of theAct of 1984 shall not apply in respect of a complaint if the appropriate authority receives from the complainant notification in writing signed by him or by his solicitor or other authorised agent on his behalf to the effect either –

(*a*) that he withdraws the complaint, or

(*b*) that he does not wish any further steps to be taken in consequence thereof.

(2) Where a complainant gives such notification as is mentioned in paragraph (1) and it relates to a complaint –

(*a*) which was transmitted to the appropriate authority by the Authority, or

(*b*) which was referred or submitted to the Authority under section 87 (1) or (2) of the act of 1984, or

(*c*) a copy of which has been sent to the Authority under section 90 (9) of that Act,

the appropriate authority shall cause a copy of the notification to be sent to the Authority.

Complaints register

12. Every chief officer of police shall cause a register of complaints against members of his force to be kept in which there shall be recorded the steps taken in dealing with a complaint and their outcome.

Delegation of functions by chief officer

13. – (1) Subject to paragraphs (3) and (4), a chief officer may delegate all or any of the functions or duties conferred on him by sections 84 to 94 of the Act of 1984 (other than his functions or duties under section 94 (3) thereof), or by Regulations made under section 99 thereof, to such an officer as is mentioned in paragraph (2).

Police (Complaints) (Informal Resolution) Regulations 1985 (SI 1985 No 671)[1]

Citation and commencement

1. These Regulations may be cited as the Police (Complaints) (Informal Resolution) Regulations 1985 and shall come into operation on 29 April 1985.

Interpretation

2. – (1) In these Regulations the following expressions have the meanings respectively assigned to them, that is to say:

'the Act of 1984' means the Police and Criminal Evidence Act 1984;

'the appointed officer' means the officer appointed for the informal resolution of complaints under section 85(4) of the Act of 1984;

'the Authority' means the Police Complaints Authority established under section 83(1) of the Act of 1984;

'chief officer' shall be construed as including a reference to a person discharging the functions of a chief officer and 'chief officer concerned' means in relation to a complaint about the conduct of a member of a police force, the chief officer of the force of which he is a member;

'complaint' means a complaint to which Part IX of the Act of 1984 applies;

'complainant' means the person by whom or on whose behalf a complaint is submitted to the chief officer concerned;

'member concerned', in relation to a complaint, means the member about whose conduct the complaint is made;

'senior officer' means a police officer of the rank of chief constable, deputy chief constable or assistant chief constable or, in the case of the City of London and metropolitan police forces, a member of the force in question of, or above, the rank of commander.

---

1 Cited throughout this work as Informal Resolution Regs; made 26 April 1985 under PACE s 99; came into operation 29 April 1985.

Application of Regulations

3. – (1) Subject to the following provisions of this Regulation, these Regulations apply to a complaint received by the chief officer concerned on or after 29 April 1985, being a complaint which he considers to be suitable for informal resolution.

(2) Nothing in these Regulations applies in the case of a complaint against a senior officer.

(3) Where under Part IX of the Act of 1984 the Authority are required or determine to supervise the investigation of a complaint it shall not be dealt with or, as the case may be, continue to be dealt with by way of informal resolution.

Procedure for informal resolution of complaints

4. – (1) Subject to paragraph (2) below, for the purpose of informally resolving a complaint to which these Regulations apply about the conduct of a member of his force, the appointed officer shall as soon as practicable –

(*a*) seek the views of the complainant and the member concerned about the matter, and,

(*b*) take such other steps as appear to him appropriate

and, without prejudice to the foregoing, where it appears to the appointed officer that the complaint had in fact already been satisfactorily dealt with at the time it was brought to his notice, he may, subject to any representation made by the complainant, treat it as having been informally resolved.

(2) The appointed officer shall not, for the purpose of informally resolving a complaint, tender on behalf of the member concerned an apology for his conduct unless he has admitted the conduct in question.

Records

5. When a complaint is dealt with by way of informal resolution under these Regulations a record shall be made of the outcome of the procedure and a complainant shall be entitled to obtain a copy thereof from the chief officer concerned if he applies for such a copy not later than the end of 3 months from the day on which –

(*a*) the informal resolution of his complaint was achieved; or

(*b*) for whatever other reason it was determined that the complaint should no longer be subject to the said procedure.

Police (Dispensation from Requirement to Investigate Complaints) Regulations 1985 (SI 1985 No 672)[1]

1. These Regulations may be cited as the Police (Anonymous, Repetitious Etc. Complaints) Regulations 1985 and shall come into operation on 29 April 1985.[2]

2. (1) In these Regulations, unless the context otherwise requires, the following expressions have the meanings respectively assigned to them, that is to say:
'the Act of 1984' means the Police and Criminal Evidence Act 1984;
'the appropriate authority' means the appropriate authority within the meaning of section 84 (4) of the Act of 1984:
'the Authority' means the Police Complaints Authority established under section 83 (1) of the Act of 1984;
'the Board' means the Police Complaints Board established under section 1 of the Police Act 1976;
'complaint' means a complaint made on or after 29 April 1985 to which Part IX of the Act of 1984 applies; and 'copy of complaint', in the case of a complaint made orally, shall include a copy of the record of the complaint;
'complainant' means the member of the public by or on whose behalf a complaint is submitted.

(2) In these Regulations, unless the context otherwise requires, any reference to a Regulation shall be construed as a reference to a regulation contained in these Regulations, any reference in a Regulation, or in the Schedule to these Regulations, to a paragraph shall be construed as a reference to a paragraph of that Regulation, or of that Schedule, and any reference in a paragraph to a sub-paragraph shall be construed as a reference to a sub-paragraph of that paragraph.

3. (1) Where the appropriate authority is of the opinion –
(a) that a complaint is an anonymous or a repetitious one within the meaning of paragraph 2 or 3 of the Schedule to these Regulations, [or

---

1 Cited throughout this work as the Dispensation Regs; note these regulations were originally known as the Police (Anonymous, Repetitous etc Complaints) Regulations 1985 (SI 1985 No 672), they were amended and renamed by the Police (Dispensation from Requirement to Investigate Complaints Regulations 1990 (SI 1990 No 1301); made 26 April 1985 under PACE 1984 s 99(2)(e); came into operation 29 April 1985.
2 Notwithstanding reg 1 the regulations are, pursuant to SI 1990 No 1301 now properly cited as described in fn 1.

that a complaint is vexatious, oppressive or otherwise an abuse of the procedures for dealing with complaints,][3] or that it is not reasonably practicable to complete the investigation of a complaint, within the meaning of paragraph 4 thereof, [or

(*aa*) that more than 12 months have elapsed between the incident, or the latest incident, giving rise to the complaint and the making of the complaint and either that no good reason for the delay has been shown or that injustice would be likely to be caused by the delay, and][4]

(*b*) [in either case,][5] that, in all the circumstances, the requirements of Part IX of the Act of 1984 (to the extent that they have not already been satisfied) should be dispensed with,

the appropriate authority may, in accordance with this Regulation, request the Authority to dispense with the said requirements as respects the complaint.

(2) The request, which shall be made in writing, shall be accompanied by –

(*a*) a copy of the complaint;

(*b*) a memorandum from the appropriate authority explaining the reasons for being of the opinion mentioned in paragraph (1); . . .

(*c*) where the appropriate authority is of the opinion that the complaint is a repetitious complaint and, as respects the previous complaint the person then the complainant gave such notification as is mentioned in Regulation 3 of the Police (Withdrawn, Anonymous Etc Complaints) Regulations 1977 or Regulation 11 of the Police (Complaints) (General) Regulations 1985 a copy of that notification unless it has previously been sent to the Board or, as the case may be, the Authority in pursuance of that Regulation [; and

(*d*) where the appropriate authority is of the opinion that the complaint is a repetitious complaint and the previous complaint has been informally resolved in accordance with the provisions of section 85 of the Act of 1984, a copy of the record of the outcome of the informal resolution procedure made under regulation 5 of the Police (Complaints) (Informal Resolution) Regulations 1985.][6]

(3) If, after considering a request under this Regulation, the Authority share the opinion of the appropriate authority, they may dispense with the requirements mentioned in paragraph (1) but they shall not reject such a request except after consultation with the appropriate authority.

(4) The Authority shall, as soon as may be, notify the appropriate authority, in writing, of their decision on such a request and, where they dispense with the requirements mentioned in paragraph (1), shall inform the complainant of their action unless the complaint is an anonymous one or it otherwise appears to them to be not reasonably practicable so to inform him within a period which is reasonable in all the circumstances of the case.

3 SI 1990 No 1301.
4 Ibid.
5 Ibid.
6 Ibid.

SCHEDULE   Regulation 3 (1)
COMPLAINTS WHICH ARE ANONYMOUS, REPETITIOUS OR
INCAPABLE OF INVESTIGATION

1.   (1) In this Schedule any reference to an injured person other than the complainant shall have effect only in the case of a complaint against a member of a police force in respect of his conduct towards a person other than the complainant; and, in such a case, any such reference is a reference to that other person.

(2) In this schedule any reference to action not being reasonably practicable shall include a reference to action which it does not appear reasonably practicable to take within a period which is reasonable in all the circumstances of the case.

2. For the purposes of Regulation 3 a complaint is an anonymous one if, and only if, it discloses (or purports to disclose) neither the name and address of the complainant nor that of any other injured person and it is not reasonably practicable to ascertain such a name and address.

3. (1) For the purposes of Regulation 3 a complaint is a repetitious one if, and only if –

(a)   it is substantially the same as a previous complaint (whether made by or on behalf of the same or a different complainant);

[(aa) the complaint was informally resolved in accordance with the provisions of section 85 of the act of 1984;][7]

(b)   it contains no fresh allegations which significantly affect the account of the conduct complained of;

(c)   no fresh evidence, being evidence which was not reasonably available at the time the previous complaint was made, is tendered in support of it; and

(d)   such action as is referred to in sub-paragraph (2) has been taken as respects the previous complaint.

(2) The condition in sub-paragraph (1) (d) shall be satisfied if, as respects the previous complaint, either –

(a)   the requirements of section 90 (5), (6) and (7) of the Act of 1984 were complied with;

(b)   the complainant gave such a notification as is mentioned in Regulation 3 (2) (c); or

(c)   the Authority, under Regulation 3, dispensed with the requirements mentioned in paragraph (1) of that Regulation.

4. For the purposes of Regulation 3 it shall not be reasonably practicable to complete the investigation of a complaint if, and only if, in the opinion of the appropriate authority or, as the case may be, of the Authority, either –

(a)   it is not reasonably practicable to communicate with the complainant or, as the case may be, the person who submitted the complaint, or any other injured person, notwithstanding that the complaint is not an anonymous one within the meaning of paragraph 2, or

(b)   it is not reasonably practicable to complete a satisfactory investigation in consequence of –

(i)   a refusal or failure, on the part of the complainant, to make a

7 Ibid.

statement or afford other reasonable assistance for the purposes of the investigation, or

(ii) a refusal or failure, on the part of an injured person other than the complainant, to support the complaint, evidenced either by a statement in writing (signed by him or by his solicitor or other authorised agent on his behalf) to the effect that he does not support it or by a refusal or failure, on his part, such as is mentioned in sub-paragraph (i) above, or

(iii) the lapse of time since the event or events forming the subject matter of the complaint.

Police (Complaints) (Mandatory Referrals Etc) Regulations 1985 (SI 1985 No 673)[1]

Citation and operation

1. These Regulations may be cited as the Police (Complaints) (Mandatory Referrals Etc.) Regulations and shall come into force on 29 April 1985.

Interpretation

2. In these Regulations –

'the Act of 1984' means the Police and Criminal Evidence Act 1984;

'the appropriate authority' has the meaning assigned to it by section 84(4) of the Act of 1984;

'the Authority' means the Police Complaints Authority established under section 83(1) of the Act of 1984;

'chief officer' shall be construed as including a reference to an officer discharging the functions of a chief officer, and references to the appropriate authority shall be construed accordingly; and

'complaint' means a complaint about the conduct of a police officer.

Application of Regulations

3. These Regulations shall apply –

   (a) to any complaint made on or after 29 April 1985, under Part IX of the Act of 1984; and
   (b) to any other matter the investigation of which the Authority determines to supervise,

being a complaint or matter where the conduct complained of or to which it relates occurred, or is alleged to have occurred, on or after 29 April 1984.

Mandatory referrals

4. – (1) Without prejudice to section 87(1)(a)(i) of the Act of 1984 (requiring reference to the Authority of any complaint alleging that the con-

---

1 Cited throughout this work as Mandatory Referrals Regs; made 26 April 1985 under PACE 1984 ss87(1)(a)(ii) and 89(5); came into operation 29 April 1985.

duct complained of resulted in the death of or serious injury to some other person), the appropriate authority shall refer to the Authority any complaint to which these Regulations apply, being a complaint alleging conduct which, if shown to have occurred, would constitute –

  (*a*) assault occasioning actual bodily harm; or
  (*b*) an offence under section 1 of the Prevention of Corruption Act 1906; or
  (*c*) a serious arrestable offence, within the meaning of section 116 of the Act of 1984.

(2) Where a complaint is required to be referred to the Authority under paragraph (1) above, notification of the complaint shall be given to the Authority not later than the end of the day following the day on which it first becomes clear to the appropriate authority that the complaint is one to which that paragraph applies.

Power of Authority to impose requirements in relation to investigations

5. – (1) Where the Authority determine, under section 89 of the Act of 1984, to supervise the investigation of a matter which is not the subject of a complaint, they shall have the like power to impose requirements in relation to the appointment of an officer to investigate the matter as they have, by virtue of subsection (4) of that section, in relation to the investigation of a complaint.

(2) Without prejudice to their powers in relation to the appointment of an investigating officer, but subject to paragraphs (3) and (4) below, the Authority may, where they undertake the supervision of an investigation of a complaint or other matter to which these Regulations apply, issue directions imposing such additional reasonable requirements as to the conduct of the investigation as appear to them to be necessary as are specified in the directions.

(3) Where at any stage of an investigation of a complaint or other matter to which these Regulations apply the possibility of criminal proceedings arises, the Authority shall not, under paragraph (2) above, impose any requirement relating to the obtaining or preservation of evidence of a criminal offence without first obtaining the consent of the Director of Public Prosecutions to the imposition thereof.

(4) The Authority shall not, under paragraph (2) above, impose any requirement relating to the resources to be made available by a chief officer for the purposes of an investigation without first consulting him and having regard to any representations he may make.

Home Office Circular 62/1992
Use of handcuffs

1   Paragraph 4.65 of Home Office circular 35/1986 seeks to prevent the use of handcuffs on prisoners unless there are 'good special reasons' for it and 'fair grounds for supposing that violence may be used as an escape is attempted'.

2   The report of the Association of Chief Police Officer's Working Party on Self-defence, Arrest and Restraint argued that Home Office circular 35/1986 was too restrictive and should be amended. Having considered the report, the Home Secretary agreed and has authorised the issue of this guidance. Paragraph 4.65 of Home Office circular 35/1986 is now cancelled.

Carrying of handcuffs
3   The decision whether or not to carry handcuffs, either routinely or in a particular case, is usually left to an individual officer's discretion, based on any guidance issued by the force concerned.

4   Chief officers will wish to ensure that officers have a personal issue of a pair of handcuffs or that there are sufficient stocks to issue to officers on request. It is not possible at present to recommend a particular type of handcuff except to say that they should not be capable of hurting the prisoner or liable to allow him or her to escape.

Use of handcuffs
5   An arrest is invariably achieved by a police officer taking physical hold of the prisoner. In many cases this may involve no real use of force and may be almost symbolic. The use of handcuffs is an additional public announcement that someone is under arrest. Any physical restraint must be justified and the degree of force used must be reasonable and the minimum necessary in the circumstances of the case.

6   In using handcuffs, *the safety of the police officer and the public and the safety and security of the prisoner are the foremost consideration*. Officers may use them when

   a)   There are reasonable grounds to believe that an unrestrained prisoner will use violence against the arresting officer(s) or bystanders; or
   b)   There are reasonable grounds to believe that the prisoner will escape custody.

Whether reasonable grounds exist will depend on the circumstances of each case, but there must be some objective basis for a decision to use handcuffs in the same way as officers must ask themselves whether they have reasonable grounds for exercising stop and search powers under PACE. Here, they must ask themselves whether there is a real threat of violence or of escape.

7   Handcuffs should only need to be used in exceptional cases for juveniles, women and elderly prisoners, but this is part of the consideration of reasonable grounds.

Flexible handcuffs

8   'Flexicuffs' may be useful in certain circumstances, but should not be used routinely or for long periods. Particular care should be taken to avoid over-tightening the flexicuffs on prisoners, and forces should ensure that cutting equipment is readily available.

DPP's advice to chief officers of police on the case of **R v Edwards** [1991] 2 All ER 266, CA

5 October 1992
A copy of this advice has been placed in the House of Commons library.

Introduction

1   I am writing to you to set out the policy which the Crown Prosecution Service, ACPO and the Home Office have agreed should be adopted in the light of the decision in *R v Edwards*. This policy supersedes the interim guidance set out in my letter to you of 10 July. I look forward to both our Services working together to implement this agreement. All parties have agreed that it is essential that the policy laid down in this letter is followed in order to ensure that a consistent approach is taken to the disclosure of potentially sensitive information about police officers' disciplinary records. I am aware of the concern which individual members of the Police Service have expressed in this area and we have sought to agree a policy within the law which takes account of those concerns.

2   In order to avoid confusion, I have distinguished in this letter between the transfer of information from the police to the CPS which is described as 'revealed' to the CPS, and the transfer of information from the CPS to the defence which is described as 'disclosed' to the defence.

3   I am advising my staff separately of the details of the agreement which has been reached. In the light of this agreement, certain other documents, such as the Manual of Guidance, will require amendment.

Finalised disciplinary proceedings

4   The decision in Edwards is authority for the proposition that the defence are entitled to cross-examine police officers about disciplinary findings proved against them. In turn, this means that the prosecution is obliged to notify the defence of such matters.

5   It has been agreed that the obligation to which I have referred is a continuing one and, accordingly, that the police are responsible for notifying the CPS of any disciplinary findings proved against any police officer involved as a witness in the case in question up to and during the course of the trial. This obligation applies to officers who are going to be called as witnesses as well as to officers whose evidence is to be read by agreement to the court. The obligation also extends to an officer whose evidence is

not relied upon by the prosecution but whose statement is disclosed to the defence as 'unused material'.

6   Having considered the matter carefully, it has been agreed that the prosecution's duty in this regard does not extend to disciplinary records which have been expunged in accordance with the relevant Police Regulations. Accordingly, disclosure of such matters is not required.

7   I am satisfied that the decision in Edwards may be restricted to a requirement to disclose those disciplinary findings which must be formally recorded under the appropriate Police Regulations. Therefore, the police need not reveal to the CPS disciplinary findings of guilt where the punishment is a caution, nor need any complaints which have not resulted in a disciplinary finding of guilt be revealed, save in those cases discussed further in paragraph 17.

8   I recognise that there are certain disciplinary offences which are unlikely ever to be relevant to the proper conduct by the defence of its case. Accordingly, I do not propose to require the police to reveal to the CPS details of disciplinary findings in respect of neglect of health, improper dress or untidiness or entering licensed premises. This is, however, subject to a specific request being made by the CPS in a case where, for any particular reason, we are concerned to know whether such findings exist.

9   Having considered the matter further, I have decided that the police should reveal to the CPS details of any disciplinary findings of guilt (except where I have specifically mentioned above that they are not required) in all cases where a full file of evidence is prepared in accordance with recommendations 11 and 12 of the Report of the Working Group on Pre-Trial Issues. It follows, therefore, that this information should be provided automatically in such cases and not only following a request from the defence. However, I am also satisfied that any request by the defence in other types of case should be compiled with by the police and the CPS. It is envisaged that such cases in which a full file is not necessary, yet the defence make such a request, should be very rare.

10 It is essential that the continuing nature of the prosecution's duty of disclosure in this regard is recognised. Accordingly, the police must assume responsibility for ensuring that they reveal to the CPS any disciplinary finding which is recorded (and which falls within the earlier paragraphs) during the lifetime of a case. By the same token, it is essential for the police to ensure that the CPS is notified of any change in circumstances which makes the previous notification of a disciplinary matter no longer pertinent. It has been agreed that the police will inform the CPS of the fact that there has been a successful appeal by the officer concerned or of the fact that a disciplinary finding revealed at the time of the submission of the full file has been expunged before the trial has started. The date of likely expunction will be supplied to the CPS with the details of the disciplinary finding. In such cases, the CPS is responsible for informing the defence, and, if necessary, the court, that any disciplinary finding has been expunged. CPS staff have been advised that the advocate in the case must be made fully aware of the need to ensure that the defence do not

seek inappropriately to refer to such matters. Prosecution advocates will be instructed to argue that, as a matter of law, expunged records are not subject to disclosure under *R v Edwards*, and, accordingly, those records which become expunged during the currency of the case but which have been disclosed should not be the subject of cross-examintion.

11   It has been agreed that the police will devise a procedure which obliges all police witnesses to indicate whether they are subject to a disciplinary finding which resulted in a recordable penalty. The Home Office is writing to Chief Officers separately about how this should be handled on a temporary basis until amendments to the Manual of Guidance can be circulated.

12   It is arguable that disclosure of the fact of a disciplinary charge and finding does not fall within the doctrine of Public Interest Immunity or breach confidentiality, but requests for further details of disciplinary cases may do. Careful consideration will be given to both issues in responding to such requests. In cases of doubt, the direction of the court will be sought before the CPS discloses such details to the defence. In all cases, information disclosed should avoid giving the name and address of the complainant unless this is absolutely necessary.

13   The question of disclosure to the defence of the information provided by the police is for the CPS. However, not all matters which are revealed to the CPS by the police will necessarily be disclosed to the defence. Whilst the CPS is mindful of its duties of disclosure in the light of recent case law, the details which the police will be able to provide in respect of the particular breach of the Discipline Code should be sufficient to enable the prosecution to make an informed decision about the relevance of the finding to the proceedings in question. When there is any doubt, the CPS will seek the direction of the Court.

14   I recognise that there may be instances when the police may wish to advise the CPS of additional information in respect of a particular disciplinary finding, but it may not be appropriate to convey that information to the CPS in a written memorandum; it may be that there are particular circumstances of which the CPS ought to be aware before deciding whether or not to disclose the fact of the disciplinary finding to the defence. It is important to note, however, that information of this nature revealed orally to the CPS may constitute 'unused material' for the purposes of disclosure to the defence and that recent case law has demonstrated the width of the prosecution's duty in this regard. In these circumstances, the supervising officer is to be responsible for noting in the file the fact that there is additional information which the CPS needs to bear in mind before reaching a decision regarding disclosure of the disciplinary finding. If the CPS considers that disclosure may be appropriate, a lawyer of not less than Gade 6 rank will consult the supervising officer to discuss the matter further. In other circumstances, it may be appropriate to ensure that full details of the earlier case are available to all from the start. The Home Office will advise Chief Officers further on this topic direct.

15 In any event, all CPS staff will be instructed to liaise with the police if there is any doubt regarding the disclosure of an officer's disciplinary record.

Disciplinary matters which have not been completed

16 I am aware that police forces already reveal details of certain complaints made against police officers which have not been completed, in accordance with local arrangements with CPS offices. The agreed policy seeks to build on those arrangements in the light of Edwards. I recognise the sensitivity which exists when considering both the revelation and the disclosure of such information; nevertheless, if the prosecution is to ensure that it complies with its duty of disclosure, it is essential that the system outlined below is followed in all Areas so that the CPS is notified of certain allegations affecting police officers who are witnesses in the case.

17 Accordingly, it has been agreed that the police shall reveal to the CPS the fact that an officer has been suspended pending completion of any enquiry being conducted into his conduct. In addition, the police shall reveal all cases in which an officer has been charged with an offence under the Discipline Code, save when the charge is solely in respect of one or more of the three disciplinary offences which are exempt from notification as per paragraph 7. Cases in which the defendant has made allegations against a police witness in his or her own case, which cannot be investigated until the case is concluded, should continue to be handled as at present.

18 There may be some cases where, although a charge has not yet been made, the nature of allegations made or under investigation is such that their non-disclosure might subsequently prejudice the current case. The ACPO officer with responsibility for discipline will be responsible for ensuring that they are revealed to the CPS where there is any likelihood that the interests of justice require this.[1] I accept that this last category is not easy to define, but I envisage that the ACPO officer with responsibility for discipline will be in a position to identify any officers under their command whose behaviour is such that the CPS ought to be made aware of any potential difficulty. The Home Office is writing to Chief Officers about interim arrangements pending the issue of amendments to the Manual of Guidance.

19 In respect of each of these categories of case which have not been completed, the CPS will first consider whether the officer's evidence is required in the instant case. Whenever it is lawfully possible to do so, the officer will not be relied upon by the prosecution. There will be cases, however, in which the officer's evidence is essential to the continued prosecution of the case. In either case, the CPS shall not disclose details to the defence of pending disciplinary matters, without consulting the

---

[1] A decision to reveal such a matter to the CPS for the purposes of complying with *R v Edwards* does not, of course, in any way prejudice the powers and responsibilities of the Police Complaints Authority under the Police and Criminal Evidence Act, 1984.

ACPO officer with responsibility for discipline. That consultation shall be undertaken by a CPS lawyer of not less than Grade 6 rank. Where a disciplinary investigation is being supervised by the PCA, the PCA supervising member should also be consulted. If a doubt remains about whether disclosure is appropriate, the CPS will seek the direction of the court. That said, it is inevitable that the defence will need to be advised of those officers who are suspended and in respect of whom it remains necessary to rely upon their evidence. The CPS shall disclose details of other matters which are not completed and which have been revealed to it in accordance with this agreement only in those cases when, and to the extent which, the current law requires it. It is irrelevant for these purposes whether or not the officer's statement forms part of the bundle of evidence relied upon by the prosecution or whether it is simply disclosed as 'unused material'.

Conclusion

20   I recognise the need to keep this agreed statement of policy under constant review. The law relating to the disclosure of information by the prosecution to the defence has been subject to considerable change in recent years. It may be that certain parts of this policy will need to be reconsidered in the light of further decisions of the courts.

21   I am confident, however, that we have achieved a practical and workable policy in the light of *R v Edwards*. To ensure that this agreed policy is consistently applied, I have instructed my staff that they must not depart from the position set out above without reference to CPS Headquarters. Equally, if there is any practical situation which is not covered in this agreement, the matter must be reported by my staff to CPS Headquarters; local arrangements should not be agreed. By this means, the agreed policy will be kept under review, and potential test cases should be identified at an early stage.

22   I look forward to receiving your full cooperation in implementing this agreed policy statement; this agreement is a very important step forward in fulfilling the prosecution's duty of disclosure to the defence. By complying with this agreement, the prospect that important cases will be lost because of a failure to comply with the decision in *R v Edwards* should diminish. In addition, cases in which the police have invested considerable time and effort in producing very compelling evidence of the accused's guilt do not run the risk of resulting in acquittal for unrelated and often technical reasons.

Useful addresses

Association of Chief Police Officers of England, Wales and Northern Ireland (ACPO)
ACPO Secretariat
Room 311
Wellington House
67–73 Buckingham Gate
London
SW1E 6BE
Tel: 0171 230 7184
Fax: 0171 230 7212

Colin Roach Centre
56 Clarence Road
London
E5 8HB
Tel: 0181 533 7111
Fax: 0181 533 7116

Citizens Advice Bureaux
Local Citizens Advice Bureaux can be found listed in the telephone directory.

Criminal Injuries Compensation Authority
Tay House
300 Bath Street
Glasgow
G2 4JR
Tel: 0141 331 2726
Fax: 0141 353 3148

GALOP
Gay London Policing Group
36 Old Queen Street
London
SW1E 9HP
Tel: 0171 233 0854

HM Inspectorate of Constabulary
Room 566
Home Office
50 Queen Anne's Gate
London SW1H 9AT
Tel: 0171 273 3246
Fax: 0171 273 4031

Home Office
50 Queen Anne's Gate
London
SW1H 9AT
Tel: 0171 273 3000

House of Commons
Westminster
London SW1A 0AA
Tel: 0171 219 3000

Inquest
Ground Floor, Alexandra National House
330 Seven Sisters Road
Finsbury Park
London
N4 2PJ
Tel: 0181 802 7430
Fax: 0181 802 7540

Interrights
The International Centre for the Legal Protection of Human Rights
Lancaster House
33 Islington High Street
London
N1 9LH
Tel: 0171 278 3230
Fax: 0171 278 4334

Justice
59 Carter Lane
London
EC4V 5AQ
Tel: 0171 329 5100
Fax: 0171 329 5055

Liberty
The National Council for Civil Liberties
21 Tabard Street
London
SE1 4LA
Tel: 0171 403 3888
Fax: 0171 407 5354

Law Centres Federation: London office
Duchess House
18–19 Warren Street
London
W1P 5DB
Tel: 0171 387 8570
Fax: 0171 387 8368

Sheffield office:
Third Floor, Arundel Court
177 Arundel Street
Sheffield
S1 2NO
Tel: 0114 2787088
Fax: 0114 2787004

Police Complaints Authority
10 Great George Street
London
SW1P 3AE
Tel: 0171 273 6450
Fax: 0171 273 6401

Press Association
85 Fleet Street
London
EC4P 4BE
Tel: 0171 353 7740
Fax: 0171 936 2363 (Editorial)

Metropolitan Police HQ
New Scotland Yard
8–10 Broadway
London
SW1H 0BG
Tel: 0171 230 1212

AIRE Centre (Advice on Individual Rights in Europe)
74 Eurolink Business Centre
49 Effra Road
London
SW2 1BZ
Tel: 0171 924 0927

Index